Kharkov/Kharkiv

# Kharkov/Kharkiv

## A Borderland Capital

Volodymyr Kravchenko

berghahn
NEW YORK · OXFORD
www.berghahnbooks.com

First published in 2023 by
Berghahn Books
www.berghahnbooks.com

© 2023, 2026 Volodymyr Kravchenko
First paperback edition published in 2026

All rights reserved. Except for the quotation of short passages
for the purposes of criticism and review, no part of this book
may be reproduced in any form or by any means, electronic or
mechanical, including photocopying, recording, or any information
storage and retrieval system now known or to be invented,
without written permission of the publisher.

**Library of Congress Cataloging-in-Publication Data**

Names: Kravchenko, V. V. (Volodymyr Vasyliovych), 1957- author.
Title: Kharkov/Kharkiv : a borderland capital / Volodymyr Kravchenko.
Other titles: Khar'kov—Kharkiv. English
Description: [Updated and revised translation]. | New York ; Oxford : Berghahn Books,
  2023. | Includes bibliographical references and index.
Identifiers: LCCN 2022053320 (print) | LCCN 2022053321 (ebook) |
  ISBN 9781800738980 (hardback) | ISBN 9781800738997 (ebook)
Subjects: LCSH: Kharkiv (Ukraine)—History. | Slobidska Ukraine (Ukraine and
  Russia)—History. | Ukraine—Foreign relations—Russia (Federation) | Russia
  (Federation)—Foreign relations—Ukraine.
Classification: LCC DK508.95.K53 K7313 2023 (print) | LCC DK508.95.K53 (ebook) |
  DDC 327.477/5047—dc23/eng/20221108
LC record available at https://lccn.loc.gov/2022053320
LC ebook record available at https://lccn.loc.gov/2022053321

**British Library Cataloguing in Publication Data**

A catalogue record for this book is available from the British Library

**EU GPSR Authorized Representative**

LOGOS EUROPE, 9 rue Nicolas Poussin, 17000, LA ROCHELLE, France

Email: Contact@logoseurope.eu

ISBN 978-1-80073-898-0 hardback
ISBN 978-1-83695-387-6 paperback
ISBN 978-1-83695-388-3 epub
ISBN 978-1-80073-899-7 web pdf

https://doi.org/10.3167/9781800738980

# Contents

| | |
|---|---|
| *List of Illustrations* | vi |
| *Preface* | viii |
| *Acknowledgments* | ix |
| *Note on Transliteration* | x |
| *Maps* | xi |
| Introduction | 1 |
| Chapter 1. The Steppe Borderland | 8 |
| Chapter 2. Town and Gown | 50 |
| Chapter 3. A Province in Search of an Identity | 92 |
| Chapter 4. City, Empire, Nation | 133 |
| Chapter 5. To the "First Capital" and Back | 174 |
| Chapter 6. Post-Soviet Borderland | 216 |
| Chapter 7. The Front Line | 254 |
| Conclusions | 291 |
| Historical Timeline | 297 |
| Selected Bibliography | 300 |
| Index | 307 |

# Illustrations

## Map

**0.1.** Sloboda Ukraine, 1762. © Dmytro Vortman, 2022.  xi

**0.2.** Kharkiv gubernia, 1914. © Dmytro Vortman, 2022.  xii

**0.3.** Ukrainian State, 1918. © Dmytro Vortman, 2022.  xii

**0.4.** Soviet Ukraine, 1942. © Dmytro Vortman, 2022.  xiii

**0.5.** Ukrainian Soviet Socialist Republic, 1991. © Dmytro Vortman, 2022.  xiv

**0.6.** Ukraine during the Russian invasion, July 2022. © Dmytro Vortman, 2022.  xv

## Figures

**1.1.** Cossack Kharko, mythical founder of Kharkiv (sculptor Zurab Tsereteli, 2004). © Vikipediia. Vil'na Entsyklopediia.  10

**1.2.** Kharkiv fortress, seventeenth century (reconstruction by L. Shmatko and I. Karas). © Wikimedia Commons.  15

**2.1.** Vasilii Nazarovich Karazin (1773–1842), enlightener, civil society activist, founder of Kharkiv University. © Wikimedia Commons.  63

**2.2.** Kharkiv University, new building (1823–31), architects E. A. Vasiliev and I. Vatelet. © Volodymyr Kravchenko, 2021.  75

**3.1.** Hryhorii Fedorovych Kvitka (Osnov'ianenko) (1778–1843), one of the founding fathers of modern Ukrainian literature. © Wikimedia Commons.  111

**4.1.** Annunciation Cathedral, the main Russian Orthodox church in Kharkiv (1888), architect Mikhail Lovtsov. © Volodymyr Kravchenko, 2008.  143

4.2. Former Land Bank in Kharkiv (1899), architect Aleksei Beketov.
© Volodymyr Kravchenko, 2008. 150

5.1. *Derzhprom*, the first Soviet skyscraper (1925–28), architects Serhii
Serafimov, Samuil Kravets, Mark Felger. © Volodymyr Kravchenko, 2021. 191

5.2. Monument to Taras Shevchenko, 1935, sculptor Matvei Manizer.
© Volodymyr Kravchenko, 2008. 192

6.1. Monument to fighters of the "Great October Socialist Revolution"
of 1917 (1976), sculptors V. I. Agibalov, Y. I. Ryk, and M. F. Ovsiankin.
Dismantled in 2011; replaced by monument to Ukrainian Independence
in 2012 (see figure 6.2.). © Volodymyr Kravchenko, 2008. 249

6.2. Monument to Ukrainian Independence, sculptors Oleksandr
Ridny and Hanna Ivanova, 2012. © Volodymyr Kravchenko, 2015. 249

6.3. Gallery and memorial steles honoring Soviet Komsomol members
engaged in anti-Nazi resistance during World War II. © Wikimedia
Commons. 250

6.4. Church of the Myrrhbearers in Kharkiv belonging to the Orthodox Church (Moscow patriarchate). It replaced competing Soviet and
Ukrainian national symbols. © Volodymyr Kravchenko, 2021. 250

7.1. Monument to Lenin, 1964, architect Aleksandr Sidorenko, erected
in place of the monument to Stalin. The monument to Lenin was
considered the largest in Ukraine. Dismantled in 2014. © Volodymyr
Kravchenko, 2011. 275

7.2. In place of Lenin, what? A failed attempt to replace the monument to Lenin with Ukrainian Orthodox symbolism. © Volodymyr
Kravchenko, 2015. 275

7.3. Overcoming history? Liberty Square. © Mikhail Protsenko, 2018. 275

7.4. The Ukrainian-Russian border before the Russian invasion.
© Volodymyr Kravchenko, 2017. 280

7.5. Russian missile near the Orthodox Church of the Assumption of
the Theotokos in the old center of Kharkiv. © Andrii Marienko, used
with permission. 282

7.6. Kharkiv oblast administration building after Russian bombardment, 1 March 2022. © Andrii Marienko, used with permission. 282

# Preface

This is an updated and revised translation of my 2010 book *Kharkov/Kharkiv: A Capital of the Borderland*, published by the European Humanities University in Vilnius. I worked on the new edition of the book roughly between 2020 and 2022, being motivated mostly by the unfading interest in the topic in the Western scholarly community. The work was basically completed before the Russian aggression against Ukraine launched by the Kremlin dictator in 2022. Main chapters required little revision except in the new literature. I only added new materials and chapters to cover the recent history of the city and region up to March 2022. My hope is that this book might contribute to a better understanding of what is going on across the vast political, cultural, and historical terrain of the Ukrainian-Russian historical borderland, which is now undergoing radical transformation.

# Acknowledgments

I am grateful to the anonymous reviewers whose comments and suggestions prompted me to think critically about the original text of the book. The book was translated and edited by Myroslav Yurkevich, who also contributed significantly to the endless process of improving the manuscript. I offer my thanks to Dmytro Vortman, who managed to prepare all the historical maps for publication in the shortest possible time, and Sulaiman Akhmad for his patience and assistance in preparing the manuscript for editing. All errors and shortcomings that the attentive reader may find in the text are of course solely the responsibility of the author. Financial support for the project was provided by the Contemporary Ukraine Studies Program (CUSP) and the Kowalsky Program of the Canadian Institute of Ukrainian Studies, as well as the Ukrainian Studies Fund (USF). Special thanks go to the European Humanities University (EHU) for transferring the translation rights for this edition and to McGill-Queen's University Press for permission to use some of my earlier published texts.

# Note on Transliteration

In this book, a simplified form of the Library of Congress romanization system is used to transliterate Ukrainian and Russian personal names and place names. This system seeks to ease reading by avoiding non-English vowel combinations, diacritics, and word endings. Consequently, in the text of the book, initial iotated vowels are rendered with a *Y* (e.g., Yurii, not Iurii); the soft sign (ь) is not indicated with the conventional prime ('); and, in masculine personal surnames ending in *uĭ*, the final *ĭ* is not transliterated (e.g., Hrushevsky, not Hrushevskyi).

In bibliographic references, on the other hand, the names of authors and editors and the titles of works written in Ukrainian and Russian are rendered in the full Library of Congress system (ligatures omitted) in order to make possible the accurate reconstruction of the Cyrillic original. In both text and bibliography, the names of individuals who devised their own English spelling of their names, not always conforming to Library of Congress romanization standards, are given according to their usage.

ALA-LC romanization tables for many languages may be consulted online at loc.gov/catdir/cpso/roman.html.

# Maps

Map 0.1. Sloboda Ukraine, 1762. © Dmytro Vortman, 2022.

**Map 0.2.** Kharkiv gubernia, 1914. © Dmytro Vortman, 2022.

**Map 0.3.** Ukrainian State, 1918. © Dmytro Vortman, 2022.

**Map 0.4.** Soviet Ukraine, 1942. © Dmytro Vortman, 2022.

**Map 0.5.** Ukrainian Soviet Socialist Republic, 1991. © Dmytro Vortman, 2022.

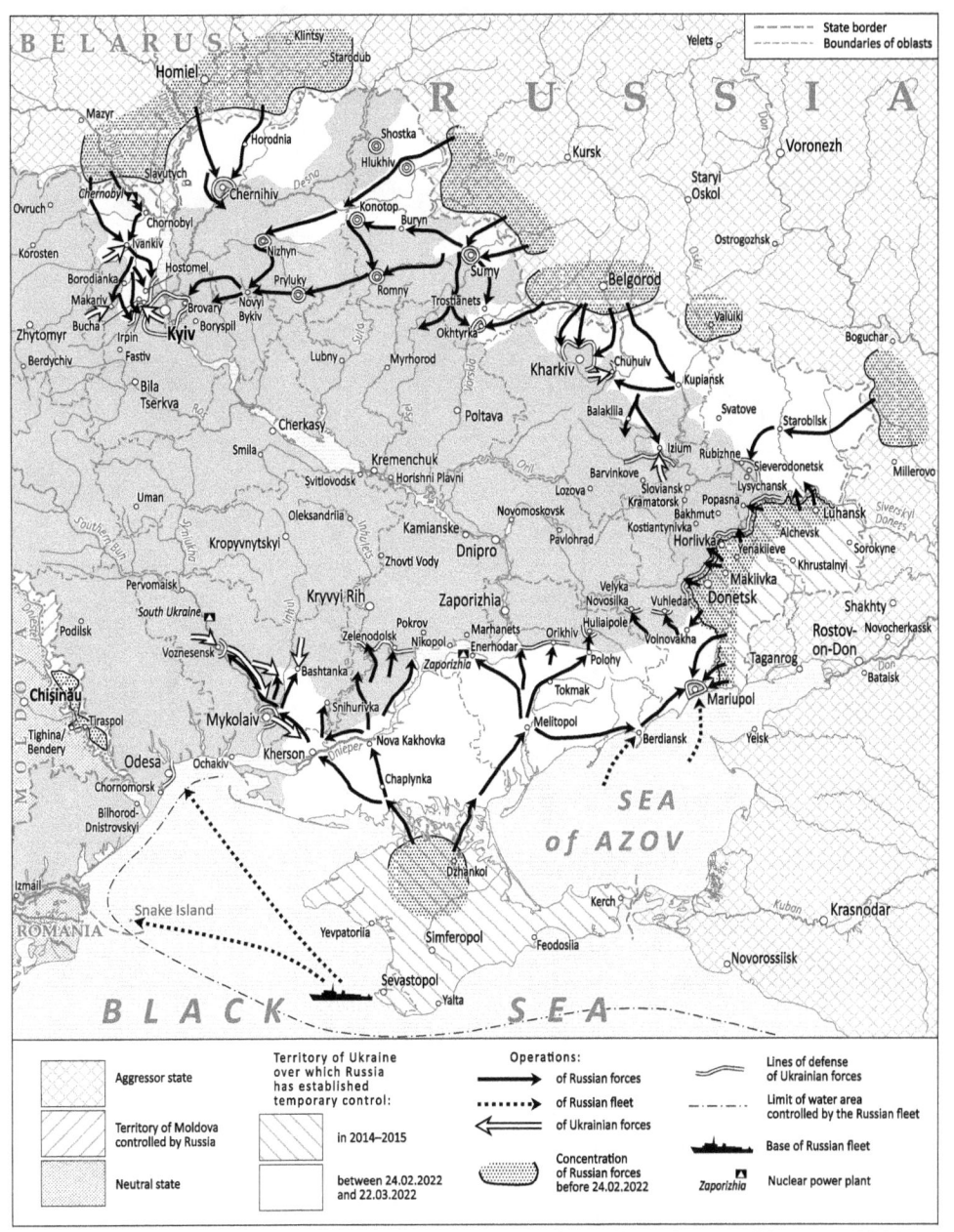

Map 0.6. Ukraine during the Russian invasion, July 2022. © Dmytro Vortman, 2022.

# Introduction

Speaking about Kharkiv, local residents sometimes say "This city is not the first, but neither is it the second." The point of the expression is that if, allegedly, we are not in first place, we do not want to settle for second. Such ambitions on the part of a city that was once the administrative capital of Soviet Ukraine are quite understandable. Kharkiv made an impetuous career in a relatively brief historical period. Having appeared on the steppe frontier of the Muscovite state in the mid-seventeenth century as a small wooden fort, over time it developed into the capital of a region known as Sloboda Ukraine, becoming the second university center after Lviv on Ukrainian territory. Kharkiv entered the modern period of its history as one of the largest cities of the Russian Empire and the Soviet Union, second only to Kyiv as an educational, industrial, and arms-production center of Ukraine.

Historically, Kharkiv belongs to two categories at once: "second" cities and border (margin-centric) cities.[1] I consider it comparable to cities like Lviv, Gdansk, Milan, or Barcelona. Geographically, Kharkiv is the most important Ukrainian urban center in the vicinity of the current Ukrainian-Russian border, which runs forty kilometers north of the city.[2] Politically, Kharkiv was at times a rival to Kyiv. From the national perspective, its public space has long been a contested ground between Ukrainian and Russian discourses of identity. No wonder Kharkiv has been rendered differently in their respective national narratives.

The Ukrainian image of Kharkiv has had several close associations: with the Cossacks; the philosopher and moralist Hryhorii Skovoroda; Kharkiv University; the national renaissance of the early nineteenth century; and Ukrainian national communism of the 1920s. In the Russian narrative, Kharkiv has often been presented as a transitional point in Russia's triumphant advance toward the Black Sea, an exemplary center of imperial education and science, as well as an industrial, commercial, and transportation center. Images of Kharkiv took shape and changed constantly, depending on the position of the observer, the various meanings attributed to one and the same phenomenon, and, of course, shifts in the city's political and cultural environments.

This book is about Kharkiv and its region, considered here as social constructs and, at the same time, as a space in which competing and even mutually exclusive discourses of identity arose, met, and interacted.³ Presented here is the history of the "imagination" of Kharkiv and its region, known as Sloboda Ukraine. It is the history of their mental (re)mapping and representation in national narratives, as well as in the public space of the city and region from their first appearance on the map in the mid-seventeenth century to the present day. Kharkiv's "cityscape" is a reflection of different discourses of identity elaborated and implemented by different political regimes—Ukrainian, imperial Russian, and Soviet—at different times.

Today the concept of identity has become all but the basic and indispensable topos of the social sciences and humanities. Regardless of certain doubts about the utility of this concept in research work, the category of identity, which is indissolubly associated with history, takes on particular significance with regard to Ukrainian themes. Like the rings of a tree trunk, contemporary Ukrainian society retains various discourses of identity that have arisen in the course of its history. Almost all of them have acquired not only a national dimension but imperial, regional, and local dimensions as well.

In this book, the concept of national identity is based on its interpretation by those historians who go beyond the era of the French Revolution in search of the roots of modern nationalism.⁴ I proceed from the concept of modern and premodern types of national identity that coexisted in parallel or were arranged in a certain hierarchy of compatible complex or hybrid structures on the broad historical expanse of the Ukrainian-Russian cultural borderland. The point is that concepts of nationalism worked out in the Western world were not and could not have been transferred to the historical territory of Orthodox Slavic Rus' without substantial revisions and limitations.

In the Russian language, the term *natsiia* (nation) has not gained acceptance as a self-description of the country and continues to amass negative connotations in Russian society to the present day; *natsiia* has been supplanted by the word *narod* (literally, "people"), a borrowing from Polish (*naród*), in which it appeared as an analogue of "nation."⁵ Translated into Russian, however, the term took on an ambiguity that it still retains today: *narod* appears in three hypostases at once—social, religious, and ethnocultural. That ambiguity is the result of retarded intellectual and cultural development as well as shallow modernization in the Slavic Orthodox world: neither the Westernized Russian nobility along with the intelligentsia nor the Marxists, nourished by Western ideas, managed to overcome the premodern syncretism of that world.

In this book, I proceed from the premise that until the mid-nineteenth century at least, no intellectuals of Russian, Ukrainian, or Belarusian origin ventured in their searches for modern national identity beyond the mental bounds of early modern "Holy Rus'," in which Great Russians, Little Russians, and White Russians were presented as "unassimilated and indivisible." The situation began to change only with the appearance of modern Ukrainian nationalism, but in the course of the last century or so, primordial religious and imperial structures have remained astonishingly persistent in this part of the world.

In the past, regional and local features were accepted as primordially equivalent to national ones. The problem of the relation between national and regional identities takes on particular significance in the southern and eastern parts of Ukraine.[6] The history of Kharkiv is inseparable from that of the Sloboda Ukraine historical region.[7] The latter took shape between the mid-seventeenth and early eighteenth centuries on the steppe frontier, control over which was contested by Russia, the Polish-Lithuanian Commonwealth, the Crimean Khanate and its vassals, and three Cossack military-democratic polities—the Hetmanate, the Zaporozhian Sich, and the Don Cossack Host. Those lands are now divided between the Kursk, Voronezh, and Belgorod oblasts (provinces) of Russia and the Luhansk, Donetsk, Poltava, Sumy, and Kharkiv oblasts of Ukraine. It must be added that the borders of the region coincided only in part with the administrative boundaries of the Kharkiv (Sloboda Ukraine) gubernia (vicegerency) in the Russian Empire and the Kharkiv oblast in the USSR and present-day Ukraine.

As a rule, historical regions have no definite borders with adjacent regions: throughout their existence, they usually play the role of specific contact zones of intensive cultural exchange.[8] The particular features of one historical region or another can therefore be defined and understood only in comparative perspective, taking account of the whole gamut of its cultural, economic, political, and sociolegal characteristics. For all the ambiguity and indeterminacy of definitions of historical regions, the use of such definitions assumes a certain territorial integrity endowed with a particular historical continuity, institutions, and symbolism reflected in regional identity.[9]

As a rule, direct links between identity and region are sustained by regional narratives that produce images of nature and landscape; by architecture, ethnocultural descriptions, evaluations of the state of the economy and relations between province and center, stereotypical images of the population (both "us" and "them"), historical texts, and so on. Regional identities are manifested not only in narratives but also in social constructions and practices, rituals and discourses bounded by particular times and places and competing with one another. In the final analysis, regional narratives enter into direct dialogue with national narratives.[10]

With the cultural turn in the humanities, regional history began to be constructed on the model of the imagination of the nation, and the very appearance of the region was interpreted as the result of intellectual projection onto the map— that is to say, mental mapping. After the collapse of the Soviet Union in 1991, the phenomenon of Ukrainian regionalism was regarded initially and primarily in the current political context.[11] In turn, the regionalization of Ukrainian political and cultural space fostered growing attention to regional aspects of Ukrainian history as a whole and to individual regions in particular. Historical regions of southern and eastern Ukraine, including the present-day Kharkiv oblast, have come increasingly into the scholarly field of vision.[12]

The Sloboda Ukraine region, of which Kharkiv became the center in the eighteenth century, has taken on different meanings at various times. It has been variously positioned on mental maps of Ukrainian, Russian, and Soviet symbolic space. In some cases it was the steppe marchland of the Muscovite state, in others a pale shadow of the Cossack Hetmanate, but most often it held the status of a borderland between forest and steppe, between the world of nomads and settled peoples, Slavs and Turkic tribes, Cossack regions and empire, Ukraine and Russia. It has encompassed the steppe frontier—the moving boundary of military settlements—or the whole gamut of multifarious divisions between Ukrainian and Russian settlements located in proximity to one another throughout the expanse of the borderland.

Although the concept of borderland is still in the process of theoretical development, it is already gaining recognition as one of the most substantial elements of nation-state building.[13] It is another question whether the borderland has been apprehended as a zone of division or contact and, if so, whether it has participated in its own right in the construction of national identities. What symbolic space has it occupied in national narratives? Has it produced a new identity space in its own right, or has it remained a mosaic, an eclectic mixture of external characteristics and attributes?

Historically, Sloboda Ukraine has been part of the Ukrainian-Russian borderland, which is the most problematic of the borderlands defining present-day Ukrainian political and national space.[14] The Ukrainian-Russian borderland is best described as a transitional or contact cultural zone, whether or not it is traversed by political or administrative boundaries. In every concrete historical instance, the Ukrainian-Russian borderland was not stable or precisely defined. It appears most often as a mental construct with a symbolic character, as well as in the form of corresponding processes, practices, and discourses arising from Ukrainian-Russian relations and endowed with their own array of symbols. The delimitation of the Ukrainian-Russian border is a problem not only and not so much of political geography or bilateral relations between states. It is, rather, a problem of national (re)identification.[15] Speaking generally, it is a problem touching on fundamental questions: what Russia is and what Ukraine is; what their mutual relations have been, are now, and might be in the future.[16]

The basic role in the formation and evolution of collective discourses of identity is played by cities and the urban cultural milieu. For that reason, the author of these pages has found it necessary to go beyond the bounds of discursive analysis and deal with particular aspects of social reality when it comes to describing such matters as the city's demography; reciprocal relations between the center and the region; the national and cultural policies of the center; the local authorities' and civil society's response to them or to the development of the Ukrainian national movement. The present book relies primarily on published sources, mainly narratives. The overwhelming majority of works devoted to the history of the city and its region belong to the genre of local history. In this regard, I was able to rely on some of my own research pertaining to the history of Sloboda Ukraine, Kharkiv, and Kharkiv University.[17]

The structure of this work is based on the chronological principle. Chapter 1 traces the history of the mental mapping and institutionalization of the Sloboda Ukraine steppe frontier to the second half of the eighteenth century, including the Catherinian reforms. Chapter 2 concerns the founding of Kharkiv University, which reflected the complexity of relations between the imperial center and the province and influenced the symbolic and cultural geography of the region in the Russian Empire. Chapter 3 is devoted to the process of reidentification of the region under the influence of imperial modernization and modern national ideas during the late eighteenth and early nineteenth centuries. Chapter 4, which encompasses the late nineteenth and early twentieth centuries, examines the urban development of Kharkiv, the changes taking place in its sociocultural space, and the progress of the Ukrainian national movement in the city. Chapter 5 deals with the history of Kharkiv from 1917 to 1991: I examine the struggle for the city in the years 1917–20, the development of Kharkiv as the capital of Soviet Ukraine, and, finally, its progress as the "second city" in the postwar period. Chapter 6 examines the reidentification of Kharkiv and region in the new political and cultural environment after the dissolution of the Soviet Union and the contradictory politics of identity as reflected in the city's public space. Chapter 7 is an attempt to trace the political and symbolic struggle for Kharkiv from 2010, when President Viktor Yanukovych's regime paved the way for the ongoing Russo-Ukrainian "hybrid war," which began in 2014, up to 2019, when the current president, Volodymyr Zelensky, came to power.

I am far from thinking that I have managed to solve all the problems touched upon in this work. Nevertheless, I shall consider my task accomplished if I manage to show the reader that Kharkiv and region, first, have their own specific places in Ukrainian historical space and time, and, second, that the project of Ukrainian nation-state building cannot be fulfilled without successful integration of the Russified border regions into the new grand narrative. This task has yet to be carried out.

## Notes

1. Jerome Hodos, "Globalization and the Concept of the Second City," *City & Community* 6, no. 4: 315–33; Jason Finch, Lieven Ameel, and Markku Salmela, "The Second City in Literary Urban Studies: Methods, Approaches, Key Thematics," in *Literary Second Cities*, ed. Jason Finch, Lieven Ameel, and Markku Salmela (London: Palgrave Macmillan, 2017), 3–20; Marcel Cornis-Pope and John Neubauer, *Towards a History of the Literary Cultures in East-Central Europe: Theoretical Reflections*, ACLS Occasional Papers 52 (2002): 1–50, here 26–27.

2. Michael T. Westrate, *Living Soviet in Ukraine from Stalin to Maidan: Under the Falling Red Star in Kharkiv* (Lanham, MD: Lexington Books, 2016); Margrethe B. Søvik, *Support, Resistance, and Pragmatism: An Examination of Motivation in Language Policy in Kharkiv, Ukraine* (Stockholm: Stockholm University Press, 2008); Oleksandr Iarmysh and Serhii Posokhov, eds., *Istoriia mista Kharkova XX stolittia* (Kharkiv: Folio, 2004); Dmitrii Bagalei and Dmitrii Miller, *Istoriia goroda Khar'kova za 250 let ego sushchestvovaniia: Istoricheskaia monografiia*, 2 vols., here vol. 1 (Kharkiv: Zilberberg and Sons, 1912, repr. Kharkiv: Kharkiv City Press, 1993).
3. Dana Arnold, *The Metropolis and Its Image: Constructing Identities for London, c. 1750–1950* (Oxford: Blackwell, 1999); Klaus Siebenhaar, "The Myth of Berlin: The Imagined and the Staged City," in *Urban Mindscapes of Europe*, ed. Godela Weiss-Sussex and Franco Bianchini (Amsterdam: Rodopi, 2006), 225–35; *Postmodern Cities and Spaces*, ed. Sophie Watson and Katherine Gibson (Oxford: Blackwell, 1995); *Imagining Cities*; *Cities of the Mind*, ed. Sallie Westwood and John M. Williams (London: Routledge, 1997).
4. "Concepts of Nationhood in Early Modern Eastern Europe," special issue, *Harvard Ukrainian Studies* 10, nos. 3–4 (December 1986): 274; Zenon E. Kohut, *Making Ukraine: Studies on Political Culture, Historical Narrative, and Identity* (Edmonton: CIUS Press, 2011), xi; Serhii Plokhy, *The Origins of the Slavic Nations: Premodern Identities in Russia, Ukraine, and Belarus* (Cambridge: Cambridge University Press, 2006), 5; Lotte Jensen, ed., *The Roots of Nationalism: National Identity Formation in Early Modern Europe, 1600–1815* (Amsterdam: Amsterdam University Press, 2016).
5. Aleksei Miller, "'Narodnost'" i 'natsiia' v russkom iazyke XIX veka: Podgotovitel'nye nabroski k istorii poniatii," *Rossiiskaia istoriia*, no. 1 (2009): 151–65; Alexei Miller, *The Romanov Empire and Nationalism: Essays in the Methodology of Historical Research* (Budapest: CEU Press, 2008).
6. Paul Pirie, "National Identity and Politics in Southern and Eastern Ukraine," *Europe-Asia Studies* 48, no. 7 (1996): 1079–1104; Anna Fournier, "Mapping Identities: Russian Resistance to Linguistic Ukrainisation in Central and Eastern Ukraine," *Europe-Asia Studies* 54, no. 3 (2002): 415–33.
7. Volodymyr Sklokin, *Rosiis'ka imperiia i Slobids'ka Ukraïna u druhii polovyni XVIII st.: Prosvichenyi absoliutyzm, impers'ka intehratsiia, lokal'ne suspil'stvo* (Lviv: Ukrainian Catholic University Press, 2019); Dmytro Chornyi, *Istoriia Slobids'koï Ukraïny: Pidruchnyk* (Kharkiv: Kharkiv University Press, 2018); Volodymyr Masliichuk, *Provintsiia na perekhresti kul'tur: Doslidzhennia z istoriï Slobids'koï Ukraïny XVII–XIX st.* (Kharkiv: Muzei Mis'koï Sadyby, 2007); Anton G. Sliusarskii, *Sotsial'no-ėkonomicheskoe razvitie Slobozhanshchiny XVII–XVIII vv.* (Kharkiv: Kharkivs'ke Knyzhkove Vydavnytstvo, 1964); Anton H. Sliusars'kyi, *Slobids'ka Ukraïna: Istorychnyi narys XVII–XVIII st.* (Kharkiv: Kharkivs'ke Knyzhkovo-Hazetne Vydavnytstvo, 1954); Dmytro I. Bahalii, *Istoriia Slobids'koï Ukraïny*, rev. ed., with preface by Volodymyr V. Kravchenko (Kharkiv: Osnova, 1990); Mykola F. Sumtsov, *Slobozhany: Istorychno-etnohrafichna rozvidka* (Kharkiv, 1918).
8. Stephan Troebst, "Introduction: What's in a Historical Region? A Teutonic Perspective," *European Review of History – Revue européenne d'histoire* 10, no. 2 (2003): 173–88.
9. Martin Jones and Anssi Paasi, eds., *Regional Worlds: Advancing the Geography of Regions* (London: Routledge, 2017); Anssi Paasi, "The Institutionalization of Regions: A Theoretical Framework for Understanding the Emergence of Regions and the Constitutions of Regional Identity," *Fennia*, no. 164 (1986): 105–46; idem, "Place and Region: Regional Worlds and Words," *Progress in Human Geography* 26, no. 6 (2002): 802–11; idem, "Region and Place: Regional Identity in Question," *Progress in Human Geography* 27, no. 4 (2003): 475–85.
10. Maiken Umbach, "Nation and Region: Regionalism in Modern European Nation-States," in *What Is a Nation? Europe 1789–1914*, ed. Timothy Baycroft and Mark Hewitson (New York: Oxford University Press, 2006), 63–80; Aleksei Miller, "Between Local and Inter-Imperial: Russian Imperial History in Search of Scope and Paradigm," *Kritika: Explorations in Rus-*

*sian and Eurasian History* 5, no. 1 (2004): 7–26; Celia Applegate, *A Nation of Provincials: The German Idea of Heimat* (Berkeley: University of California Press, 1990); Alon Confino, *The Nation as Local Metaphor: Württemberg, Imperial Germany and National Memory, 1871–1918* (Chapel Hill: University of North Carolina Press, 1997).

11. Oksana Myshlovska and Ulrich Schmid, eds., *Regionalism without Regions: Reconceptualizing Ukraine's Heterogeneity* (Budapest: CEU Press, 2019); James Hughes and Gwendolyn Sasse, eds., *Ethnicity and Territory in the Former Soviet Union: Regions in Conflict* (London: Frank Cass, 2002); Grigorii Nemiria, "Regionalism: An Underestimated Dimension of State-Building," in *Ukraine: The Search for a National Identity*, ed. Sharon L. Wolchik and Vladimir Zviglianich (Lanham, MD: Rowman & Littlefield, 2000), 183–98; Lowell Barrington and Erik Herron, "One Ukraine or Many? Regionalism in Ukraine and Its Political Consequences," *Nationalities Papers* 32, no. 1 (2004): 53–86; Oksana Malanchuk, "Social Identification versus Regionalism in Contemporary Ukraine," *Nationalities Papers* 33, no. 3 (2005): 345–68; Iaroslava Vermenych, *Teoretyko-metodolohichni problemy istorychnoï rehionalistyky v Ukraïni* (Kyiv: NANU, 2003).

12. Karen Brown, *A Biography of No Place: From Ethnic Borderland to Soviet Heartland* (Cambridge, MA: Harvard University Press, 2004); Paul Robert Magocsi, *The Roots of Ukrainian Nationalism: Galicia as Ukraine's Piedmont* (Toronto: University of Toronto Press, 2002); Hiroaki Kuromiya, *Freedom and Terror in the Donbas: A Ukrainian-Russian Borderland, 1870s–1990s* (Cambridge: Cambridge University Press, 1998); Fedir Turchenko and Halyna Turchenko, *Pivdenna Ukraïna: modernizatsiia, svitova viina, revoliutsiia (kinets' XIX st.– 1921 r.)* (Kyiv: Geneza, 2003); O. M. Sukhyi, *Halychyna: mizh Skhodom i Zakhodom. Narysy istoriï XIX–pochatku XX st.* (Lviv: Lviv National University Press,1999).

13. Anthony Cooper and Søren Tinning, eds., *Debating and Defining Borders: Philosophical and Theoretical Perspectives* (London: Routledge, 2019); Anssi Paasi, "Borderless Worlds and Beyond: Challenging the State-centric Cartographies," in *Borderless Worlds for Whom?* (London: Routledge, 2018), 21–36; Vladimir Kolossov, "Border Studies: Changing Perspectives and Theoretical Approaches," *Geopolitics* 4, no. 10 (2005): 606–32; Emmanuel Brunet-Jailly, "Toward a Model of Border Studies," *Journal of Borderland Studies* 1, no. 19 (2004): 1–18; James Anderson and Liam O'Dowd, "Borders, Border Regions and Territoriality: Contradictory Meanings, Changing Significance," *Regional Studies* 7, no. 33 (1999): 593–604.

14. Iurii Barabash, "Ėtnokul'turnoe pogranich'e: Kontseptual'nyi, tipologicheskii i situativnyi aspekty (Chuzhoe–Inoe–Svoe)," pts. 1 and 2, *Studia Litterarum* 4, no. 3 (2019): 290–329; pt. 5, no. 2 (2020): 286–321; Iaroslava Vermenych, *Terytorial'na identychnist' ukraïns'koho pohranychchia: istorychni vytoky ta heopolitychni vplyvy* (Kyiv: NANU, 2019); Vladimir Kolosov, "Radical Shifts in Russian-Ukrainian Relations and Geopolitics of Neighbourhood," *Journal of Geography, Politics, and Society* 8, no. 2 (2018): 7–15; Tatiana Zhurzhenko, *Borderlands into Bordered Lands: Geopolitics of Identity in Post-Soviet Ukraine* (Stuttgart: Ibidem Verlag, 2010); Peter W. Rodgers, *Nation, Region, and History in Post-Communist Transitions: Identity Politics in Ukraine, 1991–2006* (Stuttgart: Ibidem Verlag, 2008).

15. Peter J. Potichnyj et al., eds., *Ukraine and Russia in Their Historical Encounter* (Edmonton: CIUS Press, 1992); Valerii Smolii, ed., *Ukraïna i Rosiia v istorychnii retrospektyvi*, 3 vols. (Kyiv: Naukova Dumka, 2004); Andreas Kappeler et al., eds., *Culture, Nation, and Identity: The Ukrainian-Russian Encounter, 1600–1945* (Edmonton: CIUS Press, 2003).

16. Zenon E. Kohut, *History as a Battleground: Russian-Ukrainian Relations and Historical Consciousness in Contemporary Ukraine* (Saskatoon: Heritage Press, 2001).

17. Volodymyr Kravchenko, *The Ukrainian-Russian Borderland: History versus Geography* (Montreal, Kingston, London, and Chicago: McGill-Queen's University Press, 2022).

# CHAPTER 1
# The Steppe Borderland

## The Setting

The Sloboda region is situated at the junction of two natural and climatic zones, steppe and forest-steppe, which have no clearly defined natural boundaries and slope gently from north to south, thereby defining the direction of the region's principal rivers—the Psel, Vorskla, Siverskyi Donets, and Oskil. An exception is presented by the low Donets Ridge, which divides the rivers and their numerous tributaries into two basins, those of the Dnieper and the Don, belonging respectively to the Black and Azov Seas. The former encompassed the territory of the settled agrarian culture of the peoples of the forest-steppe zone, while the latter was more often in the sphere of influence of the nomadic peoples inhabiting the so-called Great Steppe.

Traditionally, migrants from the forest-steppe zone made use of the rivers to penetrate the black-earth steppe, which was rich in resources, and go on to the sea. The forest massifs and the marshes and lakes created by the rivers served to protect the population from the raids of steppe nomads. The latter, for their part, followed ancient overland routes (*sakmy*) that linked the rivers along the watersheds of the region's plateaus. The names of some of those routes appeared in written tradition only in the late sixteenth and seventeenth centuries: Murava, Izium, Kalmius, Bakaev. All of them reveal their Turkic roots. The names of the rivers and steppe routes may be considered the first markers of the future Sloboda region.[1]

As far as can be deduced from the available sources, the social and cultural boundaries of the region are a phenomenon of much later times. Those boundaries arose as the steppe was domesticated, and they became established thanks to the appearance of a settler population. The peoples of the steppe and forest-steppe zones had been approaching one another since time immemorial, turning the region into a broad contact zone initially devoid of clearly defined boundaries and lines of division but united by transit routes for trade, warfare, and exchange of information.

It is hardly surprising that the gaze of outside observers long traversed this expanse of territory without finding any point on which to concentrate. Until early modern times, its history and geography were not distinguished by recognizable symbols and generally attracted little notice against the background of events that had previously endowed the Crimea, the Black Sea littoral, as well as the Dnieper, Danube, and Don with symbolic meaning. The social and political communities of various peoples that arose on the territory of the Great Steppe generally made only peripheral contact on the lands of the future Sloboda region. This definitely applies to the times of the Scythians and Sarmatians; the Great Migration of Peoples and the Khazar Kaganate; Kyivan Rus'; the Pechenegs and Polovtsians; and the Golden Horde.

In the twelfth century the Dnieper portion of the future Sloboda region became the borderland of the Pereiaslav and Chernihiv-Siversk principalities of Kyivan Rus', while the Don portion was incorporated into the Cuman (Polovtsian) steppe—Desht-i-Qipchaq.[2] The conditional boundary between those territories basically coincided with the natural and climatic boundary between the steppe and forest-steppe zones. In the poetically imagined world of *The Tale of Igor's Campaign*, those two territories are distinguished as the "Rus' Land" and the "Cuman Land."[3] Some historians consider that the battle of Rus' princes with the Cumans described in that monument and mentioned in the Hypatian Codex under the year 1185 took place in the southeastern region of the present-day Kharkiv oblast in the vicinity of the town of Izium.[4] In this regard it should be noted that the "Cuman" marker of the territory subsequently known as Sloboda Ukraine and the Kharkiv region turned out to be one of the most sustainable. It left a souvenir in the form of numerous stone figures or statues erected at roadside burial mounds. The historical memory of Cuman rule long outlasted the comparatively brief sovereignty of the Golden Horde (thirteenth to mid-fourteenth centuries) over the Great Steppe.

The successors of the Golden Horde—the Crimean Khanate and the nomadic Tatar hordes subject to it in the northern Black Sea littoral—also made a lasting mark in the historical inheritance of the Steppe. It is no accident that the toponymy of the Kharkiv region retains Turkic roots to this very day: in the names of rivers (Aidar, Balakliia, Tor), ancient castle sites (Torchinovo, Azatskoe, Kukuevo), and towns (Okhtyrka, Izium, Balakliia, Burluk, Chuhuiv).[5] The greatest historian of the region, Dmytro Bahalii, had reason to claim that, to some extent at least, in the lower reaches of the Donets River, the Sloboda region was a place of permanent Tatar settlement and fortified sites where the Tatars engaged in agriculture, cattle raising, trades, hunting, and fishing. This gave them a basis to claim the territory as their own and helps explain the ferocity of the steppe wars of the late seventeenth and early eighteenth centuries.

The internecine warfare that tore apart the Golden Horde, as well as the fall of the Byzantine Empire and of Kyivan Rus', created a political vacuum in the Steppe. Attempts to fill it were soon made by new states: the Crimean Khanate; the Grand

Duchy of Lithuania, which absorbed most of the Kyivan inheritance; its principal competitor in that struggle, the Grand Principality of Moscow; and, finally, the united Polish-Lithuanian Commonwealth and the co-heir to the Byzantine Empire—the Ottoman Sultanate—which gained control of the Black Sea littoral.

In the fifteenth and sixteenth centuries, the future Sloboda region, considered in geographic perspective, was part of a large expanse of uninhabited territory, something of a buffer zone both dividing and uniting the states of the Crimea, Muscovy, and the Commonwealth. About that time, new military-democratic formations of the Cossack type—the nomadic Tatar hordes, the Don Cossack Host, and Zaporozhian Sich—arose on the periphery of each of those states. It is worth recalling that in the sixteenth and seventeenth centuries the democratic Cossack polities were serious rivals to any existing state. Without referring to well-known episodes from the history of Muscovy, the Commonwealth, and Moldavia, it suffices to mention the sad fate of the Siberian Khanate, conquered by a modest force of Cossack conquistadors.

**Figure 1.1.** Cossack Kharko, mythical founder of Kharkiv (sculptor Zurab Tsereteli, 2004). © Vikipediia. Vil'na Entsyklopediia.

Not surprisingly, each of the states contending for influence in the Steppe strove to gain the support of one Cossack host or another, while remaining mindful of the danger of such alliances to itself. The Cossack states, for their part, could be "employees" or robbers by turns. In the first case, the Cossacks would offer their services to particular warring states, receiving wages and legitimization of their own status, which they considered privileged. In the second instance, they would impose their services on one government or another or intimidate it with their strength, to say nothing of the purely pragmatic aims of such measures. The military and political situation in the Steppe changed quite frequently; hence yesterday's allies could easily become today's enemies, or vice versa.

By the mid-seventeenth century, the Muscovite state had gained the upper hand in the struggle for the Steppe.[6] Gradually, but with enviable determination, from the sixteenth century Muscovy advanced its stockades and forts southward, protecting itself against possible attack from any quarter with defensive perimeters and lines and, in turn, undertaking offensives in the steppe borderland. As a rule, the newly constructed forts and defensive lines were manned by Russian servitors. From the sixteenth to the eighteenth century, almost half the armed forces of the Muscovite state were concentrated on the southern steppe, indicating its importance to Muscovy.[7]

Hand in hand with the military advance, and sometimes anticipating it, went the Orthodox ecclesiastical colonization of the steppe. Monasteries and churches, appearing in remote and dangerous areas, defined Orthodox religious territory, as if to indicate the further course of government policy. The Sviatogorsk (Sviatohirsk) Monastery, for example, was built far out in the steppe long before its mass colonization. Moscow constantly resorted to religious argumentation in order to substantiate the "legitimacy" of its claims to the steppe not only for security reasons but also because of the need to conduct a "holy war" against the "heathen." There is mention of this, for example, in a report from the Central Office of Military Affairs to the Boyar Duma about the building of defensive structures on the Murava, Kalmius, and Noghay routes initiated at the direction of Tsar Mikhail Fedorovich as early as 1621.[8]

The gradual incorporation of the steppe into a new system of geopolitical coordinates, the appearance and interaction of various political formations on its territory, and the arrival of a settler population all, in one way or another, created a need to fill the geographic space with new social content. An indispensable aspect of that process was the delimitation and mapping of the steppe, which began toward the end of the sixteenth century and the beginning of the seventeenth.[9]

## Boundaries

Attempts to establish outer boundaries marking the steppe domains of contiguous states were undertaken at various times by the governments of Lithuania, the Commonwealth, and the Muscovite state, although that process was not and indeed could not be brought to completion by any of the interested parties until the appearance of permanent settlers. Thus, the territory of the future Sloboda region, situated in the sphere of predominant political influence of Muscovy and the Commonwealth, may be studied simultaneously with the aid of two concepts: frontier and borderland.

Michael Khodarkovsky, writing about Russian history of the sixteenth to eighteenth centuries, defines the frontier as a region constituting the periphery of a settled or domesticated territory, a particular politico-geographic area as distinct from a territory already integrated into a certain political space.[10] Jeremy Adelman and Stephen Aron define the frontier as something in the nature of a buffer or contact zone between peoples whose geographic and political boundaries are not clearly delineated.[11] In Russian, the concept of frontier (*frontir*) employed in the study of Russian history sometimes takes on not so much a geographic or cultural meaning as something of a military sense. Consequently, its closest analogue is often the broader term *porubezh'e*, which is nearer to the concept of a contact zone, while *pogranich'e* refers more to a territory defined by a political border dividing states, as well as to clearly defined cultural, religious, and linguistic regions.

If one considers the territory of the Sloboda region from the viewpoint of the Polish-Lithuanian Commonwealth, as did Guillaume Le Vasseur de Beauplan, a French engineer in the Polish service, then it takes on the character of a *pogranich'e*. Beauplan himself, who regarded the Dnieper River as the political boundary between the Commonwealth and Muscovy, recognized Moscow's right to a considerable portion of the so-called Wild Steppe on the Left Bank, which he called "Muscovite land," thereby distinguishing it from the Right Bank of the Dnieper—that is, the lands of the Commonwealth—which he called "lands of Rus'," as well as from the domains of the Crimea proper, which appeared on his map as "lands of Tartary."[12]

The boundary between the Muscovite state and the Commonwealth was also characterized by features of a *porubezh'e* or a *frontir*. It is defined in many documents as the "Putyvl *porubezh'e*," which included, among other settlements, the so-called Okhtyrka castle site, where the Cossack regimental fortified town of Okhtyrka would later be built. The Putyvl *porubezh'e* long remained a disputed territory between the Muscovite state and the Commonwealth.

It is telling that in 1634, when the Polish side proposed to mark the boundary with Muscovy by means of earthen mounds, stone pillars, and signs, the Russian government refused, pleading that "such customs are not native to the Muscovite state" and "this came about by divine will and is not for soulless posts and mounds."[13] Clearly apparent here was the shifting boundary and the possibility of changing the balance of forces in the region, taking account of the role that the Ukrainian Cossacks, then being persuaded by the Russian government to enter its permanent service, might play in such an eventuality.

It is well known that the Time of Troubles of the late sixteenth and early seventeenth centuries, in which the Zaporozhian Cossacks played an active part, delayed Moscow's advance into the steppe for some time and even moved Russia's defensive boundaries back to Belgorod, Kursk, and Voronezh. Cossack forces took part in all the wars and campaigns organized against Moscow by the Commonwealth government and the magnates in the first third of the seventeenth century. Most often, it was the borderland Russian towns and fortresses that became objects of Cossack activity.

It suffices to note that the Ukrainian Cossack leader Yakiv Ostrianyn, prior to being accepted into the Muscovite service in 1638 and becoming the founder of the fortified town of Chuhuiv, "earned" that right by seizing the Russian town of Valuiki and burning down the Belgorod stockade five years earlier.[14] Employing the services of such allies was not without risk, but at times the Muscovite government did not wish to refuse them, and at other times it could not do so. In this regard, Brian Boeck's conclusion that the policy of the Muscovite government in the steppe borderland was defined not so much by an immanent drive for expansion as by the weakness and vulnerability of Russia's position in the region appears quite convincing.[15]

If Moscow's border with the Commonwealth continued to be defined in rather approximate fashion, then its borders with the Crimean Khanate as such, in the contemporary sense of the term, did not exist at all. Nevertheless, Moscow treated the steppe frontier as a matter of tremendous significance. For evidence of the Russian government's practical and mental appreciation of its importance, one may look to the *Kniga Bol'shomu Chertezhu* (The book to the great map), produced in the late sixteenth century and constituting a detailed description of the territory adjacent to the Crimea.[16]

The territory of the future Sloboda region appears in that document as a long, thin strip linking Muscovy with the Crimea and defined basically by the steppe routes—Izium, Kalmius, and Murava—with the latter in a central position. It was here that the conditional borders of Lithuania's Kyiv Principality and, later, the palatinates of the Commonwealth came together with those of the Muscovite state.[17] What interested the compilers of the book most of all were the natural features of the region—rivers, lakes, ravines, fords—as well as defensive structures: small stockaded and fortified towns, abatis, and ditches used for defense against the Tatars. The stone figures scattered throughout the region since time immemorial were also used as points of basic orientation.

So detailed a description of the lands of the future Sloboda region in the *Kniga Bol'shomu Chertezhu* emphasizes the strategic importance that the region retained for the Muscovite authorities in the seventeenth century. And yet, in the *Kniga* it displays all the characteristics of a transitional territory with no clear lines of division or outer boundaries. Even a few decades after the formation of five Sloboda Cossack regiments, the calling card of the lands they occupied was still the Murava route. It also figures as such on Beauplan's map, reprinted by Moses Pitt in London in 1680,[18] and in a verse by the Ukrainian poet Oleksandr Buchynsky-Yaskold dating to 1678.[19]

The struggle for the steppe entered its decisive phase in the mid- and late seventeenth century, when a new Cossack state, the Hetmanate, also known under the name of "Little Russia," came into existence in the epicenter of the geopolitical quadrilateral (the Commonwealth, Russia, Turkey and the Crimea, and Sweden) under the leadership of Bohdan Khmelnytsky. Its very existence upset the established balance of forces in the region, provoking a long-term war of all against all.

The crucial and strategically important role in this new phase of struggle for the steppe was played by the Russian town of Belgorod, established in the late sixteenth century. It occupied the central position in the system of fortifications erected between 1635 and 1695, giving its name to that system.[20] The military strategic significance of that mighty fortified region, a critical bridgehead for Moscow's advance toward the Black Sea and a bastion in the confrontation with the Commonwealth, became fully apparent in the late seventeenth century, when Russian forces made use of it as their main base for the concentration of forces active both in the Ukrainian-Polish (western) and the Crimean (southern) sectors.

From the mid-seventeenth to the early eighteenth century, the war for dominance in the East European borderlands involved practically all the states of the region, as a result of which the military-bureaucratic empires of the Habsburgs, Romanovs, and Ottomans established and consolidated their superiority over states of the military-democratic (gentry-nobility and Cossack) type, including the Commonwealth, Hungary, the Crimea, and the Ukrainian Cossack Hetmanate.[21] The territory of the latter was torn to pieces by stronger neighbors, of whom Russia gained more than the rest.

These cardinal changes in the geopolitical configuration of eastern Europe were accompanied in the mid-seventeenth century by the appearance on the boundary of the steppe with the forest-steppe of a new Ukrainian (according to the ethnic affiliation of most of its permanent settlers) and, simultaneously, Russian (according to political affiliation) region—the Sloboda region. Its settlement may be considered the beginning of a new era in the history of the steppe, associated with its incorporation into the Russian Empire, as well as with the socioeconomic and cultural domestication of the steppe territory.

The mass migration of Ukrainians from the Commonwealth territories engulfed by warfare to the Muscovite-Tatar steppe frontier began after the defeat of the Cossack army at Berestechko in 1651, although particular instances of such migration had taken place earlier.[22] Every new worsening of the military and political situation on the Right and Left Banks of Ukraine sent new waves of migrants fleeing to the protection of Moscow. That process encompassed about half a century and continued, according to Dmytro Bahalii, from 1652 to 1712 inclusive.[23]

The first wave of mass emigration led to the appearance and settlement of such borderland fortified towns as Ostrogozhsk (Rybinsk), Sumy, Lebedyn, Kharkiv, Zmiiv, as well as a number of others. Two Sloboda Cossack regiments were formed simultaneously in 1652: that of Ostrogozhsk, posted on the eastern periphery of the Belgorod Line, and that of Sumy, which covered its western side. It is readily apparent that in strategic terms the first of them was aimed at the region of the Don Cossack Host and the other at the Hadiach regiment of the neighboring Hetmanate, which was continuing its suicidal war with the Commonwealth.

The Sloboda regiment of Akhtyrka (present-day Okhtyrka), formed in 1654, was posted closer to Poltava, while the Kharkiv regiment, formed at the same time, found itself in the middle, between the Dnieper and Don sectors of the new region, closer to the domain of the Zaporozhian Sich. Further waves of Ukrainian colonists taking refuge from the Ruin of the 1660s–80s led to the formation of the Izium regiment (1681) and the Balakliia regiment (formed in 1669 and disbanded in 1677),[24] which were moved to locations in the immediate vicinity of the Zaporozhian lands.

As the territory of the Sloboda regiments was settled and that of the Hetmanate, locked in a state of permanent warfare with Poland, was consolidated, the former political boundary between the Muscovite Tsardom and the Commonwealth was transformed into an administrative one, now dividing the Hetmanate from the Sloboda regiments—Cossack lands incorporated into the Russian state. As will be

**Figure 1.2.** Kharkiv fortress, seventeenth century (reconstruction by L. Shmatko and I. Karas). © Wikimedia Commons.

seen later, this administrative boundary between two Ukrainian regions proved quite stable despite constant change in the political configuration of the steppe frontier.

In retrospect, it is easy to see that by their very existence the Sloboda regiments were sharply changing the geopolitical situation on the steppe frontier in favor of Moscow. On the one hand, they protected the lands and towns of Russia proper (Great Russia) settled between the late sixteenth century and the first third of the seventeenth from Tatar raids. On the other hand, they served as a bridgehead for the Russian army, which now gained further scope to exert military and political pressure on the Cossack military polities of the Don, Zaporizhia, and the Hetmanate.

However, the appearance of permanent settlements of armed colonists on the Russian steppe frontier brought Moscow not only obvious advantages but also a certain political risk. The Russian government had to maintain constant control over the Sloboda regiments to prevent them from becoming a bridgehead for uprisings of the Cossack periphery and dissatisfied subjects against the central authorities, as had often happened in the recent seventeenth-century history of the Muscovite state.

The contradictory relations of the Cossack colonists and the Russian government make it necessary to look with fresh eyes at the celebrated fortifications—the defensive lines that Moscow built in the steppe. Many specialized studies have been written about their defensive role. Their social and political functions in the context of Russo-Ukrainian relations, however, are by no means routinely mentioned by historians. Yet it is precisely the Belgorod Line that figured as the most notable and influential feature of the frontier in the history of the Sloboda territory, fulfilling sociopolitical functions as well as strictly defensive ones.

If the author may be allowed an unintentional pun, the construction of the Belgorod Line of fortifications (*kreposti*) was accompanied by a weakening of the bonds of serfdom (*krepostnichestvo*) for Russian settlers and servitors: even runaway serfs who had already felt the weight of the Law Code of 1649 decreed by Tsar Aleksei Mikhailovich were initially accepted here. But as soon as foreign colonists—Ukrainians from the Commonwealth—made their way to the steppe frontier, the Russian government immediately restored the social barrier between serfs and freemen.[25] The Belgorod Line became the ultimate boundary for Russian settlers, legalized serfdom, and the further expansion of Russia's military-administrative system. In the future, the government would strictly maintain the distinction between Ukrainian colonists and Russian subjects proper.

It is no accident that Dmytro Bahalii defined the Sloboda region as the territory beyond the Belgorod Line of fortifications (if one considers it from Moscow's perspective) settled by Ukrainian refugees.[26] Settlers on the inner side of the Belgorod Line were often considered equals of Russian servitors, regardless of origin. As for those who settled on the outer side, protecting the line from the dangers of the steppe, they gained the right to additional privileges. The farther beyond any line of fortifications a new group of settlers ventured, the greater the number of privileges it acquired, and vice versa.

Thus, the Sloboda regiment of Ostrogozhsk, posted on the Belgorod Line itself, felt the greatest pressure from the local Russian authorities, who strove to limit the privileges granted it by the government. At the same time, colonists led by Yakiv Ostrianyn who settled the fortress of Chuhuiv, established far out in the steppe, received privileges in 1638 far beyond those granted to Russian border guards.

Other defensive structures built by the Russian government—the Izium and Ukrainian Lines—played a similar role. The Izium Line, built in 1683, promoted the establishment and consolidation of the southern boundary of the Sloboda regiments, while the construction of a new Russian "Ukrainian Line" in 1731–33 south of the present-day Kharkiv oblast and the settlement on its territory of ethnic Russian landed military formations posed a threat to the traditional privileges of Sloboda Ukrainians.[27]

It was the privileges (*slobody*) that turned out to be Moscow's most effective means of maintaining control over new settlers. Contributing to this, aside from other factors, was the political weakness of the Sloboda Cossack regiments, formed at different times by recruits from various regions and social strata of Ukrainian society and not representing a homogeneous entity. Horizontal ties among them were limited by clan loyalties or wholly personal interests, while the vertical ties that bound each of them individually to the Muscovite administration guaranteed them privileged social status and well-being. This had a decisive influence on relations between the Sloboda recruits and other Cossack military-political formations.

Relations between the Sloboda regiments and the neighboring Hetmanate (Little Russia) in a system of constantly changing geopolitical coordinates endowed the defensive line with an additional political and sociolegal character that divided the two Ukrainian Cossack regions. From the very beginning of mass colonization of the Sloboda region, it was settled mainly by individuals dissatisfied with the hetman regime. The Russian government's exploitation of the Ukrainian refugees against the Ukrainian hetmans proved much more effective than the latter's attempts to blackmail Moscow with the Russian political impostors who found refuge in the lands of Cossacks. For that reason, the Sloboda regiments presented a permanent threat to the Hetmanate by the very fact of their existence, regardless of the Hetmanate's foreign policy.

Beginning with Bohdan Khmelnytsky, Ukrainian hetmans sought either to destroy the Sloboda settlements or to subordinate them to their regimen. This became particularly apparent during the rule of Hetman Ivan Vyhovsky, highly vexed by political opponents who took refuge in the Sloboda regiments and supported Colonel Martyn Pushkar, who was loyal to Moscow. Vyhovsky's forces, commanded by Colonel Zhuchenko of Poltava, approached Sumy and Okhtyrka with Tatar allies, calling on the colonels of those towns to join them against Moscow, but without success. The supporters of the Ukrainian hetman were defeated and forced to withdraw. In general, according to Dmytro Bahalii, Vyhovsky's movement against Moscow had little influence on the Sloboda settlers.[28]

Hetman Ivan Samoilovych, who was loyal to Moscow, strove persistently but in vain to have the Sloboda regiments placed under his "regimen."[29] Another pretender to the hetmancy, Petro Ivanenko (Petryk), an official in the chancellery of the Hetmanate who arranged a military and political alliance with the Crimean khan, favored the complete abolition of the Sloboda regiments, with the takeover of the Sumy and Okhtyrka regiments by the Hetmanate and the transfer of the Kharkiv and Ostrogozhsk regiments to Right-Bank Ukraine. That would have reopened the Murava route, used for campaigns against Russia, to the Crimean khan.[30]

The political character of the boundary between the Sloboda region and the Hetmanate was demonstrated by the fact that it was precisely there, on the Kolomak River, that a political coup took place under the control of the Russian army, bringing to power Hetman Ivan Mazepa, who was initially loyal to Moscow. Mazepa had an opportunity to test the strength of that boundary when Swedish forces allied with him tried to break through the Sloboda regiments toward Moscow. They met fierce resistance in the vicinity of Krasnokutsk, Kolomak, Murafa, Kotelva, Kolontaev, and other fortresses. The Swedish-Ukrainian forces suffered heavy losses owing to partisan activity and were forced to withdraw.[31]

On the other hand, the boundaries between the Sloboda regiments and Little Russia took on a social significance.[32] In this regard the Hetmanate authorities followed the same logic as the Muscovite government, though for opposite reasons. If the tsarist government strove to divide the Ukrainian population from the Russian one so as to avoid granting its own subjects "excessive" privileges, the Hetmanate authorities, on the contrary, defended the social and political privileges enjoyed by the Hetmanate, which were far greater than those of the Sloboda region, to say nothing of Russia itself.

Territorial conflicts along the border between the Sloboda region and the Hetmanate were generally settled, with the help of the Muscovite government, in favor of the former. Such was the case of the border disputes, which had lasted many years, between the Sumy and Okhtyrka regiments on the one hand and the Poltava and Hadiach regiments on the other. The disputed lands (the towns of Kotelnia and Kolomak in particular) remained under the control of the Sloboda colonels. The appeals of Hetmans Ivan Skoropadsky and Danylo Apostol, both loyal to Moscow, proved futile.[33]

In general, mutual relations between the political elites of the two Ukrainian Cossack regions, the Sloboda regiments and the Hetmanate, remained quite complicated, not to say hostile. For the Sloboda officers and their descendants, loyalty to the tsarist throne became a matter of particular pride, an influential component of collective identity and of the mythology based upon it. For their part, patriots of the Hetmanate maintained feelings of proud superiority and outright contempt for the Sloboda settlers for almost a century and a half.[34] Such feelings, characteristic of relations between metropole and province, survived until the nineteenth century and subsequently left their imprint on Ukrainian national historiography.

The Sloboda regiments presented a threat not only to the Hetmanate but also to the Zaporozhian Host. The revolt against Moscow led by Hetman Ivan Briukhovetsky in 1668 found a much greater response among settlers of the Sloboda region than previous ones. This was most likely due to the active policy of Ivan Sirko, the Zaporozhian Cossacks' popular leader, who not only had extensive contacts in the Sloboda region but also held land and family there.[35] He was supported by residents of local towns—Tsareborysiv, Zmiiv, Valky, Murafa, and Maiatsk—and by those of the regimental center, Kharkiv. True, with the same "success," Kharkiv closed its gates to the Zaporozhians, who were soon defeated in battle at Chuhuiv. Later, in the early eighteenth century, Zaporozhian Cossacks allied with the Tatars came out against the settlers of the Sloboda region.[36]

Relations between the Sloboda Cossacks and those of the Don Cossack Host proved no less contradictory, being characterized by border disputes near the rivers Aidar, Zherebets, and Krasnaia on the one hand and coordinated action against common enemies on the other. The revolt led by Stepan Razin found support in such small towns of the Sloboda region as Tor, Maiatsk, Valuiki, Zmiiv, Zolochiv, Tsareborysiv, Balakliia, Bohodukhiv, and Chuhuiv.[37] In 1670 Colonel Ivan Dzykovsky of Ostrogozhsk, who had earlier refused support to hetmans Ivan Vyhovsky, Ivan Briukhovetsky, and Petro Doroshenko, also took part in Razin's uprising. The most likely reason is that of all the Sloboda regiments, that of Ostrogozhsk was most closely associated with the Don, and not with Zaporizhia or the Hetmanate. At the same time, the Kharkiv and Sumy regiments of the Sloboda region came out against Razin's forces, for which Moscow duly recompensed them with awards and privileges.

Something similar was to be seen during the revolt led by Kondratii Bulavin in 1707–8, which found support among the salt-workers of Bakhmut but encountered resistance from the Sloboda Cossacks. After the defeat of Bulavin's followers, the lands along the Aidar River belonging to the Don Cossacks went to the Ostrogozhsk Cossack regiment, and territories along the Siverskyi Donets River were assigned to the newly created Bakhmut province.[38]

The appearance of five Sloboda regiments that not only blocked the path of the Crimean Tatars on their campaigns of conquest but also invaded territory that the Crimeans considered their own property soon led to an abrupt deterioration of relations between Moscow and the Crimean Khanate in the late seventeenth and early eighteenth centuries. The diplomatic contrivances of tsarist diplomacy—which, in its dealings with the Crimea, avoided any mention of its claims to the "southern" lands in the new titulature of the Russian monarch introduced in 1655–66—[39] could hardly reduce tensions between the two states.

The first to feel the effects were, of course, the Sloboda colonists. Tatar hordes large and small assaulted the settlements taken over by the colonists in an effort to restore the status quo ante in that part of the steppe. In response, Moscow organized two large offensive campaigns against the Crimea, led by Prince Vasilii Golitsyn and Hetman Ivan Samoilovych, in which the Sloboda Cossacks also took part. A fierce struggle, with great losses on both sides, continued until the very beginning of the eighteenth century. It was only with the fall of the Crimean Khanate in 1783 that the danger of Tatar attacks on Sloboda Ukraine was finally lifted.

Although in practice social and even cultural boundaries between Ukrainians and Tatars often proved no less transparent than political ones, for the Sloboda colonists it was precisely the Tatars who became the basic "other," and the struggle against them took on a symbolic character. Contributing to this were the politics and rhetoric of the Orthodox Church, which strove to fill the geographic expanse of the land with sacral significance. The regional Sloboda elite, in creating its own historical mythology and list of services to the Russian throne, reserved the place of honor for the war with the Tatars (second place went to its "steadfastness" in the struggle with "traitor" hetmans).

Religious markers aside, the natural and climatic features of the region where the forest-steppe gave way to the steppe lent even greater stability to the border with the Crimean Tatars.[40] The steppe frontier made a permanent impression on the historical memory of the Sloboda settlers, yielding a rich folkloric and literary heritage. Overcoming it proved beyond the capacity even of modern Ukrainian historians, who continue to laud the achievements of the Sloboda Cossacks in the "struggle with Tatar and Turkish aggression" while maintaining a modest silence about the campaigns of conquest undertaken by "their own" heroes and their far from heroic behavior in foreign lands.

In general, the system of geopolitical coordinates within which the settlement of the Sloboda region proceeded in the late seventeenth century became one of the most important factors in the formation of the territory's regional identity. From the moment of their arrival, the Sloboda colonists felt the difference between themselves and all their neighbors, but with regard to politics they oriented themselves toward Moscow. Moreover, the Sloboda regiments never played an independent political role in the region—nor, it would seem, did they have any need to do so, considering the mixed social composition and pragmatic motivation of those who chose to settle there.

## Name

In the institutionalization and conceptualization of any new region, a fundamental role is played by its symbolic formulation—in the first instance, the appearance of the region's name, which defines its inhabitants' feeling of community and collective belonging.⁴¹ For the Sloboda region, however, the choice of name turned out to be a lengthy process in the course of which several names were applied simultaneously to one and the same territory, depending on the time period and concrete political or socioeconomic transformations of the region.

In official Muscovite documents, the lands subsequently occupied by the Belgorod Line and territory south of it, which were designated for Ukrainian settlers, had earlier been called "the steppe" (*step'*), "the Field" (*Pole*), "the Tatar routes" (*tatarskie sakmy*), and "the borderland" (*ukraina*).⁴² Thus, the Nikon Chronicle relates the building of defensive structures there in the late sixteenth century, during the reign of Tsar Fedor Ioannovich, in the following words:

> Tsar Fedor Ioannovich, seeing that there would be many wars for his state because of the Crimean people, and thinking to build fortified towns along the Tatar routes, sent his voevodas [military governors] with many warriors; it was also he who ... established the fortified towns of Belgorod, Oskol [Oskil], Valuika [Valuiki] and others in the steppe; and besides those towns, in Ukraine he established the fortified towns of Voronezh, Livna [Livny], Kursk, Kromy.⁴³

The fortified towns named here, as well as others along the borderland, were most often referred to adjectivally in Russian official documents as *ukrainnye* (of the borderland) or *polevye* (of the field).⁴⁴

The adjective *pol'skii* ("of the field," derived from *pole*) in Russian documents of the time was used quite often in reference to Belgorod and neighboring fortified towns or to public roads. In the early seventeenth century, Muscovite officials considered Voronezh, Yelets, Valuiki, and Kursk to be situated in *pol'skaia ukraina* (the steppe borderland).⁴⁵ The Ukrainian Cossack leader (otaman) Mykhailo Cherkashenyn, who earned his living in the steppe, is referred to in Russian folklore as "*pol'skii*."⁴⁶ In other words, the concepts of *step'* and *pole* were used synonymously and played the role of basic geographic markers of territory that was seen from Moscow's perspective, first and foremost, as a lethally dangerous expanse "beyond the defensive line," a borderland, a place of political exile, and, additionally, as a source of exotic fruit or game for the tsar's table.

As the Great Steppe was domesticated, the *pol'skii* terminology gradually began to go out of use in Russian official jargon. The *ukraina* terminology, on the contrary, remained in demand, not only in Muscovy but in the Commonwealth as well.⁴⁷ In time, accordingly, the notion of "two *ukrainas*," Russian and Polish, became widespread in Russian, Polish, and Ukrainian historical literature. In fact, the number of *ukrainas*—borderland territories to which that name was applied—was not limited to two. For example, the Cossack state—the Hetmanate in its borders of 1649—was also called "Ukraina," endowing the purely geographic concept of *ukraina* with added sociopolitical significance in that particular case.

Of course, it would be an obvious anachronism to speak of modern national content in the use of such terminology in the seventeenth and eighteenth centuries. The identity of ethnic Ukrainians of that day constituted a varied assortment of different markers, not always attached to a specific territory. Ethnic Ukrainians, on arriving in the Left-Bank steppe territories extending beyond the borderland Belgorod Line of fortifications, defined their new dwelling place with the aid of a mixed geographic terminology in which "Tatar" markers nevertheless played a substantial role. Examples are "in the steppe beyond the Don River in the Noghay land at the mouth of the Bitiug River"[48] or "we, your orphans, have established ourselves in the Volnoe district beyond the Vorskla River in the Crimean land, on the Tatar route, in the wild steppe."[49] According to some accounts surviving from the early seventeenth century, "Noghay" was a traditional Muscovite name for the left bank of the Siverskyi Donets River, while "Crimean" designated the right bank of that same fluvial artery of the Donets section of the Muscovite *ukraina*.[50]

The *ukraina* terminology is often encountered in the written tradition of the period with reference to the Sloboda regiments. Moreover, it was used by Russians and Ukrainians alike as a name for the borderland. In a writ from Tsar Aleksei Mikhailovich to the Sloboda regiments concerning the revolt of Hetman Ivan Samoilovych, the land occupied by the Cossack settlers was called *ukraina* and its inhabitants *ukrainskie*.[51] That usage did not change in the early eighteenth century. The Ukrainian Line was built in the Sloboda region, and the Ukrainian landed militia corps was posted there as well, as were regular formations of the Ukrainian army serving in the steppe borderland.

It is telling that on a map used by Muscovite envoys in the late seventeenth century small "Ukrainian" fortified towns in the steppe were distinguished from "Cherkasian" (i.e., Hetmanate) or Little Russian ones.[52] Inhabitants of the Sloboda region, in turn, distinguished Ukrainian, Little Russian, and Great Russian (*russkie*) fortified towns sharply from one another.[53] Nor did the Muscovite government consider that the Sloboda Ukrainian settlements belonged to the Russian lands proper. Those settlements, along with the Belgorod Line, marked the ancient symbolic boundary between Rus' and the steppe. In this regard, as mentioned earlier, one may agree with Brian Boeck, who maintains that the Moscow government clearly distinguished the metropole (the Russian lands proper) from the steppe borderland of the state.[54]

The term *ukraina*, constantly encountered in the texts of petitions and charters of the colonists themselves, as well as derivative terms (*ukrainnye goroda*, i.e., fortified towns in the borderland), were associated with Muscovite tradition and used predominantly to denote borderland (*ukrainnye*) fortified towns and territories. In the early eighteenth century, as far as may be judged from documents of local origin, *ukraina* meant the territory not only of settlements in the steppe borderland but also those of the Sloboda Cossacks.[55] At that time, however, the term did not yet carry a cultural connotation, unlike the "Little Russian" designation to be discussed shortly.

The Little Russian political and intellectual elite of the late seventeenth and early eighteenth centuries used the concept of *ukraina* synonymously with the Hetmanate or Little Russia.⁵⁶ But it would appear that the Cossack elite's geographic notion of the "fatherland" did not include the Sloboda region, which in some cases remained a territory disputed between the Hetmanate and Moscow and, in others, was considered part of Russian political space.

If one believes the text of the agreement reached by the official of the Cossack Host Petro Ivanenko with the Crimean khan, then for the two parties *Ukraina* meant the Cossack state—the Hetmanate—while the Sloboda settlements were called "Muscovite":

> if the inhabitants of the Muscovite *slobody*, transferred from *Ukraina*, refuse an alliance with us and begin to resist, then they must be treated as enemies; if an obstacle is encountered in taking the Muscovite *slobody* and joining them with *Ukraina* either by arms or by peaceful agreement, then they must be driven by force to leave the *slobody* and settle on the Right Bank of the Dnieper.⁵⁷

As we see, the concepts of *Ukraina* and the Muscovite *slobody* in this text, assuming that it is quoted accurately, are clearly distinguished.

In the eighteenth-century Cossack chronicles, the Sloboda regiments were also assigned to the Russian domains. The Eyewitness Chronicle notes that the regiments arose "on Muscovite grounds."⁵⁸ According to the most popular of the Cossack chroniclers, Hryhorii Hrabianka, Hetman Bohdan Khmelnytsky "bade the people go freely ... across the border to Great Russia so that they might settle there in fortified towns. And from that time they began to settle: Sumy, Lebedyn, Kharkiv, Okhtyrka, and all the *slobody* even as far as the Don River with the Cossack people."⁵⁹ In other words, even though the chronicler considered the Sloboda settlements to have been sanctioned by the hetman and founded by the "Cossack people," they arose on lands belonging to Moscow.

A contemporary of Hrabianka, Samiilo Velychko, a historian and "official of the Chancellery of the Host," also assigned the Sloboda settlements to Great Russia or to "Muscovite" domains with no hesitation whatever,⁶⁰ and Hetman Ivan Mazepa, obviously for the same reason, referred to the territory they occupied as "Asia."⁶¹ On the other hand, if the Sloboda region figures at all in historical texts dating from the era of the Hetmanate, then it is mentioned only episodically, in a few words, and almost never as part of the territory of the Hetmanate/Little Russia.

On maps of the late eighteenth century (Muscovite and foreign alike), the Sloboda Cossack regiments are not yet usually designated as an integral autonomous region or even shown individually, in contrast to such territories as those of the Don, Zaporozhian, and Hetmanate (Ukrainian, Little Russian) Cossacks. On Beauplan's map reprinted by Moses Pitt in London in 1680, the Sloboda settlements and regiments are not shown at all.⁶² In some cases, as on Guillaume Delisle's early eighteenth-century map of the Muscovite state, the Sloboda region is fused with the Hetmanate, both regions united under the common name *Ukraine Pays des Cosaques*, while the Zaporozhian and Don Cossacks are shown separately.[63] In other cases, they are included in the territory of the Belgorod province.

Gradually geographic (*ukraina*) nomenclature in the names of the region became supplemented by social nomenclature, in which *slobody* took pride of place. Most scholars consider that the name *slobody* is etymologically associated with the concept of *svoboda* (freedom)—in the given context, with freedom from certain traditional obligations in the interest of the state. Dmytro Bahalii, for example, notes that *slobody* referred in the first instance to concessions to colonists, and not to the settlements that they founded.[64] Subsequently, in the late seventeenth and eighteenth centuries, as the inhabitants received charters from the tsar, the territory that they occupied began to be called "*sloboda* regiments." Until the mid-eighteenth century, for example, official terminology distinguished *sloboda* fortified towns (that is, privileged ones) from those belonging to the Belgorod province, which were not endowed with similar privileges.[65]

*Slobody* turned out to be not only the most effective means for Moscow to exercise control over the colonists, as noted earlier. They also imparted some measure of uniformity to a variegated population that had arrived from various regions of Ukraine and found itself in constant motion. People moved from place to place in search of new *slobody*, settling there or returning to their previous place of residence in Left-Bank or even Right-Bank Ukraine.

This constant movement of people along and across geographic, political, and sociocultural boundaries sometimes took on the character of a way of life. It mattered little who, whither, whence, and why left his previous place of residence and settled in a new one in order to obtain or preserve a particular *sloboda* social or legal status. In either case the migrant settlers, or most of them at least, in accepting *slobody* from the Russian government, came up against the risk of eventually losing their personal freedom. Until then, however, the social mobility of the Sloboda population remained one of region's most characteristic features, defining (or, better, impeding) the demarcation of the bounds of its social space.

One more obstacle on the way to defining the boundaries of the region was the close interrelation between its military and civil administration, both Sloboda Cossack and Russian central (*prikaz*, department) and local (*voevoda*, military governor). The Military Department (*Razriadnyi prikaz*), under whose jurisdiction the Sloboda regiments initially found themselves, was simultaneously in charge of military affairs and of all the borders along the southern frontier. In 1688 the Sloboda regiments came under the administration of the Department of Great Russia (*Prikaz Velikoi Rossii*), but even now historians have not reached a consensus as to which of two offices—the Ambassadorial Office (*Posol'skii prikaz*) or the Office of Little Russia (*Malorossiiskii prikaz*)—wielded greater authority over the Department of Great Russia.[66]

The traditional historiographic commonplace according to which the name of Sloboda Ukraine existed almost from the moment of its mass settlement in the mid-seventeenth century does not appear to be sufficiently well founded.⁶⁷ The first settlers did not move to "Sloboda Ukraine." They only filled the steppe frontier with social content, organizing military-administrative units—the Sloboda regiments and settlements—with the permission of the Moscow government on a privileged basis. Those units endowed the steppe frontier with more definite boundaries, along with a new name—the Sloboda regiments.

It is telling that among the names of settlements established by Ukrainians on the steppe frontier in the late seventeenth century, anthroponyms and toponyms were dominant.⁶⁸ The former were associated with the names of their founders (*osadchi*) or owners, the latter with natural features of the site, sometimes already noted in written tradition (Kharkiv, Zmiiv, Chuhuiv et al.). In both cases, mentions of the places from which the first colonists came are very rarely to be encountered. On the contrary, one gains the impression that the colonists were determined to get a new start in their new homeland.

If names with the word "new" are encountered at all in the local toponymy of the late seventeenth and early eighteenth centuries, then they refer mainly to the newly established settlements, not to the colonists' places of origin. Nova Vodolaha and Stara Vodolaha, Novyi Merchyk and Staryi Merchyk, Novyi Burluk and just plain Burluk were all founded by settlers in their new places of residence in relatively close proximity, like the Russian Novyi Oskol and Staryi Oskol. By contrast, nothing like Novi Cherkasy, Novyi Bratslav, or, say, Novyi Fastiv appeared on the steppe frontier. Why not? The answer should probably be sought in the specific perception of the territory by the mid-seventeenth-century Ukrainians as well as the socially heterogeneous makeup of the first colonists.

## Identification

For Moscow, the identification of its new subjects was at first difficult in every respect. In the steppe, one could always encounter people of the most varied origins and occupations: hunters and fishermen, hunter-beekeepers, horse herders, traders, bandits, refugees, border guards. Social barriers between them always seemed vague. Over time, inhabitants of the borderland took on features of a general culture specific to the region and its way of life. The Belgorod and Voronezh *ukraina* was sometimes attacked by steppe raiders of Slavic origin disguised as Tatars. Nor was it unusual to encounter "bandit" Cossack formations among the Tatars roaming the steppe. Accordingly, the Muscovite border *voevodas* were instructed to keep a careful watch for marauders of both types.⁶⁹

The ethnic Ukrainians "Cossackizing" in the steppe were usually referred to in documents of the time as "Cherkasians" regardless of where they lived: in the steppe, the Commonwealth, Russian border fortresses, the Hetmanate, or the Zaporozhian Sich. Thus, the Belgorod *voevoda* complained about the "Lithuanian people, Cherkasian bandits"[70] who constantly attacked the Sevriuks of Putyvl, the Don Cossacks, and the Cherkasians of Chuhuiv, while Muscovite servitors lambasted "thieving" Cherkasians along with loyal Cherkasians of Putyvl and Livny. In time, however, the Russian authorities began to refer to Ukrainians settling the Muscovite steppe frontier as "Cherkasians arriving from Little Russian and Trans-Dnieper fortified towns."[71]

The migrants themselves, arriving in their new places of residence with established views of their homeland, used similar terms to refer to their country of origin. At first, before 1648, they spoke of Lithuania. "We did not elect you [hetman] in Lithuania," said the indignant colonists of Chuhuiv to their leader, Yakiv Ostrianyn, in 1638.[72] The Russian *voevodas* usually referred to the Ukrainians as "Lithuanian people" when reporting to Moscow about the constant vexations caused them by subjects of borderland magnates, Prince Vyshnevetsky first and foremost.[73] But by the late seventeenth century, Ukrainians asked "Where are you from?" usually replied: "From the Trans-Dnieper towns" or "From the Cherkasian towns."

The migrants of 1686 who founded the town of Volnyi said of themselves: "We have come ... from the Dnieper Cherkasian towns because of the destruction caused by Turkish and Crimean warriors."[74] Similarly, citizens of Sumy remembered almost half a century after the founding of their fortress that they had come to the new lands "from Trans-Dnieper and Hetmanate towns," settling places through which the Tatars passed on their way to "Ukrainian and Great Russian towns."[75] In both cases, the answers seem as standard as they are evasive. That probably suited both parties, arriving and receiving.

It is also striking that in the settlers' testimony Ukrainian and Great Russian towns differ from each other. Similarly, as noted earlier, the Russian authorities referred to settlements established by the "Cherkasians" on the Muscovite steppe frontier as "borderland" (*ukrainnye*) but not as "Cherkasian" (*cherkasskie*), presumably because the latter term referred specifically to the Hetmanate (Little Russia). The Hetmanate authorities, for their part, always drew a borderline between their territory and the lands of the Sloboda regiments. Thus, almost from the very beginning of the Sloboda settlements, the *ukraina* terminology took on a particular regional significance along with the broader one.

Given this distinction, the "Little Russian" and "Cherkasian" terminology served the Sloboda settlers mainly to emphasize their status as "foreigners" in the eyes of the Muscovite authorities. Bearing witness to this in particular is a petition from the Cossacks of Izium dated 1710, in which they speak of themselves as follows: "Our Little Russian people, being unaccustomed [to local conditions] because of their foreignness, unlike Russian people, can by no means bear such burdens [taxes on trades] and will all therefore go to the free Hetmanate towns, while others have already gone to towns under construction beyond the Dnieper."⁷⁶

Most often, however, the migrants preferred to call themselves Cherkasians in their new homeland, thereby substantiating their claim to possession of personal and of course ancient, "inviolable" rights and freedoms legally obtained (whether in fact or according to historical tradition was of no consequence). Those rights and freedoms, as the settlers conceived them, became known by the general phrase "Cherkasian customs" (*cherkasskie obyknosti*) and were based on tradition incorporated in the model of Cossack military democracy. In order to substantiate them, the colonists had recourse not only to Cossack but also to noble *szlachta* tradition and genealogy.

In this regard, the great mass of rank-and-file colonists appealed to Cossackdom, while the officers harked back to noble tradition and Commonwealth norms, adding the ending "-sky" (*-skii*) to their not always euphonious surnames and wrapping themselves in noble coats of arms and documents. Judging by some items of indirect evidence, it was no accident that elements of Polish heraldic tradition were employed in the official symbolism of the Sloboda regiments. And so they remained until the onset of the Russian reforms of 1734.

Settlers in the new lands brought all they could to indicate their respectability in the eyes of the Russian authorities. This might include banners symbolizing the colonists' privileged Cossack status or disassembled wooden Orthodox churches with ecclesiastical utensils, religious books, and bells. Finally, no less significance was attributed to families and servants, domestic property, and the presence of "good" people, as nobles and merchants were thought to be, in the "bands" and "trains" of migrants. All this gave new subjects the right to aspire to concessions and privileges in their new place of residence.⁷⁷

By the early eighteenth century, when the institutionalization of the Sloboda regiments as part of the Muscovite state was largely complete, and the region had received its own name, borders, system of government, and legal status; when the Cossack elite, which led regional society, had been partly integrated into the structure of the Russian imperial nobility and had created a stable network of client and clan relations, conditions arose for the symbolic framing of Sloboda Ukraine as an integral region. Logically enough, it was the Cossack officer elite that took this initiative upon itself. Since the late seventeenth century, the recognized leaders of that stratum had been the colonels of the Donets-Zakharzhevsky clan in Kharkiv.

Thanks to the clan's representative figure, the Kharkiv colonel Fedir Donets-Zakharzhevsky, the year 1705 saw the appearance of a panegyric dedicated to the officers of the Sloboda region (the first and only such work to have come down to us), written in Polish by the well-known Chernihiv poet Jan Ornowski.⁷⁸ The panegyric, entitled *Bogaty wirydarz* (The rich orchard), became the first work dedicated entirely to the Sloboda regiments. It was a heroic epic written in the ponderous and florid manner of the high baroque, containing both poetry and prose, numerous allegories and hyperboles, facts and legends drawn from local and world history.

The author's principal task, to which he dedicated all his skill and talent, was the substantiation of the noble genealogy of the Donets-Zakharzhevsky clan and its ties with the Polish nobility entitled to armorial bearings, renowned for its knightly prowess, including feats in the wars with Turkey. The basic sources indicated by the author, who was well versed in his task, were the armorial of Bartosz Paprocki, popular in the Commonwealth since 1584, and a work by Szymon Okolski, both containing data about the noble Zacharzewski/Zakharzhevsky clan.

The panegyric contains detailed descriptions of the exploits of several generations of the Sloboda Donets-Zakharzhevskys in wars with the Tatars and Swedes, as well as testimonials of their constant loyalty to the Russian throne and their energetic efforts to populate the region and build towns, fortresses, churches, and monasteries. In this regard, *Bogaty wirydarz* may be considered the first monument of the Sloboda region's historiography.

Aside from its factual data, whether authentic or born of the fantasy of the author himself or his patrons, the panegyric is of interest for its depiction of the region, to which the author refers as *slobody*, the *sloboda* region, *sloboda* towns, and so on. As the ancestral Donets-Zakharzhevsky clan took on the symbolic image of a rosebush in Ornowski's work, so the lands ruled by representatives of that clan were depicted as a rich, flowering orchard established in a onetime desert.

An engraving in the panegyric displays an Orthodox shrine in a geometrically designed orchard encircled with trees. This allegorical picture generally reflected the outward aspect of Kharkiv, the local "capital" of the Donets-Zakharzhevskys, whose name was perhaps somehow associated with the "noble" part of their family. According to architectural historians, the city plan of 1742 shows the Dormition Cathedral as the dominant feature, framed by parish churches and mud houses with thatched roofs drowning in greenery.[79]

Typically, the idea of an orchard in the desert is closely interwoven with the region's inherent rights and liberties (*libertatis*). Thus, Jan Ornowski's panegyric already contained the basic elements of the Sloboda elite's collective regional identity: the ideas of heroic warfare with the Tatars, loyalty to the Russian throne, and the rights and privileges of the local officers won by their exploits. Here one can also find the idea of the Sloboda region as a bulwark protecting Russia from the Tatars. In many ways, the new generation of local patriots that appeared in the late eighteenth and early nineteenth centuries merely supplemented and modernized Ornowski's depiction.

In 1705, at the same time as the work of the Chernihiv panegyrist, there appeared another text representing a petition from the Cossacks of Sumy to the Russian monarch. It also contained a self-description of the inhabitants of the region and an extensive presentation of their history.[80] Although the migrants' genealogy in that document is not traced back to the nobility entitled to armorial bearings but to "Cherkasian custom," that is, Cossackdom, it contains the same stable components of collective identity as those already mentioned, with dominant "Cherkasian" and "Sloboda" markers in the depiction of the region and its inhabitants.

The fusion of "Cherkasian" and "Sloboda" terminology in the description and self-description of the local population became common practice in the eighteenth century. Instances of it may be found, for example, in official documents of the times of Peter I in which Sloboda "Cherkasians" are distinguished from "Russians."[81] "Cherkasians," their "customs," and the "Sloboda regiments" survived under the successors of the first emperor of Russia until the early 1760s. In official sources contemporaneous with the reform of the military-administrative system of the Sloboda regiments in 1734, the local population appears in the capacity of "free Cherkasian people," as distinct from the "Great Russian people."[82]

At the same time, it is often the phrase "Little Russian people" that appears as a synonym of the "free Cherkasian people" in Russian official documents of the 1730s. The "Little Russian" terminology continued to circulate among the local population, reflecting the stability of Little Russian identity among various social strata in the historical regions of Ukraine. That tradition was preserved even after the liquidation of Sloboda Cossack self-government.

Even so, in the consciousness of Kharkivites, or some of them at least, the "Little Russian" genealogy could coexist peacefully with the "Polish" (*pol'skii*), now understood in the ethnopolitical rather than the geographic sense of the word. In a petition of 2 October 1780 to the empress, a citizen of Kharkiv, Sevastian Danilovich Kolosov, calls himself a "Little Russian of Polish nature."[83] It would take the passing of almost another half century before such combinations took on a humorous cast in the eyes of a new generation (the "foreigner Vasilii Fedorov" in Gogol's *Dead Souls* would hardly have seemed amusing in the late seventeenth and eighteenth centuries).

The "Cherkasians" who came to settle in Muscovite steppe *ukraina* emphasized their "foreignness" in every possible way, since it gave them a basis to claim concessions and privileges in their new home. Thus, the widow of Hetman Yakiv Ostrianyn, who had been granted special rights to settle in Chuhuiv (and was killed by his compatriots in 1641), appealing to the tsar with a petition, calls herself a "foreign widow."[84] Subsequently, memories of "foreignness" also left their mark on the consciousness of the regional elite. It was further substantiated in 1711, when Wallachians resettled in the region and swelled the ranks of the privileged local elite. As for the "Cherkasian" social identification, it may be noted that the name followed the Slobodians even when they migrated elsewhere, as for example to the Volga region.[85]

What one does not notice in the identification or self-identification of the new settlers is any word or even hint pertaining to their "Russianness," whatever the sense that might be attributed to that concept. The Ukrainians who settled the steppe frontier practically did not mix with the Russian population. Russians were not numerous in the region, and most of them were servitors. Subsequently, the Russian population increased with the arrival of soldiers posted to frontier garrisons and military settlements; Old Believers fleeing to the borderland after the reforms of Patriarch Nikon; peasant serfs brought by their masters, who had received land in the region; and, finally, with the growth of towns, representatives of the service bureaucracy, merchants, tradesmen, and others.

Russian settlements in the Sloboda region looked like spots on a solid band of Ukrainian communities. In particular, they included the towns of Valki (Valky), Slaviansk (Sloviansk), and Chuguev (Chuhuiv), as well as the villages of Russkie Tishki, Vasishchevo, Russkaia Lozovaia, Petrovskoe, Sekretarevka, Yefremovka, and a number of others located mainly on the territory of the present-day Vovchansk, Zmiiv, Kupiansk, and Kharkiv *raiony* (districts) of Kharkiv oblast.

Defending their privileged social status, the "Cherkasians" made every effort to stress their differences from "Russian people."

> For the great sovereign showed favor to those new arrivals ... he ordered that there be no Russian voevodas and officials among them in that newly built town of Kolomak ... they, the inhabitants of Kolomak, except for Russian people, are to keep taverns without quit-rent, according to their former customs. ... And they are not to take in runaway Russian servitors or people bound to communities or boyars' slaves and peasants from the Ukrainian towns.[86]

The Russian authorities, for their part, were concerned to ensure that privileges and concessions to Ukrainian colonists would not be extended to Russian subjects proper and thus promote any increase of serfs fleeing from the center of the country to the steppe borderland. Accordingly, they never tired of emphasizing the stable distinction between Russian servitors and "Cherkasians," making reminders of the need "for organizers of colonies, as well as Cossack leaders and aides-de-camp and all common people, to observe passersby intently and make certain that they are free Cherkasians, and that no Russian make his way in among the Cherkasians, and that not one Russian or Don Cossack be admitted without a passport or kept even for a day."[87]

Dmytro Bahalii asserts that the Russian government was always afraid of the conflicts that arose whenever Ukrainians and Russians settled side by side and strove as much as possible to settle them apart in order to avoid occasions for strife. As an example, he cites the incessant conflicts between the Russian and Ukrainian population of the village of Tishki (Tyshky), as a result of which the village was divided into Russkie Tishki and Cherkasskie Tishki.[88] In Kharkiv oblast, closer to the present-day border with Russia, there are still two villages not far from each other called Russka Lozova and Cherkaska Lozova.

There could be various reasons for conflict between Ukrainians and Russians, such as un-demarcated lands or reciprocal negative ethnocultural stereotypes, but most often the apple of discord was the privileges enjoyed by Ukrainian colonists that were not extended to the tsar's Russian subjects in any measure. Hence the Russian government usually granted requests from Sloboda region officers to deport Russian settlers from their territory. Not surprisingly, mutual contacts between ethnic Ukrainians and Russians were wholly inconsequential in the Sloboda region: they lived in different settlements, retained their language, clothing, and customs, cultivated mutual negative stereotypes, and rarely intermarried.[89] Those traditions were retained right up to the modern industrial era.

The boundary between Russians and Ukrainians who settled the steppe frontier was defined by *slobody*—different rights and privileges offered by the Moscow government to those who settled new lands in lieu of service. Those privileges included free possession of land, exemption from taxes, the right to duty-free trade and commerce, production and sale of liquor, the building of windmills, and several others.

"Cherkasian customs" was a broader concept relating to the sphere of traditional law, while *slobody* were narrower but more legitimate, as they were based on official juridical documents issued by Russian authorities. The Russian government usually recognized the right of its new subjects to "Cherkasian customs," readily turning a blind eye to their sometimes-checkered past.[90] Not only did it allow the colonists to develop ramified networks of clan and family ties and ignore the practice of occupying offices by inheritance, but it also promoted the cooptation of representatives of local elites into the Russian nobility. It was no accident that by the late seventeenth century practically all the Sloboda colonels had wrapped themselves in Russian boyar ranks and tsarist land grants.[91] Typically, the previously mentioned Fedir Donets-Zakharzhevsky is called a master of the table (*stol'nik*) at the beginning of the panegyric devoted to him but later becomes colonel of Kharkiv.

The political loyalty of the Sloboda regiments was rewarded with land grants, forgiveness of previous debts and offers of new loans, or confirmation of previous concessions associated with trade and commerce, and the like. *Slobody* guaranteed by the tsarist government became far more important than "Cherkasian customs." Abolishing the latter turned out to be much easier than depriving Slobodians of their *slobody*. Consequently, it was the *slobody* that long remained a basic element of their identity and lent their name to the region as a whole.

Another effective means of legitimizing the particular status of Ukrainian migrant settlers were tsarist "certificates of merit" issued by the government to Slobodians for refusing to join Cossack hetmans or warlords in the three borderland Cossack "polities" who came out against the Russian government. At a time when that government frequently denounced inhabitants of neighboring Little Russia as "traitors" or unreliable subjects, Slobodians were invariably praised for steadfastness and loyalty to the throne in the struggle against "traitors" of any kind. Over time, such propagandistic rhetoric contributed in no small measure to the formation of regional identity and would be assimilated by descendants of the Sloboda officers along with a tradition of pro-Moscow political orientation.

For the government, concessions and certificates of merit were a means of keeping the Slobodians on a short leash and gradually equalizing them in rights, or lack thereof, with its "indigenous" subjects. For the settlers, on the other hand, it was important to turn their privileged status from temporary to permanent and pass it on to their descendants. Thus, down to the early nineteenth century, relations between the Slobodians and the Russian government actually took on the character of a negotiated settlement, if an unwritten one.

That settlement was a distinctive deal struck in every particular instance by a successive reformist initiative "from above," prompting a reply in the form of a modest but friendly reminder of traditional, historically sanctified local privileges earned by courage and loyalty. It was a tradition that sometimes went unnoticed behind the fine rhetoric of both parties. For that very reason, it long outlived the Sloboda regiments themselves.

The genesis and institutionalization of the Sloboda regiments were directly associated with the long existence of the steppe frontier. The frontier created the region and gave its inhabitants a particular sociolegal status in exchange for military service to the state. The result was the appearance of a singular community distinguished from all its neighbors by the particularities of its organization.

## Institutionalization

The formal status of the Sloboda regiments and the population living on their territory changed constantly, depending not only on the geopolitical situation on the steppe frontier but also on the nature and direction of reforms at the center of the Russian state, which was developing into a centralized military-bureaucratic empire. In the late seventeenth century, the Russian government still had a poor understanding of the state conceived as a unitary sovereign territory,[92] to say nothing of a national policy. On the Sloboda frontier the state, concerned above all with security problems, strove to turn irregular military formations into regular ones and, in time, to consolidate the administration of the Sloboda territories.

But because the situation on the frontier remained unstable, given the ineffectiveness of the tsarist bureaucracy and the government's chronic lack of resources, Moscow was bound to realize sooner or later that it would be unable to carry out its plans unless it cooperated with the borderland elites. Thus, the policy of unifying and integrating the borderland generally proved inconsistent, contradictory, and dependent on the particular situation. Centralizing tendencies mixed with decentralizing ones, and vice versa. Consequently, the social niche for the existence of regional particularism might expand or contract but never disappear completely.

As territorial administrative units with particular rights, the Sloboda regiments were subordinate to the Belgorod *voevoda* from the moment of their formation. It becomes easier to understand the specificity of relations between the colonists and the government if one grasps that in the mid-seventeenth century the Belgorod *voevodstvo*, into which the Sloboda regiments were integrated, was a new type of military-administrative region of Russia with regard to its structure and management, resembling the *gubernias* (provinces) created later by Peter I, as well as the governorates-general that subsequently appeared.[93]

The novelty of that structure was the expansion of the powers of the local administration: the Belgorod *voevoda* was given authority over many military and administrative affairs previously concentrated in Moscow. Thus, from the very beginning of their existence, the Sloboda regiments became part of the modernizing expanse of the Russian Empire. From the first instant, they were ready for the reforms that followed one after the other in a country entering an epoch of radical transformation.

In 1706–8 the *voevoda* system of administration in the Sloboda region was changed to a new gubernial one. In administrative terms, the territory of the Sloboda regiments was divided between the Azov and Kyiv gubernias. Parts of the Kharkiv regiment (including Kharkiv itself) and of the Izium regiment were assigned to the Kyiv gubernia. Thus, the new administrative boundary coincided with the natural and geographic division of the Sloboda region into Donets and Dnieper sections, respectively. In 1719, however, that boundary was eliminated, as all the Sloboda territories were placed under the authority of the governor of Kyiv and thus united with Little Russia in a common administrative space. True, a year later, in 1720, the Belgorod *voevoda* again took charge of the Sloboda region, only to surrender it in 1726 to the College of War in Moscow.

In many respects, administrative reforms in the Sloboda region in the late seventeenth and early eighteenth centuries depended on the geopolitical situation in the steppe. The gubernial system of administration was introduced there immediately after the demarcation of territory between Russia and the Crimean Khanate in 1705, which established a precise boundary between them for the first time.[94] However, as subsequent developments would show, that boundary was unstable and constantly tended to turn into a frontier. The next occasion for this was the defeat of the Russian army in 1711, as the Russo-Turkish war ended and Russia lost control of the Azov region.

Russia's plans of conquest and steppe expeditions in the late seventeenth and early eighteenth centuries, regardless of their dubious political accomplishments, nevertheless had an important result. Not only did they finally determine the southern vector of the country's expansion—until then, Russia had been mainly occupied with defending that region—but they also initiated the mental appropriation of the region, previously treated as an indefinite steppe frontier with shifting boundaries, as part of Russia. Peter I's Azov campaign promoted the rise and dissemination of "southern" geographic nomenclature with regard to the lands of the Black Sea littoral recovered from the Ottoman Empire and the Crimean Khanate.

This was reflected in practice by the production of the first contemporary map of "southern and western Russia," prepared by Yakov Brius (born James Bruce) and Yurii (Georgii) von Mengden and published in Amsterdam in 1699.[95] The map, prepared according to the rules of geographic science, was the first to "make visible" the territory, including many settlements, defensive structures, and routes of communication binding Sloboda Ukraine with the Crimea.[96] Until then, those lands had been known basically from their written descriptions in the *Kniga Bol'shomu Chertezhu*, compiled before the appearance of the Belgorod Line and the Sloboda regiments.

The military-administrative transformation of the Sloboda region was accompanied by changes in its social space. The Russian government was proceeding toward the creation of a modern regular army and the reorganization of Cossack military formations into units of that army. As a result, the administrative, economic, financial, and judicial functions of the Sloboda Cossack officers were steadily reduced, while the population was gradually losing personal liberty and taking on the full burden of maintaining the empire's military and bureaucratic apparatus. In 1710 the practice of quartering soldiers was expanded to the Sloboda region, whose inhabitants would maintain a futile opposition to it for more than a century.

In 1732 the Russian government attempted a radical reform to turn local Cossack service into regular army service and limit local self-government. The strengthening of state control over the steppe periphery went hand in hand with the construction of the new defensive Ukrainian Line on the frontier in 1731–33.[97] Nevertheless, that policy did not lead to the abolition of the Sloboda regiments' traditional privileges: on the contrary, they were confirmed in 1734,[98] on the eve of the next Russo-Turkish war, which began in 1735 and ended in 1739 with the Treaty of Belgrade and a further demarcation of the steppe borderland.

On the symbolic level, changes in the status of the Sloboda regiments found reflection in the substitution of new imperial coats of arms for their old Cossack ones. They all now had a common element—the imperial crown and monogram wreathed with leaves—but also included locally specific elements reflecting the natural features or military functions of regimental fortified towns (a bunch of grapes for Izium, a cartridge bag for Sumy, a fish with a spear for Ostrogozhsk, a fortress for Okhtyrka); Kharkiv fared worst, as its name sounded odd to outsiders, and the symbol chosen for it was an outlandish "*khar'* beast" (i.e., ferret).[99]

Nevertheless, the policy of the center with regard to the Sloboda regiments remained inconsistent. The next change of government led to a complete restoration of colonists' previous rights and liberties in 1743 after their abolition or restriction a decade earlier. Such a policy not only did not erase local specificity but at times, considering the contradictory actions of the reformers themselves, it fostered the consolidation of regional elites and was attended by their cooptation into new social and administrative structures. The present-day student of this process is led to conclude that the introduction of regular military service in the Sloboda region to replace traditional Cossack service had the effect of strengthening the positions of the Sloboda officers and providing their offspring with broader access to military ranks, and consequently to ennoblement.

Subsequently, the basic components of Sloboda regional identity were enriched and consolidated thanks, however paradoxical it may sound, to the further reforms enacted by the Russian government during the integration of the steppe frontier into the empire. The Sloboda regiments began to occupy places of their own on eighteenth-century geographic maps of the Russian Empire, while a few decades earlier they had been merged either with the Hetmanate or with the Belgorod military-administrative region.[100]

The name "Sloboda regiments" first appeared on a map prepared by government surveyors in 1731.[101] Despite Russia's unstable and mutable external border in the steppe, the Sloboda region's internal administrative boundary with Great Russia remained unchanging. In 1726, for example, the Russian geodesist Yakov Isleniev prepared a map and description of the boundary line between the Sloboda region and Russian territory proper for the Senate.[102]

Mapping of the region proceeded with particular intensity in the 1730s in connection with internal reforms in the Russian Empire and a new Russo-Turkish war. In 1731 Russian surveyors compiled the *Chertezh Slobodskim polkam, lezhashchim mezhdu Donom, Oskolom, Dontsom i Vorskloiu* (Map of the Sloboda regiments lying between the Don, Oskil, Donets, and Vorskla), on which the Sloboda settlements and the new defensive lines (those of Izium and Tor) built on their territory were shown, perhaps for the first time in geographic practice.[103] Maps associated with the construction of the Ukrainian Line would not appear until the mid-eighteenth century. Sloboda Cossack settlements began to be clearly marked on maps of the steppe frontier in conjunction with the Ukrainian Line, New Serbia, and Zaporizhia.

The Sloboda Cossacks established a symbolic association with their territory by means of their new uniforms. Thus, when they received the tsar's charter restoring the rights and privileges of the region in 1743,

> the colonels, having formed the regiments according to the resolution, decided by common consent to institute uniforms that had not previously existed for every one of their regiments, to wit: Circassian topcoats with foldable sleeves decorated with silver braiding and lace were blue for all regiments, while jackets and wide trousers were different for every regiment: yellow for Kharkiv, green for Okhtyrka, red for Izium, and reddish-orange for Ostrogozhsk.[104]

Typically, as the Cossack Sloboda regiments were turned into regular hussar regiments, they lost neither their previous names nor the colors of their uniforms. New hussar regiments recruited from the native-born local population also retained distinctive regional features in their names. Thus, one of them (formed in 1757) was named the Sloboda regiment, while the other became the Ukrainian Hussar regiment.[105] To some degree or other, such symbols made it possible to maintain a certain continuity in the historical memory of the local inhabitants.

Even so, the boundary of the Sloboda regiments with Little Russia was not so stable as the one with Russia. In contemporary consciousness, the Sloboda region continued to gravitate toward "Little Russian" territory. Convincing evidence of this is to be found, for example, in a draft administrative division of the Russian Empire prepared by the Russian scholar and highly placed official Vasilii Tatishchev (1688–1750). The nomenclature of the administrative regions appearing in the draft, based on historical and geographic criteria, included the "Little Russian governorate-general," to which the author assigned the Hetmanate, the provinces of Kyiv, Orel, Donets, and Sevsk, the Belgorod "vice-gubernia," and the five Sloboda regiments.[106] As things turned out, the draft had no practical significance.

At the beginning of the Catherinian reforms, associated with the liquidation of what is conventionally known as the autonomy of the Sloboda regiments, the local population already possessed its own historical and sociolegal tradition, which formed the basis of its regional identity and found support in local privileges, confirmed by the central authorities from time to time.

Approaching the decline of their almost century-long history, approximately in the mid-eighteenth century, the Sloboda regiments already occupied their own well-defined place on the administrative political map of the Russian Empire. Their territory retained the functions and appearance of a military frontier represented by defensive structures, militarized settlements with particular rights, and, finally, a huge Russian army posted in the steppe and known by the name "Ukrainian."

As the institutionalization of the region progressed, thanks above all to the administrative and legal reforms of the Sloboda regiments initiated by the Russian government, the *ukraina* and *sloboda* terminologies were applied to them in parallel or as synonyms. In all likelihood, the union of both terms in the name of the region became firmly established only in the process of territorial administrative reform initiated by Empress Catherine II in the late eighteenth century, to be discussed in the section "Incorporation or 'Indigenization'?" below. At that time, the territory of the Sloboda regiments covered 115,000 square kilometers with about 670,000 dwellers.[107]

## The Orthodox Space

The "foreign" status of the Sloboda "Cherkasians" was emphasized initially by the particularities of Orthodox ecclesiastical culture brought by the settlers from the Commonwealth to their new place of residence. In many ways, the nature of those particularities was defined by the absence of strict social and cultural barriers between the clergy and the parishioners, as well as by the latter's active participation in church affairs and their traditions of social welfare. Hence the broad distribution of elementary parish schools with their "wandering" sextons doubling as teachers, hired and maintained by the congregations themselves, as well as the activity of church brotherhoods and hospitals in the Sloboda region.

From the very beginning, however, the Orthodox Church in the Sloboda region was not an institution capable of defending local interests. On the one hand, the first generation of Sloboda Orthodox clergy hardly surpassed the cultural level of its flock and even lagged behind it in some respects. Dmytro Bahalii recounts colorful episodes from the daily life of priests not particularly burdened with questions of education and morals but always preoccupied with the material world.[108] On the other hand, petition-bearers to the tsar's court for state salaries and assistance began making their way from Kharkiv almost from the moment of its settlement. The first Kharkiv priests, "the Cherkasy priest Yeremeishche and the newly appointed priest Vasilishche and deacon Iosipishche … rambled off … to make obeisance" in Moscow for sustenance and church construction as early as 1657,[109] and their colleagues and successors followed the beaten path. The incorporation of the new Ukrainian subjects into the Russian Orthodox world started almost immediately and was conducted smoothly.

From the very beginning, the steppe borderland of the Muscovite state, along with the Belgorod Line and the Sloboda regiments, were under the direct control of the Moscow patriarch and belonged to the so-called Patriarchal domain.[110] From 1667, that is, from the moment of the founding of the Belgorod eparchy, which was immediately elevated to the status of a metropolitanate, its administration passed into the hands of the metropolitans (from 1721, bishops and archbishops) of Belgorod and Oboian. They found themselves in charge of a massive territory neighboring on the Kyiv metropolitanate and eparchy in the Kyiv gubernia to the west and southwest, and with the Voronezh eparchy in the Azov gubernia to the east. The Belgorod arch-hierarchs were ecclesiastical analogues of the secular administration—the Belgorod *voevodas*. Their policy in the Sloboda region aimed at the unification and homogenization of the Ukrainian cultural borderland, which until then had remained a space unstable and open to the penetration of various intellectual and stylistic influences.[111]

As is well known, the Orthodoxy of the new subjects aroused strong doubts among the clerical and secular authorities of the Muscovite state. In 1658 the Kharkiv *voevoda* Ofrosimov reported to Moscow on the "scant faith" and "erroneous" conduct of services by Kharkiv settlers.[112] Consequently, the Russian Orthodox Church kept a careful watch on the borderland, bending its efforts toward combating not only the remains of pagan folk customs and the Old Believers who came to the steppe borderland in droves after the church reform of Patriarch Nikon, but also particular traditions of Orthodox spirituality and ritual developed by the Orthodox faithful and clergy on Commonwealth territory. In the latter case, the church's cultural policy on the steppe frontier was far stricter and more uncompromising than that of the secular authorities in the region.

Ecclesiastical Russification in the Sloboda region attracted the attention of those taking part in the election of the new metropolitan of Kyiv in 1685. They discussed rumors of persecution of Orthodox clergymen in the Belgorod eparchy, extortion and corporal punishment, the imposition of Muscovite baptismal customs, and the like.[113] That policy became even more rigid when the administration of the Belgorod eparchy was taken over by a representative of the local milieu, Archbishop Ioasaf (Horlenko), who was related to the Kvitka Cossack officer clan and would be canonized by the Russian Orthodox Church in 1911.

A great many old books published in Kyiv, Lviv, "and other southwestern locations" were confiscated from all the churches and monasteries of the Sloboda region and brought to the Belgorod cathedral church, whereafter, according to Archbishop Filaret, they disappeared without a trace.[114] In the late eighteenth century, the same fate would befall old icons painted in Kyiv and Lviv, which were removed from Sloboda churches by order of the Belgorod consistory and taken to Belgorod. Most likely, they were destroyed.

The incorporation of the Sloboda region into the church's spiritual territory was also accomplished with the building of new churches. The first churches, built by the colonists in the spirit of the Ukrainian baroque, including the Church of the Most Holy Theotokos in Kharkiv, have not survived to our times. Some of them were rebuilt in the image and likeness of Muscovite churches, as in the case of the Dormition Cathedral in Kharkiv, reconstructed in the late eighteenth century on the model of the five-domed Church of St. Clement in Moscow.[115]

No less important in the process of ecclesiastical unification was the role played by the appearance of local religious cults and icons. Especially prominent were the cults of the Kursk-Ozeriansk, Okhtyrka, and Kuriazh icons of the Theotokos. The Kharkiv Theological College, transferred there from Belgorod in 1726 at the initiative of Prince Mikhail Golitsyn, commander in chief of the Ukrainian army, was active in promoting Russian Orthodox Church policy in the Sloboda region.[116] In administrative terms, the college was part of the Kharkiv educational Monastery of the Holy Protection, whose prior was subordinate to the Kharkiv arch-hierarchs. In the structure of its curriculum, the Kharkiv College was a copy of the Kyiv Mohyla Academy.

The activity of the Kharkiv College, which in time became one of the greatest institutions of its type in the Russian Empire, was a major factor in creating the image of Kharkiv as an educational and cultural center. From the very beginning of its existence, the college prepared clerical cadres for the huge borderland region, including the southern black-earth and steppe periphery of the Russian Empire—the present-day Voronezh, Kursk, Belgorod, Kharkiv, Poltava, Dnipro, and Zaporizhia oblasts. In some years, the size of the college's student body exceeded even that of the Moscow and Kyiv academies.[117]

To be sure, any notion that access to the college was open to all social strata must be reined in substantially, given that the number of graduates from the lower strata averaged little more than 12 percent of the student body. Secular subjects (mathematics, European languages), which appeared in the curriculum around the 1730s, undoubtedly introduced variety into the college's system of education, but this reflected general tendencies in the development of eighteenth-century education in the Russian Empire.

As for languages in the educational process, they all increasingly felt the influence of cultural Russification. Empress Anna's charter to the Kharkiv College included a demand that the language of instruction be Russian,[118] which corresponded to the Russian government policy of rapprochement between the borderland elite and the Russian nobility. As a result, by the late eighteenth century the Kharkiv College could provide gentry estates in the Sloboda region with private teachers "who would teach children to speak Russian, and not Little Russian."[119]

The unification and Russification of religious and cultural life in the Sloboda region in the eighteenth century developed as part of the general confessionalization of religion in Russia, which had begun in the mid-seventeenth century and was accompanied by the standardization of liturgy and ritual, as well as by the elevation of the educational and cultural level of the clergy. Accordingly, such developments did not arouse resistance on the part of regional elites, whether ecclesiastical or secular.

These processes undoubtedly promoted the further incorporation of the region into the social space of the Russian Empire, but that space in turn looked more modern than the traditional local milieu. The consequences of those processes would become apparent only with the appearance and development in the late nineteenth and early twentieth centuries of the Ukrainian national movement, whose weakness was conditioned in many respects by the hostility of the Orthodox clergy toward it.

## Incorporation or "Indigenization"?

With the accession of Catherine II, there was a new turn of government policy in mutual relations between center and periphery.[120] Its defining idea, which Marc Raeff called "institutional Russification," was the gradual achievement of unification and uniformity of the imperial provinces in the administrative, economic, sociolegal, and, finally, cultural spheres.[121] With the implementation of the policy of enlightened unification, the days of Cossack self-government in the Ukrainian lands were numbered.

In 1762 a special government commission headed by Yevdokim Shcherbinin came to the Sloboda region and began carrying out yet another project of reforming the Sloboda regiments.[122] Under pressure from the commission, the Cossack leader of the Ostrogozhsk and Sumy regiments met the government halfway and, thinking to justify his own not inconsiderable malfeasance in the eyes of officialdom, renounced "our outdated Cherkasian customs" dating back more than a century and confirmed in their day with charters from the tsar.

But there was another, no less important reason why the Sloboda officers proved less than stubborn in maintaining their faded Cossack tradition. In 1762, thanks to Emperor Peter III, the nobility had been granted "freedom" from obligatory state service and began to acquire corporate rights and liberties with which the Ukrainian Cossack officers were fairly well acquainted, given their experience in the nobiliary Commonwealth. Taking this into consideration, the Sloboda elite— several hundred individuals—received a fair price for the Cossack democracy that it had long found superfluous and saw no reason to repent of its bargain. The entrance of the Cossack upper crust into the ranks of the "emancipated" Russian nobility promised further benefits in the form of the unemancipated (with no quotation marks) peasantry, which unquestionably had something important to lose.

In general, with only a few reservations, the eighteenth-century Catherinian reforms may be considered the finale of the historical epoch of the Sloboda region's autonomous existence, as is generally accepted in Ukrainian national historiography. Along with centralization and unification, those reforms completed the institutionalization of the region, which had come into existence more than a century earlier in the steppe *ukraina* of the Muscovite state within the framework of the Belgorod region of military administration. In the late eighteenth century, regional life still showed quite a few indications of continuity between the new epoch and the preceding one.

With the abolition of Cossack self-government, the Sloboda elite not only did not lose its former privileged status but even managed to consolidate its position more strongly within the framework of the noble estate's corporate self-rule. Although territorial and corporate institutions along with local privileges were not firmly rooted in the Russian borderland proper, the Ukrainian Cossack colonists long managed to maintain civic values developed through the practice of local self-government, distinguishing the Sloboda frontier from the central Russian regions.

According to contemporaries, the Sloboda gentry looked quite independent in its relations with the government even in the late eighteenth and early nineteenth centuries.[123] The practice of armed raids carried out by Polish *szlachta*, immortalized by Adam Mickiewicz, continued at one and the same time not only in the Commonwealth but also in the Sloboda region. As the German traveler Johann Georg Kohl affirmed, meetings of the local gentry, which preserved some symbolic rituals of Cossack times, might even make decisions by no means always pleasing to St. Petersburg.[124]

Considerations of both foreign and domestic policy required the cooperation of the center with local elites. The government continued its efforts to modernize a diverse country while constantly experiencing a shortage of educated secular cadres. This meant, first and foremost, the participation of representatives of such cadres in the administration of various territories, all of which continued to maintain some degree of social and cultural particularity. In the Sloboda region, as in neighboring Little Russia, representatives of the local elite took an active part in forming the imperial administration at all levels.[125]

In 1765, as the transformation of Cossack military formations into regular ones was completed, the territory of the Sloboda regiments was officially named the Sloboda Ukraine gubernia, with its center in Kharkiv. With a certain interval,[126] that name would be maintained until 1834, when it would occur to the government to do away with the last remnants of the Ukrainian lands' Cossack and gentry past. As we see, the name of the territory was not changed in principle. It merely confirmed the already existing basic features of the status of a peripheral borderland region whose inhabitants maintained their traditional privileges and freedoms.

The reign of Catherine II promoted significant population growth in the Sloboda region at a rate of more than 45 percent. In absolute figures, the population increased from 550,100 in the early 1760s to 800,100 in the early 1780s.[127] The overwhelming majority (as much as 90 percent) was ethnically Ukrainian.[128] In second place were Great Russians of all kinds, from landed gentry, bureaucrats, entrepreneurs and intelligentsia to serfs. In addition to settlers from Russia, Moldavians came to the region in the early eighteenth century (four thousand immigrated in 1711, led by Prince Dimitrie Cantemir), followed by Serbs, numbering a few hundred in the 1720s and 1730s.[129] If the Moldavian emigrants were mainly gentry landowners, the Serbs, like the Ukrainians, served as border guards in exchange for economic privileges. Finally, Germans, Frenchmen, Poles, Jews, Greeks, and Roma were also to be encountered in the towns of the Sloboda region.

The memoirs of the Kharkiv professor Christoph Dietrich von Rommel, which describe the early nineteenth century, present the social milieu of the Sloboda region as rather mixed in ethnic terms. One could encounter representatives of the local gentry, Russian landowners and officials, German tradesmen and scholars, French brokers and teachers, Polish soldiers and actors, emigrants from Europe, merchants and prisoners, Turkish and Caucasian grandees, and Polish and French officers captured in all the wars that the empire had waged in the southwestern regions of its expansion. All those people, who made the Sloboda region their permanent home, promoted the growth of what is termed "capital of diversity." During the Age of Enlightenment, the empire proved its ability to make effective use of that capital.

The Sloboda region differed from the central Russian regions in the social makeup of its population. Unlike Great Russians, the Ukrainian Slobodians retained a certain degree of social mobility and elements of civil society. True, in degree of development of the laws of serfdom, the Sloboda region stood closer to the southern territory newly conquered by Russia than to the neighboring Russian and Ukrainian lands. The proportion of serfs in the total number of peasants in the Sloboda region did not exceed 35 percent, substantially lower than in the former Hetmanate, where it fluctuated from 36 to 55 percent, and was not comparable to the Kyiv region and Right-Bank Ukraine, which were approximately at the same level as the Russian lands proper in that regard (more than 55 percent).

It is logical to assume that with Russia's increasing military and political success on its southern borders, leading to the elimination of direct threats to the Sloboda region, that region's specific features would gradually fade, and it would become integrated as part of the Russian interior, gradually merging with other Russian regions. This seems all the more likely because none of the borderland societies, as shown by the experience of the Commonwealth, Hungary, Moldavia, the Hetmanate, and the Crimea, managed to work out a feasible alternative to the policy of enlightened modernization adopted as a guide by the neighboring empires, first and foremost the Austrian and the Russian. Nevertheless, the successful modernization of the Russian Empire and its advance toward the Black Sea by no means meant the automatic liquidation of the particularities of the steppe borderland.

Russia's incorporation of new territories and subjects proceeded by means of mutual compromise, especially under conditions of chronic lack of resources. Thus, for example, as the Russian government liquidated Cossack service, enserfing part of the previously free population and wiping out the remnants of local democracy, it simultaneously promoted the institutionalization and consolidation of particular elements of regional tradition, such as the *slobody*, as well as the privileges of the social elite. Moreover, the center was not consistent in its relations with the military frontier. In this regard, it may be recalled that in the late eighteenth and early nineteenth centuries the government continued the practice of creating new Cossack forces and territories enjoying particular rights.

Government initiatives intended to promote the gradual elimination of the Sloboda region's particularity were accompanied by the modernization and transformation of the empire itself. On the one hand, this contributed to its unification; on the other hand, administrative and military reforms only scratched the surface of a community deeply rooted in the soil of the steppe, promoting its consolidation and territorial unity. The Sloboda region developed its particularity in the course of Russia's expansion into the steppe and secured individual elements of that particularity in the course of its incorporation into the empire. Thanks to this the Sloboda regiments, formed at various times, acquired a common external boundary, territory, name, symbolism, and collective identity.

The basic elements of local identity would be modified on the one hand, assimilating new elements of social reality and its intellectual representation; on the other hand, they would retain some primal symbolic nucleus. At the basis of that many-layered nucleus, one may observe, among other things, the borderland "Ukrainian" (*ukraina*) component associated with the geography and geopolitical history of the region, defined by its immediate proximity to the steppe, the sense of the steppe, and the historical memory of the steppe. No less important a component of local identity was Cossackdom, which had absorbed the "Cherkasian" and "foreigner" rhetoric associated with the origin and sociolegal status of the settlers. Finally, the geopolitical orientation toward Moscow may be considered one of the most influential components of the Sloboda region's identity.

The key role in the sociopolitical self-identification of the Sloboda elite was played by the interrelated discourses of "loyalty" manifested in the struggle against Tatars and "traitors" and the *slobody* earned from the throne in return for that loyalty. To this, one should probably add the specific political culture, based on clan and kin, associated with isolation from political activity and pragmatic self-limitation to practical affairs. Finally, it may be added that the Sloboda settlers were initially less burdened with tradition and showed themselves open to innovations promoting the modernization of the region in the late eighteenth and early nineteenth centuries.

## The Economy

Local privileges confirmed at various times by Russian monarchs and associated mainly with various trades, especially liquor distilling and milling, as well as exemption from certain taxes, were decisive in forming the economic identity of the Sloboda region.[130] Other contributing factors were fertile soil, an environment conducive to stock raising, less onerous conditions of serfdom, unusually well-developed market trade in all goods, and the region's relatively late entry into the all-Russian economic system because of poorly developed transportation.

The broad development of market trade may be considered one of the particular features of the Sloboda region's economic life. This was promoted by concessions received by the inhabitants, particularly the exemption of goods from customs duties, as well as the region's favorable geographic location, which attracted merchants from Russia, Little Russia, the Don Cossack Host, Poland, and the Crimea. The building of Black Sea ports and the settlement of the steppe and the Black Sea littoral increased the Sloboda region's significance as a hub of commerce between the new region of Southern Russia and the regions of trade and industry in central Russia.

The same condition promoted the influx of Russian merchants into the region, who gradually took over all large-scale business, including wholesale trade, on the steppe frontier.[131] This was due mainly to their degree of organization and professionalism, surpassing that of the Ukrainian colonists, ties with industrial regions in Russia, the low price of goods, and to some degree the presence among them of Old Believers, who were united by a strong work ethic.

This was the period in which a discourse began to arise about the periphery lagging behind the center of the empire, along with the view that local Ukrainian inhabitants had a congenital indisposition to commercial activity, were prone to be satisfied with little, and were naively credulous—characteristics conventionally attributed to natives of newly discovered lands. At the end of the twentieth century, that view would be reformulated by the "natives" themselves precisely to the contrary.

The region's economic identity found symbolic reflection in the system of coats of arms awarded to the towns of the Kharkiv vicegerency in 1781. All of them, aside from the towns' own markers, mainly drawn from local flora and fauna (plums, cherries, pears, blackthorn or wolf, swan, and the like), contained obligatory elements of Kharkiv's new civic symbolism: a horn of plenty and a caduceus indicating the flowering of the town thanks to trade and stock raising.[132]

## Notes

1. Alla Perepecha and Artur Iareshchenko, eds., *Toponimichnyi slovnyk Kharkivshchyny* (Kharkiv: Derzhavna naukova biblioteka Korolenka, 1991).
2. Iaroslav Dashkevych, "Pokraini notatky pro Ukraïns'ki stepy u 'Heohrafiï' Ptolomeia 1562 r.," in *Boplan i Ukraïna: zbirnyk naukovykh prats'* (Lviv, 1998), 86.
3. Norman W. Ingham, "*Zemlia Russkaia* and *Zemlia Polovetskaia* in the Poetic Structure of '*Slovo o Polku Igoreve*,'" *Russian History/Histoire Russe* 19, nos. 1–4 (1992): 97–114, here 102.
4. Mikhail F. Getmanets, *Taina reki Kaialy: "Slovo o polku Igoreve,"* 2nd ed. (Kharkiv: Izd. Khar'kovskogo universiteta, 1989), 3rd ed. (Kharkiv, 2003).
5. Perepecha and Iareshchenko, *Toponimichnyi slovnyk Kharkivshchyny*.
6. Matvei Liubavskii, *Obzor istorii russkoi kolonizatsii s drevneishykh vremen i do XX veka* (Moscow, 1996); Aleksei A. Novosel'skii, *Bor'ba Moskovskogo gosudarstva s tatarami v pervoi polovine XVII veka* (Moscow: AN SSSR, 1948); Anna Khoroshkevich, *Rus' i Krym: ot soiuza k protivostoianiiu: konets XV–nachalo XVI v.* (Moscow: Editorial URSS, 2001); John P. LeDonne, *The Grand Strategy of the Russian Empire, 1650–1831* (New York: Oxford University Press, 2004).
7. Stephan Hedlund, "Vladimir the Great, Grand Prince of Muscovy: Resurrecting the Russian Service State," *Europe-Asia Studies* 58, no. 5 (2006): 775–801, here 780.
8. Liubavskii, *Obzor istorii*, 302.
9. Valerie Kivelson, *Cartographies of Tsardom: The Land and Its Meanings in Seventeenth-Century Russia* (Ithaca, NY: Cornell University Press, 2006), 9.
10. Michael Khodarkovsky, "From Frontier to Empire: The Concept of the Frontier in Russia, Sixteenth-Eighteenth Centuries," *Russian History/Histoire Russe* 19, no. 1–4 (1992): 115.
11. Jeremy Adelman and Stephen Aron, "From Borderlands to Borders: Empires, Nation-States, and the Peoples in Between in North American History," *American Historical Review* 104, no. 3 (1999): 814–41, here 815. See also John Mack Faragher, ed., *Rereading Frederick Jackson Turner: "The Significance of the Frontier in American History" and Other Essays* (New York, 1994); Daniel Power and Naomi Staden, eds., *Frontiers in Question: Eurasian Borderlands 700–1700* (New York: St. Martin's Press, 1999); Steven G. Ellis and Raingard Esser, eds., *Frontiers and the Writing of History, 1500–1850* (Hanover-Laatzen: Wehrhahn, 2006); Ihor Chornovol, *Komparatyvni frontyry: svitovyi i vitchyznianyj vymiry* (Kyiv: Krytyka, 2015).
12. Iaroslav Dashkevych, "Velykyi kordon Ukraïny za kartamy Boplana (politychni ta konfesiini vidnosyny)," in *Istorychne kartoznavstvo Ukraïny*, ed. Iaroslav Dashkevych (Lviv, Kyiv, and New York: M. Kots', 2004), 106–8.

13. Sergei Solov'ev, *Sochineniia v 18 knigakh. Istoriia Rossii s drevneishykh vremen*, vols. 9–10, bk. 5 (Moscow: Nauka, 1990), 171.
14. Viktor Brekhunenko, *Moskovs'ka ekspansiia i Pereiaslavs'ka Rada 1654 roku* (Kyiv: Instytut istoriï Ukraïny, 2001), 171.
15. Brian J. Boeck, "Containment vs. Colonization: Muscovite Approaches to Settling the Steppe," in *Peopling the Russian Periphery: Borderland Colonization in Eurasian History*, eds. Nicholas B. Breyfogle, Abby Schrader, and Willard Sunderland (London: Routledge, 2007), 45.
16. *Kniga Bol'shomu Chertezhu* (Moscow and Leningrad: Nauka, 1950), 49; cf. Denis J. B. Shaw, "Mapmaking, Science and State Building in Russia Before Peter the Great," *Journal of Historical Geography*, no. 31 (2005): 415–20; Kivelson, *Cartographies of Tsardom*, 32.
17. Dashkevych, "Velykyi kordon," 107.
18. *Land of the Cossacks: Antiquarian Maps of Ukraine (Zemlia kozakiv: starovynni karty Ukraïny)* (Winnipeg: Ukrainian Cultural and Educational Centre, 1987), 23.
19. *Ukraïns'ka literatura XVII st. Synkretychna pysemnist'. Poeziia. Dramaturhiia. Beletrystyka* (Kyiv: Naukova Dumka, 1987), 311.
20. Vladimir Zagorovskii, *Belgorodskaia cherta* (Voronezh: Izd. Voronezhskogo universiteta, 1969).
21. William H. McNeill, *Europe's Steppe Frontier, 1500–1800* (Chicago and London: University of Chicago Press, 1964), 126–27.
22. In 1638 the Cossack leader Yakiv Ostrianyn fled to Russia with his Cossacks and established the Chuhuiv fortress on the Russian steppe frontier. It stood until 1641, when the Cossacks rebelled and returned to the Polish-Lithuanian Commonwealth.
23. Dmytro Bahalii, *Istoriia kolonizatsiï Slobids'koï Ukraïny (Vybrani pratsi v 6 tomakh*, vol.1, ed. Volodymyr Kravchenko) (Kharkiv: Golden Pages, 2007), 320.
24. Volodymyr Masliichuk, *Balakliis'kyi Polk (1669–1677)* (Kharkiv: Kharkiv Private Museum of the City Estate, 2005).
25. Boeck, "Containment vs. Colonization," 47.
26. Bahalii, *Istoriia kolonizatsiï*, 205, 288.
27. Hryhorii P. Zaika, *Ukraïns'ka Liniia* (Kyiv and Poltava: Arkheolohiia, 2001); Volodymyr Masliichuk, *Provintsiia na perekhresti kul'tur (doslidzhennia z istoriï Slobids'koï Ukraïny) XVII–XIX stolit'* (Kharkiv: Kharkiv Private Museum of the City Estate, 2007), 118.
28. Bahalii, *Istoriia kolonizatsiï*, 325, 347.
29. Bahalii, *Istoriia kolonizatsiï*, 280–81.
30. *Tysiacha rokiv ukraïns'koï suspil'no-politychnoï dumky: v 9 tomakh*, ed. Taras Hunchak [Hunczak] (Kyiv: Dnipro, 2001), 3: 332–36.
31. Oleksander Ohloblyn, *Het'man Ivan Mazepa ta ioho doba* (New York, Paris, and Toronto: OOChSU, Liga Vyzvolennia Ukraïny, 1960), 341, 343.
32. Oleksandr Hurzhii, *Ukraïns'ka kozats'ka derzhava v druhii polovyni XVII–XVIII st.: kordony, naselennia, pravo* (Kyiv: Osnovy, 1996).
33. Bahalii, *Istoriia kolonizatsiï*, 408–9.
34. Samiilo Velychko, *Litopys* (Kyiv: Dnipro, 1991), 370.
35. Volodymyr Masliichuk, *Altera Patria: Notatky pro diial'nist' Ivana Sirka na Slobids'kii Ukraïni* (Kharkiv: Muzei Mis'koï Sadyby, 2004); Volodymyr Masliichuk and Iurii Mytsyk, *Koshovyi Otaman Ivan Sirko* (Kyiv: PP Nataliia Brekhunenko, 2007).
36. Filaret, *Istoriko-statisticheskoe opisanie Khar'kovskoi eparkhii, v 3 tomakh*, 2nd ed., vol. 2 (Kharkiv: Muzei Mis'koï Sadyby, 2005).
37. Petro Lavriv, *Istoriia Pivdenno-Skhidnoï Ukraïny* (Kyiv: Ukraïns'ka vydavnycha spilka, 1996), 81.
38. Lavriv, *Istoriia Pivdenno-Skhidnoï Ukraïny*, 83–85.
39. Sagit Faizov, "'Gde Moskva, Gde Vostok, Gde Zapad?': Geograficheskaia Polemika mezhdu Krymskim Khanom Mukhammedom IV i Tsarem Alekseem Mikhailovichem v 1655–1656,"

in *Ukraïna–Rossiia: Istoriia vzaimootnoshenii*, eds. Aleksei Miller, Vladimir Reprintsev, and Boris Floria (Moscow, 2003), 128–45.
40. Bahalii, *Istoriia kolonizatsiï*, 280.
41. Anssi Paasi, "Bounded Spaces in the Mobile World: Deconstructing 'Regional Identity,'" *Tijdschrift voor Economische en Sociale Geografie* 93, no. 2 (2002): 140.
42. Michael Khodarkovsky, "Frontier and Non-Christian Identities in Early Modern Russia," in *Mappa Mundi: Zbirnyk naukovykh prats' na poshanu Iaroslava Dashkevycha z nahody ioho 70-richchia* (Lviv, Kyiv, and New York, 1996), 178–98, here 181; Serhii Plokhy, *The Origins of the Slavic Nations: Premodern Identities in Russia, Ukraine, and Belarus* (Cambridge: Cambridge University Press, 2006), 317.
43. Bahalii, *Istoriia kolonizatsiï*, 90.
44. Liubavskii, *Obzor istorii*, 307–8.
45. Bahalii, *Istoriia kolonizatsiï*, 91, 195.
46. Bahalii, *Istoriia kolonizatsiï*, 148.
47. Plokhy, *The Origins*, 317–19; Volodymyr Kravchenko, "In Search of 'Ukraine' in the Russian Empire (Late Eighteenth and Early Nineteenth Centuries)," in *Eighteenth-Century Ukraine: New Perspectives on Social, Cultural, and Intellectual History*, eds. Frank Sysyn, Zenon Kohut, and Volodymyr Sklokin (forthcoming).
48. Plokhy, *The Origins*, 294.
49. Plokhy, *The Origins*, 310.
50. *Kniga Bol'shomu Chertezhu*, 68–78, 81–87.
51. Dmitrii Bagalei, *Materialy dla istorii kolonizatsii i byta stepnoi okrainy Moskovskogo gosudarstva (Khar'kovskoi i otchasti Kurskoi i Voronezhskoi gubernii) v XVI–XVIII stoletii, sobrannye v raznykh arkhivakh*, vol. 2 (Kharkiv: Izdanie Istoriko-Filologicheskogo Obshchestva pri Khar'kovskom Universitete, 1890), 171.
52. Leo Bagrow, *A History of Russian Cartography up to 1800*, ed. H. W. Castner (Wolfe Island: The Walker Press, 1975), 10.
53. Bahalii, *Istoriia kolonizatsiï*, 280, 287, 308, 321.
54. Boeck, "Containment vs. Colonization," 49.
55. Filaret, *Istoriko-statisticheskoe opisanie*, 300.
56. Kravchenko, "In Search of 'Ukraine' in the Russian Empire."
57. Bahalii, *Istoriia kolonizatsiï*, 349.
58. *Istoriia kolonizatsiï*, 266.
59. *Istoriia kolonizatsiï*, 267–68.
60. Velychko, *Litopys*, 2: 282, 426.
61. Orest Subtel'nyi, *Ukraïna: istoriia* (Kyiv, 1994), 203. In Moscow's mental map of the world, it was the Don River, not the Dnieper, that divided Europe and Asia. Mark Bassin, "Russia between Europe and Asia: The Ideological Construction of Geographical Space," *Slavic Review* 50, no 1 (1991): 4.
62. *Land of the Cossacks*, 36–37.
63. *Land of the Cossacks*, 23.
64. Bahalii, *Istoriia kolonizatsiï*, 322.
65. Hnat Khotkevych, "Do istoriï Slobozhanshchyny (protses saltivtsiv z Pasiekamy)," *Naukovi zapysky naukovo-doslidnoï katedry istoriï ukraïns'koï kul'tury*, no. 6 (1927): 85.
66. Dmytro Bahalii, *Istoriia Slobids'koï Ukraïny* (Kharkiv: Osnova, 1990), 83–84.
67. Brian L. Davies, *Warfare, State and Society on the Black Sea Steppe, 1500–1700* (London and New York: Routledge, 2007), 102; Artur Iareshchenko, *Ukraïns'kyi Feniks* (Kharkiv: Prapor, 1999), 45.
68. Iareshchenko, *Ukraïns'kyi Feniks*; Viktoriia Sadovnycha, "Antroponimiia Slobozhanshchyny XVII st.: zahal'nyi ohliad," *Visnyk L'vivs'koho Universytetu* 34, no. 2 (2004): 185–90; Iuliia Abdula, *Stanovlennia oikonimiï Slobozhanshchyny (na materiali Kharkivshchyny). Avtoreferat dysertatsiï* (Kirovohrad, 2008), 11.

69. Brekhunenko, *Moskovs'ka ekspansiia*, 280.
70. *Moskovs'ka ekspansiia*, 261.
71. Iareshchenko, *Ukraïns'kyi Feniks*, 50.
72. Bahalii, *Istoriia kolonizatsii*, 186, 188–91.
73. *Istoriia kolonizatsii*, 260–61, 264.
74. *Istoriia kolonizatsii*, 310.
75. *Istoriia kolonizatsii*, 321.
76. Filaret, *Istoriko-statisticheskoe opisanie*, 304–5; Volodymyr Masliichuk, "Dialoh 'Ukraïns'koho' ta 'Rosiis'koho' na peretynakh Slobids'koï Ukraïny (druha polovyna XVII st.)," in *Ukraïna i Rosiia: problemy politychnykh i sotsiokul'turnykh vidnosyn: zbirnyk naukovykh prats'*, ed. Valerii Smolii (Kyiv, 2003), 436.
77. Bahalii, *Istoriia kolonizatsii*, 259; Ivan Saratov, *Istoriia khar'kovskikh gerbov: uchebnoe posobie* (Kharkiv: Maidan, 2000), 142–43.
78. Jan Ornowski, *Bogaty w parantelę, sławę y honory wirydyarz herbownemi Ich Mościow Panow P. Zacharzewskich*... (Kyiv: Lavra Press, 1705); Ihor Ia. Losiievs'kyi, "'Bahatyi sad' Iana Ornovs'koho 1705 r.: Pershyi khudozhn'o-dokumental'nyi tvir pro Slobids'ku Ukraïnu," in *Pol's'ka diaspora u Kharkovi: Istoriia ta suchasnist'; Materialy naukovoï konferentsii*, 2nd ed. (Kharkiv: Maidan, 2004), 97–118.
79. [Anonimus], "350 let khar'kovskoi arkhitektury," in *Arkhitektory Khar'kova*, ed. S. Chechel'nyts'kyi (Kharkiv, 2008), 6.
80. Bahalii, *Istoriia kolonizatsii*, 333.
81. Vadim Passek, "Istoriko-Statisticheskoe Opisaniie Khar'kovskoi Gubernii XVIII Stoletiia," in *Materialy dlia statistiki Rosiiskoi imperii*, vol. 1 (Kharkiv, 1839), 41–42; Izmail Sreznevskii, *Istoricheskoe obozrenie grazhdanskogo ustroeniia Slobodskoi Ukrainy so vremeni ee zaseleniia do preobrazovaniia v Khar'kovskuiu guberniiu* (Kharkiv: Kharkiv Gubernia Press, 1883), 13, 18–19.
82. Bagalei, *Materialy*, 2: 160, 171, 172–78.
83. Hurzhii, *Ukraïns'ka kozats'ka* derzhava, 92.
84. Bahalii, *Istoriia kolonizatsii*, 177.
85. Vladimir F. Gorlenko, *Stanovlenie ukrainskoi etnografii kontsa XVIII–pervoi poloviny XIX st.* (Kyiv: Naukova Dumka, 1988), 198.
86. Bahalii, *Istoriia kolonizatsii*, 312, 317.
87. *Istoriia kolonizatsii*, 187.
88. *Istoriia kolonizatsii*, 217.
89. *Istoriia kolonizatsii*, 206.
90. Dmitrii Bagalei and Dmitrii Miller, *Istoriia goroda Khar'kova za 250 let ego sushchestvovaniia: Istoricheskaia monografiia*, 2 vols. (Kharkiv: Zilberberg and Sons, 1912. Repr. Kharkiv: Kharkiv City Press, 1993), 1: 21.
91. Masliichuk, "Dialoh," 443.
92. Willard Sunderland, "Imperial Space: Territorial Thought and Practice in the Eighteenth Century," in *Russian Empire: Space, People, Power, 1700–1930*, eds. Jane Burbank, Mark von Hagen, and Anatolyi Remnev (Bloomington: Indiana University Press, 2007), 33–67, here 35.
93. Davies, *Warfare, State and Society*, 93.
94. G. A. Sanin, "Iuzhnaia granitsa Rossii vo vtoroi polovine XVI–pervoi polovine XVIII v.," *Russian History/Histoire Russe* 19, nos. 1–4 (1992): 442.
95. Denis J. B. Shaw, "Geographical Practice and Its Significance in Peter the Great's Russia," *Journal of Historical Geography* 22, no. 2 (1996): 164.
96. Vasyl' Pirko, *Kartohrafichni materialy Pivdnia Ukraïny XVIII stolittia* (Lviv: NTSh Press, 1997), 406.
97. Vasyl' Pirko, "250-richchia z chasu sporudzhennia Ukraïns'koï linii," *Ukraïns'kyi istorychnyi zhurnal*, no. 8 (1986): 139–42.

98. Pirko, "250-richchia," 136.
99. Saratov, *Istoriia khar'kovskikh gerbov*, 147–48.
100. Rostyslav Sossa, *Istoriia kartohrafuvannia terytoriï Ukraïny* (Kyiv: Instytut Istoriï Ukraïny NAN Ukraïny, 2007), 90–91.
101. Pirko, *Kartohrafichni materialy*, 406.
102. Hurzhii, *Ukraïns'ka kozats'ka derzhava*, 67.
103. Pirko, *Kartohrafichni materialy*, 406–8.
104. Grigorii Kvitka, *Khar'kov i uezdnye goroda: Khar'kovskaia starina* (Kharkiv: Kharkivs'ka Starovyna, 2005), 186.
105. Kvitka, *Khar'kov i uezdnye goroda*, 188–89.
106. *Ėkonomicheskaia geografiia v SSSR. Istoriia i sovremennoe razvitie*, ed. Nikolai Baranskii (Moscow, 1965), 251.
107. Volodymyr Sklokin, *Rosiis'ka imperiia i Slobids'ka Ukraïna u druhii polovyni XVIII st.: prosvichenyi absoliutyzm, impers'ka intehratsiia, lokal'ne suspil'stvo* (Lviv: Ukrainian Catholic University Press, 2019), 28–29.
108. Bahalii, *Istoriia Slobids'koï Ukraïny*, 188–89.
109. Bagalei and Miller, *Istoriia goroda Khar'kova*, 1: 321.
110. *Istoriia goroda Khar'kova*, 1: 319, 324.
111. Liudmila Sofronova, "Funktsiia granitsy v formirovanii ukrainskoi kul'tury XVII–XVIII v.," in *Ukraina–Rossiia: Istoriia vzaimootnoshenii*, eds. Aleksei Miller, Vladimir Reprintsev, and Boris Floria (Moscow, 1997), 101–14.
112. Bagalei and Miller, *Istoriia goroda Khar'kova*, 1: 320–21.
113. Solov'ev, *Sochineniia v 18 knigakh. Istoriia Rossii s drevneishykh vremen*, vols. 13–14, bk. 7: 375.
114. Filaret, *Istoriko-statisticheskoe opisanie*, 1: 16; Bagalei and Miller, *Istoriia goroda Khar'kova*, 1: 330.
115. "350 let khar'kovskoi arkhitektury," 6.
116. Liudmyla Posokhova, *Kharkivs'kyi kolehium (XVIII – persha polovyna XIX st.)* (Kharkiv: Business-Inform, 1999).
117. Posokhova, *Kharkivs'kyi kolehium*, 41, 46, 48–49.
118. Bagalei and Miller, *Istoriia goroda Khar'kova*, 1: 392.
119. Grigorii P. Danilevskii, *Ukrainskaia starina: Materialy dlia istorii ukrainskoi literatury i narodnogo obrazovaniia* (Kharkiv: Izdanie Zalenskogo i Liubarskogo, 1866), 298.
120. Sklokin, *Rosiis'ka imperiia*; Zenon Kohut, *Rosiis'kyi tsentralizm i ukraïns'ka avtonomiia. Likvidatsiia Het'manshchyny, 1760–1830* (Kyiv: Krytyka, 1996).
121. Kohut, *Rosiis'kyi tsentralizm*, 78.
122. Masliichuk, "Dialoh," 141–56.
123. Kristof Ditrikh fon Rommel' (Christoph Dietrich von Rommel), *Spohady pro moie zhyttia ta mii chas*, comp. and ed. Volodymyr V. Kravchenko, trans. Volodymyr Masliichuk and Nataliia Onishchenko (Kharkiv: Maidan, 2001).
124. Johann G. Kohl, *Russia. St. Petersburg, Moscow, Kharkoff, Riga, Odessa, the German Provinces on the Baltic, the Steppes, the Crimea, and the Interior of the Empire* (London: Chapman and Hall, 1842), 509–10.
125. Stephan Velychenko, "Identities, Loyalties, and Service in Imperial Russia: Who Administered the Borderlands?" *Russian Review* 54, no. 2 (1995): 188–208.
126. Between 1781 and 1796, the Sloboda Ukraine gubernia was renamed the Kharkiv vicegerency (*namestnichestvo*).
127. Vladimir M. Kabuzan, *Zaselenie Novorossii (Ekaterinoslavskoi i Khersonskoi gubernii v XVIII–pervoi polovine XIX veka (1719–1858 gg.)* (Moscow: Nauka, 1976), 192.
128. Kabuzan, *Zaselenie Novorossii*, 211.

129. Bahalii, *Istoriia kolonizatsii*, 394–98; Pavel Rudiakov, *"V sluzhbu i vechnoe poddanstvo...": Serbskie poseleniia Novaia Serbiia i Slavianoserbiia na ukrainskikh zemliakh (1751–1764)* (Kyiv: ArtEk, 2001).
130. Colum Leckey, "Provincial Readers and Agrarian Reform, 1760s–1770s: The Case of Sloboda Ukraine," *Russian Review* 61 (2002): 535–59, here 549.
131. Dmitrii Bagalei, "Iarmarki Khar'kova v 18 stoletii," in idem, *Ocherki iz russkoi istorii*, 2 vols. *Monografii i stat'i po istorii Slobodskoi Ukrainy* (Kharkiv, 1913), 2: 76.
132. Saratov, *Istoriia khar'kovskikh gerbov*, 156–57.

CHAPTER 2

# Town and Gown

The search for an optimal administrative strategy to manage territories distant from the center and the need to integrate them into the empire were closely intertwined with new tasks and challenges produced by the expansion of the Russian Empire toward the south and west. In this case, imperial expansion was closely associated with modernization, which in turn looked like the reverse side of westernization. The reformation of an empire tremendous in size and diverse in population inevitably assumed a different character in different regions, taking local particularities into account.

The Russian government's strategies of modernization in the Sloboda region in the late eighteenth and early nineteenth centuries were fully reflected in the history of the city of Kharkiv and Kharkiv University, which became the most recognizable symbols of the whole region from that time on. The question arises in that regard: to what extent did the civic and university reforms reflect local and regional particularities? Did the imperial reforms influence the cultural and geographic identification of the city and region in their own right? But before proposing answers to these and related questions, we must generally note the basic vectors of central policy in the southern steppe borderland of the empire during the period under discussion.

This new region of the Russian Empire was to become a bridgehead for further military and economic expansion toward the Caucasus and the Balkans. As the military frontier in Southern Russia gradually evolved into a settlement frontier,[1] the Russian government undertook a new large-scale project intended to transform the southern steppe borderland in the spirit of the European Enlightenment. New towns and administrative territories began to appear in the northern Black Sea littoral and in the Crimea. They were planned and built according to models of antiquity as these were understood in Russia during the Age of Enlightenment. In time, they would constitute a historical region known under various names: Southern Russia, New Russia, the northern Black Sea littoral, Southern Ukraine, and Steppe Ukraine.[2] The appearance of the new region and the place it assumed on the new cultural and political map of the Russian Empire attested, in the words of Andrei Zorin, to the global reorientation of Russian politics, culture, and self-consciousness in general.³

The newly acquired region was to become a model of successful Russian modernization, a showcase of Europeanism. But that was only one side of the coin. The other side was represented by the search for cultural and civilizational sources of the Byzantine legacy, perceived in that regard as a basis for the revival of the Orthodox world under Russian leadership. The "South Russian" cities became centers of new institutions established for the training of Greek and Balkan Slavic youth, such as the Corps of Foreign Coreligionists, transferred in 1779 from St. Petersburg to Kherson or, more than half a century later, the South Slavic Boarding School in Nikolaev (Mykolaiv).⁴

The southern direction of Catherine II's domestic and foreign policy was accompanied by the search for a new capital of the Russian Empire, now to be located in the south as a counterweight to the northern capital of St. Petersburg.⁵ At first Kherson is likely to have pretended to that role, as Catherine II herself noted repeatedly.⁶ According to the empress's intention, Kherson was to become the main port of the new region, a "southern St. Petersburg."⁷ It is no accident that the city was built by the godson of Peter I, General Ivan Gannibal. The Kherson and Slaviansk eparchy of the Russian Orthodox Church, endowed with an exclusively high status, was established in the new city in 1775. True, it later became apparent that the government had botched the historical data, concluding that this was the location of ancient Chersonesus, the legendary site of the christening of Grand Prince Vladimir (Volodimer, Ukr. Volodymyr) of Kyiv.⁸

In time, Kherson was replaced in official planning by Katerynoslav (Yekaterinoslav), whose cornerstone was laid in 1787 by the Russian empress herself in the presence of Emperor Joseph II of Austria. The city's very name appeared to be a supplementary argument in favor of the prime role reserved for it in the empire's future (as compared with Peter's city, St. Petersburg). The particular status of Katerynoslav was also emphasized by an imperial ukase of 1784 on the establishment of a university in the city intended to educate not only Russian subjects but also Slavs residing in the Ottoman and Austrian Empires.⁹ The sum of 300,000 rubles was appropriated for the building of the university, and the first professors were appointed. Although the project was not realized, it undoubtedly had an influence on the idea of Kharkiv University.

It is curious, however, that in the search for a new alternative to St. Petersburg as capital of the Russian Empire, the gaze of imperial politicians did not turn at first to Kyiv, which had pretended to that role in the mid-seventeenth century. This was despite the cult of pre–Petrine Rus' that was developing during the rule of Catherine II, in which Kyiv was assigned the role of basic symbol of the "organicism" of the empire's historical development, supposedly breached by Peter I. A favorite of the empress, Platon Zubov, conjuring up chimerical plans for redrawing the map of the whole world, immediately identified six sites for the capital of the future "universal" Russian Empire but found no place for Kyiv among them.[10] Thus contemporary Kyiv (like Moscow, with its burden of presecular historical and cultural tradition) remained uninteresting to the Russian government: the Kyivan idea seemed much more important.

Traveling through the Sloboda region, Empress Catherine II favored the town of Kursk, for example, with an observation regretting that Peter I had not established the capital there, for, "passing through these places, one imagines the times of Volodimer I, in which there were many inhabitants in these lands."[11] Kharkiv did not inspire anyone to reflections of that kind. It simply had no visible place in the eighteenth-century system of cultural coordinates pertaining to antiquity and old Rus'.

## A Borderland City

The significance of Kharkiv for the empire was initially based mainly on military and geopolitical considerations. It had long been the headquarters of the commander in chief of Russia's border troops in the "southern land," which had been transferred first to Poltava, then to Kremenchuk, and finally to Yelisavetgrad (present-day Kropyvnytskyi) toward the end of Catherine II's reign.[12] The placement of Kharkiv in the symbolic space of "Southern Russia" reflected the expansionist aspect of the imperial center's policy on the territory of the former steppe borderland. It was this very circumstance that gave Kharkiv priority in the struggle for the right to call itself the administrative and cultural capital of the new southern region of the empire and allowed it to outstrip no less serious competitors—Belgorod, Sumy, and Yekaterinoslav (Ukr. Katerynoslav, present-day Dnipro).

In that struggle the town of Sumy, which exceeded Kharkiv in population and in intensity and volume of trade with Russia, could be considered its first and most serious competitor in the Sloboda region. It was no accident that in 1732 Sumy became the residence of the first reformer of the Sloboda region, Prince Aleksei Shakhovskoi. The city's geographic proximity to Russia made it the empire's foremost strongpoint in the Sloboda region at a time when the government's priorities remained the annexation and incorporation of the steppe borderlands, including those inhabited by the Cossacks.

But in the latter half of the eighteenth century, when the Cossack military administrative formations no longer appeared to present a military threat to the empire, the government's political priorities changed. Southward expansion toward the Black Sea took pride of place. In military strategic and geopolitical terms, Kharkiv turned out to be preferable to Sumy as a strongpoint of imperial policy. Kharkiv was granted the status of Sloboda Ukraine gubernia center in 1765. This status was reestablished in 1796, after some brief experimentation with administrative reform, during which (1780–95) Kharkiv was elevated to the level of center of the vicegerency (*namestnichestvo*).

Imperial expansion toward the Black Sea opened new prospects for Kharkiv, especially in connection with the constant threat of war with Turkey and the development of the Serbian and Greek national movements in the early nineteenth century. The Russian government was cultivating far-reaching plans for strengthening its political influence in the Balkans, and Kharkiv therefore took on further significance as a bridgehead and transit point in the southern vector of imperial policy.

From the eighteenth century onward, there was a growing concentration of migrants from the Balkans in the Ukrainian steppe borderland, and they received various privileges from the Russian government according to the Ukrainian example.[13] These were mainly Serbs and Wallachians who filled the ranks of the local elite, the officer corps, the higher clergy, and the intelligentsia. Migrants from Serbia studied and taught at the Kharkiv College and then at the university. On the eve and in the course of the Russo-Turkish war of 1806–12, Serbian deputations and Russian emissaries passed through Kharkiv in opposite directions.

It should be noted that from the moment of Kharkiv's elevation to the status of capital of the Sloboda region, its influence was never limited to the administrative borders of the gubernia or vicegerency. For example, the authority of the military governor of the Sloboda Ukraine gubernia extended far beyond its bounds, encompassing the Belgorod, Voronezh, Kazan, Saratov, and Astrakhan gubernias, as well as the Don Cossack Host.[14] The frontier status and local privileges granted to the permanent inhabitants were the only factors that allowed these extremely diverse territories to be considered as an administrative unit.

Kharkiv's importance as a strategic and military administrative hub at the crossroads of the most important routes linking the capitals with the southern borderlands of the empire was supplemented by its functions as an ecclesiastical administrative center of a large region, especially after the Belgorod Theological College, which trained inhabitants of the imperial borderlands as Orthodox clergymen, was transferred there in 1726. It was the college that distinguished Kharkiv among other gubernia centers of the Russian Empire. In 1799 Kharkiv became the center of the new Sloboda Ukraine eparchy.

In other words, Kharkiv became not only the administrative center of the Sloboda Ukraine gubernia but also the regional capital of the whole former steppe borderland of Russia, which was distinguished from the "internal" Russian regions by its established privileges (*slobody*). In that regard Kharkiv rather quickly gained supremacy over Belgorod, which had been regarded since the seventeenth century as the military administrative center of Russian control over the steppe borderland, and assumed its characteristic place between the more traditional towns of Little Russia and the new towns of Southern Russia.

The growth of Kharkiv was considerably promoted by market trade. From the moment of its founding, the city began to develop actively as a site of wholesale markets, which were very soon counted among the largest in the empire.[15] If at first Sumy was the basic commercial center of the region, given its closer proximity to Russia and the relative safety of its greater distance from the steppe borderland, then Russia's southward expansion led to the elevation of Kharkiv as a large center of wholesale market commerce. Thus, Kharkiv's commercial interests began to associate it more closely with the newly developing region of "Southern Russia," and not with the central regions of the empire.

This was well understood by the Kharkiv deputies to the Legislative Commission in 1767–68. They came out in particular against the reorientation of Russian external trade toward St. Petersburg, obviating Poland, and found allies for their position among deputies from neighboring Little Russia.[16] At the same time, the local interests of Kharkivites diverged significantly from those of the inhabitants of Little Russia and the Zaporozhian Sich because of their competition in southern trade, which, considering the country's generally poor communications network, was of the greatest interest to local merchants.

For more than a century after its founding, Kharkiv remained a fortified location with only individual features of urban identity in the form of "truncated" civic self-government, craft guilds, and church brotherhoods. This was clearly insufficient to equate Kharkiv with other Ukrainian cities, which were governed by Magdeburg law, especially as the Cossacks quickly and completely subjected the townspeople to themselves.

For a long time Kharkiv lacked even the external attributes of an urban milieu, remaining a fortified free settlement undistinguished in any way from other settlements on the steppe frontier. The founders of Kharkiv—"rabble and country bumpkins," in the contemptuous expression of a local Russian governor—continued their accustomed way of life in the new location, establishing outlying farms and engaging in rural trades, distilling, and commerce.

At the point of its initial settlement, Kharkiv had a population of 1,500 to 1,800, the absolute majority of whom were ethnic Ukrainians.[17] But the population of the fortress changed frequently because of the constant rotation of Russian troops and the migration of Ukrainian colonists in search of new free settlements. The city long remained sparsely populated: in the early nineteenth century, only 5,373 males were registered there, and Kharkiv was exceeded in population by Valky (5,392 males) and Okhtyrka (6,309 males).[18]

In and of itself, the number of inhabitants did not make a settlement a city. Suffice it to say that contemporary Dorpat had a population even smaller than Kharkiv's, but that did not stop it from being considered a city. A much more important factor characterizing the urban milieu was the social structure of its population. In the early nineteenth century, the absolute majority of Kharkivites were peasants owned by the state—*gosudarstvennye*, otherwise known as *kazënnye* or *voennye obyvateli* (military residents)—or by landowners (*pomeshchich'i*). Taken together, they numbered more than 7,500. They were followed, in descending order, by townspeople and guild tradesmen (more than 1,500), merchants (not many more than 800), gentry and clergy (fewer than 500).[19]

Unsurprisingly, Kharkiv looked like a typical free settlement whose inhabitants were basically employed in agriculture, small trades, and commerce, just as described by the early nineteenth-century Russian traveler Ivan Dolgoruky.[20] Crooked lanes, wooden houses with thatched roofs, filthy streets legendary even by provincial standards, foul-smelling rivers and, as a result, a lethal microclimate and unsanitary conditions—all these aspects of Kharkiv made a profound impression on Dolgoruky's contemporaries.

Professor Illia Tymkovsky, on first seeing Kharkiv in 1803, wrote: "The city . . . is only beginning to emerge from savage ignorance."[21] The reason for such a harsh reaction was evidently the huge amount of manure that, year after year, was simply dumped into the river or scattered on the streets "to reduce dirt." Tymkovsky's contemporary, Professor Ludwig Jakob, who came to Kharkiv from the German city of Halle in 1807, addressed the university's academic council with an official statement in which he wrote:

> The amount of dirt and manure on our streets keeps growing from day to day to such an extent that one must beware lest it bury not only people and animals but even houses. This huge amount of dirt, from which pedestrians can hardly ever make their way out, while horses and carriages plow through it only with difficulty, is destroying all the advantages of dwelling in the city and even threatening the lives of its inhabitants.[22]

Washed out with water and mixed with dirt, this waste product of the famous Kharkiv markets constantly poisoned the air and water, producing many epidemic diseases, the most widespread of which were typhus, fever, malaria, rheumatism, and respiratory ailments. In the early nineteenth century, mortality exceeded natality in the city. On settling in Kharkiv, migrants from the provinces soon came to resemble the local inhabitants, stricken with pallor and chronic eye infections. Most of all, sanitary and living conditions in Kharkiv proved lethal to foreigners arriving from Europe: many of them soon died or were compelled to leave the city of "healthful climate."

The Polish historian Ludwik Janowski considered that in the early nineteenth century Kharkiv as a city was worse than neighboring Belgorod, Voronezh, or Kursk.[23] His opinion was confirmed in particular by the Russian traveler Pavel Sumarokov, to whom Kharkiv, with the attractions enumerated previously, seemed "not in the least like Great Russian cities."[24] There was every reason to hold such an opinion, for during the first century and a half of Kharkiv's existence its sociocultural space actually merged with that of the surrounding free settlements, whose inhabitants continued to lead the traditional way of life associated with agrarian society.

Kharkiv's urban space took shape very slowly. Its first streets, to judge by their names, seemed mere extensions of the routes traversing the city: Moscow, Sumy, Zmiiv, Chuhuiv, Poltava, Belgorod and, later, Katerynoslav, Taganrog, and so on. The city's sociocultural space was also marked by the names of Orthodox churches, residents' estates and professional occupations (basically tradesmen, merchants, and soldiers), foreign settlers (Germans, Armenians) or the most prominent homeowners (Klochko). Until the early nineteenth century, however, the streets and squares of Kharkiv had no permanent names.

The first attempt to give Kharkiv streets permanent names was made in the early nineteenth century by the gubernia administration in the person of its head, Ivan Bakhtin.[25] The enlightened governor demanded that the council install posts with iron signs marking the appropriate street names. Unfortunately, it is not known whether the order was carried out—most likely not, for three decades later the local authorities again issued a directive to place tablets with exact street names on city houses.[26]

By the early nineteenth century, the outer boundaries of Kharkiv were no longer defined by fortress walls, as earlier, but by socioeconomic conditions associated with state encroachment on local liberties, the most important being the liquor trade, which made the greatest contribution to the imperial budget. In Kharkiv itself by that time, tax-farmers dealing in liquor had taken control of the trade, establishing monopoly prices in the city. In the villages, however, which continued to enjoy liberties, the price of liquor was still established freely and thus more cheaply than in the city. Accordingly, in 1807 Kharkiv barricaded itself against the province with makeshift customs offices at which all passing inhabitants presenting a potential threat to state interests were searched.[27] For those wishing to drink themselves under the table, however, there was no prohibition on going beyond the municipal boundary and coming back across it some time later, completely satisfied.

As with the Sloboda region in general, only permanent residents, united by common interests, could promote the consolidation and symbolic delineation of urban territory. Catherine II, striving to sequester urban residents from rural ones and stimulate the growth of cities, imported contemporary Western legislation into Russian imperial space. The Charter to the Cities, endowing city dwellers with the right of self-government, was adopted in 1785. It turned out, however, that the ground of the Russian Empire had been poorly prepared for experiments of that kind.

To begin with, the cities themselves had to be "created," and city dwellers along with them. To that end, the status of many imperial settlements of the empire, such as Kharkiv, was elevated: they began to be called cities. Their residents, in turn, were assigned to civic social estates, with clearly defined rights for each of them. But breathing life into enclaves of civil society planned by the government of a "service" empire with its serfdom, barely competent and corrupt bureaucracy, conservative church, and absence of rule of law turned out to be a difficult task.

City dwellers had no corporate interests in common. They remained divided by social estate, with first place reserved for the gentry. Kharkiv's civic space was divided into distinct quarters—yesterday's free settlements—whose residents joined together on the basis of estate membership, type of occupation, way of life, and so on: the Zakharkiv free settlement, Moskalivka, Chuhuivka, and others. Clearly, no collective civic identity could arise under such conditions.

Civic self-government was taken in hand by a single estate—the merchants,[28] who often ignored the interests of the overwhelming majority of Kharkivites. The gentry and bureaucracy in turn, along with the police and the church, practically ignored the city council, which was reduced to an appendage of the gubernia administration. In fact, the city was administered directly by the governor and his loyal police. Not surprisingly, councillors elected to the agencies of civic self-government regarded that honor as a burdensome duty and strove to rid themselves of it at the first convenient opportunity.

On the other hand, democratic self-government, developed by the enlightened authorities on the basis of Western models, long remained incomprehensible and unnecessary to the fledgling civic ("civil") society. The historian Dmytro Bahalii, who devoted many sorrowful lines to the condition of Kharkiv's civic self-government and its feeble resistance to the imperial bureaucracy, was nevertheless constrained to admit that it was largely the merchants themselves—assertive individuals, but generally crude, accustomed to bowing to authority and settling affairs with the aid of bribes—who were largely responsible for the lamentable state of that self-government. Understandably, initiatives meant to defend civic interests remained a rarity, often subject to retribution.

Nevertheless, after the appearance of the Charter to the Cities it became possible at least to define the nature and extent of particular civic interests, even if they were based entirely on social estates and limited to the commercial sphere. Almost from the moment of its formation in 1787, the Kharkiv city council set about protecting the interests of local merchants from competition, striving to keep Great Russian, Little Russian, and Jewish traders, as well as visiting peasants, out of the city's market.[29] To the accompaniment of the city council's struggle against Jewish traders in Kharkiv, a Jewish cemetery was established and even managed to grow old.[30]

Before the city council and the merchants began to exercise a palpable influence on the development of the urban milieu and cultural life of Kharkiv in the first half of the nineteenth century, the city was obliged for its progress above all to the enlightened initiatives of the imperial government. In a depiction of the city dating to 1787, it is clearly apparent that the civic landscape is still dominated by churches, monasteries, and wooden houses of city residents, but the center is already occupied by the residence of the governor general, along with the gubernia council and the governor's mansion.[31] True, the city council and assembly are still practically inconspicuous; some time later the experimental development of civic self-government would be halted completely by Emperor Paul I and renewed only with the accession of Alexander I in 1801. Nevertheless, the following century and a half of the city's history would become a time of impetuous progress, in which civic self-government would play a notable role.

In the second half of the eighteenth century, a public space for secular culture appeared in Kharkiv and began to develop with the dissemination of the new Enlightenment culture and ideology throughout society. Kharkiv's transformation into the administrative center of the Sloboda region was conducive to the appearance of the city's first theater, which found a permanent home in 1791. The theater enjoyed broad support in civic society, which contributed generously to its outfitting and filled the hall for any presentation, especially comedies, vaudeville, and comic operas, mainly by Russian and some Western authors: Aleksandr Sumarokov, Yakov Kniazhnin, Denis Fonvizin, Denis Diderot, Beaumarchais, and Voltaire.

Kharkiv's first printing press made its appearance in 1793 at the gubernia office of social assistance. Among its first publications historians make particular mention of an ode written by students of the Kharkiv College in honor of the patron of that educational institution, Prince Aleksandr Golitsyn (1795), as well as Berdychiv calendars translated from the Polish by the prefect of the Kharkiv College, Andrii Prokopovych, and published in 1797 and 1799.[32]

The Kharkiv free settlement's acquisition of an urban identity found expression in the active formation of the city's mythology, created mainly through the efforts of the local cultural elite. The first step in that direction was probably taken by the Donets-Zakharzhevsky colonels of Kharkiv, who commissioned the Chernihiv poet Jan Ornowski to write a panegyric to their clan. The panegyric contained the image of an "orchard city" in the wild steppe. In the late eighteenth century, the Kharkiv College and the famous philosopher Hryhorii Skovoroda also contributed a good deal to the formation of a new image of Kharkiv as an urban center of learning.[33]

Skovoroda, whose *Basni Khar'kovskie* (Kharkiv fables) brought renown to the Sloboda region in general, referred to Kharkiv as Zakharpolis and the city of the sun, prophesying an illustrious future for it. However, if one accepts Dmytro Bahalii's opinion that Skovoroda's well-known song "Vsiakomu horodu nrav i prava..." (To every city its customs and laws) is a depiction of Kharkiv,[34] then it must be admitted that contemporaneously with the vision of a "city of the sun" an image arises of Kharkiv as a "city of sin," from which the philosopher fled, as from fire, to the "groves," fields, and outlying farms.

A paramount element of the Kharkiv myth was the city's genealogy. On the cusp of the eighteenth and nineteenth centuries, it took shape in two basic forms, folkloric and literary. The former was associated with a legend about the founder of the city, a certain Cossack Kharko, who had established an outlying farm under his name that developed in time into the city of Kharkiv. "Portraits" of Cossack Kharko, armed and garbed in highly distinctive fashion, mounted and holding a pike, were abundantly to be found at local markets and in the homes of Kharkiv residents.

The subject was taken up by the Kharkiv literary figure Vasyl' Maslovych, who published a sentimental poem, *Osnovanie Khar'kova* (The founding of Kharkiv, 1816), concerned less with history than with the love of Kharko's daughter, Hapka, for the farm laborer Yakiv.[35] Even so, the author emphasizes the direct link between past and present by means of details of the urban landscape recognizable to his contemporaries. Dialogues between the main characters include Ukrainian words and expressions, giving the work a certain local color appreciated by Russian-speaking readers.

Another version of the history of Kharkiv's founding was produced by the Ukrainian writer Hryhorii Kvitka, a contemporary of Maslovych also concerned with requited love, but with somewhat different social accents. In this work the founder was no longer the Cossack Kharko but a distinguished noble, the son of a Muscovite boyar and a German woman brought up in the household of a Polish governor of Kyiv and nicknamed Kvitka (Flower) because of his handsome appearance. Having fallen in love with the governor's beautiful daughter, as the conventions of the genre require, Kvitka flees with her across the border, where he enters the service of the Russian tsar and establishes the outlying farm of Osnova (Foundation), which gives rise to the city of Kharkiv.

What attracts attention in this story, if anything, is the noble "foreign" descent of the city's "founder," raised on a gentry estate. From the late eighteenth century, the city of Kharkiv—the new imperial administrative and cultural center in the borderland—began actively to influence the "marking" of the whole region, among whose names, along with "Sloboda region" and "Ukraine," that of "Kharkiv region" soon appeared. The thought inevitably occurs that the "Kharkiv" marker in the region's name indicated integrationist tendencies in its political and cultural life, while the "Sloboda Ukrainian" marker emphasized local particularities, at first in the capacity of a border region with special rights, and subsequently as part of Ukrainian national space, to be discussed in the following sections.

## A University for Ukraine

The founding of Kharkiv University in 1805 may be considered the central event in the history of the Sloboda region in the first half of the nineteenth century.[36] The university became one of the most recognized symbols of the city and region as a whole, notably influencing the cultural and even administrative topography of the Ukrainian-Russian borderland. It is presented in the Ukrainian grand narrative as the first Ukrainian university and the main center of the early national revival.[37] In this chapter, I approach the issue in the context of mutual center-periphery relations as well as the center's cultural policy in the southern borderlands of the empire.

The development of modern education in the Ukrainian lands in the eighteenth and early nineteenth centuries remains a controversial problem. According to David Saunders, "it may have lagged behind education available in the West, but it was a long way ahead of most of the education available in Russia."[38] Nevertheless, one cannot ignore numerous complaints of contemporaries attesting to their view that the educational system in the Ukrainian lands was incapable of meeting the practical needs of society. Many of them preferred to travel to German university centers to obtain diplomas rather than enroll in Orthodox collegiums in Kyiv, Kharkiv, or Chernihiv. The only Russian university in Moscow also attracted numerous Ukrainians from the Cossack lands.

The Little Russian elite of the Hetmanate well understood the connection between secular university education and the social status associated with it. Education and service were the routes whereby representatives of the former Cossack officer class were supposed to consolidate their new status as members of the Russian nobility, especially those whose claims to nobility appeared dubious. Military service remained the most important means of acquiring nobiliary rights and powers, but a civilian professional education was also gradually beginning to create opportunities.

The last Ukrainian hetman, Kyrylo Rozumovsky, had begun to develop plans for the establishment of a university in his capital, Baturyn.[39] In his dual role as Ukrainian hetman and president of the St. Petersburg Academy of Sciences, Rozumovsky followed the model of German universities of the day, with their corporate autonomy. The first university professors and staff members would be invited to Ukraine from the German lands. The principal goal of Baturyn University was to be the education of a new secular generation of the Little Russian intellectual elite—teachers, doctors, and professors. It proved impossible to realize this project after Rozumovsky's resignation.

The same fate awaited efforts to establish a university in other urban centers of the former Hetmanate, such as Chernihiv, Pereiaslav, and Lubny.[40] It is significant that at least some of these projects were elaborated in cooperation with the imperial Russian authorities or even initiated by the latter. The newly established Katerynoslav, imagined in the role of southern capital of the Russian Empire, was also projected as a university center. The city was supposed to become a center of gravity for Orthodox Slavs in the Balkan peninsula, and the university was to play an important role in drawing them into Russian cultural space. But the idea of Katerynoslav University perished with the death of its main promoter, Prince Grigorii Potemkin.

The Sloboda region gentry also expressed itself in favor of secular education during the elections to the Legislative Commission of 1768 and in the course of its work. However, the local elites appeared to be less ambitious than their Little Russian neighbors. They only proposed expanding the curriculum of the Kharkiv Orthodox Collegium to include, in particular, modern languages, mathematics, and military science.⁴¹ Such a modest program seemed acceptable to the imperial authorities. The Kharkiv College was expanded to include a state secular educational institution known as "supplementary classes," "classes," a "state school," or even a "gymnasium."⁴²

Basically intended for children of the gentry, it was in fact independent of the college and directly subordinate to the gubernia (provincial) government, that is, to the gubernia administration. The curriculum of the "supplementary classes" lent itself to turning the school into a military college, which was fully in keeping with the desires of the local gentry. It was no accident that contemporaries compared the Kharkiv state school with a cadet college.⁴³ The secular system of education soon expanded with the opening of the Main Public School in Kharkiv in 1789.

To understand the subsequent course of events, which led to the founding of Kharkiv University, one has to interpret them in a political context. Emperor Alexander I, who was brought to power by a gentry conspiracy, reinstated the Charter to the Nobility (1785) and the inviolability of gentry privileges in 1801. The tsar supported a Senate initiative by reestablishing the practice of convoking gubernia gentry assemblies and allowing them to submit collective petitions to the government, earlier forbidden by Paul I. The Charter to the Cities was reinstated in the same year. The new monarch needed to resume the dialogue with gentry society in order to promote his own agenda of enlightened reform.

The gentry of the ill-assorted provinces of the empire, for its part, once awakened to participation in social affairs, usually hastened to voice its own needs and demands, which were sometimes at variance with official efforts to unify the state. This sequence came into play whenever a period of official reaction was followed by a policy of liberal reform. The unambiguous signals sent by the center were duly received in the regions. This in turn led to the activation of somnolent gentry initiative. As in the elections to the Legislative Commission in 1767, the Ukrainian gentry began to articulate its traditional rights and freedoms.

The gentry of the Sloboda region, having learned of the restitution of the Charter to the Nobility, hastened to convoke an extraordinary assembly on 31 May 1801 to express its deep appreciation to the new emperor. The imperial rescript on the matter, dated 29 December 1801, included all the requisite mentions of "our constant appreciation of the steadfast loyalty, diligence, and merits of the Sloboda Ukraine gentry" and the "affirmation and assurance of all the rights and privileges conferred upon it at various times and existing without revocation to the present day."⁴⁴ The townspeople followed in their footsteps, celebrating the restitution of the Charter to the Cities.

A step toward the satisfaction of the Sloboda gentry's corporate interests was the governmental project to establish a military academy (cadet college) in Kharkiv, which was made public in mid-August 1801. It contained an appeal for voluntary donations to help build the institution. Since the wishes of the central authorities in the Russian Empire were always interpreted locally as routine calls for action, the Sloboda gentry obliged itself to collect 100,000 rubles for the new project over three years.

True, some of the landowners protested that sum, considering it excessive,[45] but that was not the main thing: relations between the local provincial gentry and the throne began to be determined once again, as previously, by the practice of direct dialogue and mutual compromise. In that regard the gentry of the Sloboda region followed the protocol of relations with the government worked out by long practice: initiatives were to come "from above," and the response to them presupposed a positive reply "from below," along with a modest reminder of local needs and wishes.

The landed gentry of the Sloboda region decided to seize the opportunity to approach the government on the question of restoring the local rights and privileges set forth in tsarist charters of the seventeenth and early eighteenth centuries but abolished during the reign of Catherine II. According to the practice of earlier years, the gentry, followed by the merchants, selected their deputies, who were supposed to greet the new emperor in person with his election to the throne and represent the gubernia at his coronation. The deputies elected by the gentry were the marshal of the Sloboda region nobility, Volodymyr Donets-Zakharzhevsky, the Sumy landowner Fedir Kukol-Yasnopolsky, and the Bohodukhiv landowner Vasilii Karazin, then living in St. Petersburg, who was embarking on his impetuous career at court.

## Karazin

The biography of Vasilii Karazin is veiled in mystery and legend, and the man himself played a significant role in creating and preserving his personal mythology.[46] Much of what we know about his youth and the breakneck speed and trajectory of his career at the tsarist court comes from Karazin's own statements issued at various stages and twists and turns of his complicated life. This trove of information shows distinct traces of a fluctuating civic and political state of affairs. Quite a few historians who studied Karazin's life came under the influence of the polemical and subjective views of the educator himself or his ideological opponents. This situation gave rise to many conflicts, exaggerated views, ambiguities, and unresolved mysteries that are the stuff of the literature about him.[47]

Karazin was the son of a Balkan emigrant who made his way up the military career ladder to the rank of colonel and became the owner of a large estate in Sloboda Ukraine.[48] His father's service to the Russian throne allowed Karazin to enter the elite Semenovsky Life Guards Regiment. His restless and turbulent nature led him, however, from military service to academia and freethinking, from embarking on journeys throughout Russia to an attempt to escape across the border. Arrested while trying to make an illegal crossing of Russia's western border and imprisoned in the Shlisselburg Fortress, by a stroke of luck Karazin obtained a pardon from Tsar Paul I and a sinecure in St. Petersburg.

**Figure 2.1.** Vasilii Nazarovich Karazin (1773–1842), enlightener, civil society activist, founder of Kharkiv University. © Wikimedia Commons.

After Alexander I acceded to the throne, Karazin was granted a personal audience with the new Russian emperor and earned his trust in the process. The circumstances behind this metamorphosis remain veiled in mystery to the present day. It may be inferred that Tsar Alexander, surrounded by conspirators who had murdered his father, badly needed people personally devoted to him. Karazin, the son of an immigrant, a person who hailed from the borderland, and an outsider who was not afraid of taking risks, had enjoyed the favor of Paul I even though he had no influential patrons at court and was not dependent on the various competing groups and clans. He was thus eminently suited for the role of trusted assistant to the emperor. Holding the modest post of secretary of various committees and commissions developing projects of university reform, Karazin was simultaneously a confidant of the emperor with direct access to him. To a certain extent, all this goes to explain the political and cultural phenomenon of Karazin at the Russian court, the degree of his influence on current affairs, and the role he played in the founding of Kharkiv University.

Regardless of his fairly low rank and office, Karazin wielded much greater influence than might be observed from outside. He was sometimes given secret assignments requiring particular delicacy, notably the investigation of instances of corruption among high-ranking officials. On the orders of Alexander I, Karazin gathered compromising materials about Dmitrii Lopukhin, the odious governor general of Kaluga, who was notorious for his criminal actions and abuse of power. These materials enabled the state commission headed by Gavriil Derzhavin to prosecute Lopukhin, even though the latter had many friends and high-ranking patrons.[49] Most of those who were in the habit of taking bribes and engaged in the abuse of power began to fear Karazin, who, according to predictions, was slated to become the tsar's favorite.[50] In addition, he was formally appointed secretary of the committee that had been charged with drafting a new statute for higher educational institutions and the Academy of Sciences.

For a brief period Karazin played a dual role: as an unofficial agent, he served as the sovereign's eyes and ears, and as a representative of the nobiliary community of Sloboda Ukraine who stood next to the throne, he was the spokesman of its thoughts and moods. In addition, he was formally appointed secretary of the committee charged with drafting a new statute for higher educational institutions and the Academy of Sciences. Karazin soon justified the expectations of his countrymen in his role as deputy. Thanks to his support, on 29 December 1801 they received a monarchical charter confirming their former rights and privileges granted to them by various monarchs in different periods. At the same time Karazin, on his own initiative, presented a proposal to the gentry of Sloboda Ukraine to support the idea of founding a university in Kharkiv with donated funds.

It is hard to say when this idea occurred to Karazin, especially considering that he wrote about it in vague terms.[51] I have not found any evidence that such a plan existed in 1801, as the historian Yakov Abramov, one of Karazin's biographers, has written.[52] However, one may concur with Dmytro Bahalii that, one way or another, the idea of a university was connected with Karazin's work in the statute-drafting committee; therefore, the idea of founding a university in Kharkiv possibly emerged no earlier than 1802, that is, after the gentry of Sloboda Ukraine obtained confirmation of its privileges.[53]

On 2 May 1802 Karazin sent a private letter to the Kharkiv priest and enlightener Vasyl' Fotiiev, which states in part:

> Having been deemed worthy of a conversation with the good Sovereign shortly after my return to St. Petersburg, I ventured to tell him

about the idea of establishing a university in Kharkiv that would be organized better than the Moscow one and worthy of being called the educational centre of southern Russia. My idea was received positively, and I set about drafting a plan for it.[54]

Karazin states further: "This idea has utterly captivated my soul, and I am only waiting for the gentry company's assent in order to act."[55] As far as I have been able to determine, this is the first documented mention of the idea of founding a university in Kharkiv.

There is an established notion in the scholarly literature that at the time the choice of Kharkiv as a university town could not have occurred to anyone but Karazin.[56] And indeed, it must be accepted that almost until the last moment the society of the Sloboda region had not the slightest inkling of the fate prepared for it in the capital. The gentry of the Sloboda Ukraine guberniia, expecting that a cadet college would be opened in Kharkiv, was simultaneously preparing for its general assembly in order to offer ceremonial thanks to the emperor for reinstating local privileges. The marshal of the guberniia nobility, planning that occasion, advised in a letter of 20 June 1802 that a supplementary donation of funds be made, either to open a forty-bed hospital in Kharkiv or to provide scholarships for twenty children of the gentry or, in the last instance, for aid to the poor.[57] As yet, however, there was no mention of a university in those letters.

In July 1802, when Karazin convinced the tsar that the local gentry fully supported the idea of Kharkiv University and was prepared to prove it with generous voluntary donations, he had no formal right to do so, as he had not obtained the preliminary agreement of the gentry corporation.[58] Dmytro Bahalii, a historian of Kharkiv University, found himself obliged to admit that Karazin, "with his characteristic enthusiasm ... had already informed the sovereign of the Kharkiv gentry's desire to make a donation for the university" long before the official decision of the gentry assembly.[59]

It may be assumed that certain promises of a private or public nature had been given to the Kharkiv gentry on Karazin's part in return for its agreement to support the university project. The carefully prepared and regulated ceremonial character of the assembly of guberniia gentry on 30 August 1802 strikes one as noteworthy in that connection. It was meant to remind those present yet again, if reminder were needed, that the main reason for the event and the idea at its heart was not, after all, the university but the charter of gentry privileges graciously presented by the monarch.

That precious document was carried publicly on a crimson pillow, sprinkled with holy water, and displayed in the most prominent places in church and in administrative premises. Against that background, subsequent donations for the university appeared as mere gestures of gratitude on the part of society in response to yet another monarchical favor. It would be fair to assume that the organizers of the gentry assembly were mindful of the fact that 30 August was the saint's day of Alexander, after whom the monarch was named. That day became the date of the official university holiday, in commemoration of the gentry assembly of the Sloboda gubernia in 1802 at which the restitution of some of their rights and privileges was celebrated.

Regardless of all the preparatory measures, opposition to the university project arose among the gentry of the Izium and Vovchansk districts of the Sloboda Ukraine gubernia, who considered that it had been "handed down from above" without preliminary consultation, at the government's initiative. More precisely, this was just a continuation of the previous opposition, when the smallholders protested what they considered the excessive sum of 100,000 rubles specified as a voluntary donation for the military academy that the government was planning for Kharkiv. The new sum of a million rubles suggested by some of the gentry as a total contribution to the building of the university looked utterly unrealistic in comparison.

The paradox of this situation was that the opposition—supported, by the way, by the governor of Sloboda Ukraine, A. K. Artakov, who was acting in accord with previous governmental instructions—was conducting itself lawfully in formal terms, citing an official ban on donations of an involuntary nature. Moreover, the opponents noted procedural infringements in the course of preparations and conduct of the gentry assemblies. They pointed out in particular that the emperor had not issued an edict permitting such assemblies to be conducted, which cast doubt on the legality of their decisions.

Karazin, for his part, did all he could to obtain a positive resolution from the gentry assembly of 31 August 1802. His speech, abounding with fervent and genuine emotion, and replete with passionate rhetoric in the spirit of the time, concluded with the forthright words: "It now depends on you, most esteemed assembly, to justify me or consign me to shame and despair. I stand here before you either as your friend or as a criminal."[60] Karazin had to make desperate efforts to come up with a verdict favorable to himself in the matter. He was running across a bridge that was collapsing behind him.

In that situation the gentry did not wish and would scarcely have dared to turn the tsar's favorite from a friend into an enemy, thereby risking a fiasco with the reinstatement of its local privileges. The Sloboda gentry, having listened to Karazin the official, hastened to express to him—their deputy at the tsar's court—a whole series of supplementary petitions concerning their traditional privileges (*slobody*). Nor did they neglect to reduce the sum of their voluntary donations for the university to 400,000 rubles, including their unpaid debts to the state and their personal donations to the cadet college. Participants in the assembly defined their position in a separate document, approved on 1 September 1802, which was to serve as an instruction to Karazin with regard to his subsequent actions.

Thus, in the consciousness of the Sloboda gentry, Karazin's university project turned out to be closely associated with their own corporate desires—those already confirmed by the government and those they expected to realize. So widespread was this attitude that even the marshal of the local nobility, Volodymyr Donets-Zakharzhevsky, a descendant of a well-known line of Cossack colonels, appealing to the neighboring Little Russian gentry to do its part in contributing financially to the establishment of Kharkiv University, gave it as his prime argument that new governmental favors could be expected for the region: "The gentry of the Sloboda Ukraine gubernia had the good fortune to receive a charter of confirmation of the rights and privileges of this land, Most Highly granted by His Imperial Majesty."[61]

Karazin himself, given the ambiguity of his status vis-à-vis the emperor, appeared by turns in the role of an official in the imperial capital endowed with plenary powers and a deputy of the Sloboda Ukraine gentry at court. The draft university statute written by Karazin corresponded in the first instance to the corporate interests of the local gentry, inasmuch as it made particular provision for maintaining the principle of segregation by social estate in the educational process, special prerogatives for students of gentry descent, the inclusion of military training in the university curriculum, and so on. According to the draft statute, all higher and more elementary schools in the Sloboda region were to be supervised by a director elected from the local gentry with the assistance of a committee of university professors. Other estates were thus deprived of influence on university affairs. Karazin's draft endowed the university with a thoroughly gentry character.

Karazin could not have been unaware that at the beginning of 1802 Alexander I had personally struck out of the draft statute for Dorpat (Tartu) University all items proposed by the local gentry in its own interests and all that might restrict the academic freedom of the university corporation. The tsar confirmed his position on the matter yet again during a visit to Dorpat University in May 1802. Karazin was in fact going against the current by coming out against the updated model of the German university, with its fundamental principles of academic freedom and autonomy, toward which the imperial bureaucracy of the capital, the most influential grouping at court, oriented itself. But Karazin took the risk deliberately because he had no alternative. He became a hostage of his dual role as imperial agent and regional patriot. At all costs he needed to incline the Sloboda gentry toward a voluntary "patriotic" donation for the founding of Kharkiv University, persuading them to abandon any intention of opening a military academy in the city, for which some funds had already been collected. And it was precisely the support of the local gentry that was supposed to become the decisive argument capable of convincing the government to open a university in Kharkiv.

Following the gentry's example, the Kharkiv municipal administration supported the idea of founding a university in the city but supplemented it with its own desires and petitions. The merchants, for instance, petitioned to end military quartering in the city. Other estates, particularly the townspeople and guild tradesmen, followed the example of the gentry and the merchants, even though they had declined to make financial contributions. Unlike them, the local Cossacks declared a voluntary donation of a parcel of land in the city for Kharkiv University, not forgetting to remind the authorities that it would be desirable to renew their own corporate privileges associated with the production and sale of spirits, the abolition of certain taxes, the tax-farming system, and the like.[62]

Thus, as the historian Ludwik Janowski justly noted, the idea of Kharkiv University was closely bound up from the very beginning with the exclusive corporate interests of local society, which was so contrary to the wishes of the enlightened Russian government.[63] In that regard the Sloboda gentry did not differ from its Little Russian, Baltic, or Polish-Lithuanian counterparts. The situation that had come into existence at the beginning of Catherine II's reign was being repeated in miniature: social initiative in the localities, awakened "from above," was going beyond the framework envisaged by the authorities.

In this case, the situation contradicted certain fundamental principles of the state policy of centralizing and unifying the regions of the empire. That is precisely why the governor of Kharkiv, Andrei Artakov, reacted so strongly to the demand of Kharkiv merchants concerning military quartering. The emperor himself did not dare to abolish that policy. Moreover, the demands of local estates with regard to the reinstatement of their traditional "liberties," especially the production and free sale of spirits, affected the interests of the imperial treasury and the local administration, which realized considerable income from the state monopoly on vodka.

Finally, the very circumstances attending the preparations and proceedings of the gentry assembly of August 1802 in Kharkiv, opposition complaints about legal infractions by a group of the richest and most influential representatives of the local gentry corporation, and similar complaints by Artakov against the actions of Karazin himself and the municipal government, which supported him, called into question the legitimacy of the second component required for the success of Karazin's project—the "unexpected and, to date, the only patriotic outburst of its kind" in the form of the gentry's voluntary financial contribution to the university.[64]

In a special rescript of 30 September 1802, Alexander I thanked the Sloboda gentry for its patriotic action in rather restrained terms, without a word about its petitions of a regional corporate nature, emphasizing particularly that he would agree to accept the funds only on condition that they not lead to a new tax on serfs. The government even found it necessary to open an official investigation, supervised by the minister of the interior, Viktor Kochubei, of the circumstances in which the assemblies of the Sloboda gentry were held. However, the government needed to proceed cautiously.

The decision of the Kharkiv gentry and townspeople to donate voluntarily in the interests of the university had already become public knowledge. The government found it more useful to turn that decision to its own advantage by presenting it as an expression of support for its policy on the part of the provincial gentry and evidence of active social participation in governmental reforms. The principal motive officially put forward for establishing a university in Kharkiv was the "patriotic donation" of the gentry and citizens of the Sloboda Ukraine guberniia.

The new tsarist rescript of 31 January 1803 to the Sloboda gentry differed sharply from the one of 31 August 1802, in which Alexander I had reacted to the decision of the general assembly of the Sloboda Ukrainian gentry. This time it was couched in an exceptionally gracious tone, with thanks and compliments addressed to particular individuals who had acted in the interests of the university. The emperor distributed awards to its most active supporters. Those opposed to the university project—the marshal of the Izium nobility, Zakharashevych-Kapustiansky, and Governor Andrei Artakov—suffered a defeat. Some time later the former was publicly rebuked by the emperor, while the latter was soon dismissed from his post. Both suffered for sticking to the letter of the law.

The issue of Kharkiv University had in fact already been decided in its favor by the end of 1802, when Karazin and the future administrator of the Kharkiv educational district, Count Seweryn Potocki, began the selection of the first university professors. The formal decision to confirm the list of university towns and educational districts in the Russian Empire was taken in January 1803 with a special legislative act, "Preliminary Regulations of Public Education," on the foundations of a new system of education for the empire.

The other reason why the Kharkiv University project gained official status instead of being shelved for many years—the fate that had befallen many earlier university projects and even ukases promulgated by Catherine II—was regional geopolitics. These came to the fore in September 1802, when discussions of the university project were initiated in the government committee entrusted with drafting a new statute for higher educational institutions and the Academy of Sciences at the behest of the school commission on which Karazin served as secretary.

## Regional Geopolitics

It appears that, initially, Karazin was the only one championing Kharkiv's interests. He acted on the basis of his position as spokesman of Russia's southward expansion, in which Kharkiv could play an important strategic role. The city had a unique geopolitical location, situated as it was at the very heart of strategic communication routes linking central Russia with New Russia (*Novorossiia*), the Crimea, and the Caucasus. In this connection, Karazin wrote: "Kharkiv, insignificant in its own right ... could not boast of anything but its central location in the southern gubernias."[65] However, it was Kyiv, not Kharkiv, that many considered an obvious choice for the university project.

The leading Western specialists invited by the Russian government, including the Swiss Frédéric-César de La Harpe, and a well-known educational reformer from the Austrian Empire, the Serb Teodor Janković-Mirijevski, gave preference to Kyiv, placing it on the same level as Moscow, Dorpat, Vilnius, St. Petersburg, and Kazan.[66] The Little Russian landed gentry, however, raised the question of founding a university in Chernihiv and expressed its desire to donate a certain sum of money from its private income for that purpose. Some time later, Lubny and Novhorod-Siverskyi emerged as contenders for the status of university towns. It is not clear in what way the idea of a university was connected with the local nobles' social and regional privileges. It is much clearer that these projects were ill coordinated.

Illia Tymkovsky, a Little Russian gentleman who worked together with Karazin on the Kharkiv University project, tried to convince his compatriots that there was no point in petitioning for a university in Poltava or Chernihiv, given that the Kharkiv institution was to be "built near [Little Russian gentry] and in a land inhabited by its relatives."[67] Such arguments did not help: in the eyes of the regional elites, ethnic commonality took second place to particular corporate privileges. Disappointed by such course of events, Karazin went so far as to assert that in the future he would be guided exclusively by the interests of his own "small homeland," the Sloboda region, and not Little Russia, which was allegedly mocking his efforts.[68] The story with the university project was repeated several years later, when the Sloboda gentry, developing a project for the founding of an institute of noble maidens in Kharkiv, even proposed that it be called a "Little Russian" institute; they invited the gentry of the neighboring Little Russian gubernias to take part in establishing it, but the latter declined this second proposal as well.[69]

It is interesting to note that highly placed Little Russians, such as the ministers Petro Zavadovsky and Viktor Kochubei, who presumably could lobby for the Little Russian university project, did not lift a finger to support their compatriots. Both sought openly or covertly to undermine Karazin's plans. They rejected university reform in principle and advocated the alternative lycée system, which was closer to aristocratic preferences than the more socially inclusive university model of education. However, when the old-fashioned minister of public education, Count Petro Zavadovsky, was replaced by his compatriot Count Oleksii Rozumovsky, a descendant of the last hetman of Little Russia, the latter raised for discussion the issue of moving the university from Kharkiv to Kyiv.

Professor Ferdinand Shveikart, a member of Kharkiv University's scholarly council, wrote in 1814:

> The university should be transferred to the ancient location of learning and source of Little Russian culture, that is, to Kyiv. This is required by the city's glory, the multitude of inhabitants of every estate, the great commerce that goes on there, and the resulting comforts of life, especially the proximity of places where learning flourishes. Foreign scholars invited from abroad will of course more readily go to Kyiv than to Kharkiv. No argument against such a transfer can be derived from the delineation of the district of our university. After all, Kharkiv was cho-

sen not because it is located in the center of the district, but the district was created after Kharkiv was chosen.[70]

Almost half the members of the council also expressed themselves in favor of Kyiv.

The attempt yielded nothing. A similar fate, evidently for the same reasons, awaited the last nineteenth-century attempt to transfer the university from the Sloboda region to Little Russia. It was undertaken in the latter half of the 1820s by the administrator and supervisor of the Kharkiv educational district, Aleksei Perovsky, yet another descendant of the last hetman of Little Russia. As an alternative to Kharkiv, he suggested Novhorod-Siverskyi, the former administrative capital of Little Russia, but it appears that the proposal was not even considered by the academic council of Kharkiv University.

The choice between Kharkiv and Kyiv in connection with the reform of secular education was not a sham, as some historians suppose.[71] It had a clearly delineated political subtext. Kharkiv became the center of a university educational district because it was less associated with the regional historical privileges of the gentry than any city in either Little Russia or the Polish borderlands (*kresy*). From the viewpoint of the center, Kharkiv appeared to be a fulcrum for official policy intended to overcome the corporate and regional diversity of the southern and western borderlands of the empire and bring about their cultural and legal unification.

The Kharkiv educational district was made up of diverse regions of contemporary Russia and Ukraine, differing in traditions and ethnic composition: the Russian military borderland; the Cossack territories of the Sloboda region; Little Russia; the Don Cossack and Black Sea Cossack Hosts; the Crimean Khanate; New Russia; and even part of the Caucasus.[72] It is striking that, as noted earlier, the sphere of administrative responsibility of the supervisor of the Kharkiv educational district at the moment of its delineation practically coincided with the territory subordinate to the military governor of the Sloboda Ukraine gubernia in the late eighteenth century. This was the borderland of Russian modernization.

It is worth mentioning in this regard that while the Little Russian gentry refused to support Karazin's university project, it found favor in two South imperial gubernias, those of Katerynoslav and Kherson. The gentry of Katerynoslav, to whom the idea of a university had not been alien since the times of Prince Grigorii Potemkin, and who did not find "South Russian" regional identification incompatible with local tradition, resolved in January 1803 to donate more than 100,000 rubles to Kharkiv University in the course of a decade. Some time later, in 1806, the gentry of another southern gubernia, that of Kherson, also resolved to donate slightly more than 40,000 rubles to Kharkiv University.[73]

The Kharkiv University project had tremendous influence on establishing the further intellectual cartography not only of the Sloboda region but of all the southern regions of the Russian Empire. Karazin, considering the university in Kharkiv and the boundaries of its educational district, stressed that it should be "the focus of enlightenment of southern Russia."[74] In declaring the pretensions of "insignificant Kharkiv" to figure as the "focus of the southern gubernias,"[75] Karazin was virtually relaying to the city the baton of Katerynoslav, which had failed to become the southern capital of the empire and a university center, as noted earlier. Not surprisingly, Karazin, with his affinity for Balkan problems because of his origins and family traditions, maintained that his plan for the founding of Kharkiv University provided for the education of students from Greece. All in all, Kharkiv University was assigned the task of acculturating the new territories annexed to the Russian Empire in the course of its southwestern expansion.

The western dimension of imperial politics also played a certain role in the history of the Kharkiv University project. In this case, the Polish factor turned out to be the most influential. The project of founding a university in Kharkiv won the support of the "Polish" party, headed by Prince Adam Czartoryski, which was influential at court. The motives guiding the Polish nobleman in his decision to support Kharkiv against Kyiv have not remained obscure to historians. In the opinion of James T. Flynn, Czartoryski expressed apprehension that the opening of a university in Kyiv might hamper his plans to reestablish a university in Vilnius.[76]

There certainly appeared to be grounds for Czartoryski's apprehension. From the end of the eighteenth century, Russian educational institutions played a particular role in the integration (*splochenie*) of the western and Baltic lands into the Russian Empire. It was no accident that the Russian government established the first public schools in the empire in 1789 in the Polatsk and Mahilioŭ gubernias and in Kyiv. In December 1801 the educational commission presented a memorandum to the emperor recommending the reform of Polish schools in the western gubernias on the model of Russian public schools "in order to bring annexed Poland into close union with Russia."[77]

During the reign of Alexander I, the development of the educational system in the Right-Bank Ukrainian, Lithuanian, and Belarusian gubernias was in the hands of officials such as Petro Zavadovsky, for whom corporate, regional, and political considerations took precedence over modern national ones. Given the precipitous rise of French power and the impending war with Napoleon, Alexander I, for his part, did not wish to annoy the Polish gentry yet again. The Kharkiv University project presented no direct threat to Polish cultural dominance.

According to Ivan Lysiak-Rudnytsky, "Ukrainian national interest would have required favoring Kyiv," as that would certainly have promoted the development of the Ukrainian national project, especially the cultural unification of Right- and Left-Bank Ukraine and the undermining of Polish gentry influence on the Right Bank.[78] As the Ukrainian historian writes,

> Prince Czartoryski was right, as a Polish patriot, when he attempted to prevent the founding of a university in Kyiv. He was intent on including the three Right-Bank gubernias—Volhynia, Podilia, and Kyiv—in

the Vilnius educational district and thereby consolidating Polish cultural hegemony in those territories. And he managed to do so with the active assistance of the Ukrainian Karazin.[79]

In fact, Karazin was a "Ukrainian" only in the geographic sense. His role was not that of a Ukrainian nationalist but of one who favored cultural and legal Russification. In a letter to the governor general of Little Russia, Prince Aleksandr Kurakin, Karazin weighed the chances of various cities—Poltava, Kyiv, Kharkiv, and Chernihiv—with regard to the founding of a university. He stressed that Kyiv lay in the sphere of influence of the Polish gentry, while Poltava maintained "some kind of unconquerable alienation from the Great Russian inhabitants" and was too far removed from the Russian towns of Orel, Kursk, and Voronezh.[80] The Sloboda region, in Karazin's opinion, had none of those blemishes.

But Kharkiv University did not become a regional gentry institution. There was initially nothing in its statute, structure, or teaching staff that reflected specific features of the locality or the region. Nor did the structure of the educational process and curriculum contain anything specially oriented toward local history, geography, or culture, or anything designed to encourage students to think of their native history and culture in terms of Ukrainian national or Sloboda regional identity. The only detail reminiscent of the university's location was the intention to establish a department of military science in order to satisfy the wishes of local gentry donors.

The establishment of the university reflected the triumph of the doctrine of imperial centralization over regional and social particularism. The opening ceremony at the beginning of 1805 was intended to highlight the leading role of the government in the establishment of Kharkiv University. All present were reminded of that role by the medallion specially struck for the occasion, which featured the allegorical figures of Alexander I alongside Apollo, as well as the names of the emperor and the first supervisor of the Kharkiv educational district, Count Seweryn Potocki.

The local gentry was represented at the celebration only in the capacity of obedient and grateful subjects showered with the graces of the supreme powers. There was nothing to remind one of the initiatives of the gentry themselves in establishing the university. The most eloquent instance of aposiopesis in this regard may be considered the absence from the celebration of Vasilii Karazin himself, the author of the idea of Kharkiv University. In other words, the scenario of public representation of state power did not, in this instance, include those for whom it was actually intended, thereby reflecting the common practice of the imperial authorities.

It seems that the final act of the dialogue between the imperial center and the gentry of Sloboda Ukraine turned out to be a profound disappointment for the latter. Not only did the government actually ignore the gentry's corporate interests, but it completely removed the gentry elite from direct influence on university affairs, concentrating control over them in its own hands. Government officials would long find themselves obliged to explain to the citizenry that just because the university bore the name of their city, that did not give the local gentry any right to take part in its administration.

No wonder that the Sloboda gentry quickly lost interest in the university. The assembly of marshals of the nobility of the Sloboda Ukraine gubernia held on 21 April 1803 declined Karazin's proposal to establish a public committee to audit financial contributions, as stipulated particularly on 1 September 1802. Financial contributions to the university fell off sharply. Two decades later, the Sloboda gentry was still in arrears amounting to more than 100,000 rubles—an amount approximating that of initial donations for the desired cadet college in Kharkiv. The government had to resort to administrative repression, collecting money from debtors with the aid of the police and courts. For a quarter century afterward, there were unceasing complaints from the disgruntled gentry that the funds collected were being spent on the university and not on a cadet college. But the government remained unyielding until it had extracted almost the entire amount of the debt from the unfortunate patrons. Yet again, the well-known Russian proverb was reaffirmed: any initiative other than an official one is reprehensible. Local donations did not create an endowment: financially, the imperial Kharkiv University was totally dependent on the state.

In 1811, on the eve of Napoleon's invasion of Russia, Karazin tried to revise the status of Kharkiv University and strengthen the features of its statute associated with the gentry and the region. He proposed that the government replace the supervisor of the educational district with a permanent director chosen from the ranks of the local gentry and obliged to live in Kharkiv. Karazin planned to occupy the position himself. At the same time, he raised the question once again of establishing a department of military science, a theological faculty, and a boarding school for gentry students at Kharkiv University. This time, as well, the local gentry's proposal of university reform was rejected by the imperial center.

The first supervisor of the Kharkiv educational district, Count Seweryn Potocki, asserted in his speech at the ceremony that Kharkiv University was organized "on the model of Oxford and Cambridge, to which the sons of the first English lords come to learn how to defend the rights of their country in Parliament; on the model of Göttingen, Jena and others, where the prince-electors and reigning princes do not find it shameful to send their children."[81] In general, however, the government oriented itself on the German or, more precisely, the Göttingen model, which had become the most popular in central and eastern Europe at the time.[82] It was closely associated with the state. The latter regarded universities as effective instruments in its struggles with the church, the aristocracy, traditional legislation, and regional particularism. Thus, the Kharkiv University project, associated from the outset with the ideas of traditional regional identity and estate privileges, was realized in a form directed against those ideas.[83] Interestingly, Dorpat University, initiated by the Baltic German landed nobility, was also integrated into the imperial educational structure over time and turned from a *Landesuniversität* into a *Reichsuniversität*.[84]

**Figure 2.2.** Kharkiv University, new building (1823–31), architects E. A. Vasiliev and I. Vatelet. © Volodymyr Kravchenko, 2021.

## The Academic "Colony"

The inclusion of universities in the system of state institutions automatically brought their staff members and graduates into the bureaucratic hierarchy according to the Table of Ranks, while master's and doctoral diplomas became equivalent to certificates of gentry status. It should be recalled that until then scholars and professors had been considered members of the so-called third estate and could count only on the status of "distinguished citizens" granted them according to the Charter to the Cities (1785).[85] From that time on, not only a professorial career but also a university diploma opened the path to personal and even hereditary nobility. This was a great step forward from the times when, according to Christoph Rommel, certain landowners were quite incapable of grasping the difference between professors and actors.[86] With the passing of another quarter century, the title of university professor would finally become prestigious and honorable in the eyes of nineteenth-century Russian society.

For the most part, the first professors and instructors of Kharkiv University were recruited abroad. The instruction issued by the minister of public education, Petro Zavadovsky, provided that invitations to Russian universities would be issued first and foremost to scholars from the Slavic lands of the Austrian Empire, for whom the Russian language was supposedly not a foreign tongue.[87] Searches undertaken by Seweryn Potocki in the Austrian Empire, notably in Lviv, Krakow, and Vienna, for candidates to fill professorial chairs produced very modest results. At first he managed to recruit only one professor of Slavic descent, the Serbian physicist Atanasije Stojković, who would soon become rector of Kharkiv University. His countryman Teodor Filipović (pseudonym Božidar Grujović), a lawyer by education, was elected an adjunct of Kharkiv University in 1804. It is not known whether he managed to initiate any courses of instruction, as he returned to Serbia in 1805 and became the author of the first Serbian laws and a draft of state organization (constitution) for the country.

Much greater success attended searches for qualified candidates in the German lands and in France, then involved in the conflagration of warfare and a radical rebuilding of the whole social, governmental, and cultural order. The famous German universities were in deep crisis because of the French occupation. The best German scholars, including the famous Johann Wolfgang von Goethe and Johann Gottlieb Fichte, helped their countrymen and colleagues search for new places of employment and move to the outskirts of the Russian Empire, including Kharkiv and Kazan.[88] It was in Germany that most of the instructors prepared to abandon their homeland for a career in provincial Kharkiv were recruited. This ran counter to Zavadovsky's instructions but was wholly in keeping with the general orientation of Russian reformers toward German models of education. Another source of cadres for Kharkiv University was France, which provided a considerable percentage of emigrants dissatisfied with the revolution and the Napoleonic reforms.

The Russian government successfully exploited the situation in European states drawn into the maelstrom of the Napoleonic Wars. The material conditions in which Russian university professors lived, along with certain social privileges, seemed quite attractive, at least to some of the applicants. Moving to the newly established university gave both foreigners and Russian subjects the opportunity to climb the ladder of a career in government service more quickly by obtaining a professorial post, thereby raising one's social status and gaining the right to join the gentry. But it turned out that the first cohort of Kharkiv professors also included individuals with a sense of cultural mission, noble idealists inspired by the prospect of extending education to culturally untilled and seemingly virgin lands. These were Germans for the most part, brought up in the spirit of Enlightenment philosophy that prevailed in the universities of their homeland.

The staff of professors and instructors at Kharkiv University proved extraordinarily diverse by origin. Germans were dominant among them, followed by Slavs from the Austrian Empire and Frenchmen. Thus, unlike Moscow University, where immigrants from Germany formed a strong and solidary corporation, Kharkiv University drew its foreign professors from different regions of Europe: they were divided into a variety of groups by origin, religious and national affiliations, educational qualifications, and political loyalties. In this regard, the academic staff at Kharkiv University resembled the one at Kazan University. Russian subjects, who made up no more than one-third of the instructors, were also of various ethnic origin, including Russians, Ukrainians, Germans, and Poles. At first, the only ethnic Ukrainian on academic staff was Professor Illia Tymkovsky, who was also the only nobleman among the Russian subjects.

Understandably, this diversity of the Kharkiv professoriate gave rise to constant arguments, intrigues, and conflicts among individuals and cliques concerning problems of infinitely less than global significance. As always in such circumstances, questions of politics and worldview became closely intertwined with injured self-esteem, personal ambition, and conflict of interest. The constant enmity between French and German professors proved especially dramatic. The former were led by Antoine Jeudy Dugour (Degurov), a subtle political operator and deft intriguer who later became rector of St. Petersburg University. The leader of the opposing party was Johann Baptist Schad, a professor of philosophy and a dazzling polemicist, frenzied and passionate in his undiplomatic behavior, who was ultimately deported from Russia. The Germans freely accused their French colleagues of being politically untrustworthy and harboring pro-Napoleonic sympathies, while the French sought to catch their opponents out in freethinking.

Most of the Russian subjects were divided from the foreigners by established prejudice and poorly concealed hostility. "The Russians and the foreigners differed in everything," noted Professor Christoph Rommel.[89] The former, in his view, were distinguished by "great hypocrisy and cunning. Cold-bloodedly awaiting their chance in debate, as if preparing an ambush, they all knew, to the detriment of the open-hearted foreigners, how to exploit every moment when the latter heatedly allowed themselves incautious phrases; in barbaric cunning they outdid even the French."[90] The foreigners, for their part, were no innocent victims of local "barbarism" but appealed to the higher authorities at every turn, showing off their own merits. Most foreigners of the "first enrollment" kept their distance from the Russian professors.[91] They united in groups that were closed to outsiders. Christoph Rommel, for example, mentions a bachelors' club of German professors that admitted only two non-Germans, Atanasije Stojković and Abram Kalkau. Johann Schad held Latin evenings at home for colleagues at which German literature was discussed.

There were outstanding specialists to be found among the Kharkiv professors, although it may be, as James Flynn considers, that the Kharkiv professoriate was inferior in scholarly quality to its colleagues in the universities of Dorpat, Vilnius, and Moscow,[92] and was on the level of Kazan University in that regard. The leading scholars, representing the philosophical and social disciplines, were concentrated in the department of ethics and politics. Outstanding among them were the Fichtean philosopher Johann Schad (1758–1834);[93] the economist and lawyer Ludwig Jacob (1759–1827), a former rector of the University of Halle; and the economist Joseph Lang (1775 or 1776–1819), whom the Nobel laureate in economics Wassily Leontief considered one of his intellectual forebears.[94] The Russian subjects Timofei Osipovsky (1766–1832) and Mykhailo Ostrohradsky (1801–1862) excelled in mathematics.

The results of the scholarly work carried out by academic staff at Kharkiv University in the early period of its existence were conditioned both by the modest needs and resources of a provincial university and by the general nature of scholarship in the Age of Enlightenment. The Kharkiv University milieu acted as an intermediary distributing the latest scholarly knowledge from the more advanced Western centers to the European cultural periphery, which included Sloboda Ukraine at the time. The scholarly activity of the first Kharkiv professors came down in practice to teaching and popularizing in the spirit of the Enlightenment. Their publications—textbooks, manuals, lecture courses, translations, official speeches, and more than modest dissertations—substituted for independent scholarly research.

Most probably, the foreign professors generally felt that that there was little demand in Kharkiv for the kind of scholarship they had produced at home. This is eloquently illustrated by the fate of Professor B. Reit's work on the history of Kyivan Rus'. His Latin-language book, published in Kharkiv, remained unnoticed or deliberately ignored by his colleagues. No less eloquent in this regard is the example of Joseph Lang, whose works, also published in Kharkiv, were read by no one. Indeed, they lay with their pages uncut even in German libraries for almost a century and a half. Also lost to scholarship were the years spent in Kharkiv by such specialists as the agriculturalist Karl Noeldechen and the veterinarian Martin-Heinrich (Fedor) Pilger, who came to the university full of creative plans and ideas but very soon lost enthusiasm. In Kharkiv the historian Christoph Rommel produced mainly educational materials, but after his return to Germany he published a major work on the history of Kassel.

A scholar undertaking to study the influence of Kharkiv professors on Ukrainian or Russian scholarship and education will most probably end up disappointed. Transplanted from abroad to local soil, the exotic plant proved not so fruitful as in its homeland. It is the presence of scholarly traditions, currents, and scientific schools that determines the profile and influence of any educational institution. In this regard, the first Kharkiv professors did not create conditions for the development of those factors. For most of them Kharkiv proved just a temporary stop on the way to the Russian capitals or back home after the Napoleonic Wars. If, for example, Ludwig Jacob barely endured about two years in Kharkiv, then Antoine Dugour became a Russian subject and even Russified his surname (Degurov), which later allowed him to make a brilliant career as rector of St. Petersburg University.

## The University and Local Society

The privileges granted to the professorial corporation of the university provoked envy and jealousy among the local gentry. Typical in this regard was an episode that occurred in 1826, when the corpse of Emperor Alexander I was being transported through Kharkiv. A dispute arose between the local governor and the professors: who was to follow the emperor's coffin, and in what order? When the authorities ranked the professors below the officials of the gubernia court and the medical council, there was a sharp objection from the district supervisor, Aleksei Perovsky. As a result, it was decided that the professors were worthy of a place alongside the officials of the gubernia administration and would walk in pairs with them in the funeral procession.

Corruption was commonplace in the imperial bureaucracy at all levels. The memoirs of Professor Christoph Rommel contain much that is instructive in this regard. His acquaintance with the local "guardians of law and order" began when "unknown" criminals stole two of his horses. "When I told the town governor about it," recalled Rommel, "he asked how much I would give. We soon came to an agreement; he sent a policeman who brought my horses directly from the criminals' barn in the neighboring town [Bohodukhiv] the following night and returned them to me in almost perfect condition."[95] With unconcealed irony Rommel described the life-loving head of the criminal court, who would ride through the streets of the town collecting the usual tribute from merchants in the form of gifts, exactly as Gogol would later describe it in his *Inspector General*.[96]

The newly arrived foreigners were rather quick to adopt local customs and habits. When it became clear that university diplomas had a notable influence on service careers and even on social status, and appointments to educational institutions and even the censorship began to depend on the university professoriate, then corruption soon found its way into the university corporation. One of the richest landowners in Sloboda Ukraine, General Osip Khorvat, asked Professor Rommel to prepare his illegitimate son, Pavel Degai, for university examinations. Rommel recalled:

> At the time, I had no idea of the traditional method of bribery. As the examination of the young Degai for the doctoral degree drew near, he told me of having heard that I apparently wished to buy his marvelous new two-horse carriage. I denied this, and that seemed to be the end of the matter. But soon I happened to see a Russian colleague of mine riding in that expensive carriage, and later, in St. Petersburg, I learned how they had ridiculed my honesty.[97]

Less than two decades later, Kharkiv University would consider it a privilege to elect the same Pavel Degai, by then a department head in the Ministry of Justice and later a state secretary, senator, and member of the censorship committee, as an honorary member. Besides its moral significance, bribe-taking among the professoriate had something of a social regulatory nature, indicating the university's adjustment to the social environment of its locality and their mutual adaptation.

In one way or another, the learned colonists sought to adapt to an unfamiliar sociocultural environment. Some of the foreign professors in Kharkiv began learning Russian immediately. The Frenchman Jacques Belin de Ballu would go to the local bazaar for that purpose, holding a Russian dictionary in his hands but obviously failing to grasp that the bazaar with its *surzhyk* (patois) was the last place in Kharkiv to try learning literary Russian. The saleswomen would make fun of his pronunciation and his quaint mannerisms. The German Johann Schad, an avid drinker, took a liking to local invective, excitedly calling it "politeness arrayed in coarse and vulgar form." He even attempted to translate expressions that he found especially colorful into Latin.[98]

The fact that many professors married local women may be taken as an indication that their adaptation to Kharkiv society was proceeding well. The old Russian or Ukrainian gentry might confuse professors with actors or tradesmen, but most landowning dynasties of the Sloboda region, some of them quite well off though still relatively young in the ranks of the Russian gentry, were eager to enter into relations with university instructors, who had acquired unheard-of and previously unseen advantages. Furthermore, there were a good many young unmarried professors aged from twenty-two to slightly over forty. Those among them who could not boast gentry origins hoped to improve their material and social status by means of family ties with "true" nobles—the only privileged social estate in the empire. That was the route taken by the Russian Ivan Rizhsky, the Serb Atanasije Stojković, and the Frenchman Antoine Dugour. Professors Pavlovych and Christoph Rommel married local female landowners, as did the music instructor Gustav Adolf Hess de Calve.

Unfortunately, most of the marriages contracted by professors in Kharkiv turned out unsuccessfully for personal reasons. The cultural gap between learned men and provincial women proved too great. Thus, Professor Fedor Pilger's marriage with a simple and poorly educated Ukrainian woman closed the doors of local "high" society to him. A similar misalliance was Johann Schad's marriage to a Russified German woman who could not even write without errors. The third rector of Kharkiv University, Timofei Osipovsky, married a beautiful young Ukrainian woman who found learned society boring and once, in a fit of temper, threw into the fire a scholarly treatise over which her taciturn husband had spent many long evenings. A mere month after coming to Kharkiv, Christoph Rommel, a confirmed bachelor, married a woman from the influential gentry clan of the Kovalinskys. The captive of the Ukrainian Circe suffered a few years before divorcing his wife, whose world was limited to religious feasts, gossip, and card games.

## A "National University"?

The original mission of Kharkiv University had been to disseminate the achievements of Enlightenment culture throughout the newly acquired and not yet domesticated provinces of the empire. It is interesting to note that more than half of its first-year students came from the Sloboda Ukraine gubernia, the rest from the neighboring Kursk and Voronezh gubernias, and only a few individuals from neighboring Little Russia and the southern gubernias. The preponderance of local graduates over all others remained, regardless of the constant growth of the student body in absolute numbers. At the moment Kharkiv University was opened, it had a total enrollment of 57 students, 33 of whom were subsidized by the state, while 24 paid their own way. The subsequent growth of the student body was slow. Thus, there were 86 students in 1811, 159 in 1819, and 358 in 1825.[99] For comparison, it may be noted that Kharkiv fared better than Kazan but was far behind Vilnius and Dorpat Universities.[100]

The scholarly activity of the first Kharkiv professors was not confined to the Sloboda Ukraine gubernia but embraced the whole educational district, which included much of the territory of Little Russia and the southern gubernias. The first supervisor of the Kharkiv educational district, Count Seweryn Potocki (who, appropriately enough, owned a southern estate called Severinovka in the Kherson gubernia), called for the establishment in Kharkiv of a historical museum to display all artifacts discovered on the territory of the Black Sea littoral. The French professor Antoine Dugour devoted a special study to the history and culture of the Noghay Tatars.

Educated foreigners attracted by the newly established Kharkiv University at the beginning of the nineteenth century naturally took an interest in the local historical and cultural tradition. The doctoral dissertation of the musicologist and folklorist Gustav Adolf Hess de Calve, a former Habsburg subject, brought local Ukrainian topics into academic scholarly discourse.[101] The German scholars Bernhard Reit and Christoph Rommel took an interest in the history of Ukrainian (Little Russian) Cossackdom. An instructor at Kharkiv University, the writer and journalist Razumnik Gonorsky, translated into Russian and published in 1818 an excerpt of the *Annales de la Petite-Russie* by the French scholar Jean-Benoît Scherer and the doctoral dissertation of Hess de Calve, written originally in German. But all these cases are distant from the Romantic passion for the folk.

Initially, it was the strong current of conservative imperial Russian patriotism in the period of the Napoleonic Wars that promoted interest in Slavic-Rus' history, language, and tradition. It was a reaction to Western, mostly French, influence that inspired Russian university professors to show an interest in the local and, to their mind, "Russian" folklore and language. It is telling, however, that in the field of history it was not so much the relatively new Sloboda region or other parts of the Kharkiv educational district that claimed their attention as neighboring Little Russia, with its ancient history and rich folklore tradition.

The Russian historian Gavriil Uspensky became the first university scholar in the empire to publish, in 1811, a description of the governmental institutions and ranks of the former Cossack Hetmanate. *The Pis'ma o Malorossii* (Letters about Little Russia, 1816) by the Kharkiv University student Aleksei Lëvshin followed.

A senior official of the Kharkiv educational district, the ethnic Georgian Nikolai Tsertelev, issued the first specialized publication of Ukrainian/Little Russian folk songs in 1819.

From the very beginning of his administration, the first rector of Kharkiv University, Ivan Rizhsky, continued the policy of linguistic Russification initiated earlier by the rectors of Kharkiv Theological College.[102] In 1805 the University Council resolved, on Rizhsky's motion, "to endeavor to have teachers from among the Great Russians in the district in order to avoid habits of incorrect pronunciation of the Russian language among the students."[103] The efforts of the university professoriate proved not to have been fruitless, as shown by the eloquent testimony of the local pedagogue Timofei Selivanov: "Already in 1807 we found teachers in the schools of Kharkiv itself who simply jabbered with the pupils in Ukrainian, so we, that is, teachers newly arrived from teachers' colleges, following the authorities' directions, broke them and trained them to speak Russian."[104]

At the same time, besides its communicative function, the Ukrainian language had a symbolic and cultural one. In that capacity it was regarded first and foremost as a survival of ancient "Slavic-Rus'" tradition untouched by the leveling influence of European and urban civilization. By the same token, the Ukrainian language attracted the constant attention of Russian archaizing traditionalists: concerned about Western cultural influence, they turned to the Ukrainian cultural and historical heritage, especially to language. It was none other than the Russifier Ivan Rizhsky who set about searching for local Ukrainian-language manuscripts and studying them. Rizhsky's successor in the chair of Russian language and literature, Professor Ivan Sreznevsky, was distinguished by similar qualities. Standing in the ranks of the "Russian party" on the university board, he is less known today than his son, the famous Russian philologist and leader of the Kharkiv Romantics Izmail Sreznevsky.

Thus, along with the Russification of teaching and of the system of training pedagogical cadres, early nineteenth-century Kharkiv University, fully in the spirit of the time, helped promote an awakening of interest in the local Ukrainian vernacular, which continued to be spoken by the ethnic Ukrainians who constituted the main mass of the university's student body. Individual professors born in neighboring Little Russia, especially Illia Tymkovsky and Pavlo Shumliansky, also spoke the vernacular well. The latter particularly liked to spice his language with Ukrainian colloquialisms and jokes. Shumliansky was also the first to try using the Ukrainian language in teaching at Kharkiv University, although for comic effect, in the spirit of *Kotliarevshchyna*.

Aleksei Lëvshin, a graduate of Kharkiv University, appealed to educated people to bend their efforts toward perfecting and developing the Ukrainian literary language. Petro Hulak-Artemovsky, who became a professor of history and rector of Kharkiv University, would realize Lëvshin's appeal in practice, becoming one of the founders of modern Ukrainian literature. But almost a hundred years would pass before the Ukrainian professoriate in the person of Mykola Sumtsov attempted to introduce the Ukrainian language into the teaching process at Kharkiv University.

In the first half of the nineteenth century, a cultural contact zone of Ukrainian-Russian literary bilingualism developed around Kharkiv University and its publications. Local authors who used the Ukrainian language in their works—Vasyl' Maslovych and Petro Hulak-Artemovsky—also wrote in Russian. They were perfectly capable of speaking one language and writing in the other, but, mixing the two languages or marking one of them with colloquialisms or expressions borrowed from the other, or styling their works in the genres of burlesque, parody, or irony in reaction to the new literary canon, they endowed their writing not so much with a communicative as with a symbolic meaning. Russian speech spiced with the Ukrainian language functioned as a marker of local borderland identity on regional and personal levels.

The intermediary role of Kharkiv University in the creation of a new cultural space became especially striking with the appearance and rapid growth of periodical publications in the city.[105] They were initiated in 1812 thanks to the German professors on staff and focused mostly on general information and economics. Much more popular than the practical publications were the literary and scholarly journals *Ukrainskii vestnik* (*Ukrainian Herald*, 1816–19), *Khar'kovskii Demokrit* (*Kharkiv Democritus*, 1816), and *Ukrainskii zhurnal* (*Ukrainian Journal*, 1824–25). It was no accident that literary journals appeared in Kharkiv during and after the Napoleonic Wars. They reflected the rise of patriotic as well as anti-Western attitudes in local and, more broadly, Russian society. To bring provincial literature to life, a European intellectual challenge was required. As for reorienting it to local subjects, national-patriotic pathos proved quite sufficient.

All these journals had to be Russian-language publications, but they were intended mainly for a local readership and occasionally featured Ukrainian-language items and stories on local subjects. From time to time, Kharkiv periodicals published Ukrainian material, including a cycle of satirical verses by Hryhorii Kvitka under the title *Shpyhachky* (Digs), literary works by Vasyl' Maslovych titled *Osnovanie Khar'kova* (The founding of Kharkiv) and *Pesn' semeistvu* (A song to the family), a series of poetical works and translations by Petro Hulak-Artemovsky, as well as a number of others. The Ukrainian-language texts often appeared in reaction to the intrusion of the Russian-speaking milieu into the everyday life of the Sloboda province.

Kharkiv journalism became a forum for creative encounters between intellectuals from various regions of the university educational district. The proud Little Russian nobles could look down on the Sloboda Ukraine upstarts, but Ukrainian men of letters from both neighboring regions used the opportunity to discuss Little Russian history and geography publicly in the pages of *Ukrainskii vestnik* and *Ukrainskii zhurnal*. In 1819 the former published a prose work by the historian, writer, and adjunct of Kharkiv University Petro Hulak-Artemovsky titled "Something about That Harasko" that included a citation from the "manifesto" of Little Russian nationalism, the famous *Istoriia Rusov* (History of the Rus' people).[106]

Thus, if in the late eighteenth and early nineteenth centuries patriots of the Sloboda region and Little Russia still quarreled with one another about local rights and privileges and competed in efforts to open "their" university, after somewhat more than a decade following the establishment of Kharkiv University they began to unite their efforts in the cultural process, transitioning from a socioregional to an ethnic conception of nation and territory. This would hardly have become possible if the Kharkiv educational district had not united various regions of Ukraine within its boundaries. While Kharkiv journals were published in Russian, by no means did they eliminate manifestations of local color and regional patriotism; on the contrary, they activated local subjects in the cultural process.

## Polish Connections

Although the Polish lobby at court supported the Kharkiv University project because of its remoteness, Kharkiv was not isolated from Polish cultural influences. They reached Sloboda Ukraine together with Ukrainian migrants in the mid-seventeenth century. From that point of view, Kharkiv remained in the sphere of the Polish-Ukrainian cultural borderland. Not only had that borderland not disappeared with the partitions of the Polish-Lithuanian Commonwealth in the late eighteenth century, but it had become even more prominent in the early nineteenth century with the formation of the Vilnius educational district (1803) and the establishment of the Krzemieniec Lyceum (1805). After the Napoleonic Wars, Kharkiv University's contacts with Polish educational institutions and intellectuals became even more intensive.[107]

The elective teaching of Polish language and literature at Kharkiv University was initiated in 1818 by Petro Hulak-Artemovsky, an adjunct instructor at the university and a graduate of the Kyiv Mohyla Academy who came from Right-Bank Ukraine, where he had made his living for some time as a domestic teacher on Polish gentry estates. He became a Ukrainian writer in Kharkiv, but many of his best works of serious literature, which opened new generic and thematic possibilities for the Ukrainian language, were influenced by Polish writers, especially Ignacy Krasicki and Adam Mickiewicz. In his early period as a writer, Hulak-Artemovsky maintained active contacts with Polish intellectuals and was even elected a member of the Royal Society of Friends of Learning in Warsaw.

In 1831, after the crushing of the Polish revolt, Kharkiv professors were enlisted in the "reorganization" of the educational system in the Polish-Ukrainian borderland. The Right-Bank Ukrainian gubernias of Podilia and Volhynia were temporarily transferred to the jurisdiction of Kharkiv University. After the closing of Vilnius University and subsequent persecution of Polish culture, contacts between the Kharkiv and Polish intellectual milieux became even more intensive. Many Polish students found shelter in Kharkiv, and in some years they accounted for as much as one-third of the student body at the local university.[108] Some Polish professors also found themselves constrained to move there from Vilnius. Since Kharkiv was farther from the Right Bank than Kyiv or Odesa, the attitude of the local administration toward Poles was, as a rule, fairly measured.

The boundaries of the Kharkiv educational district did not substantially change the position of the region on the imperial map as compared with the preceding century. They merely consolidated its traditional contiguity with other borderlands: Little Russia, the Don and Black Sea regions, and the former Polish-Lithuanian Commonwealth. Proximity to restless Poland on the one hand, to the warlike Caucasus on the other, and, through the Crimea and the Black Sea littoral, to the Ottoman Empire on the third, only served to emphasize the region's borderland status.

\* \* \*

The fact of Kharkiv University's location on Ukrainian ethnic territory and the interest of its professors and students in Ukrainian studies have prompted notions of the Ukrainian character of that educational institution. If the first foreign professors at Kharkiv University imagined its symbolic geography through the "southern," ancient, and "Cossack" markers, then by the second quarter of the nineteenth century the latter were replaced with ethnic "Little Russian," *khokhol*, and "Ruthenian" symbols. Thus, in a letter of October 1829 to Joachim Lelewel, Michał Bobrowski called Kharkiv the "capital of the *khokhly*."[109] The Russian scholar Yakov Grot, in correspondence with Petr Pletnev, saw Kharkiv's basic difference from Odesa in the fact that people there spoke "in *khokhol*." Ivan Aksakov, speaking of Kharkiv University, shrugged his shoulders, stating it as self-evident that "the university is poor, of course, but the *khokhly* probably place it above all others."[110]

Although Ukrainian national space figures under a variety of names, Kharkiv University is located within it in the role of a national educational center. For that reason, a member of the Ruthenian Triad, Ivan Vahylevych, called Kharkiv the "focus of Ruthenian enlightenment,"[111] while the Polish historian Reverend Walerian Kalinka, who was close to Prince Adam Czartoryski, called the Sloboda region "the heart of Ruthenian nationality."[112] Unquestionably, such rhetoric creates an illusory perspective. Between the founding of Kharkiv University *in* Ukraine and its transformation into a *Ukrainian* institution there lies a long road that has not yet been traveled to the end.

As a whole, the Kharkiv University project corresponded to the policy of enlightened modernization and unification of the Russian Empire, which presupposed the elimination of historical boundaries between the regions of the empire. On the one hand, the founding of Kharkiv University reflected the triumph of the doctrine of enlightened centralization over regional and social particularism. From the very beginning, the university was a state institution subject to a supervisor appointed directly by the emperor, not a local gentry corporation. There was at first nothing in the university structure, teaching staff, or curriculum reflecting a local, regional particularity. Kharkiv University did not have the appearance of a campus or a "small town of learning," as intended by its founder, Vasilii Karazin. Initially it was housed in government buildings along one of the central streets and only gradually expanded its presence in the city through the purchase and construction of new premises scattered throughout Kharkiv.

On the other hand, however, the transformation of Kharkiv into a university town emphasized the specific character of the region. The success of the Kharkiv University project was dependent in many ways on the regional patriotism and enthusiasm of its initiator, Vasilii Karazin. It gained a response in local society mainly because the idea of the particular privileged status of the region was still vital in its various strata. Even the idea of university autonomy for a distinct corporation endowed with the right of self-government was quite easily assimilated into the familiar local model of settlement on the basis of particular rights.

Kharkiv University, having relieved itself of its missionary functions of enlightenment in the distant southern and western regions, became localized in time as a truly regional university for the Sloboda region. The role of "Russifier" of the Polish *kresy* of Right-Bank Ukraine ultimately fell to Kyiv. The geographic location of Kharkiv turned out to be unsuitable for carrying out such a mission. When the new St. Vladimir University was promptly established in 1834, some Kharkiv professors were transferred to Kyiv to strengthen it as a bastion of Orthodox Slavic-Rus' influence in the Polish-dominated region. Kyiv University, for its part, became a link between the Right Bank and the Sloboda region, promoting the cultural consolidation of Ukrainian ethnic territory on the one hand and its direct contact with Polish cultural space on the other. Later, in 1865, the new university space on Ukrainian territory would be joined by yet another institution, the University of New Russia in Odesa.

Thanks to the university, the city's landscape was organically enriched in the first half of the nineteenth century by botanical and civic gardens, a boulevard, and new places of public rest and recreation. The merchants in turn promoted the city's progress with the construction of new brick houses and commercial buildings, the laying of boulevards, and the development of the service sector. Along with the university there appeared professors and members of staff who acquired homes of their own in the city. German tradesmen invited by Karazin for the needs of the university even managed to lay the foundations of a new German Street.

The diverse ethnic and denominational composition of the university's academic and student body, merchants, tradesmen, and soldiers led to the establishment in the city, along with Orthodox churches, of Lutheran (1830) and Catholic (1832) churches and, adjoining them, cemeteries of the corresponding denominations. Besides Christian churches, synagogues and mosques, along with their cemeteries, made their appearance in Kharkiv. Until the mid-nineteenth century, however, it was the state and church that defined the transformation of Kharkiv's civic space. It may be considered that the symbol of their indissoluble union was the construction in 1844 of Kharkiv's tallest building in the city center—the bell tower of the Dormition Cathedral, raised in honor of Emperor Alexander I and the victorious expulsion of Napoleon and his multinational army ("twelve languages") from Russia in 1812.

To what extent the example of Kharkiv may be considered typical of "many middle-size and even large Russian cities of the time" is a debatable question.[113] The German scholar August von Haxthausen, who passed through Kharkiv in July 1843, subtly noted the particular features of the city's landscape. He described in detail the "three sources and three composite sections" of Kharkiv that presented themselves to his inquiring mind as he approached the center: the "countryside with orchards and flower beds" with which it began; the "city of Catherine II," built in the spirit of the Moscow suburbs with their long, straight, unpaved streets, Russian tradesmen, taverns, and shops; and, finally, the city of the times of Nicholas I, located in the center of that layer cake—modern, wholly European, with straight, partly paved streets, large squares and palaces, but lacking life and movement.[114]

It may be assumed that this depiction reflected Haxthausen's concept of the Russian Empire as a whole—the idea of progress in the absence of organicism. "Three cities in one" unfold before the reader of the German scholar's travel notes in the form of a successively ascending panorama: from nature (the plant kingdom) to trades (the mineral kingdom), and from there to contemporary civilization, that is, from the village through the commercial center to the contemporary city; however, on arriving at its center, the traveler finds himself in an unpopulated place. Moreover, every new spiral of the city's history continues its existence autonomously, unconnected with its other segments.

Contemporaries compared Kharkiv with Odesa as an example of a "European" university town, differing from similar towns only in the Ukrainian accent of its population. Haxthausen wrote of Kharkiv as one of the most important, beautiful, and richly promising towns of Southern Russia, comparable with Odesa to the same degree as Moscow might be compared with St. Petersburg.[115] The constant comparisons of Kharkiv with St. Petersburg belong to the same context and are largely to be explained by the role of regional capital that Kharkiv began to play from the moment of its transformation into the administrative center of Sloboda Ukraine.

## Notes

1. Andreas Kappeler, "Iuzhnyi i vostochnyi frontir Rossii v XVI–XVIII vekakh," *Ab Imperio*, no. 1 (2003): 47–64.
2. O. Repan, ed., *Narysy z istoriï osvoiennia Pivdennoï Ukraïny XV–XVIII st.: kolektyvna monohrafiia* (Kyiv: K.I.S., 2020); Fedir Turchenko and Halyna Turchenko, *Pivdenna Ukraïna: Modernizatsiia, svitova viina, revoliutsiia (kinets' XIX st.–1921)* (Kyiv: Heneza, 2003).

3. Andrei Zorin, *Kormia dvuglavogo orla: Russkaia literatura i gosudarstvennaia ideologiia v poslednei treti XVIII–pervoi treti XIX veka* (Moscow: NLO, 2001), 108.
4. Zorin, *Kormia*, 106.
5. Vera Proskurina, *Mify imperii: Literatura i vlast' v epokhu Ekateriny II* (Moscow: NLO, 2006), 114, 145.
6. Zorin, *Kormia*, 115.
7. Patricia Herlihy, *Odesa: Istoriia mista, 1794–1914* (Kyiv: Krytyka, 1999), 16.
8. Zorin, *Kormia*, 105–8.
9. Dmitrii Iavornitskii, *Istoriia goroda Ekaterinoslava* (Dnipropetrovsk, 1989), 54.
10. Those mentioned were St. Petersburg, Moscow, Berlin, Vienna, Constantinople (Istanbul), and Astrakhan (Proskurina, *Mify*, 146).
11. Proskurina, *Mify*, 145.
12. Dmitrii Bagalei and Dmitrii Miller, *Istoriia goroda Khar'kova za 250 let ego sushchestvovaniia*, 2 vols. (Kharkiv: City Press, 1993), 2: 130.
13. Pavel Rudiakov, "V sluzhbu i vechnoe poddanstvo. . .": *Serbskie poseleniia Novaia Serbiia i Slavianoserbiia na ukrainskikh zemliakh (1751–1764)* (Kyiv: ArtEk, 2001).
14. Oleksandr Hurzhii, *Ukraïns'ka kozats'ka derzhava* (Kyiv: Osnovy, 1996), 102; Izmail Sreznevskii, *Istoricheskoe obozrenie grazhdanskogo ustroeniia Slobodskoi Ukrainy so vremeni ee zaseleniia do preobrazovaniia v Khar'kovskuiu guberniiu* (Kharkiv: Kharkiv Gubernia Press, 1883), 22.
15. Bagalei and Miller, *Istoriia goroda Khar'kova*, 1: 291.
16. Dmytro Bahalii, *Istoriia Slobids'koï Ukraïny* (Kharkiv: Osnova, 1990), 136, 140–41.
17. Bagalei and Miller, *Istoriia goroda Khar'kova*, 1: 55.
18. *Istoriia goroda Khar'kova*, 2: 114.
19. Dmitrii Bagalei, *Opyt istorii Khar'kovskogo universiteta (po neizdannym materialam)*, 2 vols. (Kharkiv: Kharkiv University Press, 1893–98), vol. 1 *(1802–1815)*, 1023.
20. Ivan Dolgorukii, *Slavny bubny za gorami ili puteshestvie moe koe-kuda 1810 goda* (Moscow: Moscow University Press, 1870), 50–53.
21. Nikolai Lavrovskii, "Vasilii Nazarovich Karazin i otkrytie Khar'kovskogo universiteta," *Zhurnal Ministerstva Narodnogo Prosveshcheniia*, no. 2 (1872): 202.
22. Bagalei, *Opyt istorii*, 1:1002.
23. Ludwik Janowski, *Uniwersytet Charkowski w początkach swego istnienia (1805–1820)* (Krakow, 1911), 45–46.
24. Bagalei and Miller, *Istoriia goroda Khar'kova*, 2: 2.
25. *Istoriia goroda Khar'kova*, 2: 9.
26. *Istoriia goroda Khar'kova*, 2: 17.
27. *Istoriia goroda Khar'kova*, 2: 9.
28. *Istoriia goroda Khar'kova*, 1: 135–36; 2: 26–261.
29. Dmitrii Bagalei, *Ocherki iz russkoi istorii*, 2 vols. (Kharkiv, 1913), 2: 69; Bagalei and Miller, *Istoriia goroda Khar'kova*, 1: 76.
30. Bagalei and Miller, *Istoriia goroda Khar'kova*, 2: 2.
31. *Istoriia goroda Khar'kova*, 1: 106–7.
32. *Istoriia goroda Khar'kova*, 2: 476–77.
33. Volodymyr Masliichuk, *Provintsiia na perekhresti kul'tur (doslidzhennia z istoriï Slobids'koï Ukraïny XVII–XIX stolit'* (Kharkiv: Kharkiv Private Museum of the City Estate, 2007), 349.
34. Dmytro Bahalii, *Ukraïns'kyi mandrovanyi filosof Hryhorii Skovoroda*, 2nd ed. (Kyiv, 1992), 328.
35. Igor' Losievskii, *Russkaia lira s Ukrainy: Russkie pisateli Ukrainy pervoi chetverti XIX veka* (Kharkiv: Oko Press, 1993), 65, 130–32.
36. The following part of this chapter was published under the title "A University for Ukraine" in my collection of articles *The Ukrainian-Russian Borderland: History versus Geography* (Montreal, Kingston, London, and Chicago: McGill-Queen's University Press, 2022),

170–204. I wish to thank the publisher for permission to reprint the text of the article, with changes, in this book.
37. Vitalii Sarbei, "Istoryko-heohrafichni rehiony Ukraïny v protsesi natsional'noho Vidrodzhennia kintsia XVIII–pochatku XX st.," *Dnipropetrovs'kyi istoryko-arkheobrafichnyi zbirnyk*, no. 1 (2001): 357–61; Paul Robert Magocsi, *A History of Ukraine*, 2nd rev. ed. (Toronto: University of Toronto Press, 2011), 381; Iaroslav Hrytsak, *Narys istoriï Ukraïny: Formuvannia modernoï ukraïns'koï natsiï XIX–XX stolittia* (Kyiv: Heneza, 1996), 30.
38. David Saunders, *The Ukrainian Impact on Russian Culture: 1750–1850* (Edmonton: CIUS Press, 1985), 42.
39. Grigorii Teplov, "Proekt k uchrezhdeniiu universiteta Baturinskogo, 1760 goda," *Chteniia v Obshchestve istorii i drevnostei rossiiskikh*, no. 2 (1863): 67–85.
40. Viktor Korotkyi and Vasyl' Ul'ianovs'kyi, eds., *Z imenem Sviatoho Volodymyra*, vol. 1 (Kyiv, 1994), 27–36.
41. S. V. Rozhdestvenskii, *Ocherki po istorii sistem narodnogo prosveshcheniia v Rossii v XVIII–XIX vekakh*, vol. 1 (St. Petersburg, 1910), 285.
42. Bagalei and Miller, *Istoriia goroda Khar'kova*, 1: 404.
43. *Istoriia goroda Khar'kova*, 1: 421.
44. Bagalei, *Opyt istorii*, 1: 55.
45. *Opyt istorii*, 1: 44–49.
46. Anatolii Bolebrukh, Serhii Kudelko, and Anton Khridochkin, *Vasyl' Nazarovych Karazin (1773–1842)* (Kharkiv, 2005); Nikolai Tikhii, *V. N. Karazin: Vinovnik uchrezhdeniia universiteta v Khar'kove* (Kharkiv, 1905); Vasilii N. Karazin, *Sochineniia, pis'ma i bumagi* (Kharkiv: Kharkiv University Press, 1910).
47. Bagalei, *Opyt istorii*, 1: 5–37.
48. Dmitrii Bagalei, "Nazarii Aleksandrovich Karazin i ego kolokol," *Kievskaia starina*, no. 11 (1892): 163–75.
49. It is worth recalling that the celebrated Russian poet and high-ranking official Gavriil Derzhavin also owed his career to the struggle against corruption in the highest ranks of the imperial government and his close relations with the Russian monarch. He was later banished from the court because of his temperament and his refusal to obey the unwritten rules of court etiquette. A similar fate later befell Karazin.
50. He was soon promoted to the rank of collegiate counsellor, receiving a diamond ring as a sign of the monarch's favor.
51. Karazin, *Sochineniia*, 539.
52. Ia. Abramov, *V. N. Karazin, ego zhizn' i obshchestvennaia deiatel'nost': Biograficheskii ocherk* (St. Petersburg, 1891), 35.
53. Bagalei, *Opyt istorii*, 1: 54.
54. *Opyt istorii*, 1: 53.
55. *Opyt istorii*, 1: 54.
56. Nikolai Lavrovskii, "Vospominanie o Vasilii Nazaroviche Karazine (1773–1873)," *Zhurnal Ministerstva Narodnogo Prosveshcheniia*, no. 2 (1873): 301; Dmitrii Bagalei, Nikolai Sumtsov, and Vladislav Buzeskul, *Kratkii ocherk istorii Khar'kovskogo universiteta za pervye sto let ego sushchestvovaniia (1805–1905)* (Kharkiv: University Press, 1906), 1; Janowski, *Uniwersytet Charkowski*, 45–46.
57. Bagalei, *Opyt istorii*, 1: 55–57.
58. *Opyt istorii*, 1: 71.
59. *Opyt istorii*, 1: 68.
60. *Opyt istorii*, 1: 70.
61. Ivan Pavlovskii, "Pis'mo V. N. Karazina k kniaziu A. B. Kurakinu o privlechenii malorossiiskogo dvorianstva k pozhertvovaniiu na Khar'kovskii universitet," *Trudy Poltavskoi Uchenoi Arkhivnoi Komissii*, no. 11 (1914): 185.
62. Bagalei, *Opyt istorii*, 1: 85.

63. Janowski, *Uniwersytet Charkowski*, 31.
64. Bagalei, *Opyt istorii*, 1: 91.
65. Karazin, *Sochineniia*, 539.
66. Bagalei, *Opyt istorii*, 1: 14.
67. Masliichuk, *Provintsiia na perekhresti kul'tur*, 351.
68. Karazin, *Sochineniia*, 38.
69. Bagalei and Miller, *Istoriia goroda Khar'kova*, 2: 700.
70. Bagalei, *Opyt istorii*, 1: 1017–18.
71. Fedor A. Petrov, *Rossiiskie universitety v pervoi polovine XIX veka: Formirovanie sistemy universitetskogo obrazovaniia*, 4 vols. (Moscow: Khristianskoe Izd-vo (vol. 1) and State Historical Museum (vols. 2–4), 1998–2001), 1: 299; 2: 192.
72. Bagalei, *Opyt istorii*, 1: 225.
73. *Opyt istorii*, 1: 88.
74. *Opyt istorii*, 1: 101.
75. Karazin, *Sochineniia*, 539, 622.
76. James T. Flynn, "V. N. Karazin, the Gentry, and Kharkov University," *Slavic Review* 28, no. 2 (1969): 209–20, here 212.
77. Sergei Rozhdestvenskii, *Istoricheskii obzor deiatel'nosti Ministerstva Narodnogo Prosveshcheniia, 1802–1902* (St. Petersburg: Ministry of Education Press, 1902), 24.
78. Ivan Lysiak-Rudnyts'kyi, *Istorychni ese*, 2 vols., 2nd repr. ed. (Kyiv: Dukh i Litera, 2019), 1: 212.
79. Lysiak-Rudnyts'kyi, *Istorychni ese*.
80. Pavlovskii, "Pis'mo V. N. Karazina k kniaziu A. B. Kurakinu," 179–85.
81. Irina Zhuravleva, "Ideal popechitel'stva: graf Severin Pototskii," in *Kharkiv i Pol'shcha: Liudy i podii* (Kharkiv: Maidan, 2006), 57–75.
82. John Gascoigne, *Science, Politics, and Universities in Europe, 1600–1800* (Brookfield, VT: Ashgate, 1998), 9.
83. Marc Raeff, "Ukraine and Imperial Russia: Intellectual and Political Encounters from the Seventeenth to the Nineteenth Century," in *Ukraine and Russia in Their Historical Encounter*, ed. Peter J. Potichnyj et al. (Edmonton: CIUS Press, 1992), 69–85, here 79.
84. Peter Dhondt, "Ambiguous Loyalty to the Russian Tsar: The Universities of Dorpat and Helsinki as Nation Building Institutions," *Historical Social Research* 33, no. 2 (2008): 99–126, here 103.
85. Iurii D. Margolis and Grigorii A. Tishkin, *Otechestvu na pol'zu, a rossiianam vo slavu* (Leningrad: Leningrad University Press, 1988), 193–94.
86. Kristof Ditrikh fon Rommel' (Christoph Dietrich von Rommel), *Spohady pro moie zhyttia ta mii chas*, comp. and ed. Volodymyr V. Kravchenko; trans. of *Erinnerungen über mein Leben und meine Zeit* by Volodymyr Masliichuk and Nataliia Onishchenko (Kharkiv: Maidan, 2001); Edgar Hösch, "An Episode from German-Ukrainian Scholarly Contacts: Dietrich Christoph von Rommel," in *German-Ukrainian Relations in Historical Perspective*, eds. Hans-Joachim Torke and John-Paul Himka (Edmonton: CIUS Press, 1994).
87. Mikhail I. Sukhomlinov, *Materialy dlia istorii prosveshcheniia v Rossii v tsarstvovanie imperatora Aleksandra I* (St. Petersburg: F. S. Sushchinskii, 1866), 71.
88. Serhii Stel'makh, *Istorychna dumka v Ukraïni XIX – pochatku XX stolittia* (Kyiv: Akademiia, 1997), 70–81.
89. Rommel', *Spohady*, 120.
90. *Spohady*, 121.
91. Leonid Nichpaevskii, "Vospominaniia o Khar'kovskom universitete, 1823–1829 gody," *Russkaia starina*, no. 8 (1907): 376.
92. James T. Flynn, *The University Reform of Tsar Alexander I, 1802–1835* (Washington, DC: Catholic University of America Press, 1988), 53.

93. Karl Klaus Walther, "Johann Baptist Schad in Russland," *Jahrbücher für Geschichte Osteuropas* 40, no. 3 (1992): 340–65.
94. Götz Uebe, "The First Flow of Funds Table: Lang's Tableau of 1815," *History of Political Economy* 24, no. 2 (1992): 435–53.
95. Rommel', *Spohady*, 129.
96. *Spohady*, 129.
97. *Spohady*, 131.
98. N. A. Lavrovskii, "Ėpizod iz istorii Khar'kovskogo universiteta," *Chteniia v Obshchestve istorii i drevnostei rossiiskikh*, no. 2 (1873): 39.
99. Bagalei, *Opyt istorii*, 1: 793; 2: 110, 857.
100. Flynn, *The University Reform*, 60–62.
101. Gustav Gess de Kal've, *Teoriia muzyki, ili rassuzhdenie o sem iskusstve...*, trans. Razumnik Gonorskii, 2 vols. (Kharkiv, University Press, 1818).
102. Grigorii P. Danilevskii, *Ukrainskaia starina: Materialy dlia istorii ukrainskoi literatury i narodnogo obrazovaniia* (Kharkiv: Izdanie Zalenskogo i Liubarskogo, 1866), 298.
103. *Ukrainskaia starina*, 307.
104. *Ukrainskaia starina*, 307.
105. V. S. Kiselev and T. A. Vasil'eva, "Ėvoliutsiia obraza Ukrainy v imperskoi slovesnosti pervoi chetverti XIX v.: Regionalizm, ėtnografizm, politizatsiia," *Vestnik Tomskogo gosudarstvennogo universiteta: Filologiia* 26, no. 6 (2013): 61–77; Susan Smith-Peter, "Ukrainskie zhurnaly nachala XIX veka: Ot universalizma Prosveshcheniia do romanticheskogo regionalizma," in *Istoriia i politika v sovremennom mire*, eds. I. G. Zhiriakov and A. A. Orlov (Moscow: MGOU Press, 2010), 447–61; Ihor L. Mykhailyn, *Istoriia ukraïns'koï zhurnalistyky XIX stolittia* (Kyiv: Tsentr Navchal'noï Literatury, 2003).
106. Petro Hulak-Artemovs'kyi, *Poetychni tvory*; Ievhen Hrebinka, *Poetychni tvory, povisti ta opovidannia* (Kyiv: Naukova Dumka, 1984), 51–52.
107. Artur Kijas, *Polacy na Uniwersytecie Charkowskim, 1805–1917*, 2nd rev. ed. (Poznań: PTPN Press, 2008).
108. Fedor Neslukhovskii, "Iz moikh vospominanii," *Istoricheskii vestnik*, no. 4 (1890): 116–53.
109. Bagalei and Miller, *Istoriia goroda Khar'kova*, 2: 130.
110. Sergei Beliakov, *Ukrainskaia natsiia v ėpokhu Gogolia* (Moscow: AST, 2016), 41.
111. *"Rus'ka triitsia" v istoriï suspil'no-politychnoho rukhu i kul'tury Ukraïny* (Kyiv: Naukova Dumka, 1987), 110.
112. Lysiak-Rudnyts'kyi, *Istorychni ese*, 1: 425.
113. Dzh. Khosking [Geoffrey Hosking], *Rossiia: narod i imperiia (1552–1917)* (Smolensk, 2000), 258.
114. Baron von Haxthausen, *The Russian Empire, Its People, Institutions, and Resources*, vol. 1 (London: Chapman & Hall, 1856), 394.
115. Haxthausen, *Russian Empire*, 1: 397.

CHAPTER 3

# A Province in Search of an Identity

During the reign of Catherine II, the political map of eastern Europe changed profoundly. As Willard Sunderland has noted, Russia's borders with the Polish-Lithuanian Commonwealth, the Ottoman Empire, and the Crimean Khanate changed six times between 1772 and 1795 as a result of wars and annexations.[1] That number certainly increases if one takes account of the borders of the Ukrainian lands of the Hetmanate, the Zaporozhian Sich, and the Sloboda region, which were constantly redrawn in the course of incorporation and reformation of the empire's steppe borderland.

The newly incorporated regions in the west and south had yet to be intellectually "domesticated" and accommodated in the imperial cultural and national space. However, the symbolic space of "Russianness" was only gradually taking modern shape in the nineteenth century. Russian nation-building lagged significantly behind empire-building. The process was rendered difficult by the unceasing expansion of Russia's territory on the one hand and the shallow and selective modernization of its empire on the other. The lack of well-articulated intellectual tools may be considered yet another obstacle on the path to the national reidentification of Russia as a whole. These were the factors mainly responsible for the enduring contradiction between the secular and presecular conceptions of "Russianness."

Despite the development of modern geographic, ethnographic, historical, and statistical research, "Russian" nomenclature of the late eighteenth and early nineteenth centuries was truly in a state of chaos. One and the same region, whose administrative and mental boundaries remained changeable, might be called entirely different names, as was also the case with the population living on its territory. The example of Ukraine—Little Russia—Rus'—Russia—Southern Rus'—Southern Russia—was quite typical in that regard. Students of other regions that had once been part of the historical and cultural space of Rus' faced the same confusion. That is understandable if one considers that none of the criteria for defining Russian identity—historical, ethnic, linguistic, geographic—was employed at the time with sufficient consistency to endow that "imagined" identity space with more or less definite features.² "Russia" was in fact perceived as an aggregate of the historical regions of ancient Rus'.³

The search for the identity of the Russian Empire in the late eighteenth and early nineteenth centuries was defined by two contradictory tendencies: on the one hand, enlightened unification on the basis of European models and secularization of the cultural process; on the other, anti-Western discourse and a turn toward Russian Orthodox tradition.⁴ This contradictory fusion of what might provisionally be called "westernizing" and "Slavophile" orientations, which did not take ideological form until the second third of the nineteenth century, distinguished the policy of the imperial center to the same degree as the succession of centralizing and decentralizing tendencies in its activity. From the height of the capital, provincial culture in that changing map of the world took on a variety of aspects, from that of a sleepy bear's den into which no ray of Enlightenment could penetrate to that of a life-giving source of "native" Slavdom unsullied by modern Europeanism.

## The South Russian "Challenge"

The annexation of the Black Sea littoral and the Crimea obliged the Russian authorities to modify the traditional representation of the historical regions of Rus'/Russia already discussed. The former steppe borderland attracted particular attention: numerous authors produced investigations in the syncretic genre of area and population studies, including historical, geographic, ethnographic, socioeconomic, and legal data. As the intellectual appropriation of the new steppe territories proceeded, "southern" terminology increasingly began to define the geographic, historical, and cultural dimension of the country. The "south–north" system of cultural coordinates came into use in Russia about the same time as it was replaced in other European countries by "east–west" coordinates.⁵ The new administrative and symbolic geography of the Russian Empire began to acquire additional substantiation in the empress's historical writings: "Northern Russia" was embodied by ancient Novgorod and "Southern Russia" by the Kyiv Principality.⁶

What had to be clarified first and foremost was the relation between the newly annexed southern lands and the neighboring regions of Little Russia and Sloboda Ukraine. The administrative answer to that question was initially determined by the institutionalization of New Russia (constituted as the New Russia gubernia from 1764 to 1783 and then from 1796 to 1804, and subsequently as the governorate-general of New Russia and Bessarabia from 1822 to 1874).⁷ But that raised the further question of whether "New Russia" could be considered synonymous with "Southern Russia."

That did not appear to be the case, considering that the southern "belt" of the Russian Empire, established by Catherine II along with the "northern" one, turned out to be much broader than New Russia. It comprised all the territories south of the middle "belt," whose center was Moscow. Consequently, New Russia, as well as the much older Sloboda Ukraine and Little Russia, were all faced with the problem of reconciling their local identity with that of the new "Southern Russia." Particular evidence of this is to be found in the series of topographic descriptions of the "southern" vicegerencies prepared in the late 1780s.

Evidently, representatives of "New Russia" found themselves in the easiest situation. It is apparent from the preface to the atlas of the Katerynoslav vicegerency, prepared in Kremenchuk in 1787, that the whole history of this new administrative entity could be reduced to four lines: "This land, having been subjected since ancient times to various changes and, so to speak, having served as a spectacle of misfortune and destruction by Turkish and Tatar invasions, has now, under the peaceful and felicitous rule of Great Catherine, been brought into safe and flourishing condition."[8] This account, which mentioned only the historical Turco-Tatar "yoke," did not associate "New Russia" with the legacy of ancient Rus'. But that did not satisfy the imperial center, which sought to legitimize its new territorial acquisitions by turning to history.

The historical legacy and mythology of ancient Kyivan Rus', along with that of antiquity, was actively employed in Russia's intellectual "domestication" of the former Crimean Tatar and Turkish domains. Suffice it to recall searches for the semi-legendary Tmutarakan Principality, with the aid of which Moscow pressed its claims to the Khanate of Astrakhan at one time.[9] Was it an accident that the *Tale of Igor's Campaign*, which describes a struggle of ancient Rus' warriors with Polovtsian steppe nomads, was conveniently discovered by the Ober-Procurator of the Apostolic Governing Synod, Aleksei Musin-Pushkin, in 1795 and published with the assistance of two highly placed imperial scholars, Nikolai Bantysh-Kamensky and Aleksei Malinovsky, in 1800?

The constant administrative transformations of the southern and western borderlands of the Russian Empire promoted their symbolic consolidation around Kharkiv, Odesa, and Kyiv. The governorate-general of New Russia and Bessarabia was established in 1822. Some time later, the Kherson, Tavriia, and Katerynoslav gubernias were assigned to the Odesa educational district. By that time, the Kharkiv educational district had lost its Transcaucasian territories. However, the Russian government's administrative reforms had not yet taken full account of ethnic considerations. Curiously, in 1832 the minister of education, Karl Liven, based his attempt to exclude the New Russia provinces from Kharkiv's jurisdiction on the mixed ethnicity of their population, which meant that they could not be considered Russian. Emperor Nicholas I rejected Liven's proposal, asserting, as it were, that he knew perfectly well that those lands were indeed "Russian."[10]

Nevertheless, as "Southern Russia" began to appear quite distinctly on maps of the empire, it remained without a regional center of its own for a long time. Three cities—Kharkiv, Kyiv, and Odesa—pretended to that role. According to the new Russian minister of education, Sergei Uvarov, who replaced Karl Liven in that office, it would be appropriate for Kyiv, the "real . . . center of education of Southern Russia," to assume that role.[11] Yet Kharkiv continued to enjoy that status in public opinion.[12] In fact, the role of regional center was gradually accruing to Odesa, which was positioning itself more confidently than any other city in the southern cultural space.

Unlike Kharkiv or Kyiv, Odesa had no problem of conflicting local identities. It had never belonged to Little Russia or Sloboda Ukraine. From the very beginning of its existence, Odesa had a southern "residence permit." The first Russian-language periodical publication in multiethnic Odesa, which appeared in 1821, was titled *Vestnik Iuzhnoi Rossii* (South Russian courier), and the first society similar to the Philotechnical, founded in 1828, was known there as the Agricultural Society of Southern Russia. True, the university established in Odesa in the latter half of the nineteenth century was called New Russian, not South Russian, but that was merely a reflection of the unending struggle for primacy between cities in the South Russian symbolic space, as well as its ongoing fragmentation.

## The Little Russian Challenge

The symbolic annexation of the southern lands by St. Petersburg met with political and intellectual resistance from the Little Russian elite. Kyiv had already established itself as the historical center of the Little Russian region (i.e., the former Cossack Hetmanate) and, as such, became the main symbol of early modern Little Russian identity.[13] Moreover, Little Russian intellectuals had traditionally defended their exclusive claim to the historical and cultural legacy of ancient Rus'. Little Russia was most often identified with Kyivan Rus' as a whole or with the Kyiv Principality, which was considered the "true Rus'" and the center of the "Slavic-Rus'" world. The historical space of "Little Russia" also included the possessions of the former Zaporozhian Host, which now came under direct imperial control, and the settlements of Sloboda Ukraine, as described earlier.

Compared to "Great Russia," "Little Russia" appeared better defined owing to its administrative boundaries, but its symbolic boundaries remained diffuse. Some authors, regardless of origin, define Little Russia mainly with reference to the administrative framework of the Poltava and Chernihiv gubernias, as well as the governorate-general of Little Russia (Left-Bank Ukraine as a whole), prevailing in their lifetimes. For other authors, oriented more toward historical and ethnocultural rather than dynastic and administrative considerations, Little Russia was not limited to the Left Bank but included the Right Bank of the Dnieper, the Sloboda region, New Russia, and additional territories.

Mykhailo Antonovsky, a coauthor of Johann Gottlieb Georgi's well-known *Description of All Peoples Inhabiting the Russian State* (1799), wavered between the traditional historical criteria and the new ethnographic ones in defining the territory of Little Russia.[14] The Russian scholar Khariton Chebotarev, by contrast, experienced no such doubts. According to him, Little Russia encompassed not only the lands of the former Hetmanate but also the territory of the Sloboda region, along with the Belgorod and New Russia gubernias.[15] In terms of geography, Little Russia in its broadest extent was most often identified with Southern Russia.

The identification of Little Russia with Southern Rus' on the basis of history and ethnicity became a commonplace in the works of nineteenth-century authors of Ukrainian origin, including Yurii Venelin, Osyp Bodiansky, Mykola Hohol/ Nikolai Gogol, Mykhailo Maksymovych, Amvrosii Metlynsky, Taras Shevchenko, Panteleimon Kulish, and many other contemporaries. This was the period in which the terms "South Russian people" and "South Russian language," as well as the literature written in that language, began to circulate widely, distinguishing the "South Russian" historical tradition from the "North Russian" one.[16] The "dispute between southerners and northerners about their Russianness" (Yurii Venelin) prefigured Ukrainian-Russian polemics concerning their common historical and geographic heritage.

## Sloboda Ukraine

Sloboda Ukraine underwent a series of administrative reforms with Kharkiv as its newly established center. The very name of the Sloboda Ukraine gubernia, which came into existence in 1765, contained both centralizing (gubernia) and regional (Sloboda Ukraine) elements, which attests eloquently to the imperial center's contradictory policy in the borderland. In 1780 the Sloboda Ukraine gubernia was renamed the Kharkiv vicegerency (*namestnichestvo*), consisting of fifteen districts (Bilopillia, Bohodukhiv, Chuhuiv, Izium, Kharkiv, Khotmyzhsk, Krasnokutsk, Lebedyn, Myropillia, Nedryhailiv, Okhtyrka, Sumy, Valky, Vovchansk, Zolochiv).

When the pendulum of official policy swung in the opposite direction, in 1796, the Kharkiv vicegerency was abolished and the Sloboda Ukraine gubernia reestablished on its territory. It consisted of ten districts: Bohodukhiv, Izium, Kharkiv, Kupiansk, Lebedyn, Okhtyrka, Sumy, Valky, Vovchansk, Zmiiv. Another thirty years would pass, and in 1834 the Sloboda Ukraine gubernia would become the Kharkiv gubernia, roughly within the same boundaries, this time for a longer period, until the end of the Russian Empire.

Depending on the changing integrationist or expansionist priorities of imperial policy, the Sloboda region was integrated by turns into larger administrative entities—general governments uniting several neighboring provinces. In the early 1780s the Kharkiv vicegerency was ruled by governors general (Petr Rumiantsev-Zadunaisky in 1780–81 and Yevdokim Shcherbinin in 1781–82), whose principal task was the complete elimination of Cossack self-government in the Hetmanate and the Sloboda region respectively.[17]

For a very brief period, the Kharkiv vicegerency was joined to the Voronezh vicegerency. In a few years, however, the Kharkiv and Sloboda regions were shifted southward again. In 1787 the Kharkiv vicegerency came under the rule of Prince Grigorii Potemkin, the governor general of the Katerynoslav and Tavriia vicegerencies, who was occupied with the project of establishing New (Southern) Russia. Officially, Kharkiv remained the administrative center of the Sloboda Ukraine gubernia and was identified with the borderland (*ukraina*) in that capacity.

The use of the term "Ukraine" was almost always determined by its context.[18] In the overwhelming majority of historical and geographic texts of the late eighteenth and early nineteenth centuries, "Ukraine" was a synonym of historical "Little Russia" on both sides of the Dnieper, most often in the form of Cossack territory so as to designate its peripheral, borderland character. The parallel use of the toponyms "Little Russia" and "Ukraine" may be encountered in many texts of the period, regardless of the authors' origin. Sometimes "Ukraine" was divided into two parts, "Muscovite" or Left Bank and "Polish" or Right Bank; at other times into three, if one adds the borderland steppe belt of historical Little Russia. In some cases, Ukraine recovered its integrity in geographic terms, figuring as the continuous borderland of Muscovite Rus' and the Commonwealth. In other cases, its integrity was maintained in ethnocultural as well as political and geographic terms.

The "Ukrainian" localization of Kharkiv and the Sloboda region was associated with the notion that they constituted a cultural borderland as seen from the capitals of the Russian Empire. For example, in the St. Petersburg satirical journal *Zhivopisets* (Painter), "Ukrainian" geographic space was marked in 1772 by mentioning the names of cities—Poltava, Kharkiv, and Holtva—as well as an imaginary local newspaper entitled *Ukrainskie vedomosti* (Ukrainian news). The "mores" of the cultural borderland are depicted ironically in the journal: they are represented by the local gentry, busily hunting with hounds and enjoying banquets, and a mentally unsound landowner searching for someone to whom to sell his conscience. The same motifs occur in satirical texts written by the famous philosopher and moralist Hryhorii Skovoroda, briefly discussed later.

An academician of the St. Petersburg Academy of Sciences, Vasilii Zuev, who passed through Kharkiv in 1781, after it had become the center of the vicegerency, also commented on Kharkiv "mores." The city's satraps mocked him so severely that the offended traveler gave free rein to his emotions, describing his ordeals and concluding that while he had thought of Kharkiv as belonging to central—that is, civilized—Russia, it turned out that the manners prevailing there characterized it as part of the wild borderland, where a traveler's life was in constant danger.[19]

However, since the late eighteenth century, when local elites "took root" in their estates and developed their regional consciousness, the cultural climate in Sloboda Ukraine had improved. There were several intellectual enclaves in the milieu of the local landed gentry, whose members discussed literature, the arts, and science.[20] Among them were the Russian writer Aleksandr Palitsyn from the Popivka estate;[21] the enlightener and founder of Kharkiv University, Vasilii (Vasyl') Karazin from Kruchik; the scientist and traveler Fedor Bibershtein (Friedrich August Freiherr Marschall von Bieberstein) from Merefa; Hryhorii Kvitka from Osnova; and Mykhailo Kovalinsky from Pan-Ivanivka. In parallel with the circles of landed gentry, some Russian officers billeted in Sloboda Ukraine also formed literary gatherings. Rufin Dorokhov, a friend of Aleksandr Pushkin, known for his poetry and duels, was one of the most active participants in the officers' circle of the Chuhuiv garrison. When the Russian traveler Prince Ivan Dolgoruky visited Kharkiv in 1820, he was somewhat surprised to encounter fashionable and refined society, which entertained him with music and Boston (a card game).[22]

The "Ukrainian" identification became the most obvious choice for the Sloboda Ukrainian gentry. The titles of journals that appeared in Kharkiv in the early nineteenth century were distinguished by the "Ukrainian" marker: *Ukrainskii vestnik* (Ukrainian herald), *Ukrainskii zhurnal* (Ukrainian journal). Vasilii Karazin, contemplating plans for the study and public education of Southern Russia with Atanasije Stojković, a Serbian professor at Kharkiv University, envisaged the publication of a journal under the title *Sobesednik iz Ukrainy* (Interlocutor from Ukraine).

The "Ukrainian" identification of Kharkiv and gubernia had become firmly established, officially and unofficially, in various segments of Russian society. For example, the *Statistical Description of the Russian Empire* compiled by Yevdokim Ziablovsky in the early nineteenth century says of the Sloboda Ukraine gubernia that "the land constituting this gubernia is called Ukraine to this day, and this because it lay on the very borders, limits, or edge of Russia."[23] In the strictly geographic sense, the Kharkiv region was called *ukraina* by the Russian Decembrist Nikita Muraviev.[24] He worked out plans for the federative restructuring of the Russian Empire in which Kharkiv figured as the capital of a kind of "state" named "Ukraine," while Kyiv was to become the center of a kind of "Buh [River]" state and Odesa of a "Black Sea" state.[25]

Kharkiv was referred to as the "capital of Ukraine" in the notes of the German traveler Johann Georg Kohl, who passed through the city in 1838.[26] The well-known Russian literary critic Vissarion Belinsky repeated Kohl's reference. In the early 1840s he, too, had recourse to the "capital" metaphor in order to express his impression of the city: "Kharkiv, in its populousness and beauty as compared to other gubernia towns, is in a way the capital of Ukraine, and hence the capital of Ukrainian literature, of Ukrainian prose and, in particular, of Ukrainian verse."[27]

## Sloboda Ukraine and Little Russia

The reforms of Catherine II and Alexander I in the late eighteenth and early nineteenth centuries did not supplant the traditions of regional estate particularism. Those traditions found reflection in the few works devoted to Ukrainian history in the late eighteenth and early nineteenth centuries, which basically retained a regional character and reproduced the administrative boundary that continued to divide historical Little Russia from the Sloboda region. Most authors of those works confined their attention to the territory of Little Russia/the Hetmanate, passing over the Sloboda region and, indeed, other lands settled by ethnic Ukrainians. At best, a few lines were devoted to the Sloboda region, covering the formation of the Sloboda Cossack regiments in the mid-seventeenth century. In the Little Russian historical narrative, that region was depicted as a borderland of the Little Russian metropole, settled by "upstarts" from the common people brazen enough to make totally unfounded claims to membership in the Cossack gentry.

Highly typical in this regard is a satirical poem written in the Ukrainian vernacular by an unknown patriot of Little Russia/the Hetmanate on the cusp of the eighteenth and nineteenth centuries. The author mocks the self-identification of the inhabitants of the Sloboda region as "Little Russians, steppe Ukrainians, and fine Slobodians," attributing highly unflattering characteristics to them ("unbaptized Gypsies," "filth, shepherds, homeless vagabonds"), accusing them of cowardice and offering the following advice: "Go ahead and graze sheep, plow the land, and be carters, / But don't even think of crawling into Cossackdom! / Settle the free lands but pay us rent! / And if not, we'll drive you from the steppes: shoo, shoo!"[28]

The attitude of the Little Russian Cossack elite to that of the Sloboda region was reflected even more strongly in the famous historico-publicistic pamphlet *Istoriia Rusov* (History of the Rus' people), written approximately at this time by an unknown author. He maintained that the Sloboda region had belonged historically to Little Russia, attributing the formation of the Sloboda regiments to the Ukrainian hetman Bohdan Khmelnytsky and asserting that those regiments had settled on Little Russian lands and were under the jurisdiction of the Hetmanate authorities. According to the author, it was only since the times of Hetman Ivan Samoilovych that the "local hetmans, preferring that every one of them be a small autocratic hetman rather than submit to the great hetman, had petitioned that the tsar's court or, better, Prince Golitsyn, who was then in charge of everything, to grant each of them particular rights independent of Little Russian subordination."[29]

It is telling that the author of the *Istoriia Rusov* categorically rejected the name "Ukraine" for his fatherland, considering it contemptuous, if not degrading, and maintaining Little Russia's right of "Rus'" primogeniture vis-à-vis Great Russia. Generally speaking, the Little Russian historical narrative retained negative stereotypes with regard to Sloboda Ukraine that had grown out of the experience of political struggle in the mid- and late seventeenth century, when the paths of the two Ukrainian Cossack regions sometimes diverged quite considerably. Other texts of the period show that the author of the *Istoriia Rusov* was no exception in his attitude toward the Sloboda region.³⁰

Quite naturally, historians of the Sloboda region hastened to refute their Little Russian opponents by insisting on the noble origins of the local elite. The region's historical mythology was based on the feats of the "little hetmans" in loyal and irreproachable service to the Russian throne and the unbroken sequence of favors and privileges that the Slobodians had received from Russian monarchs. Naturally, that loyalty shone all the more brightly against the somber record of the "traitors"—the Little Russian hetmans Ivan Vyhovsky, Ivan Briukhovetsky, and Petro Doroshenko. In other words, the historical record of the Sloboda region was created in opposition not to the Russian imperial but the Little Russian regional historical narrative.

The first attempt at a synthesis of the views of the Sloboda Ukrainian gentry concerning their history was the work of Illia Kvitka on the Sloboda regiments, published in 1812—a banner year for the Russian Empire.³¹ In character, content, and style, that rather concise publication resembles the historico-archival-geographic compendia of the late eighteenth century devoted to Little Russia, with their authors' characteristic feelings of local and estate patriotism, heightened attention to ethnogenetic constructions of various kinds, and scrupulous enumerations of the services rendered by the "noble estate" to the monarchical throne.

The *Notes on the Sloboda Regiments* actively employ the discourse of the "foreign" origin of the first settlers, already mentioned in chapter 1, while saying comparatively little about their kinship with the neighboring Little Russians. According to the author, the Slobodians consisted of "Poles, Polish Ukrainians" and representatives of "other foreign peoples" who took on the general appellation of "Cherkasians," derived from the place of origin of the first families to arrive, in order to "distinguish their settlements and kin, a mixture of various tribes, from other peoples inhabiting Russia."³²

Such assertions were meant to help the author establish the "noble" origin of the Sloboda officers, most of whom, in his opinion, traced their ancestry from the Polish nobility (including, to be sure, the founder of the Kvitka clan).³³ Curiously, the author denies the claim of noble origin to the famous Kharkiv colonel and master of the table (*stol'nik*) Hryhorii Donets, celebrated in a poem by Jan Ornowski as a scion of the potent Zacharzewski/Zakharzhevsky clan.

Kvitka maintains that the lands of the Sloboda region belong to the local gentry by right of conquest and not historical inheritance. He denies that the region was inhabited even in the times of Kyivan Rus' and enters into polemics with his predecessors on that score; in his opinion, the first settlers found those lands empty, located "beyond the boundaries of Russia" and ruled by the Crimean Tatars. Having arrived from the Polish-Lithuanian Commonwealth, the settlers "subjected this land to the rule of the Russian monarch," thereby earning the right to the tsar's favors, licenses for enterprises, and privileges.[34] Thus the claims of the descendants of the Sloboda Cossacks to the Sloboda lands acquired a dual basis—by virtue of the "right of conquest" and tsarist grants.

With heavy implication, Kvitka stresses that the main reason prompting the ancestors of the Slobodians to leave their homeland and become subjects of the Russian monarch was his just administration of the law, which was known to all, and by no means the religious persecution of the Orthodox in the Commonwealth, which Kvitka does not even mention in the basic text of the work.[35] According to the author, the Slobodians came to be known as subjects of the tsar of their own free will, and not by compulsion. In these postulates one may discern the influence of the discourse of "equal rights," widespread among the Cossack elite, according to which their ancestors had pledged allegiance to other states exclusively as "equals with equals and freemen with freemen."

The legitimizing historical myth of the Sloboda Cossacks' services to the Russian throne included not only proofs of their courage and martial valor but also the virtue of "loyalty" manifested in the course of the rebellions of "traitors"—Hetmans Ivan Briukhovetsky and Ivan Mazepa. In the former instance, according to the author, the Slobodians did not yield to persuasions to join the rebellion and suffered at the hands of the Zaporozhians; in the latter, they stoutly defended Russia's borders against Mazepa's forces. That myth proved to be one of the most stable and influential components of regional discourse, surviving robustly to our own day.

Not surprisingly, Kvitka unconditionally condemns all encroachments of local Russian authorities on the privileges of the Sloboda regiments, as in the case of the "Belgorod *razriad* [department]," which limited the rights of settlers to distill liquor. If crowned heads permitted themselves such encroachments, they generally pass without comment in Kvitka's work, as, for example, in the passage devoted to "changes in the Sloboda regiments" during the reign of Anna Ioannovna. By contrast, all instances of lifting restrictions and reinstating privileges in the Sloboda region, as well as new tsarist favors bestowed on the Sloboda regiments, are described in detail on the basis of the relevant charters and manifestos.

Clearly, Kvitka's work is directly continuous with the historical conceptions of the local elite of the early eighteenth century. In that depiction of the past, the Sloboda region is still restricted in time and space: its history begins only in the mid-1640s, and its territory is defined with the aid of sociolegal markers; if the account manages to include, for example, the Ostrogozhsk regiment, then it is only with very significant reservations. In that regard the *Notes on the Sloboda Regiments* are not contemporaneous not only with the early nineteenth century, that is, with the time of their publication, but even with the late eighteenth century.

Nevertheless, Kvitka admitted at times that the Sloboda region might be part of the historical space of Little Russia. In 1816, in the pages of the Kharkiv journal *Ukrainskii vestnik*, he expressed the opinion that the name "Little Russia" belonged to the whole Left Bank of the Dnieper River, while the Right Bank continued to be known as "Ukraine."[36] The Chernihiv historian Mikhail Markov, who polemicized with Kvitka, indicated that both could extend to either bank of the Dnieper, but that the latter term was more closely associated with Cossackdom.[37] The Sloboda region had no particular ties with either term.

Can one discern an evolution of Kvitka's views on this basis? Most likely, new realities and conceptions did not supplant old ones in the consciousness of regional elites but joined them, creating a unique symbiosis whose internal contradiction did not particularly trouble the authors as it does the present-day reader. In any case, the notion of the death of the "old" regionalism in the early nineteenth century should be accepted only in a limited sense. Not only did the old regionalism not fade into oblivion, but it even gained a new impulse under the influence of historical, geographic, and ethnographic research.

The notion of the unity of historical Ukrainian regions had certainly arisen long before the dissolution of Cossack regional autonomy. Indeed, as noted in chapter 1, the "Little Russian" ethnocultural component, which united the inhabitants of the Sloboda region with their countrymen in the Hetmanate, had been present in the settlers' consciousness from the very beginning of their occupation of the land. Thus, in the historico-topographic description of Kharkiv submitted to the Catherinian commission charged with drafting the new Law Code of 1767, the city is said to have been founded by "freemen of the Little Russian people summoned from Trans-Dnieper and Little Russian towns according to privileges in order to defend the boundaries against the Crimean Tatars."[38]

Thus Andrei Aleinikov, a deputy from the Khopersk fortress to the Catherinian commission of 1767, spoke of one "Little Russian people in Little Russia and in the Sloboda regiments."[39] Educated migrants from Little Russia, for their part, also noted the historical and ethnocultural commonality of Slobodians and Little Russians. Hryhorii Kalynovsky, for example, described "Ukrainian wedding rituals of the common people" that were common to inhabitants of Little Russia and the Sloboda region.[40] Although the famous philosopher, moralist, and poet Hryhorii Skovoroda stood removed from new conceptions of the people as an ethnocultural community, his wandering helped give rise to the notion that this territory had a commonality marked on the one hand by the monasteries of Kyiv and Voronezh and, on the other, by the estates of the ancestral Cossack and gentry clans. In both cases this was mainly the territory of Little Russia and the Sloboda region. It was as if Skovoroda were demonstrating their historical and cultural affinity while simultaneously recognizing the differences between the two regions, calling the first his mother and the second his aunt.[41]

Much more productive in this regard were Russian and foreign travelers, including contemporaries of Skovoroda. Visiting the Sloboda region for the first time, and reflecting an "outsider's" view of it,[42] they noted differences not between Slobodians and Little Russians but between Little Russians and Russians. Comparative descriptions of the two peoples became something of a calling card of the Sloboda region. That circumstance in turn made it possible to reveal the ethnocultural boundary between the Sloboda region and the Great Russian lands proper, which until then had had a purely legal administrative status.

Most interesting in this regard is the testimony of Johann Güldenstädt, who traveled the Sloboda region in 1774.[43] Passing through the lands of Izium province along the so-called Ukrainian Line, established in 1732, he wrote that "all the aforementioned free lands (along the Donets) belong to Izium province and are settled by Little Russians, with the exception of smallholding free lands ... belonging to Katerynoslav province. Between those two lands there are constant border disputes, and indeed, one can hardly expect the merging of Muscovites with *khokhly*, as they jokingly call each other, that is, of Russians with Cherkasians or Rusnaks."[44] More than half a century after Güldenstädt, August von Haxthausen partly confirmed that conclusion, noting that villages in the Kharkiv gubernia were "wholly Little Russian" and differed from Great Russian villages, which were more reminiscent of German villages.[45]

The Russian traveler Vasilii Zuev, passing through the Sloboda region in 1781, described in detail the "first plainly Little Russian" settlement on his route—the small town of Lyptsi in the Kharkiv vicegerency, not far from its border with Kursk.[46] The people of that settlement were "completely different from the Russians as in speech and clothing, so in actions," but "not different from the Little Russians in any way." Zuev did not dwell on that in detail, considering ethnographic distinctions between Little Russians and Russians a well-known fact.

Another Russian traveler, Pavel Sumarokov, following the same route in 1803, also considered Lyptsi a border settlement; for him, the striking differences between ethnic Russians and Ukrainians probably were not such well-known facts as they were for Zuev, otherwise he would hardly have given free rein to his emotions and eloquence, describing how "in the tidy and merry house I find different faces, different habits, different clothes on the owners, different arrangements, and hear a different language. Can it be that this marks the boundary of the empire? Am I not entering another state?"[47]

The historian and diplomat Dmitrii Bantysh-Kamensky, passing through the Sloboda region six years after Sumarokov, in 1809, also delineated the ethnographic boundary between Ukrainian and Russian settlements quite clearly but located it "thirty-five versts from Kursk": "In the free settlement of Medvenka, where I changed horses, I saw for the first time Little Russian cottages whitened with clay inside and outside. This free settlement ... is inhabited entirely by Little Russians. ... When I asked one of the local peasants why their homes were whitened with clay, he answered me: 'We are not like the Muscovites; we like cleanliness.'"[48]

Contemporaries of Bantysh-Kamensky, particularly Prince Ivan Dolgorukov, who traveled through Kharkiv in the years 1810–17; the well-known historian and writer Mikhail Pogodin, who visited the Kharkiv region a decade later; and the ethnographer and statistician Vadim Passek also placed the provisional boundary between Russian and Ukrainian areas of settlement not far from present-day Kursk or Belgorod. In 1843 the German scholar August von Haxthausen placed the ethnographic boundary of Little Russia somewhere in the vicinity of the present-day town of Staryi Oskol in Belgorod oblast.[49] Thus, one may conclude that in terms of sociolegal status Sloboda Ukraine kept its distance from neighboring Little Russia but shared its ethnicity.

The relations of Sloboda Ukraine with the emerging South Russian region were different. As the latter became ever more clearly defined on the map, enthusiastically reformed by the most esteemed of Russian empresses, Catherine II, and developing into something of a model space of enlightened modernization, the Sloboda region became more closely associated with the south imagined as a space of modernity. Indeed, Sloboda Cossack regiments had been part of the south since the moment of their appearance in the mid-seventeenth century; as noted in the previous chapter, that process was associated from the outset with the military and administrative reform of the steppe borderland. It was as if Sloboda Ukraine were anticipating the paths of development of all Southern Russia, acting as a mediator between it, neighboring Little Russia, and Russia proper.

For many Russian travelers who passed Kharkiv on their way southward, following the route of Catherine II's famous journey to the Black Sea in 1787, Kharkiv was a southern city. Their travelogues symbolically united the Russian black-earth lands with the ethnically Ukrainian territories, as well as New Russia, the Black Sea littoral, and the Crimea, in the single virtual space of "Southern Russia." But the meaning of the latter was not clearly articulated. From the second half of the eighteenth century, some observers began to pay more attention to the ethnic characteristics of the local inhabitants. In the late 1780s, these observations led the author of the *Topograficheskoe opisanie Khar'kovskogo namestnichesta* (Topographic description of the Kharkiv vicegerency) to draw interesting conclusions.

## A New Vision?

Most students of the *Topographic Description* incline to the view that it was written by Ivan Pereverzev, the director of the public school in Kharkiv and a graduate of the local theological college.[50] The work contains, in particular, a comparative description of the Ukrainian and Russian inhabitants of the territory, as well as a historical outline of the Sloboda region and an attempt, unique for its time, to formulate the idea of the ethnocultural unity of Ukrainians regardless of their place of residence, political or even religious affiliation, on the basis of a "South Russian" definition.

It may be assumed that in some measure the *Topographic Description* became the reply of a local author to the comparative description of Ukrainians and Russians in the *Trudy Vol'nogo Ėkonomicheskogo Obshchestva* (Works of the Free Economic

Association) of 1768. In that publication, Sloboda Ukrainians are depicted in generally positive fashion as simple-hearted, tidy, reasonable, and god-fearing, but also "inept," "always seeking liberty," and indolent as compared to Great Russian serfs. In the opinion of the compilers or editors of the text, the "Cherkasian people" or "Cherkasians" were not so assiduous and industrious as Russian peasants because of "their former liberty."[51] They were said to be inclined to drunkenness, inactivity, and carelessness, inasmuch as they wandered from place to place, invoking their ancient privileges.

The interpretation of the same problem in the *Topographic Description*, published twenty years later, in 1788, looks entirely different. The author observes that it was precisely the local Ukrainians who taught their Great Russian neighbors better methods of husbandry and daily living, and that it was not their faults but their virtues that led them to be "careless"—a preference to be satisfied with little, "lack of envy," and "Spanish trustfulness."[52]

The general characterization of the "common temper of Ukrainian inhabitants" in Pereverzev's work is more in the nature of a panegyric: "The spirit of European benevolence, alien to Asiatic savagery, nourishes inner feelings with some kind of delight; the spirit of ambition, turning into a hereditary quality of the inhabitants, prevents slavish degradation and irresolution; it obeys the voice of the authorities voluntarily, without slavishness. The spirit of general competition bars the way to despotism and monopoly."[53] Similar panegyrics to the "native . . . not newly arrived . . . Slobodian," to borrow the words of Hryhorii Kvitka, would subsequently be interpreted and repeated in a wealth of variations by almost all local patriots of the region. In that regard, the influence of the *Topographic Description* on the formation of the local regional narrative can hardly be overestimated.

The author's position is hard to explain exclusively on the basis of local patriotism, given that Russian peasants had lived in the region for quite a long time and become part of the locality along with the Ukrainians. One can only surmise that the "pro-Ukrainian" assertions of Ivan Pereverzev, if indeed he was the author of the *Topographic Description*, were influenced to some degree by opposition to serfdom. The injustice of the enserfment of Ukrainian peasants was fully apparent even to the local gentry. Maintaining that they were inferior to Great Russian serfs in aptitude and way of life meant indirectly justifying that condition.

But the significance of Pereverzev's ethnographic observations rose above the regional level. He wrote his work at a time when the Kharkiv vicegerency was becoming part of the South Russian administrative and cultural space that was taking shape in the lands annexed to Russia—Little Russia, Zaporizhia, the Black Sea littoral, and the Crimea. Pereverzev also included the Sloboda region in the same South Russian space. Like his contemporary Opanas Shafonsky, he identified Southern Rus' with Kyivan Rus'. But Pereverzev did not reduce that space to historical or contemporary Little Russia, nor to the territories annexed to the Russian Empire in the late eighteenth century.

As the basis of his work Pereverzev took not the confessional, social, and administrative markers of the territory but the ethnocultural features of the population living there. On that basis he concluded that the inhabitants of the whole ethnic territory of contemporary Ukraine were historically and ethnoculturally one people, including those in the western lands, then living beyond the borders of the Russian Empire and belonging, at least in part, to the Uniate and not the Orthodox Church.

> The inhabitants of Southern Russia, separated from one another by distance between places, foreign rule, different administrations, civic customs, and speech, some also by religion (the Union), attract the gaze of the not unknowledgeable observer. When they gather for worship in Kyiv from the east, from the Volga and the Don, from the west, from Galicia and Lodomeria, and from places closer to Kyiv, they regard one another not as speakers of different languages but as if they were countrymen, yet with much that is foreign in words and actions, which seems strange to both parties; but in general all these scattered countrymen maintain filial piety toward the mother of their ancient dwelling places, the city of Kyiv, up to the present day.[54]

A comparison of Illia Kvitka's views concerning the Sloboda region with those of his predecessor, Ivan Pereverzev, allows one to discern both similarity and substantial difference. Like Kvitka, the author of the *Topographic Description* legitimized the "noble genealogy" of the first settlers: "all the ranks of the Sloboda region were largely of noble descent or children of officers, and rarely of the common people, but even for this outstandingly worthy qualities and merits were required."[55] At the same time, while Kvitka, following tradition, thought that the first settlers had established their forts and settlements "on the Tatar side," the author of the *Topographic Description* referred to the lands of the Kharkiv vicegerency as the "deserted legacy of their ancestors,"[56] thereby locating them in the historical space of Kyivan Rus'. Hence Southern Russia, which Pereverzev defines by reference to historical analogies with the Grand Principality of Kyiv, turns out de facto to be one and the same Little Russia.

In speaking of the unity of what would now be called Ukrainian national territory, Pereverzev stresses its difference from the Russia proper, defined by the "Great Russian" and "northern" markers. "This fateful division of Southern from Northern, or Great, Russia has transformed those inhabitants forever in such a way that from the latter there has come forth as if some kind of foreign nation; from the former there has developed the Little Russian Ukrainian dialect as an appanage language of a Slavic tribe."[57]

Roman Szporluk considers that the Kharkiv author managed to go beyond the traditional historico-geographic bounds of Little Russia and imagine a new map of Ukraine close to the one that exists today, including Kharkiv, Kyiv, and Lviv and based on an acknowledgment of the national unity of the local population residing in those lands.⁵⁸ Nevertheless, the Kharkiv scholar's intellectual innovation still needs to be explained. Can one consider that Pereverzev was ahead of his time, or were the views that he expressed typical of the intellectual milieu that developed in Kharkiv in the latter half of the eighteenth century?

It would be fair to assume that the author might have been in contact with scholars from Moscow University, among whom the previously mentioned Khariton Chebotarev had already established his reputation as one of the leading specialists in Russian geography. But there is no doubt that the observations about Ukrainian history and ethnography belong to the author or local correspondent of the *Topographic Description*. In any case, the idea of the geographic, historical, and ethnic coherence of Ukrainian territory in the west–east framework became conventional wisdom in the first half of the nineteenth century.⁵⁹

In the early 1820s, the notion of "Ukraine from the Carpathians to the Don, settled by a Ukrainian population of many millions," was expressed by the writer, historian, and educator Pavlo Biletsky-Nosenko of Chernihiv in a letter to the editors of the Kharkiv journal *Ukrainskaia zhizn'* (Ukrainian life).⁶⁰ It may be assumed that Biletsky-Nosenko was familiar with the *Nachertanie statistiki Rossiiskogo gosudarstva* (Statistical outline of the Russian state, 1818–19) by the Russian scholar Konstantin Arseniev, which divided the Russian Empire into ten regions. One of them was the Carpathian region, which included the lands extending from Warsaw to the Don River, encompassing all of present-day Ukraine together with the Crimea and the Black Sea region.⁶¹

## What Tongue Will Land You in Kharkiv?

The dissemination and inculcation of the Russian literary language in local society may be considered a cardinal element of the policy of cultural Russification conducted by the imperial center in the borderlands. Its transmitters were first and foremost the army, the bureaucracy, the courts and the system of law enforcement, as well as the institutions of religious and secular education. In the early nineteenth century, imperial Russian culture and its language had not yet attained distinct national parameters and norms. They were in the process of formation, of intellectual and aesthetic ferment, bringing together various components of the Orthodox Slavic (including Ukrainian) cultural tradition with Western intellectual innovations.

Members of the local gentry were glad to continue speaking colloquial Ukrainian with one another. In gentry salons and gatherings, local color made itself apparent through Ukrainian words and phrases with which the educated public sometimes liked to pepper its conversation, as well as through Ukrainian songs and melodies. This was insufficient to create a competitive Ukrainian-language milieu but quite enough to make the Ukrainian language a marker of a certain local distinctiveness and cultural specificity as compared to the language of the ethnic Great Russians who occupied various niches of modernized cultural space in the city and region.

In the first half of the nineteenth century, the Ukrainian vernacular generally prevailed over Russian in the Sloboda region. Speakers of Ukrainian and Russian continued to find difficulty in understanding one another even in the upper echelons of local society. It was no accident that Russian officials, intellectuals, and scholars on the one hand and Ukrainian publishers and authors of works of literature, history, and local lore on the other supplied their historical, literary, and ethnographic publications with Ukrainian-Russian glossaries intended to explain the particularities of the local language to the Russian-language reader.

Although the Ukrainian vernacular of the early nineteenth century remained poorly comprehensible to Russians, they did not find it a hostile or alien element. Moreover, besides its communicative function, the Ukrainian language had a symbolic and cultural one. In that capacity it was regarded first and foremost as a survival of ancient "Slavo-Rossian" tradition untouched by the leveling influence of European and urban civilization. By the same token, the Ukrainian language attracted the constant attention of archaizing Russian traditionalists concerned about Western cultural influence who sought to combat it by turning to the sources of "authentic" "folk" Slavo-Rossianism, that is, to the provinces. Furthermore, Ukrainian-language works were intended not only for elites. They were also supposed to reach the uneducated mass of the common people. That is why the Ukrainian language was not trampled under the hooves of the "Russian troika" immortalized by Nikolai Gogol. The foregoing explains why university professors and their students, coming to Kharkiv from Russia, set about learning the Ukrainian language and gathering the Ukrainian-language historical and literary heritage.

The works of Kharkiv authors of the early nineteenth century reflected the local cultural elite's search for a language capable of expressing the specifics of the region. At first this was literary Russian, though somewhat archaic in style, interspersed with vernacular Ukrainian words and phrases. True, Ukrainian was used basically to produce burlesque and parodistic humorous literature, but even such writing promoted the creation of a new literary Ukrainian on the basis of a living vernacular and the formation of a cultural fellowship inclined to use it.

Works of this nature often appeared in reaction to the intrusion of the Russian-speaking milieu into the everyday life of the Sloboda province. The year 1812 saw the premiere in St. Petersburg of a patriotic play by Aleksandr Shakhovskoi titled *Kazak-stikhotvorets* (The Cossack versifier), whose protagonist was a Cossack of the Kharkiv Sloboda regiment, the writer and poet Semen Klymovsky. The play, which aroused fervent sympathy among Russian audiences on the eve of the war with the "twelve languages" (the Napoleonic armies), was staged in Kharkiv in 1817. But there its reception was completely different. The reason was the language in which the Ukrainian characters in the play expressed themselves, which proved so incomprehensible to the local public that it felt itself insulted.[62]

A colorful sketch of the prevailing attitude toward the Russian vernacular in the everyday life of early nineteenth-century Kharkiv was left by Petro Hulak-Artemovsky, then one of the publishers of *Ukrainskii vestnik* and an instructor at Kharkiv University:

> Oh! They're already jabbering about who knows what in their own lingo! There's that outlandish language of theirs! Sometimes it happens that you stand in front of him for a good hour, and he minces and chops at you! What? The hell you can understand whatever it is he's chattering and going on about! You just think you catch him saying that *vot-s*, and *shto-s*, and *da-s*, and *net-s*, and *gavariu-kazhu, gavariu-kazhu* ["I say" in phonetic Russian spelling and correct Ukrainian], but what it is he's saying, you won't make sense of even with a priest![63]

The cultural orientations of the educated Sloboda elite in the late eighteenth and early nineteenth centuries reflected a generally contradictory fusion of particular elements of the European Enlightenment and the traditionalist's reaction against it, later strengthened by the influence of Romanticism. On the one hand, the gentry of that region gained the opportunity to make direct contact with the West by traveling abroad, arranging for their children to learn foreign languages in boarding schools maintained by foreigners, socializing with migrants from western Europe who settled among them, importing Western intellectual, economic, and material culture, and so on.

On the other hand, there was a constantly growing negative reaction in local society against Western fashions and culture: works by patriotically inclined Russian satirists, writers, and playwrights who had declared open warfare on "Gallomania" and incessantly mocked "Russian Parisians" in their works enjoyed considerable success in the region, including the Kharkiv theater. They inspired imitations by local writers, such as Akim Nakhimov, Vasilii Karazin, Hryhorii Kvitka, Petro Hulak-Artemovsky, and others.

Patriotic motifs, delving into Old Rus' antiquity and mythology, drawing on folklore, and struggling against Western cultural influence were characteristic traits of the work of Kharkiv writers and poets in the early nineteenth century. When the newly discovered *Tale of Igor's Campaign* was published in 1800, it immediately found ardent admirers in the Sloboda region, and the local landowner Aleksandr Palitsyn wrote perhaps the first poetic adaptation of its text in Russian. Local members of his literary circle maintained close connections with the conservative Russian Academy of Literature and its president, Aleksandr Shishkov, who opposed Nikolai Karamzin from the nationalist ("Slavo-Rossian") perspective.[64]

As "ancestral" ("Slavo-Rossian") culture was counterposed to Western culture, it became the practice to conceive of the cultural opposition between town and country in national terms. It was in the countryside—the new idealized microcosm of the local Russian gentry—that people sought the sources of old-fashioned

"Slavo-Rossian" culture, embodying liberty, morality, simplicity, and humaneness, as opposed to the "corrupt" Western influence of the town, with its hypocrisy, artificiality, imitativeness, envy, and the like. Naturally, the ideas and works of Jean-Jacques Rousseau found a receptive milieu and gained broad popularity in the "cultural nests" of educated landowners in the Sloboda region.

What has been said previously largely explains the success enjoyed in the Sloboda region by the Ukrainian philosopher, writer, and musician Hryhorii Savych Skovoroda (1722–94). Even now, the personality and works of the wandering philosopher, moralist, and poet do not lend themselves to a definitive treatment and can hardly be interpreted in terms of modern national culture.[65] Nor is there any need for that. Suffice it to say that the phenomenon of Hryhorii Skovoroda may be examined in a context conditioned by the reaction of the local Sloboda Ukrainian milieu to the modernization of the social and cultural life of the empire carried out by the Russian government in the era of Catherine II under the watchwords of the European Enlightenment.

Skovoroda remained halfway between the cultural epochs of the old Orthodox baroque tradition and the new secular culture of the Western Enlightenment. Wandering the territory of the former Sloboda regiments, like the descendants of the first colonists of the region, he did not fit into a society divided into estates. His works and way of life were clearly continuous with the historical period in which local society, not yet divided into castes, participated actively in church affairs, the small-town milieu was not opposed to that of the province, and spirituality rarely exceeded the bounds of religion. Perhaps that vital link with the bygone pre-Catherinian Sloboda region played no less a role in the posthumous cult of Skovoroda than the consonance of his ideas and way of life with the Rousseauist enthusiasms of the local gentry.

Skovoroda's name became widely known thanks to the efforts of representatives of the local cultural elite, beginning with his pupil and biographer, the landowner Mykhailo Kovalinsky, as well as his contemporaries Ivan Vernet and Gustav Adolf Hess de Calve, immigrants who had found a second homeland in the Sloboda region. Vasilii Karazin proudly asserted that "beneath a forelock and in a Ukrainian peasant jacket we had our own Pythagoras, Origen, and Leibniz."[66] By the early 1830s and 1840s, the name of Skovoroda, the "Ukrainian Diogenes," had already become almost the basic distinguishing cultural marker of the region, a symbol both of local color and of "Slavo-Rossian" patriotism. Subsequently, the philosopher's work would be inscribed in Ukrainian national discourse.

## Hryhorii Kvitka: Between Russia and Little Russia

Illia Kvitka's nephew Hryhorii Kvitka, a well-known public figure of the Sloboda region, an educator and one of the pioneers of modern Ukrainian literature, ac-

**Figure 3.1.** Hryhorii Fedorovych Kvitka (Osnov'ianenko) (1778–1843), one of the founding fathers of modern Ukrainian literature. © Wikimedia Commons.

tively studied the history of the region and its capital, Kharkiv.[67] Because it was Hryhorii Kvitka who took on the publication of his uncle's *Notes on the Sloboda Regiments*, that work was long attributed to him. In 1840 he published an article "On the Sloboda Regiments" in the journal *Sovremennik* (The contemporary) that turned out to be nothing other than a creative reworking of Illia Kvitka's text.

As one compares Hryhorii Kvitka's work with his uncle's publication, the similarities and differences in their views are readily apparent.[68] What makes them similar is both authors' conception of the Sloboda region as "valiant and loyal," deserving of the Russian monarchs' favor and of its modest rights and privileges. A common element in their accounts may also be discerned in their conviction that the first settlers came "from abroad" and in their insistent efforts to prove the "noble" origins of the regional gentry and not to conceal the particular merits and distinction of their ancestors from posterity.

The differences in tonality between the two publications derive largely from the greater influence on Hryhorii Kvitka than on his uncle of the ethnocultural components of the national discourse that was developing in his time, which led him to take a different approach to certain key aspects of the region's history. I note immediately that the influence turned out to be profoundly contradictory. Above all, Hryhorii Kvitka actively affirmed that the Sloboda region belonged to the "all-Russian" historical and cultural space. He did not follow in the footsteps of his predecessor, who had denied that the region belonged to Kyivan Rus' and had calmly "given away" its territory to the Tatars. On the contrary, Hryhorii Kvitka attempted to prove the "Russian" allegiance of the Sloboda region from ancient times (since the first centuries of the Common Era, "if not earlier"), declaring that the lands of Sloboda Ukraine had never "constituted possessions of ... the Tatars," while Polish claims to that territory could simply be dismissed as "invalid and imaginary."[69]

The theme of "return to one's own home," whose relevance to the settlers was denied by Illia Kvitka but affirmed by Ivan Pereverzev, thus found its continuation in the work of Hryhorii Kvitka. This allows one to grasp his interpretation of the reasons for Ukrainian resettlement of the steppe borderland. It turned out that the main reason was not the "legal preferences" of the juridically enlightened Slobodians but the religious persecution of the Orthodox in the Commonwealth, to which the historian of the Age of Enlightenment Illia Kvitka, apparently out of absent-mindedness, attached no particular significance.

Despite his stress, in the spirit of official ideology, on the motifs of "Russianness" and Orthodoxy in the interpretation of regional history, Hryhorii Kvitka went against the current in the direction of deepening the historical and cultural differences between Sloboda Ukraine and Little Russia. According to him, the Slobodians, fortunate under the paternal rule of Russia, "cared nothing at all" for the fate of their former homeland, Little Russia, and played no part in the upheavals taking place there at the time, their only goal being to "remain faithful to the government, which was benevolent to them. No circumstances could deter them from this: neither disturbances and danger from the Tatars nor urgings of fellow tribesmen who, having become subjects of Russia, often wavered in maintaining their oath in complete purity."[70]

In a letter of 28 December 1841 to Andrei Kraevsky, Hryhorii Kvitka asserted:

> We Slobodians do not constitute Little Russia. They, the Little Russians, were still hemming and hawing over how to disengage from the impious Poles and thinking to whom it would be more advantageous to attach themselves when our ancestors, not pausing for thought, got up and went to their own father, the Russian tsar, settled the free lands along the border ... and began fighting off the Tatars and shielding Russia with their own bodies.[71]

The same idea is to be found in his "Tatar Invasions," accompanied by caustic remarks about the Little Russians, who had "gone mad for some time and veered off the true path," trying to get the Slobodian settlers to "do their dirty work" for them.[72]

Even so, Hryhorii Kvitka's Sloboda regional discourse was based not only on historico-political but also on ethnocultural factors. He agreed that "the peoples who settled the present-day Kharkiv gubernia were mainly Ukrainians and had the same language and customs as the Little Russians"; he was even prepared to admit that the Little Russians were the elder brethren of the Slobodians, although he emphasized that the Slobodians "since the time of their settlement here had diverged from them considerably, resulting in a notable difference."[73]

Kvitka, who wrote works in both Russian and Ukrainian, even insisted on the difference between the language of the Slobodians and that of the Little Russians, asserting that the former was "much more purified than Little Russian" and that the local inhabitants did not understand many Little Russian words.[74] It may have been precisely under Kvitka's influence that the Russian publisher of the Kharkiv almanac *Utrenniaia zvezda* (Morning star), Ivan Petrov, emphasized the difference between the Little Russian and Ukrainian dialects.[75]

It is readily apparent that in this case the "Slobodian" vernacular was assigned the role that the "Little Russian" language had played in relation to "Russian": the "purified" language was considered the one not "distorted" by foreign borrowings and thus closer to the primordial "Slavic" base. Emphasizing what distinguished the vernacular of the Slobodian commoners both from Little Russian, "spoiled" by Polish loan words, and from Russian, which contained French words, the Sloboda patriot Hryhorii Kvitka strove to endow it with a higher status among the provincial sources of "native" Slavo-Rossian antiquity. Hypothetically, it may have been just such assertions that aroused objections from Taras Shevchenko, who noted that Kvitka "did not lend an ear to the language, perhaps because he had not heard it in the cradle from his mother."[76]

Touching on the question of the Slobodians' ethnic composition, Kvitka had recourse to the same discourse of "foreignness" that his predecessor Illia Kvitka had used, endowing it not with social but ethnocultural content by stressing that "the inhabitants of these Sloboda regiments began calling themselves 'Cherkasians' in order to distinguish themselves from Little Russians, Poles and others, thereby creating something in the nature of a distinct people."[77] That "something in the nature of a distinct people" possessed not only a name, genealogy, and history of its own but also a fully delineated territory. It is another matter that Kvitka defined the ethnic space of the Sloboda region no longer in opposition to Little Russia but to Russia proper (Great Russia).

In Kvitka's works, the territory of the "small motherland" takes on an integral character and a unique ethnicity, including not only Kharkiv but also such settlements as Derhachi, Vilshana, Kolomak, and Borisovka (the latter a village in Kursk gubernia known for its painters of religious art). For the Russian traveler Pavel Sumarokov, the small town of Lyptsi symbolized the transition from Russia to Little Russia, while for Kvitka, observing Lyptsi from the opposite side of the "boundary," that small town was marked by a tavern—a symbol of "Raseia" and "Muscovite nature."[78]

The construct of regional Sloboda identity created by Kvitka on a historico-cultural basis was crowned with his characterization of the "ideal Ukrainian"—an inhabitant of the Sloboda region. In his article "Ukrainians," published in the St. Petersburg journal *Sovremennik* in 1841, Kvitka wrote as follows on the subject: "The Slobodian ... is tidy, hospitable, sincere, polite"; he is honest and sincere, thanks to which he is unable to cheat anyone but often falls victim to a swindle himself; he is obedient and devoted to authority, without which he does not want to take a step; he aspires to learning and has no few achievements in that domain, especially the local clergy, which may be considered exemplary "with regard to knowledge and morals"; he loves music and art and has an aptitude for them.

> From the very beginning of their settlement here to the present day, there has been nary a sound of any notable criminal offenses or violations of the cardinal rules of religion and loyal fulfillment of duty to authority among the Slobodians, and no inhabitant of this gubernia, neither in the army nor outside the gubernia or the fatherland, has anywhere or in any instance forgotten his duty to the throne or besmirched this gubernia, always loyal and devoted to those in authority.[79]

Both the differences and the similarities of this portrait of the "Ukrainian" to the one produced half a century earlier by the author of the *Topographic Description* are readily apparent. In Kvitka's depiction, the ideal Slobodian of the times of Nicholas I more closely resembles a loyal subject than a courtier described by Pereverzev, brimming with the sense of his own dignity, "obeying the voice of the authorities voluntarily, without slavishness." Along with this, it may be noted that in the "Slobodian portrait" drawn by Kvitka it is social and not ethnic characteristics that take pride of place, which is equally true of Pereverzev's sketch.

The foregoing permits the assumption that Kvitka—delineating the boundaries of the Sloboda region both in the north, with Russia, and in the west, with Little Russia, seeking to establish the presence of a particular territory, an ethnic genealogy, a historical past, and specific features of the language spoken by the local inhabitants—was thereby creating certain conditions for the formation of ethnocultural regionalism. And yet Kvitka went no further along that path. He stopped when, in his literary work, he turned to the conversational vernacular of the Ukrainian commoners of the Sloboda region.

Kvitka, who wrote in both Russian and Ukrainian, repeatedly described tragicomic situations produced by mutual incomprehension between Russians and Ukrainians. In one of his stories, he describes a meeting in the imperial capital between a Russian soldier "discharging his duties" and a Ukrainian landowner from the Cossack officer class. After a series of amusing misunderstandings resulting from their interaction, the disheartened soldier hears out a lecture from his older companion on the subject of who the Little Russians are: "After all, they, like Turks and Tatars, are a different people, and they have a language of their own"; they are "not ours" and only pretend to be Orthodox out of guile and fear of Russia.[80] And so it is language again that shows the presence of a dividing line between Ukrainian and Russian cultural space, now on the level of "high" culture.

It was indeed the language chosen by Kvitka for his literary work that placed a symbolic limit on the cultural integration of the Ukrainian Sloboda region into the common space of the Russian Empire. It is the Little Russian language and not the Slobodian regional dialect that Kvitka calls "ours": it is in this sense that he writes in a letter of 28 December 1841 to Andrei Kraevsky of a translation "from our language into Russian"; that "we should and must write in our language"; of the "schism perpetrated by Russian journals against our language"; finally, he affirms the historical priority of "our" language over Russian, basing that priority on the closeness of the language to "native Slavic."[81] Notable with regard to the latter instance is Kvitka's polemic with Nikolai Tikhorsky in the conservative Slavophile journal *Maiak* (Beacon) in the early 1840s. In one of the replies to his opponent, Kvitka expresses himself utterly in the spirit of linguistic nationalism, close in character to the *Istoriia Rusov*, with its exclusive claims to the historico-cultural legacy of Rus'.[82]

In the final analysis it was precisely the Little Russian language, which the "Ukrainian" writer Hryhorii Kvitka chose for his work, that proved conducive to the unification of Sloboda Ukraine with Little Russia in the process of nation-building, which transformed the cultural and linguistic space of the "Slavo-Rossian people." But Kvitka's national and linguistic choice was not the only possible one. Another variant may be seen in the example of the life and activity of Vasilii Karazin, a contemporary of Kvitka.

## Vasilii Karazin: Between Russia and Southern Russia

The formation of Slobodian regional discourse at the beginning of the nineteenth century is indissolubly associated with the name of another eminent representative of the Sloboda gentry elite, Vasilii Karazin, the educator and innovator who initiated and inspired the Kharkiv University project. His role in the founding of the university was discussed in the preceding chapter. Here it must be noted that Karazin had much in common with Hryhorii Kvitka: both men were ardent patriots of the Sloboda region; both acted under the watchwords of enlightenment and modernization; as public figures, both possessed outstanding leadership qualities; and, finally, both were loyal subjects of the empire with conservative political views.

At the same time, compared to the "humanist" Kvitka, Karazin took a greater interest in practical questions associated with politics, economics, technology, and the natural sciences, with much less of a bent for folklore and popular "traditions."

It was perhaps Karazin who, for the first time in the intellectual life of the region, formulated the notion of its territory as a "small fatherland," a *patria*, part of the "great fatherland"—Russia. In 1802, in his speech to the Sloboda gentry on the need to establish a university in Kharkiv, Karazin described the Sloboda region as follows:

> The location of our gubernia makes it the center of the most fertile southern lands. ... The aptitudes of our countrymen are well known; people in the capitals have become used to respecting talent as our natural possession. Our air is salutary, our climate gentle, capable of enticing even foreigners, whom we will invite to join us. The land shows tremendous readiness for enterprise of every kind—the arts and sciences will establish themselves in our homeland; they will consider it their own; they will bethink themselves of Greece, the land sacred to them, which originally bequeathed them to the southern land of Russia at a time when the rest of Europe was still drowning in ignorance and barbarously spilling the blood of nations.[83]

The "Greek" allusions with regard to the Sloboda region, scattered throughout many of Karazin's works, doubtless reflected his aspiration to celebrate his homeland, to single it out from other provinces of the empire with the aid of outstanding, familiar symbols of Enlightenment culture. He was not alone in that aspiration and proceeded along trodden paths. The Polish philosopher and educator Stanisław Staszic, for example, believed his motherland to be the nation that should play the role of Greece for the Russian Empire, which, by the way, struck a receptive chord among at least some Russian intellectuals. Comparisons of various cities of the empire with Athens were also popular. Considering that Athens figured as the most common embodiment of Greece as a center of culture and enlightenment, the Russian traveler to "Southern Russia" Vladimir Izmailov assigned the role of the Russian Athens, naturally enough, to his native Moscow.

And yet references to Athens did not exhaust the "Greek" discourse of Enlightenment culture. Aside from militant Sparta, it was also represented by Arcadia—a symbol of happy, carefree patriarchal life against the background of a nature benevolent to man. For example, a contemporary of Izmailov, the Russian traveler Petr Shalikov, discovered "Arcadia" in Poltava, a city in the vicinity of Kharkiv.[84] Reminiscences of antiquity, familiar in Enlightenment cultural discourse, would be used several decades longer to mark Ukrainian territories until they were crowded out by new historical and geographic symbols introduced by Romanticism and realism.

Returning to Karazin, it must be emphasized that his own patriotic doctrine, while following changes in the cultural and political life of the empire, always made place for its author's dual identity, which combined love for the "small motherland" that was his home with the common fatherland—the Russian Empire. As he wrote, "My life belongs to the whole fatherland, but in particular to the land that was the cradle of my ideas. I am already blessed a hundredfold if chance has made it possible for me to do the slightest good for my beloved Ukraine, whose welfare is so closely bound up in my understanding with the welfare of gigantic Russia."[85]

Karazin's notions about the past of the Sloboda region corresponded in many ways to those expressed at various times by Pereverzev and Kvitka. They included, in particular, a patriotic aspiration to prove that the land belonged to the historical space of Kyivan Rus', a conviction of the profound antiquity of its settlement, the thesis of the persecution of the Orthodox in the Polish-Lithuanian Commonwealth as the main reason for their resettlement in the Sloboda region, and the view that the Cossack officers were of noble descent, meritorious in the struggle against the "Crimean barbarians."[86]

Like Kvitka, Karazin sought to substantiate the ethnocultural differences between the Slobodians and the Little Russians. Publishing his "Zamechaniia o Slobodsko-Ukrainskoi gubernii" (Observations on the Sloboda Ukraine gubernia) in 1820, Karazin wrote that "the people of the Sloboda Ukraine gubernia, though belonging to the Little Russians from ancient times and having the same language and customs as they, have changed considerably over the time of their settlement in these places."[87] In his opinion, they had drawn closer to the "general mass of the Russian people," as a result of which "the local people and gentry have become more Russified ... than their neighbors,"[88] which had influenced their language as well.

At the same time Karazin, unlike Kvitka, regarded ethnic Ukrainians as if from a distance, explaining to his reader, for example, that the local people were known to the Great Russians as *khokhly* but were in fact the same Slavo-Rossians, only they had migrated from Red Rus' and come to the region in the late sixteenth century.[89] Karazin himself often used the term *khokhol* or even *khokhlik* with reference to the local population, but not in the derogatory sense, given that he spoke of the aptitude of the *khokhly* for the arts and sciences.

Speaking of the "Russification" of the Slobodians and their drawing together with the "general mass of the Russian people," Karazin nevertheless did not renounce the practice of offering comparative descriptions of the Ukrainian and Russian population, as had been done since the latter half of the eighteenth century. Those descriptions were generally based on the principle of mutual complementarity and not opposition of ethnic Russians and Ukrainians: "The Great Russian is more industrious and ready to serve. The inhabitant of Kharkiv is tidier, hospitable, and polite. The Ukrainian is more charitable, aspires more to learning, and has greater aptitude for the arts; the Great Russians for crafts," and so on.[90] Nevertheless, the very comparison of Ukrainians and Russians, which obliged the author to formulate their collective distinguishing features, created opportunities to place them in opposition and thereby to deepen cracks in the space of "Slavo-Rossian" culture under the influence of national ideas.

Not long before his death, Karazin—after efforts to develop the Ukrainian literary language on the basis of local vernaculars had become apparent—was faced with the inevitability of defining his attitude toward the language problem. It was this very inevitability that divided Kvitka and Karazin—patriots of the Sloboda region hitherto united by commonality of regional, estate, and educational interests. Karazin discerned political sedition in Taras Shevchenko's Ukrainian verses dedicated to Kvitka and, as was his wont, did not hesitate to inform the higher authorities about them.[91] At the same time, he came out against Ukrainian-language publications in the almanac *Molodyk* (New moon), not because he found them politically dubious but merely because they were written in Ukrainian and contained material drawn from Ukrainian folklore.

"It is unfortunate that he [Ivan Betsky, the founder of the Kharkiv almanac *Molodyk*] named it in the *khokhol* language, against my advice," wrote Karazin to the famous Russian historian Mikhail Pogodin in 1842. "That name, which forces one to suspect that it will take only *khokhol* pieces, of which everyone has already had enough, and which, believe me, our Kharkivites (who have long proudly identified themselves with old Russia) prize less than anyone else, gives pause to many."[92]

Karazin's position in this case is wholly comparable to Vissarion Belinsky's view on the lack of prospects for Ukrainian literature and the need for the linguistic Russification of Ukrainians. Karazin had dreamed of the time when his fatherland would change its "Ukrainian" name to "Kharkivite," becoming completely integrated into the renovated cultural space of the Russian Empire and forgetting its borderland past. But this did not mean that the Slobodian educator was cutting his ties with his "small motherland."

Unlike Belinsky, Karazin believed that provincial culture, merging with all-Russian culture, had both the capacity and the duty to enrich the latter with its own cultural uniqueness and thereby promote its further development, renewal, and cultural enrichment. By the same token, Karazin promoted the development of conceptions of his homeland's regional specificity. The direction of development of imperial discourse that he advocated—from the bottom up, from borderland to capital, from province to center—assumed, one way or another, not the leveling of local particularities but their cultivation.

## The Dilemma of Russian Nationalism

With the coming to power of Nicholas I (1825–55), the situation in the Russian Empire changed substantially. The reforms of the new government were meant to promote the further unification of the geographic, sociolegal, and national space of the Russian Empire. In the Ukrainian lands, the last remnants of local sociolegal particularities in the form of the court system based on the Lithuanian Statute, Magdeburg law, and certain Cossack and gentry privileges were liquidated.⁹³ In connection with this, a new governmental program for the study of local history, geography, the economy, and statistics was mounted along the Ukrainian-Russian border from the late 1830s. It was comparable in scale perhaps only to the "scientific expeditions" and "topographic descriptions" of the times of Catherine II.

The conception of territorial integrity or regional specificity again turned out to be closely associated with empire- and nation-building. In the times of Nicholas I, nationality policy was predicated on Russia's opposition to western Europe and based mainly on historical and religious factors. In the doctrine of Count Sergei Uvarov, formulated as "Orthodoxy, autocracy, *narodnost'*," the last link was the most enigmatic and weakest because of its vagueness, simultaneously dissolving the national essence in imperial, social, and religious factors under the umbrella of "all-Russianness." In the words of Serhy Yekelchyk, the formula was a reaction but not a response to the new idea of the nation.⁹⁴

But Russian society, though weighed down by the imperial burden, turned out to be ahead of its government in matters of nation-building. It found its own national heartland, the historical and cultural nucleus of the Russian Empire, by no means in the Black Sea steppes, as the Russian government probably wished, and even less on the territory of "Little Russia," as patriots of the former Hetmanate probably would have liked, but in Moscow, which remained the principal and traditional meeting place for the provincial gentry and thus took on the role of "natural" center of provincial Russia, as opposed to cosmopolitan, Europeanized St. Petersburg.⁹⁵

It was precisely in Moscow in the early 1830s that perhaps the boldest effort ever was made to reformulate Russian imperial history in terms of modern Russian nationalism. It came in 1830 in the form of a review by the Russian historian and writer Nikolai Polevoi of Dmitrii Bantysh-Kamensky's *History of Little Russia*.⁹⁶ Polevoi, approaching history not from the dynastic viewpoint, as did his predecessor Nikolai Karamzin, but with an ethnocultural standard, drew a dividing line between Russian and Ukrainian (Little Russian) history and culture for the first time in Russian historiography, asserting that "to the present day the Little Russians merely profess the Greek faith, speak a particular dialect of the Russian language, and belong to the political structure of Russia, but by nationality they are not Russian at all."⁹⁷ The Little Russians were "a people completely different from us, pure Russes. Their language, clothing, facial structure, everyday life, dwellings, opinions, and popular beliefs are not ours at all! We shall say more: even now they take an unfriendly view of us there."⁹⁸

In fact, Polevoi was renouncing notions, as widespread as they were archaic, of the common "Russianness" of the Little Russians, Great Russians, and Belarusians, cultivated since the times of the *Synopsis* mainly by representatives of the Little Russian clerical and secular elites. He attacked those notions from the viewpoint of exclusive modern nationalism, deconstructing the premodern "Slavo-Rossian" identity by adopting only the "Great Russian" elements included in it and rejecting everything else, in this case "Little Russian," as superfluous.

Nevertheless, this attempt to create a modern Russian national discourse and replace the imperial one was supported neither by the imperial government nor by the conservative camp of the intellectual elite, whether Great Russian or Little Russian. Little Russian intellectuals, including Mykhailo Maksymovych, Mykola Hohol/Nikolai Gogol, and other contemporaries hastened to contribute their own regional page to the annals of the "Slavo-Rossian people," lightly revised since the times of the *Synopsis*. Hryhorii Kvitka was no exception in that regard, although, comparing Polevoi's cited remarks with the previous quotation from Kvitka's story about the conversation of two Russian soldiers about Little Russians, we shall not encounter all that many differences.

Yet the first step had been taken toward secularizing the concept of the "Slavo-Rossian people." National ideas, increasingly influential in Russian society, were setting Ukrainian and Russian intellectuals apart. The umbrella of "Russianness," tugged in opposite directions by "Little Russians" and "Great Russians," finally ended up in the hands of the latter. But that did not by any means entail the disappearance of Little Russian identity. It continued to exist alongside Ukrainian national identity and even began a fierce struggle with the latter in the late nineteenth and early twentieth centuries.

On the other hand, the Russian "westernizers," prizing modernization above searches for Slavic antiquity, were also not about to disappear from the social and cultural life of the empire. Starting approximately from the latter half of the 1830s, their voices grew ever louder in the general chorus of well-intentioned but not always concordant subjects of Emperor Nicholas I. The example of Vissarion Belinsky is not superfluous in that regard. From that time on, the ratings of the provinces began to fall in the opinion of the capital as, one after another, the literary clichés of "Italy," "Switzerland," "Arcadia," and other illusions pleasant to the ear were dispelled by the sight of scenes from the daily lives of "dead souls" and "Old World landowners" vividly described by Hohol/Gogol.

## The Kharkiv Romantics

With the development of a system of secular education, learning, and the expansion of public space for secular culture in the cities, the basic role in the promotion of modern national consciousness passed to the intelligentsia, which had close ties with the gentry.[99] University towns became the main channels for the transmission of European culture and learning to the provinces, as well as centers for the rise and development of national ideas and institutions. This allowed the intellectual elite, including its representatives in the provinces, to participate directly in the formation of modern national consciousness in the Russian Empire in its various iterations.

Romanticism as an essential precondition for the reception and reproduction of national ideas in the Ukrainian context is very often associated with German influences disseminated by Kharkiv University, which allegedly inspired the younger generation of intellectuals to collect local folklore and experiment with the vernacular. This view requires considerable limitation, as it reflects the intellectual situation of the 1830s–40s and should not be extrapolated to the early nineteenth century, when intellectual life was still influenced by the European Enlightenment rather than nascent Romanticism.

It was at this time that Romanticism aroused a new wave of interest in folk culture in local Kharkiv society. The assimilation of Romantic culture, mainly through Russian and Polish "mediation," led to the formation in Kharkiv of new intellectual circles in the late 1820s and early 1830s that consisted mainly of students, graduates, and instructors of the university. Quite a few Polish students took part in Kharkiv literary evenings devoted to the discussion of Ukrainian themes and subjects. During his time at Kharkiv University, Professor Ignacy Daniłowicz did much to promote interest in Ukrainian ethnography and history among local students.[100] Among his students there was the beginning Ukrainian Romantic writer Levko Borovykovsky, who studied Polish language and literature and translated works of Adam Mickiewicz into Ukrainian.

Another graduate of Kharkiv University, Nikolai/Mykola Kostomarov, turned in his early work to the theme of the historical Polish-Ukrainian borderland, Cossack revolts, and religious conflict in the Polish-Lithuanian Commonwealth of the sixteenth and seventeenth centuries. His dissertation on the religious union caused a reaction more typical of borderland mentality than the calm assurance of the imperial center. At the insistence of Metropolitan Innokentii of Kharkiv, the dissertation was not approved for defense and burned, fortunately without involving the author in the flames.[101]

The literary and scholarly circle headed by Izmail Sreznesky may be considered the calling card of Kharkiv Romanticism. It served to unite graduates of Kharkiv University who were enthusiastic about ideas of "nationality" and "Slavdom," wholly in the spirit of the official policy proclaimed by Sergei Uvarov. Their activities led to the development of Ukrainian-language prose, poetry, criticism, and dramaturgy, as well as historiography and ethnology. In Kharkiv the basic tribunes of the new generation of intellectuals were the literary almanacs that replaced the Kharkiv journals of the early nineteenth century.[102] The first of them was *Ukrainskii al'manakh* (1831), which published, among other material, texts of Ukrainian folk and epic songs, works on Ukrainian history, and poetic variations on the Cossack theme. It was continued in 1834 by two issues of the almanac *Utrenniaia zvezda* (Morning Star), with the second issue containing exclusively Ukrainian-themed and mainly Ukrainian-language publications by Hryhorii Kvitka, Petro Hulak-Artemovsky, Ivan Kotliarevsky, Yevhen Hrebinka, and Izmail Sreznevsky.

Another serial prepared by Izmail Sreznevsky was *Ukrainskii sbornik* (Ukrainian Miscellany), whose two issues included the texts of Ivan Kotliarevsky's popular plays *Natalka-Poltavka* (Natalka, the girl from Poltava, 1838) and *Moskal'-charivnyk* (The Muscovite-sorcerer, 1841). In the 1840s several issues of the almanac *Molodyk* (New moon) were published with the participation of mainly Ukrainian authors. Most of the works printed in those publications came to be regarded as classics of the new Ukrainian literature.

The thematic miscellany *Zaporozhskaia starina* (Zaporozhian antiquity), six issues of which appeared between 1833 and 1838, is considered the best known and most influential publication of the Kharkiv Romantics. It featured historical, folkloric, and literary items in various genres devoted to the history of Ukrainian Cossackdom. A good portion of them turned out to be stylizations of folkloric and manuscript sources by contemporary authors in the spirit of traditional epics and historical fiction. The geography associated with that history took in not only the neighboring Little Russian gubernias but also the lands of the former Zaporozhian Sich, as well as Right-Bank and, in part, western Ukraine. In other words, the "Little Russia" of the Kharkiv Romantics rose above the traditional boundaries of historical regions and was basically coterminous with Ukrainian ethnic territory.

The Kharkiv Romantics functioned as cultural communicators, mediators, and "gatherers of the cultural heritage" rather than conscious promoters of the Ukrainian national revival. Their intellectual associations remained extraordinarily fluid, diffuse, and ambivalent.[103] Their writings fitted comfortably into the framework of the official imperial doctrine of "Orthodoxy, autocracy, *narodnost'*" and even helped the careers of those members of the circle who subsequently devoted themselves to government service. They contributed to the development of Ukrainian studies within the broad pan-Russian intellectual framework.

It was no accident that the leader of the circle, Izmail Sreznevsky, carefully distanced himself from anything reminiscent of idealization of the Ukrainian Cossack past even before his transfer to St. Petersburg. In his *Historical Survey of the Civil Organization of Sloboda Ukraine from the Time of Its Settlement to Its Transformation into the Kharkiv Gubernia*, Sreznevsky referred to the times of Cossack self-rule in the spirit of Nikolai Polevoi and Vissarion Belinsky as "half-savage independence" and a "semi-nomadic type of civilization."[104] After that, almost half a century would pass before the history of the Sloboda region in Cossack times was reinterpreted in a different and positive manner in the works of Dmytro Bahalii, Mykola Sumtsov, and their followers.

The late 1830s and 1840s turned out to be a crossroads from which the paths of the Ukrainian and Russian intellectual elites began to divide. From the same period, one can speak of diverging cultural orientations among the older generation of the Slobodian intelligentsia, particularly apparent in the example of Hryhorii

Kvitka and Vasilii Karazin. Thus, the priority of political loyalty over language and religion, hitherto the basic principle of relations between the monarchy and local elites, began gradually to give way to ethnocultural versions of collective and personal identity during the rule of Nicholas I. Often despite the regional (Sloboda Ukrainian) and imperial (Slavo-Rossian) patriotism of the gentry elite, this process emphasized the Little Russian identity of the local inhabitants. This identity, expressed in the Ukrainian language, could not help but influence the perception of Sloboda Ukraine as a specific region, a borderland between Ukraine/Little Russia and Russia/Great Russia.

## Border or Borderland?

From the beginning of the nineteenth century, writings about the Sloboda region began referring to it as "inauthentic" Little Russia, which was distinguished at the same time from "authentic" Great Russia. The character of Sloboda Ukraine had already been termed ethnoculturally ambivalent by the aforementioned Dmitrii Bantysh-Kamensky in his travel notes of 1810: in his words, the inhabitants of the Sloboda region, living, "so to speak, on the border dividing Great from Little Russia ... differ greatly as from native Little Russians, so from Russians, from whom they have adopted certain customs."[105] In the early nineteenth century, the thesis that the local population was being Russified became one of the most commonly encountered assertions in writings and comments on the subject by local intellectuals.

The subject of the Russification of the Sloboda region entered not only scholarly and artistic but also official discourse. In this regard one might mention the statements of the governor of Kharkiv, Vasilii Muratov, who noted that the residents of the gubernia entrusted to his care "differ considerably from Little Russians."[106] Nevertheless, if one examines his argumentation closely, it becomes apparent that he basically limited those differences to the institutional and cultural aspects of community life. It turns out that "Kharkivites" differed from their relatives in Poltava and Chernihiv mainly in that 1) Slobodians were subordinate to one government; 2) many Russians—landowners, officials, and merchants—had settled in the Kharkiv region and its gubernia center; and 3) the headquarters of the commander of troops "in the southern land" were located in Kharkiv. In other words, the learned governor attached no particular importance to ethnocultural affairs in the course of his activity.

Kharkiv travelers heading for Russia, for their part, confirmed the existence of an ethnocultural boundary between Ukrainians and Russians but perceived it differently from Russian travelers. Thus, the Kursk gubernia, which most Russian travelers saw as marking the boundary between Great Russia and Little Russia, was similarly perceived by their countryman Izmail Sreznevsky. But because a Kharkiv man of letters was crossing it from the other, "Little Russian" side, he was delighted to find "everything Russian, everything absorbing" in Kursk: the Russian peasant women's headdresses (*kokoshniki*) and dresses (*sarafany*) made his "ardent" heart beat faster.[107]

Such observations prompt the conclusion that the ethnic boundary between Ukrainians and Russians, which was becoming better defined, did not differ greatly from the one that had arisen previously on the basis of particular privileges (*slobody*) enjoyed by local inhabitants. Furthermore, the provisional boundary between the Sloboda region and Great Russia was turning into a border between Little Russia and Great Russia under the influence of ethnocultural characteristics. But this was a rather distinctive border, delineated not by swing-beam barriers or sentry boxes but by such markers, which would later become stereotypical, as picturesque landscapes, tidy white cottages, dress, language, the way of life of the local population, and the like.

Nevertheless, it may be assumed that by the mid-nineteenth century the cultural Russification of the region had achieved a measure of success. It may also be assumed that for that very reason Dmitrii Kachenovsky, a "westernizer" and professor of Kharkiv University, and shortly afterward the Russian publicist and Slavophile Ivan Aksakov as well, drew a provisional line dividing the borderland Sloboda region from the "native," "authentic" Little Russia between Kharkiv and Poltava in the vicinity of the town of Valky, located about 50 kilometers from Kharkiv. But the cultural Russification of the Sloboda region by no means entailed the loss of its regional specificity.

The Russian intellectual toolbox of the mid-nineteenth century simply lacked the requisite definitions to specify the particularities of the cultural borderland. Hence Sloboda Ukraine often found itself deprived of clearly expressed characterizations, as it combined attributes of both historical Little Russia and Russia proper. Consequently, the region took on features of an ethnoculturally amorphous, diffuse space on the one hand while, on the other, it combined a number of boundaries superimposed on one another.

It was probably the Russian historian, ethnographer, and writer Vadim Passek who became the first student of the Sloboda region to apply the term "indeterminacy" to it.[108] Thereafter, the word would be encountered with amazing frequency in comments of local and visiting intellectuals about the region and its center, Kharkiv. More precisely, it would be used in that context no less frequently than "Russian," "Little Russian," and "Ukrainian" terminology, long enough to become customary. Indeed, this went on long enough to permit the assumption that in the first half of the nineteenth century the development of the region was defined not so much by its integration, that is, by unidirectional merging with some imagined imperial center, as by the formation of a particular borderland regional discourse.

From the late eighteenth century, the city of Kharkiv—the new imperial administrative and cultural center in the borderland—began actively to influence the "marking" of the whole region, among whose names, along with "Sloboda region" and "Ukraine," that of "Kharkiv region" soon appeared. The university was officially named "Kharkovian," not "Ukrainian" or "Little Russian." The thought inevitably arises that the "Kharkiv" marker in the region's name indicated integrationist tendencies in its political and cultural life, while the "Sloboda Ukrainian" marker emphasized local particularities, at first in the capacity of a border region with special rights, and subsequently as part of Ukrainian national space, to be discussed later. In 1835 the name of the gubernia was changed definitively from "Ukrainian" to "Kharkiv."

The position of Vasilii Karazin, who persistently sought the integration of his "small motherland" into the empire, deserves attention in that regard. After the Sloboda Ukraine gubernia was renamed the Kharkiv gubernia, Karazin found it necessary to delineate the position of the Kharkiv region on the map of the Russian Empire once again. In an article "On the Significance of Kharkiv for Southern Russia," published in 1840, he mentions the Kharkiv gubernia in the same breath as the Chernihiv and Poltava gubernias, not dividing the Sloboda region from Little Russia.[109]

The geographic image of the region constructed by Karazin was no longer based on the central location of Kharkiv in the region of "Southern Russia," as it had been previously, but on its "middle position between the north and south of the empire," on "the road from the north and the capitals to the south, and from the east and the nomadic plains into educated Europe." Even the soil of the Sloboda region, in his view, "differed from the soil of the southern land and the northern land."[110] Karazin, thinking about the significance of Kharkiv, defined it with the metaphor of a "crossroads town,"[111] which became firmly established in local cultural tradition from then on. The development of transportation routes connecting Kharkiv with the central Russian gubernias merely enhanced its reputation as a city mediating between Moscow and "Ukraine, Little Russia, New Russia, the Don region, the towns of the southern littoral, and the Caucasus."[112]

The borderland character of the region was also emphasized by the profusion of ethnonyms with the aid of which authors of the late eighteenth and early nineteenth centuries sought to define its population. It turned out that the "Cherkasians," known there from ancient times, could be known not only as "Little Russians" but also, to restrict oneself to a review of the works of Ivan Pereverzev, Hryhorii Kvitka, and Vasilii Karazin, as "Slobozhanians," "Ukrainians," "Ukrainian inhabitants," "Southern Russians," "Russians," "Rusyns," the "Rusyn nation," and the "Rus' people," as well as "Kharkiv inhabitants," "inhabitants of this gubernia," and "regionals."

Among the names for local Ukrainians, Johann Güldenstädt noted *khokhly*. In a letter of October 1829 to Joachim Lelewel, Michał Bobrowski, informing him of Ignacy Daniłowicz's move from Kharkiv to Vilnius, also uses the term, calling

Kharkiv the "capital of the *khokhly*."[113] Corresponding with Petr Pletnev, Yakov Grot sees the essential difference between Kharkiv and Odesa in the fact that the "*khokhol* language" is spoken in Kharkiv. Vasilii Karazin's use of the term in his works has already been mentioned in this chapter.

Most often, the term *khokhly* was used as an "outward" description of ethnic Ukrainians comprehensible to their neighbors, the Poles and Russians. In a letter of 1832 to Izmail Sreznevsky, Opanas Shpyhotsky complained that the local booksellers had behaved with him "like *moskali* with a *khokhol*."[114] At the same time, representatives of local society as different in origin as Gustav Adolf Hess de Calve and Vasilii Karazin readily called themselves Ukrainians but never *khokhly* or Little Russians. In this they differed, for example, from Viktor Kochubei, the minister of internal affairs, who referred to himself in correspondence with the governor general of Little Russia, Prince Nikolai Repnin, as a "*khokhol* by birth."

Nevertheless, from the viewpoint of the imperial center, the distinguishing traits of ethnic Ukrainian regions appeared insignificant, dissolving into the Ukrainian space well known to the Russian public and used for self-identification on the "we-they" principle. Arriving in the capitals of Russia, Karazin or, for example, Sreznevsky, neither of whom was or considered himself an ethnic Ukrainian (*khokhol*, *maloros*), were now taken for Little Russians.[115] For the Siberian-born Russian writer and historian Nikolai Polevoi, who lived in Moscow, all natives of the Sloboda region—Vasilii Karazin, Aleksandr Palitsyn, Hryhorii Skovoroda, Hryhorii Kvitka—were "notable natives of Little Russia."[116]

Thus, in the hierarchy of ethnonyms used to denote Ukrainians in the Russian Empire of the late eighteenth and early nineteenth centuries, one may discern a number of supplementary nuances.[117] In the Russian language of the time, *khokhol* was perhaps the only ethnonym used exclusively to emphasize certain ethnocultural particularities of inhabitants of some Ukrainian territories; while *maloross* or *ukrainets* carried a certain ethnocultural connotation, they might also have purely geographic significance. As for the ethnocultural element of that terminology, however, "Little Russian" was used much more often than "Ukrainian."

Thus, one may conclude that in the late eighteenth and early nineteenth centuries Sloboda regional discourse took shape in the process of the institutional and cultural transformation of the former steppe frontier of the Russian Empire. In that process the local intellectual elite, regardless of ethnic origin and consciousness, played no less a role than the imperial government, at least until the 1830s and 1840s, when under the influence of modern nationalism language began to take on the role of the basic ethno-differentiating factor, confronting the educated elite of the former Cossack borderland regions with the problem of national choice.

The Sloboda regional discourse contained a clearly expressed modernizing component. In that framework it might be interpreted in either an integrationist or a region-centric manner. The two interpretations did not oppose each other and developed in parallel, differing only in attitude toward local regional distinctions of a sociolegal, cultural, and ethnic nature. Karazin, for instance, attached much less importance to those distinctions than Kvitka. Accordingly, regional differences between the Sloboda region and Little Russia were clearly less significant to Karazin than to Kvitka.

Nevertheless, both these eminent representatives of the local gentry who flourished in the early nineteenth century promoted the formation of Slobodian discourse by studying the region's history, ethnography, and culture, as well as by selflessly developing the public sphere, without which it would have been impossible to formulate the basic elements of regional identity. The active participation of representatives of local society in the modernization of the region and the support that governmental initiatives found there partly "regionalized" the new imperial institutions, symbolically "domesticating" them.

The regional identity of the Sloboda region and its administrative and cultural center, Kharkiv, remained unstable, mutable, and dependent on the changing imperial context. Russian government policy in the region left sufficient space for the cultivation of local particularities. In any case, the church looked like a much more consistent agent of Russification than the enlightened secular elite, which was only beginning to feel national ground beneath its feet. In this regard, Sergei Uvarov's national doctrine was rather tolerant toward provincial culture, situated for the time being mainly in the conservative spectrum of the Russian Empire's cultural life and closely associated with its Orthodox Slavophile segments. Thus, regardless of the policy of institutional, cultural, and linguistic Russification, the Sloboda region retained its borderland status.

In general, the reforms undertaken by the imperial center in the late eighteenth and early nineteenth centuries, intended to promote the modernization and cultural unification of the country, should have led to the disappearance of the old regional borders and rapprochement between the borderlands and the imperial center. Sloboda Ukraine in turn, having lost its local self-government and become a gubernia (after spending some time as a vicegerency and governorate-general), should have played the role of regional leader in the process of institutional and cultural Russification of the former steppe borderland. A special role in that process was reserved for Kharkiv University, considering the importance of education in the policy of the imperial center.

Nevertheless, the cultural integration of the periphery into the empire was accompanied by the appearance of new boundaries that did not coincide with administrative ones but also did not eliminate them. The reason for this was, first and foremost, that the policy of the center toward the periphery was contradictory and inconsistent. Its centralizing tendencies kept changing to decentralizing ones, and vice versa. But the basic reason for this contradiction must be sought not in the lack of continuity in the policy of the imperial elite but in the continuing expansion of the Russian Empire. Thus Kharkiv, as an administrative and cultural center, gained unusually broad powers going far beyond the bounds of Sloboda Ukraine.

In and of itself, the liquidation of the military frontier did not remove the border as a factor in the life of the region, and the elimination of the administrative boundary between the historical Sloboda and Little Russian regions led not to their "dissolution" in some common space of the Russian Empire but to increasing closeness and the transformation of Kharkiv into the administrative and cultural center of Little Russia.

Even in the first half of the nineteenth century, after the opening of Kharkiv University, the Sloboda region, as seen from the center, remained a borderland. Considerations of military strategy played a substantial role in that view, if one recalls that after the Napoleonic Wars it was the Sloboda region that was chosen as a place to experiment with military settlements, which were established in the Kharkiv, Izium, and Zmiiv districts of the gubernia in 1817. Chuhuiv became the capital of the military settlements. The government probably assumed that reminiscences of such settlements on the steppe frontier were no less popular among the inhabitants of the region than reminiscences of Cossackdom.

It was not just anywhere but in a military camp near Chuhuiv that a meeting took place in 1859 between the imam Shamil, taken captive in the Caucasian mountains, and Emperor Alexander II. With this meeting the emperor sought not only to show respect for an enemy but also to make a symbolic gesture of appeasement with regard to the Caucasian military border. The former Sloboda Ukraine, a borderland from the viewpoint of the capitals and a domesticated cultural space as seen from the borderland, was perfectly suited to that purpose.

## Notes

1. Willard Sunderland, "Imperial Space: Territorial Thought and Practice in the Eighteenth Century," in *Russian Empire: Space, People, Power, 1700–1930*, eds. Jane Burbank, Mark von Hagen, and Anatolii Remnev (Bloomington: Indiana University Press, 2007), 52.
2. Vera Tolz, *Inventing the Nation: Russia* (London: Arnold Press, 2001); Liah Greenfeld, "The Formation of the Russian National Identity: The Role of Status Insecurity and Ressentiment," *Comparative Studies in Society and History* 32, no. 3 (July 1990): 551, 583.
3. Marina V. Loskoutova, "A Motherland with a Radius of 300 Miles: Regional Identity in Russian Secondary and Post-Elementary Education from the Early Nineteenth Century to the War and Revolution," *European Review of History* 9, no. 1 (2002): 7–22; Leonid E. Gorizontov, "The 'Great Circle' of Interior Russia: Representations of the Imperial Center in the Nineteenth and Early Twentieth Centuries," in *Russian Empire: Space, People, Power, 1700–1930*, 67–93.
4. Greenfeld, "The Formation of the Russian National Identity," 551, 583.
5. Larri Vulf, *Izobretaia Vostochnuiu Evropu: karta tsivilizatsii v soznanii épokhi Prosveshcheniia* (Moscow, 2003), 35.
6. *Sochineniia imperatritsy Ekateriny II* (St. Petersburg, 1901), vol. 8, pts. 1–2: 64.
7. Fedir Turchenko and Halyna Turchenko, *Pivdenna Ukraïna: Modernizatsiia, svitova viina, revoliutsiia (kinets' XIX st.–1921)* (Kyiv: Heneza, 2003), 12–13; Valentyna Shandra, *Heneral-hubernatorstva v Ukraïni, XIX–pochatok XX st.* (Kyiv: NASU Institute of Ukrainian History, 2005), 164–264.

8. "Opysy Stepovoï Ukraïny ostann'oï chverti XVIII–pochatku XIX stolittia," in *Dzherela z istoriï Stepovoï Ukraïny*, vol. 10 (Zaporizhia, 2009), 141.
9. Aleksandr Filushkin, "Problema genezisa Rossiiskoi imperii," in *Novaia imperskaia istoria postsovetskogo prostranstva* (Kazan: Ab Imperio Press, 2004), 389.
10. James T. Flynn, *The University Reform of Tsar Alexander I, 1802–1835* (Washington, DC: Catholic University of America Press, 1988), 180.
11. Flynn, *The University Reform of Tsar Alexander I*, 223.
12. Mikhail Zhdanov, *Putevye zapiski po Rossii v dvadtsati guberniakh* (St. Petersburg, 1843), 100.
13. Zenon E. Kohut, "The Development of a Little Russian Identity and Ukrainian Nation-Building," *Harvard Ukrainian Studies* 10, nos. 3–4 (1986): 559–76.
14. Iogann Gotlib [Johann Gottlieb] Georgi, *Opisanie vsekh obitaiushchikh v Rossii[skom gosudarstve] narodov: Ikh zhiteiskikh obriadov, obyknovenii, odezhd...*, 2nd ed. (St. Petersburg, 2007), 708.
15. Khariton Chebotarev, ed., *Geograficheskoe metodicheskoe opisanie Rossiiskoi Imperii s nadlezhashchim vvedeniem k osnovatel'nomu poznaniiu zemnogo shara i Evropy voobshche...* (Moscow: Universitetskaia tipografiia, 1776), 103–4.
16. Iurii Venelin, "O spore mezhdu iuzhanami i severianami naschet ikh rossizma," *Chteniia v Obshchestve istorii i drevnostei rossiiskikh*, no. 4 (1847): 1–16.
17. Sergei Posokhov and Aleksandr Iarmysh, *Gubernatory i general-gubernatory* (Kharkiv: Acta, 1996), 152.
18. Volodymyr Kravchenko, *The Ukrainian-Russian Borderland: History vs Geography* (Montreal, Kingston, London, and Chicago: McGill-Queen's University Press, 2022), 17–46.
19. Vasilii Zuev, *Puteshestvennye zapiski ot Sankt Peterburga do Khersona v 1781 i 1782 godu* (St. Petersburg, 1787), 184–85.
20. Ol'ha Biriova, *Pomishchyts'ki sadyby Kharkivs'koï huberniï (persha polovyna XVIII–pochatok XX stolittia), Avtoreferat dysertatsiï ... kandydata istorychnykh nauk* (PhD diss., Karazin National University of Kharkiv, 2009).
21. Mykhailo Teslia, *Oleksandr Oleksandrovych Palitsyn i "Palitsyns'ka akademiia"* (Sumy: Mak-Den, 2010).
22. Dmitrii Bagalei, *Opyt istorii Khar'kovskogo universiteta (po neizdannym materialam)*, 2 vols. (Kharkiv: Kharkiv University Press, 1893–98), vol. 1 *(1802–1815)*, 1025.
23. Evdokim Ziablovskii, *Statisticheskoe opisanie Rossiiskoi imperii v nyneshnem eia sostoianii s predvaritel'nymi poniatiiami o statistike i o Evrope voobshche v statisticheskom vide*, 3 vols. (St. Petersburg, 1808), 1: 128.
24. Militsa V. Nechkina, *Dvizhenie dekabristov*, 2 vols. (Moscow: Izdatel'stvo Akademii Nauk SSSR, 1955), 1: 389, 423.
25. Nechkina, *Dvizhenie dekabristov*, 1: 389, 423.
26. Johann G. Kohl, *Russia. St. Petersburg, Moscow, Kharkoff, Riga, Odessa, the German Provinces on the Baltic, the Steppes, the Crimea, and the Interior of the Empire* (London: Chapman and Hall, 1842), 186, 505.
27. Vissarion Belinskii, *Polnoe sobranie sochinenii: V 13 tomakh* (Moscow: Izdatel'stvo Akademii Nauk SSSR, 1953–59), vol. 8 (Moscow, 1955), 89.
28. I. O. Dzeverin et al., ed., *Ukraïns'ka literatura XVIII stolittia* (Kyiv: Naukova Dumka, 1983), 215–16.
29. *Istoriia Rusov ili Maloi Rossii*, attributed to Heorhii Konys'kyi (Georgii Koniskii) (Moscow: Moscow University Typography, 1846), 108.
30. Oleksandr I. Hurzhii, *Ukraïns'ka kozats'ka derzhava v druhii polovyni XVII–XVIII st.: Kordony, naselennia, pravo* (Kyiv: Osnovy, 1996), 8.
31. Volodymyr Masliichuk, *Provintsiia na perekhresti kul'tur: Doslidzhennia z istoriï Slobids'koï Ukraïny XVII–XIX st.* (Kharkiv: Kharkiv Private Museum of the City Estate, 2007), 256–88.

32. Illia Kvitka, *Zapiski o slobodskikh polkakh s nachala ikh poseleniia do 1766 g.* (Kharkiv, 1812; 2nd ed., 1882).
33. Kvitka, *Zapiski*, 11–12.
34. *Zapiski*, 4–9, 19.
35. *Zapiski*, 11–12.
36. Oleh Zhurba, *Stanovlennia ukraïns'koï arkheohrafiï: liudy, ideï, instytutsiï* (Dnipropetrovsk, 2003), 148–49. See also *Ukrainskii vestnik*, no. 2 (1816): 145–46; no. 3 (1816): 304–14.
37. *Ukrainskii vestnik*, no. 8 (1816): 121–37; no. 10 (1816): 138–40.
38. Dmytro Bahalii, *Vybrani pratsi*, vol. 5, pt. 1: *Istoriia kolonizatsiï Slobids'koï Ukraïny* (Kharkiv: Golden Pages, 2007), 300.
39. *Sbornik Imperatorskogo Russkogo istoricheskogo obshchestva*, vol. 8 (1871): 375.
40. G. Kalinovskii, *Opisanie svadebnykh ukrainskikh prostonarodnykh obriadov* (St. Petersburg: Tipografia H.F. Klena, 1777).
41. Dmytro Bahalii, *Ukraïns'kyi mandrovanyi filosof Hryhorii Skovoroda*, 2nd ed. (Kyiv, 1992), 77.
42. Amanda Gilroy, ed., *Romantic Geographies: Discourses of Travel, 1775–1844* (Manchester: Manchester University Press, 2000); Andreas Schoenle, *Authenticity and Fiction in the Russian Literary Journey, 1790–1840* (Cambridge, MA: Harvard University Press, 2000); Vladyslav Verstiuk, Viktor Horobets', and Oleksii P. Tolochko, *Ukraïns'ki proekty v Rosiis'kii imperiï: Narysy*, vol. 1 of *Ukraïna i Rosiia v istorychnii retrospektyvi*, 3 vols, ed. Valerii Smolii (Kyiv: Naukova Dumka, 2004), 266–331.
43. Dmitrii Bagalei, *Materialy dlia istorii kolonizatsii i byta stepnoi okrainy Moskovskogo gosudarstva XVI–XVIII stoletii*, 2 vols. (Kharkiv, 1890), 2: 319–98.
44. [Iohann] Gil'denstedt (Johann Anton Güldenstädt), "Dnevnik puteshestviia po Slobodsko-Ukrainskoi gubernii v avguste i sentiabre 1774 goda," in *Khar'kovskii sbornik*, vol. 5 (1891): 71.
45. Baron von Haxthausen, *The Russian Empire, Its People, Institutions, and Resources, by Baron von Haxthausen*, vol. 1 (London: Chapman & Hall, 1856) (first published in German, 1847–52), 411.
46. Zuev, *Puteshestvennye zapiski*, 184.
47. As quoted in Vasyl' Sypovs'kyi, *Ukraïna v rosiis'komu pys'menstvi*, pt. 1, *(1801–1850)* (Kharkiv: DVU, 1928), 36.
48. Dmitrii Bantysh-Kamenskii, *Puteshestvie v Moldaviiu, Valakhiiu i Serbiiu* (Moscow, 1810), 30–31.
49. Haxthausen, *Russian Empire*, 392–93.
50. *Opysy Kharkivs'koho namisnytstva kintsia XVIII st.: Opysovo-statystychni dzherela*, comp. Vasyl' O. Pirko and Oleksandr I. Hurzhii (Kyiv: Naukova Dumka, 1991), 5–8; Vladimir Gorlenko, *Stanovlenie ukrainskoi étnografii kontsa XVIII–pervoi poloviny XIX st.* (Kyiv: Naukova Dumka, 1988), 65–67.
51. *Trudy Vol'nogo Ėkonomicheskogo Obshchestva*, pt. VIII (1768): 40–41, 50, 53, 55.
52. *Opysy Kharkivs'koho namisnytstva*, 30, 32, 34, 36.
53. *Opysy Kharkivs'koho namisnytstva*, 36.
54. *Opysy Kharkivs'koho namisnytstva*, 18.
55. *Opysy Kharkivs'koho namisnytstva*, 24.
56. *Opysy Kharkivs'koho namisnytstva*, 21.
57. *Opysy Kharkivs'koho namisnytstva*, 19.
58. Roman Szporluk, "Mapping Ukraine: From Identity Space to Decision Space," *Journal of Ukrainian Studies* 33 (2008): 448–51.
59. Kravchenko, *The Ukrainian-Russian Borderland*, 17–47, 107.
60. Bagalei, *Opyt istorii*, 1: 773.
61. Konstantin Arsen'ev, *Trudy uchenykh, ili literatura rossiiskoi statistiki*, vol. 1 of *Nachertanie statistiki Rossiiskago gosudarstva* (St. Petersburg, 1818).

62. "Iz vospominanii Mikhailovskogo-Danilevskogo," *Russkaia starina*, no. 6 (1897): 476.
63. Petro Hulak-Artemovs'kyi, *Poetychni tvory*; Ievhen Hrebinka, *Poetychni tvory, povisti ta opovidannia* (Kyiv: Naukova Dumka, 1984), 51.
64. Bagalei, *Opyt istorii*, 1: 771–73.
65. *Dva stolittia skovorodiany: bibliohrafichnyi dovidnyk*, comp. Leonid Ushkalov, Serhii Vakulenko, and Alla Yevtushenko (Kharkiv: Acta, 2002).
66. Bagalei, *Opyt istorii*, 1: 84.
67. Nikolai Sumtsov, "Slobodsko-ukrainskoe dvorianstvo v proizvedeniiakh G. F. Kvitki," *Kievskaia starina*, no. 6 (1884): 201–9; Dmitrii Bagalei, *Zametki i materialy po istorii Slobodskoi Ukrainy* (Kharkiv, 1893), 46–56.
68. Grigorii Kvitka, *Khar'kov i uezdnye goroda. Khar'kovskaia Starina* (Kharkiv: Kharkivs'ka Starovyna, 2005), 166–90.
69. Kvitka, *Khar'kov i uezdnye goroda*, 166–67.
70. *Khar'kov i uezdnye goroda*, 166–67.
71. Hryhorii Kvitka, *Istorychni, etnohrafichni, literaturno-publitsystychni statti, lysty*, vol. 7 of *Zibrannia tvoriv u 7 tomakh* (Kyiv: Naukova Dumka, 1981), 143–44.
72. Kvitka, *Istorychni*, 143–44.
73. Grigorii Kvitka (Hryhorii F. Kvitka-Osnov'ianenko), "Ukraintsy" in idem, *Stat'i istoricheskie*, vol. 4 of *Sochineniia* (Kharkiv, 1890), 460.
74. Kvitka, "Ukraintsy," 460.
75. Taras Koznarsky, "Kharkiv Literary Almanacs of the 1830s: The Shaping of Ukrainian Cultural Identity" (PhD diss., Harvard University), 160.
76. Taras Shevchenko, *Kobzar* (Kharkiv: Shevchenkove, 1996), 10.
77. Kvitka, *Khar'kov i uezdnye goroda*, 170.
78. Hryhorii F. Kvitka-Osnov'ianenko, *Povisti ta opovidannia. Dramatychni tvory* (Kyiv: Naukova Dumka, 1982), 31.
79. Kvitka, "Ukraintsy," 461.
80. Hryhorii F. Kvitka-Osnov'ianenko, "Story (1841)," in *Istorychni, etnohrafichni, literaturno-publitsystychni statti, lysty*, vol. 6 of *Zibrannia tvoriv u 7 tomakh* (Kyiv: Naukova Dumka, 1981), 9.
81. Kvitka, *Zibrannia tvoriv u 7 tomakh*, 7: 272–73.
82. Hryhorii F. Kvitka-Osnov'ianenko, "Otvet Tikhorskomu na ego stat'iu v sentiabrskoi knizhke Maiaka, za 1842 god," *Maiak*, no. 10 (1843): 34.
83. Bagalei, *Opyt istorii*, 1: 113.
84. Koznarsky, "Kharkiv Literary Almanacs," 39–40, 42.
85. Bagalei, *Opyt istorii*, 1: 114.
86. Anatolii Bolebrukh et al., *Vasyl' Nazarovych Karazin (1773–1842)* (Kharkiv: Avto-Enerhiia, 2005), 271.
87. Karazin, *Sochineniia*, 448.
88. *Sochineniia*, 449.
89. *Sochineniia*, 584, 600.
90. *Sochineniia*, 484–85.
91. Kvitka, *Zibrannia tvoriv u 7 tomakh*, 7: 290, 295.
92. *"Ia smelo mogu stat' pred sudom potomkov...": Karazinskii sbornik* (Kharkiv, 2004), 282.
93. Zenon Kohut, *Rosiis'kyi tsentralizm i ukraïns'ka avtonomiia. Likvidatsiia Het'manshchyny, 1760–1830* (Kyiv: Krytyka, 1996), 207.
94. Serhy Yekelchyk, "The Grand Narrative and Its Discontents: Ukraine in Russian History Textbooks and Ukrainian Students' Minds, 1830s–1900s," in *Culture, Nation, and Identity: The Ukrainian-Russian Encounter (1600–1945)*, eds. Andreas Kappeler, Zenon E. Kohut, Frank E. Sysyn, and Mark von Hagen (Edmonton: CIUS Press, 2003), 234.
95. Viktor Zhivov, "Chuvstvitel'nyi natsionalizm: Karamzin, Rostopchin, natsional'nyi suverenitet i poiski natsional'noi identichnosti," *Novoe Literaturnoe Obozrenie*, no. 91 (2008),

https://magazines.gorky.media/nlo/2008/3/chuvstvitelnyj-naczionalizm-karamzin-rosto pchin-naczionalnyj-suverenitet-i-poiski-naczionalnoj-identichnosti.html.
96. Volodymyr Kravchenko, "Nikolai Polevoi i zvychaina skhema 'rus'koï istoriï"(persha tretyna XIX st.,″ *Journal of Ukrainian Studies* 33–34 (2008–2009), *Tentorium Honorum: Essays Presented to Frank E. Sysyn on His Sixtieth Birthday*, 303–15.
97. Nikolai Polevoi, "Malorossiia, ee obitateli i istoriia," *Moskovskii telegraf*, no. 18 (1830): 229.
98. Polevoi, "Malorossiia," no. 17: 77.
99. This extract from the chapter was published in Kravchenko, *The Ukrainian-Russian Borderland*, 200–2.
100. Jerzy Hawryluk (Iurii Havryliuk), "'Podlasianie ruskiego plemienia' w epoce narodowego romantyzmu," *Nad Buhom i Narvoiu: Ukraïns'kyi chasopys Pidliashshia*, no. 2 (2003).
101. Ieremiia Aizenshtok, "Persha dysertatsiia Kostomarova," *Ukraïna*, no. 3 (1925): 21–27; James T. Flynn, "The Affair of Kostomarov's Dissertation: A Case Study of Official Nationalism in Practice," *Slavonic and East European Review* 52, no. 127 (1974): 188–96.
102. Ahapii Shamrai, ed., *Kharkivs'ka shkola romantykiv*, 3 vols. (Kharkiv: DVU, 1930).
103. Koznarsky, "Kharkiv Literary Almanacs," 246.
104. Izmail Sreznevskii, *Istoricheskoe obozrenie grazhdanskogo ustroeniia Slobodskoi Ukrainy so vremeni ee zaseleniia do preobrazovaniia v Khar'kovskuiu guberniu* (Kharkiv: Kharkiv Guberniia Press, 1883).
105. Bantysh-Kamenskii, *Puteshestvie*, 30–31.
106. Quoted in: Dmitrii Bagalei and Dmitrii Miller, *Istoriia goroda Khar'kova za 250 let ego sushchestvovaniia*, 2 vols. (Kharkiv: City Press, 1993), 2: 130.
107. Vsevolod Sreznevskii, "Iz perepiski I. I. Sreznevskogo, 1829–1839 gody," *Kievskaia starina*, no. 6 (1901): 325.
108. Vadim Passek, *Ocherk Khar'kovskoi gubernii* (Kharkiv: [not available], 1839), 53.
109. Vasilii N. Karazin, *Sochineniia, pis'ma i bumagi* (Kharkiv: Kharkiv University Press, 1910), 483–84, 485.
110. Karazin, *Sochineniia*, 485.
111. *Sochineniia*, 485.
112. Bagalei and Miller, *Istoriia goroda Khar'kova*, 2: 973.
113. Artur Kijas, *Polacy na Uniwersytecie Charkowskim, 1805–1917*, 2nd rev. ed. (Poznań: PTPN Press, 2008), 53.
114. Koznarsky, "Kharkiv Literary Almanacs," 82.
115. Venedikt Figlarin, *Pis'ma i agenturnye zapiski F. V. Bulgarina v III otdelenie* (Moscow, 1998), 546.
116. *Severnaia pchela*, no. 120 (29 May 1844): 479.
117. Andreas Kappeler, "Mazepintsy, Malorossy, Khokhly: Ukrainians in the Ethnic Hierarchy of the Russian Empire," in *Culture, Nation, and Identity: The Ukrainian-Russian Encounter*, 162–81.

## CHAPTER 4
# City, Empire, Nation

The "great reforms" of the late nineteenth century opened a new historical epoch for the Russian Empire, which initiated a successive stage of the "revolution from above" and proceeded under the influence of the ideas of modernization and nationalism. Modern national discourses of the peoples of the Russian Empire took shape mostly on an ethnocultural basis, interacting not only with one another but also with modernized imperial nationalism. The boundary between the regional and national discourses remained very subtle, and the differences between them were sometimes hard to distinguish. This chapter will examine the influence of those processes on the symbolic geography of the Kharkiv region and the city as well as the way in which local discourse was constructed in the new historical narrative and reflected in the urban landscape.

### "Southern Russia"

In the late nineteenth and early twentieth centuries, the region of "Southern Russia" associated with the most urbanized and industrialized Donbas, as well as the Azov Sea and Black Sea littoral, was considered something of an economic entity. It included, aside from Kharkiv, such cities as Katerynoslav and Odesa. Each of those cities could claim the role of regional capital. By that time each of them had acquired a marked "southern" geographical identification that became visible in the names of new civic institutions, periodicals, and industrial enterprises. In Katerynoslav, for example, there was a South Russian Union of Labor Anarchist Communists, and the Bolsheviks published the newspaper *Southern Worker*[1]; a South Russian Union of Labor was active in Odesa in 1875; and the newspaper *Southern Proletarian* was published in Kyiv.[2] But Kharkiv had an incontestable advantage over all its competitors because of its location, since it was closest to the Russian imperial capitals.

The role of Kharkiv was promoted by the active building of railways, which were extremely important for the economic integration of the Ukrainian lands into the all-Russian market.³ The new Kursk–Kharkiv–Azov (later Sevastopol) railway was inaugurated on 22 May 1869. Railways fanning out from Kharkiv to Sumy and Kremenchuk (1871), Kyiv and Rostov (1873), and Sevastopol (1875) linked the city not only with the imperial center but also with the Crimea and the Black Sea basin. Typically, a considerable number of railway lines crossing the Sloboda region followed the ancient steppe routes.

Having established rail connections with all the major regions and cities of the Russian Empire, Kharkiv became one of the country's major transportation hubs, increasing its traditional role as a staging post and transit point in the communications network of the empire's central and southern gubernias—in a word, the city of crossroads advertised by Vasilii Karazin. Alfred Rieber has shown that the heated debates developing in St. Petersburg in the early 1860s concerning the choice of direction of railway lines were not only based on strictly economic and military strategic considerations; they were also endowed with national meaning.⁴ According to Pavel Korf, "It is not just goods that travel by rail but also books, ideas, customs and attitudes.... Great Russian and Little Russian capital, Great Russian and Little Russian ideas, attitudes and customs will blend, and these two already close peoples will become very much alike."⁵

Local Ukrainian elites took an active part in determining the direction of railway construction, based first and foremost on their own regional interests. These points can be illustrated to some extent by correspondence carried on in 1866 by the well-known writer, public figure, and patriot of the Sloboda region Grigorii Danilevsky with a native of Kharkiv, the composer Petro Sokalsky, then living in Odesa. Sokalsky warned Danilevsky, for example, that in agitating for the development of a railway line from Kharkiv to the Sea of Azov, he should not come out against the building of the Kharkiv-Odesa line, as that might affect the interests of neighboring New Russia and turn the governor general of New Russia and Bessarabia, Paul von Kotzebue, against Kharkiv. Sokalsky wrote:

> Your path is clear: to lobby for your [Azov] line and *not touch* the one from Kharkiv to Odesa. On that basis, you will encounter an ally and an active assistant in the governor general of New Russia and Bessarabia.... To speak truly, there is decidedly no need and no profit for you in denouncing the Khar[kiv]-Odes[a] line. Do not denounce it and defend your own, and the New Russ[ian] side will help you; otherwise you yourself will bring down an enemy upon you.... I am writing this to you with the utmost seriousness and with a view to the benefit of Kharkiv. Go hand in hand with New Russia, do not trample in the mud what does not concern you, and you will find friends here.⁶

In the end it was the Azov-Crimea line, intended to connect the center and the Left-Bank Ukrainian gubernias with the Black Sea ports, that gained the upper hand in government circles over the southwestern project, in which the central places were reserved for Kyiv and Odesa. In that case economic expediency took precedence over engagé nationalist considerations, and Kharkiv won the battle for priority construction of a railroad to the sea, which served its interests better than a connection with Odesa. The Kharkiv-based management of the southern railroads controlled all connections with the main Kursk–Kharkiv–Sevastopol and Kharkiv-Mykolaiv lines, whose total length was almost 4,000 versts.

The strength of Kharkiv's position in the dynamically developing industrial and resource-rich region of "Southern Russia" was increased by the rise of the Donets-Kryvyi Rih coal and metallurgical basin.[7] It was ultimately Kharkiv that became the administrative and financial center of the Donets Basin and an intermediary in its connections with the central regions and capitals of Russia. In that regard, Kharkiv gained uncontested superiority over Katerynoslav, which had also aspired to the role of regional "capital of the Donbas."[8]

Kharkiv became the headquarters of the Congress of the Mining Industry of Southern Russia, an organization with considerable influence not only on the domestic but also on the foreign policy of the Russian Empire. The congress included entrepreneurs who controlled one of the empire's most powerful cartels, the *Prodamet* or Association for the Sale of Products of Russian Metallurgical Plants. It was formed in 1902 on the basis of the five largest metallurgical factories in the empire's southern lands, and on the eve of World War I it included close to 90 percent of all the metallurgical enterprises in the country.[9]

Although Kharkiv ceased to be the administrative capital of the governorate-general of Little Russia in 1856, the city remained the regional administrative, economic, and cultural center of the former borderland territories, encompassing the Russian Central Black-Earth Zone, the Sloboda region, Little Russia, New Russia, and the Black Sea littoral. As before, the sphere of activity of many administrative, economic, scholarly, and cultural institutions coming into existence in Kharkiv went far beyond the boundaries of the Kharkiv gubernia. Thus, in the late nineteenth century, the Kharkiv factory district—one of the six into which the empire's territory was divided—encompassed, along with the Kharkiv gubernia, those of Voronezh, Kursk, Orel, Penza, Tambov, Tula, Kaluga, Katerynoslav, Baku, Kutaisi, and Tiflis, along with the domains of the Don and Black Sea Cossacks.[10]

In 1867 Kharkiv became the judicial center not only of its own gubernia but also of those of Kursk, Voronezh, Orel, and parts of the Tambov and Katerynoslav gubernias, with a total population of as many as seven million. In the early twentieth century the jurisdiction of the Kharkiv high court tribunal extended to the Poltava gubernia and part of the Tavriia gubernia, as well as to the Don Cossack Host, and the total population of the territory subject to Kharkiv in judicial terms increased to seventeen million.[11] It is readily apparent that the territory of the Kharkiv judicial district in the early twentieth century was quite comparable to that of the century-old Kharkiv educational (university) district.

Railway transport combined with Kharkiv's convenient location to promote a large influx of labor, goods, and financial investment coming from Russian capitals as well as from Belgian, French, and German cities. Branches of large imperial Russian and foreign banks, which controlled almost 90 percent of investment in the industrial enterprises of Southern Russia, were opened in Kharkiv.[12] They included, in particular, branches of the international Azov-Don, Volga-Kama, and St. Petersburg banks, while the local joint-stock Merchant and Land Bank competed successfully with them. The bank became part of the financial and industrial empire of Aleksei/Oleksii Alchevsky, a Sumy-born businessman and philanthropist who, along with his friend Ivan Vernadsky, became one of the contributors to the nascent Ukrainian national movement.[13]

In the late nineteenth and early twentieth centuries, Kharkiv developed as a center of agricultural and transport machine-building, metalworking, and light industry, following the general growth of a capitalist market economy in the Russian Empire. Kharkiv began to take on the characteristics of a modern industrial center closer to the end of the nineteenth century, especially as construction began of an industrial giant: the Kharkiv locomotive factory. It was joined by other machine-building plants and factories established by foreign investors (Melgose, Helferich-Sade). At the new Kharkiv enterprises, wages of qualified workers were among the highest in the Russian Empire, yielding only (but not always) to those in the new plants and factories of the capital. In general, industrial wage levels in Kharkiv were closer to those of the new industrial centers of Southern Russia.[14]

## Mapping the Region

Did the development of large-scale industry, transport, communications, and mass media in Kharkiv, which was becoming a modern industrial city, mean the further integration of the region into the imperial center; the city's penetration, along with other cities and regions of Ukraine, into some nucleus of the Russian Empire?[15] I would give only a partly positive answer to this question. The rapid modernization of the Russian Empire firmly established Kharkiv in the swiftly developing economic space of Southern Russia. It remained basically the same historical Sloboda region that had encompassed the territory of the Kharkiv educational district, but it was now acquiring a more pronounced industrial profile.

The foregoing raises the question of the formation of a particular regional identity in the late nineteenth and early twentieth centuries developing on a territorial and economic basis in the course of the intensive modernization of the southern steppe periphery of the Russian Empire. Apart from the Kharkiv region, that space included the Donbas, New Russia, and the northern Black Sea littoral. All of them came under the sphere of interests and activities of the Congress of the Mining Industry of Southern Russia, which held regular meetings in Kharkiv. Individual structural elements of the region's cultural identity were apparent in local periodicals, museums of local history, scholarly and educational societies, and local archives.

The growth of Kharkiv's economic influence was accompanied by the enhancement of the "southern" components of its symbolical geographic identification. In the early twentieth century, a popular guidebook to Kharkiv presented it as the economic, cultural, and educational center of Southern Russia.[16] There were community organizations in Kharkiv with "southern" markers in their names: the Society of Assistance to Miners in Southern Russia, the Congress of the Mining Industry of Southern Russia, the South Russian Acclimatization Society, the South Russian Automobile Club, and the Consumer Association of Southern Russia. Their publications also appeared in Kharkiv: *South Russian Miners' Leaflet* (1880–87), *News of the South Russian Technological Association* (1896–1917), *News of the South Russian Acclimatization Society* (1901–10), *South Russian Agricultural News* (1895–1918), *South Russian Consumer* (1914–17), and several others.

The Administration of Southern State Railways, also located in Kharkiv, issued periodicals with a "southern" flavor at various times: *Echo of Southern Roads, Southern Railway Echo, Southern Railway Courier*. The word "southern" figured in the title of the largest Kharkiv newspaper, *Iuzhnyi krai* (Southern land) and was constantly repeated in lesser-known local publications: *Southern Life* (1906), *South* (1910), *Southern Voice* (1911), and *Southern Copeck News* (1914–15).[17] The Technological Institute, founded in Kharkiv in 1871, was also described as South Russian. The Bolsheviks, who established a Kharkiv office of their newspaper *Iskra* (The Spark), in 1901, called it "southern."

It was Kharkiv that met all travelers heading southward from central Russia as the first representative of the "South." In this regard one may cite the testimony of Ivan Bunin, who came to Kharkiv from Russian Orel. Upon arrival, the beginning writer found exactly what he expected to find:

> the first thing that impressed me in Kharkiv was the mildness of the air and the fact that there was more light there than in our parts. . . . I looked around and immediately felt in everything something not entirely ours, softer and bright, even seemingly springlike. . . . There was no sun but plenty of light; more, in any case, than usual for December, and its warm presence behind the clouds promised something very good. And everything was softer in that light and air.[18]

As the political situation in the Russian Empire grew more acute in the early twentieth century, the developing regional identity of Southern Russia tended toward politicization. During the Revolution of 1905, the idea arose in Odesa to create a South Russian or Black Sea Republic including the southern lands of present-day Ukraine and the Crimea, as well as Volhynia and Podilia.[19] But because the region of Southern Russia had no definite geographic and cultural center, and no clearly delineated administrative boundaries, its politicization found no ideological substantiation comparable to Siberian or Cossack-based (Don and Kuban) regionalisms. Nevertheless, the very appearance of a holistic image of Southern Russia and the popularization of that geographic concept endowed local Sloboda identity with a new spatial and symbolic dimension, removing it from the familiar bipolar "Great Russia–Little Russia" system of coordinates.

The southern dimension of the regional identity of Kharkiv and vicinity, developing on an economic and geographic basis in the process of modernization, was only partly related to another, more traditional type of southern identification that was mainly historical and ethnocultural in nature. It had evolved on a Little Russian basis, continuing the old "dispute between southerners and northerners about their Russianness" into the late nineteenth and early twentieth centuries.[20] In the Russian Empire, South Russian terminology was used much more often than Ukrainian terminology, with reference to Little Russia and all things Little Russian. As before, however, the boundary between the regional and ethnocultural content of that terminology remained transparent and not always well defined.

Wavering between territorial and ethnic aspects of the region's identification is apparent in a programmatic article in the Ukrainian journal *Osnova* (Foundation), published in St. Petersburg in 1861–62. It reads:

> The land to whose study *Osnova* will be devoted is inhabited mainly by the South Russian people. Although in Bessarabia, the Crimea, and the land of the Don Cossack Host the dominant population is not South Russian, we include those regions in the scope of our study as well, both because they do not yet have their own print publications and because they are engaged in direct industrial and commercial relations with the neighboring South Russian lands.[21]

The publishers of *Osnova* most often used the "South Russian" designation as synonymous with "Little Russian." Mykola Kostomarov wrote Ukrainian history in the guise of "Southern Rus'" history, a tradition continued by the Russian historian of Ukraine Aleksandra Yefimenko and the Polish historian Aleksander Jabłonowski. Taras Shevchenko called his primer of the Ukrainian language, published in 1861, "South Russian." The imperial minister of internal affairs, Petr Valuev, identified "Little Russian parlance" with the "South Russian dialect." There is no question that in all these instances South Russian terminology was employed in an ethnocultural context extending beyond the administrative boundaries of Little Russia and the Sloboda region.

It was on the basis of South Russian terminology that Panteleimon Kulish, publishing his *Zapiski o Iuzhnoi Rusi* (Notes on Southern Rus') in 1856, included the cities of Kyiv, Kharkiv, and Odesa in a coherent national space.[22] The same three cities figured as administrative centers of the corresponding regions in the projected federal restructuring of the Russian Empire proposed by Mykhailo

Drahomanov.²³ Thus, the three largest and most developed cities of what is now Ukraine marked the new national space that was actively being shaped in the late nineteenth and early twentieth centuries.

In the historical and geographic conceptualization of the first generation of Ukrainian intellectuals, including Heorhii Andruzky, Mykhailo Drahomanov, and, to some extent, Mykhailo Hrushevsky, the southern lands were thought of as an integral space sometimes called the Black Sea region (*Chornomoria*). But by the time the Ukrainian People's Party issued its political program in 1905, the southern lands also embraced the Kuban region established and inhabited by ethnic Ukrainians after the liquidation of the Zaporozhian Cossack Host. Shortly afterward, the region of "Southern Russia" would come to be known in the Ukrainian national narrative as "Southern Ukraine."

The mental remapping of Ukrainian national space was promoted in many ways by the prolific writer, native, and patriot of the Sloboda region Grigorii Danilevsky, who lived on his estate in the village of Pryshyb, now in the Balakliia raion of Kharkiv oblast.²⁴ In the 1850s and early 1860s, he continued the line of local writing initiated by Hryhorii Kvitka, turning to subjects drawn from the history of the Sloboda steppe borderland in such works as *Slobozhane* (Slobodians, 1853), *Iz Ukrainy* (From Ukraine, 1860), and *Beglye v Novorossii* (Refugees in New Russia, 1862). He also studied and popularized the historical and cultural heritage of the Sloboda region, concentrating mainly on the early nineteenth century, in such works as *Osnov'ianenko* (1856) and, in particular, *Ukrainskaia starina* (Ukrainian antiquity, 1866).²⁵

In 1861 Danilevsky published the collection *Ukrainskaia starina* (Ukrainian antiquity), including material mainly of local content pertaining to the life and work of Hryhorii Skovoroda, Vasilii Karazin, and Hryhorii Kvitka, as well as to the history of education in the Kharkiv region. The region was presented to the reader as an enlightened borderland, "our so-called Ukrainian antiquity," as stated in the editor's foreword. An analysis of ethnic nomenclature in the texts of the collection shows that in this case the term *ukraina* predominantly retains its geographic significance, although the author also uses it as a synonym for both Little Russia and Southern Russia.

Unlike Kvitka, Danilevsky no longer counterposes the Sloboda region to Little Russia. For him, figures such as Skovoroda, Karazin, Kvitka, and Ivan Kotliarevsky are representatives of Ukrainian society and Ukrainian literature and are, simultaneously, "the first true intellectual movers of Little Russian society." Thus, in the new historical and literary narrative created by Danilevsky, the internal boundaries between historical Ukrainian regions are effaced, but their common boundary with Great Russia remains as before. The writer emphasizes the modernizing aspects of the development of the Sloboda region, paying special attention to the future and not the past, to the spirit of enterprise and not the language of daily intercourse. In effect, he replicates the panegyric to Sloboda Ukrainians created by Ivan Pereverzev almost a century earlier, supplementing it with his own explanations of the difference between Ukrainians and Russians.

Danilevsky followed the path of rapprochement between the regions of Ukraine and Southern Russia, wearing down the conditional boundary between those regions by employing the ethnotoponym *ukraintsy*, whom he favored with the epithet *nashi* (our), endowing them with "the whole breadth of the steppe, from Chernihiv to the Crimea and from Kharkiv to Zaporizhia" as their habitat.[26] Moreover, Danilevsky consciously shifted emphasis from ethnocultural factors to social ones in differentiating the inhabitants of the two regions, old and new.

Noteworthy in that regard is his sketch "Pennsylvanians and Carolinians," in which the "Carolinians," described as Little Russian traditionalists, are counterposed to "Pennsylvanians," progressive and enterprising colonists, alien to all conservatism, vital and bold, resourceful and practical, reminding the author of American farmers and entrepreneurs and portrayed in the sketch as "steppe Yankees."[27] Danilevsky regarded the "mixing of social estates and peoples" in the "steppe *ukraina*" as a factor in the progressive development of society on the American model and, in the spirit of Taras Shevchenko, looked forward to the appearance of future Washingtons in the "steppe Yankee" milieu.

Regardless of the popularity of South Russian discourse, neither South Russian nor Ukrainian terminology eliminated the use of the Little Russian lexicon in Ukrainian historiography. Consequently, Kharkiv could figure simultaneously in two South Russian regional discourses, one superimposed upon the other: economic and geographic, as noted in the preceding section, and Ukrainian national, not yet finally differentiated from "South Russian" and "Little Russian."

On administrative maps and in geographic descriptions of the Russian Empire produced in the late nineteenth and early twentieth centuries, Kharkiv is assigned to Little Russia along with Poltava and Chernihiv.[28] The same is apparent on ethnographic maps produced in Lviv in the late nineteenth century: there, the eastern boundary of Ukraine runs along the external borders of the Kharkiv and Katerynoslav gubernias. In an illustrated description of the Russian Empire published in the United States in the mid-nineteenth century, the Kharkiv gubernia is also included in Little Russian geographic and administrative space.

In their turn, Russian and foreign travelers passing through Kharkiv in the late nineteenth and early twentieth centuries assigned the Kharkiv region to Little Russia, as their many predecessors had done in the late eighteenth and early nineteenth centuries.[29] For example, the English traveler Annette Meakin describes the Kharkiv region by invoking recognizable Little Russian stereotypes, including such distinguishing characteristics of Little Russia as clean and neat houses, the poetic disposition of their inhabitants, the closeness of Little Russians to Slavic "roots," which supposedly distinguished them from Russians, and the like.[30]

The availability of multiple definitions of one and the same territory and of the "native" population identified with it allows one to speak of the undeveloped state of national discourse in the "pre-national" Russian Empire. The rise and development of regional and national components of identity did not eliminate representations of Orthodox Slavic imperial "Russianness" existing at the time, although such representations found themselves increasingly under the pressure of more modern concepts of the nation, both Ukrainian and Russian.

## The Ukrainian-Russian Borderland

At the regional level, of course, the acculturation and nationalization of the rural population did not proceed so intensively as in Kharkiv. In the Kharkiv gubernia, the ratio of ethnic Ukrainians to Russians was 80.6 percent to 17.7 percent, respectively.[31] On the eve of World War I, it changed even more in favor of the Ukrainians (almost 86 percent to 13 percent, respectively).[32] In practice, this simply meant the deepening of the breach between city and province: Ukrainian peasants preferred to resettle in other regions of the Russian Empire, primarily the North Caucasus, the Far East, and Siberia, instead of going to Kharkiv; furthermore, in the late nineteenth and early twentieth centuries Kharkiv Ukrainians moved from the center to the suburbs, making way for more enterprising migrants from other regions of the Russian Empire.[33]

The breach between the gubernia center and the province with regard to literacy was no less striking in the Kharkiv region: if in Kharkiv itself more than half the population was able to read and write by the end of the nineteenth century, the figure in the gubernia was almost three times lower (16.85 percent).[34] By that standard, the Kharkiv gubernia yielded substantially to those of Katerynoslav (21.5 percent literacy), Kherson (25.9 percent), and Tavriia (27.9 percent), surpassing only Podilia.[35] Thus it is not surprising that while scholars of world reputation were at work in Kharkiv University, natives of the Kharkiv villages were still engaging in witch hunts. The low cultural and educational level of the rural population of the Kharkiv gubernia may be considered the basic obstacle to its cultural Russification.

Nevertheless, given the influence of modernization and urban culture, the reciprocal influence of ethnic Russians and Ukrainians in the region was becoming more apparent. Professor Andrei Krasnov of Kharkiv University, traveling through the region in 1902 and noting the unquestionable affinity and kinship of "Little Russians" in the Kharkiv and Poltava regions, emphasized the interaction of Russians and Ukrainians in that territory: "The traditional hostility between the *khokhly* and the *moskali*—the basic distinction between their social bases in the Kharkiv region—is beginning to abate, though by no means fully as yet. In any case, these completely different peoples are beginning to show mutual influence." Thus, Russians were beginning to speak the *"khokhol"* dialect" and *khokhly* to wear Russian dress, and there was a rising rate of intermarriage.[36]

Along with already traditional assertions about inhabitants of the Kharkiv region as an ethnoculturally mixed population on the border of Ukraine and Russia, in the latter half of the nineteenth century, attempts were being made to establish a different ethnocultural identification of Slobodians, going beyond the framework of Ukrainian-Russian dualism. That is how an ethnographic sketch of Kharkiv gubernia by Aleksandr Rittikh, published in 1880, may be interpreted. The author emphasizes that the Kharkiv gubernia is "wholly Russian and Orthodox" but notes nevertheless that in language, character, way of life, "composition," and "notions," the local population, differing from both Great Russians and Little Russians, represents the same ethnographic type as the one predominant in the region of New Russia.[37] But Rittikh considered this "new phenomenon" not yet fully formed; hence he could not assign the Kharkiv region to any definite ethnographic territory. Similar conclusions were reached by another ethnographer of the Sloboda region, Petro Ivanov, who studied the life and beliefs of peasants in the Kupiansk district of the Kharkiv gubernia.[38]

It may be assumed that both Rittikh and Ivanov clearly lacked a theoretical arsenal sufficient to conceptualize their observations within the framework either of a regional identity taking shape in Southern Russia to supplement its already existing spatial geographic and economic dimensions, or of Ukrainian ethnocultural identity, or of a particular borderland identity of the population of the Kharkiv region. In any case, one may assume that dominant among the local rural population at the time was a congeries of local variants of a premodern "Slavo-Rossian" Orthodox identification, including Little Russian but not coterminous with it or with other "lower" forms of identity.[39]

## The All-Russian Orthodox Discourse

As the imperial government familiarized itself with national ideas in the course of the late nineteenth and early twentieth centuries, Russian nationalist notes began to sound ever more openly in its policy. However, the Russian imperial elite of that day was unable to come to terms with the idea of modern nationality and go beyond religious notions in comprehending it. The deputy minister of public education under Emperor Alexander III, Prince Mikhail Volkonsky, seeking to define criteria for membership in the "Russian nationality," was unable to come up with anything better than the following declaration: "Only an Orthodox was considered truly Russian, and only a Russian could be truly Orthodox."[40] Russian public opinion paid increasing attention to the difference between the empire, with its ethnic diversity, and the Russian geographic nucleus. But the boundaries of the latter remained diffuse and undefined.

If, like representatives of the upper imperial bureaucracy, one considered Orthodoxy the token of Russianness, then on the symbolic map of the empire

Kharkiv belonged unconditionally to the nucleus of Orthodox Russia. In that regard, Kharkiv hardly differed from the large cities of central Russia. At the same time, it differed substantially from cosmopolitan Odesa, for example, or from the Polish-Jewish towns of Right-Bank Ukraine, which, viewed from the center, were fraught with hidden danger to imperial Orthodox identity. In Kharkiv, it must be considered that there was no such threat.

When Archbishop Antonii (Khrapovitsky) of Volhynia and Zhytomyr, known for his political activity, was appointed to Kharkiv, the press of Volhynia considered it a move "from the Volhynian periphery to the center of Russia" on the part of the hierarch,[41] somehow reminiscent of a retreat from the front line to the rear. True, the Kharkiv Orthodox clergy did not rest on its laurels, but instead of combating the powerful Catholic Church or converting Judaists, they were busy with small religious sects of different varieties or, for example, with the activists of the Tolstoyan movement, to say nothing of left-wing secular ideologies and parties.

Imperial Orthodox symbolism defined Kharkiv's civic cultural space in many ways, filling it with churches in the neo-Russian Byzantine style, public rituals of multitudinous official feasts, ecclesiastical and secular, and every conceivable kind of mass ceremony on the occasion of historical jubilees of Slavic literature (1885), the baptism of Rus' (1888), and name days of members of the imperial family

**Figure 4.1.** Annunciation Cathedral, the main Russian Orthodox church in Kharkiv (1888), architect Mikhail Lovtsov. © Volodymyr Kravchenko, 2008.

and associated events. The wreck of the tsar's train near Borky, in the vicinity of Kharkiv, in 1888 gave Kharkiv gubernia greater prominence on the symbolic map of Orthodox Russia and found reflection in the city's cultural life.

The emperor survived it, although he suffered various degrees of trauma. The Orthodox Church hastened to clothe the incident in the appearance of a miracle. A chapel was erected on the site of the wreck, and in less than two full years about 100,000 rubles were raised in donations for its construction. Vasilii Karazin's grandson, the painter Nikolai Karazin, dedicated an epic painting to the subject, and the local photographer Alfred Fedetsky prepared an album of photographs concerning the accident that he ceremoniously presented to King Christian of Denmark, while the Kharkiv clergy had a silver bell cast to mark the occasion and installed in the bell tower of the Dormition Cathedral.[42]

As the imperial Orthodox discourse felt the increasing influence of political radicalism, it responded with ever-increasing militancy. In the early twentieth century, Kharkiv became an arena of activity of Russian imperial nationalist organizations, the Russian Assembly and the Union of the Russian People.[43] Professors of Kharkiv University, particularly Andrei Viazigin, became leaders of the Black Hundreds in Kharkiv and actively propagandized their ideas in periodicals such as *Mirnyi trud* (Peaceful labor), *Glas naroda* (Voice of the people), and *Chernaia sotnia* (Black hundred). By early 1907 formal membership in the Kharkiv chapter of the Union of the Russian People had reached almost four thousand, while the gubernia as a whole had about twelve thousand members.[44] But one should not be misled by these figures. Russian nationalists in Kharkiv could hardly count on mass support in the relatively modernized space of a university town lacking such a strong irritant to the benighted mob as compact settlements of unassimilated Jews in their quarters.

In Kharkiv, many activists of the Polish and even the Jewish national movements encountered a much more tolerant attitude than in the outlying towns, which were bastions of Orthodox nationalism. The "foreigners" most visible to the local population—Germans and Jews—turned out to be sufficiently integrated into the city's cultural space. They were represented first and foremost by the scholarly, cultural, and entrepreneurial business elite, not by small merchants and tradesmen in direct contact with semi-rural lumpen elements. Owing to the large number of Jewish students, the city became one of the first Zionist centers with a global reputation. In 1882 Jewish students of Kharkiv University established the BILU Society ("The House of Yaakov, arise and let's go!") and became pioneers of Jewish settlements in Ottoman-ruled Palestine (Eretz Israel). The Zionist movement that arose in Kharkiv did not have a radical character there. The same may be said about the Polish intelligentsia of Kharkiv.

The basic criteria for creating an image of "foreigners" in mass consciousness were still traditional religious and ethnic stereotypes characteristic of the premodern era. In the late nineteenth century, local Russian nationalists sounded the alarm about the "conquest" of Kharkiv first by Jews, then by Germans, and in the twentieth century, especially during World War I, they added Ukrainians as well. In general, however, as noted earlier, Kharkiv avoided the extremes of modern nationalism in all its manifestations.

Unlike Katerynoslav or Odesa, Kharkiv did not become an arena of bloody Jewish pogroms or interethnic conflicts. It was of course possible, in the spirit of official policy, to change the name of the city orchard from Bavarian to Slavic, or change the name of German Street to Pushkin Street, as was done in Kharkiv in the late nineteenth century. One could guarantee victory for members of the Black Hundreds—large landowners, peasants, and Orthodox priests—elected from Kharkiv gubernia to the Third State Duma, as happened in 1907. It should be noted, however, that even Black Hundreders in Kharkiv had the reputation of being more or less "civilized."[45] They were inclined to avoid armed conflict with their opponents.

Aside from confessional, imperial, and anti-Western components, the discourse of modern Russian nationalism in Kharkiv included an ethnocultural—that is, Great Russian—element. As early as the 1860s, for example, contemporaries distinguished "Slavophiles" working in Kharkiv "in the name of the Great Russian nationality" from "Ukrainophiles" acting "in the name of the Little Russian nationality."[46] The latter were in the majority. Khrystyna Alchevska recalled that in Kharkiv, along with a Ukrainian circle, there was a Great Russian circle led by someone named Yuriev, and she spoke of a certain rivalry between them. Members of both circles organized a competitive choral performance at which the public was restrained in its attitude to the Ukrainians while calling for an encore from the (Great) Russian choir.[47]

Unfortunately, Alchevska did not identify the audience or judges at the concert, nor did she say anything about the program or the membership of the Great Russian circle. Indeed, the very scarcity of information about the event is quite telling. By all accounts, Great Russian ethnofolklorism, regardless of its choral achievements, yielded in popularity to "all-Russian" secular culture, which was closer to the imperial than to the ethnocultural variant of nation-building. The exponents of that type of culture were mainly the city's liberal-democratic middle strata, which had preponderant influence in bodies of local self-government, community organizations, cooperatives, higher educational institutions, as well as professional, women's, labor, and student movements. According to Michael Hamm, it was thanks to their influence that local politics were relatively free of significant ethnic conflict and odious personalities.[48]

In the late nineteenth century, even representatives of the imperial administration in Kharkiv reacted much more calmly to the Ukrainian national movement than their colleagues in Kyiv. It is a question whether this toleration should be considered a consequence of the democratic traditions of local society, capable of overcoming nationalist extremes,[49] or of confusion between Little Russian and

Ukrainian identities, or simply of indifference to nationality in its modern form. The question remains open, and a search for answers to it is beyond the scope of the present work.

## Demography

The population of Kharkiv increased in geometric progression, mainly owing to new arrivals. Thus, in 1866 the city had a population of 60,788, and in 1912 already 238,466.[50] Kharkiv yielded in size of population only to Kyiv and Odesa, with which it had traditionally been compared since the nineteenth century, but it also withstood comparison to Lviv (almost 160,000 by the end of the nineteenth century). In the Russian Empire, Kharkiv held ninth place after St. Petersburg, Moscow, Warsaw, Odesa, Kyiv, Łódź, Riga, and Tiflis; as for foreign cities, Kharkiv was comparable in population to such cities as Minneapolis or Prague.[51]

The ethnic structure of Kharkiv's population reflected its mainly Ukrainian-Russian character. The all-Russian census of 1897, in which language served as the main criterion of ethnic differentiation, showed that Russians constituted 63.2 percent of the city's population and Ukrainians 25.9 percent (all others taken together made up 11.8 percent).[52] In percentage weight of Ukrainians compared to other ethnic groups, Kharkiv outdid all large cities on the territory of what is now Ukraine. Ethnic Ukrainians accounted for slightly more than 22 percent of the population of Kyiv, more than 18 percent in Lviv, and three times more than 5.7 percent in Odesa.[53] Otherwise, an exception might be made only for Poltava—the only gubernia city in the Russian Empire in which ethnic Ukrainians made up more than half the population.

It should be noted, however, that there is now a somewhat different estimate of the ethnic composition of Kharkiv's population. According to recent research, the two most numerous ethnic groups in the city, Ukrainians and Russians, were roughly equal: the former constituted about 43 percent, the latter about 42 percent.[54] But neither ethnic origin nor language of choice can serve as the main criteria of national identification in this period. Citizens of Kharkiv combined premodern components of identity with modern ones or simply ignored them altogether.

The constant growth of the Russian population in Kharkiv was due mainly to migration. In the late nineteenth century, for example, new arrivals, many of them peasants, accounted for slightly more than 60 percent. The basic contingent of migrants came from the neighboring Great Russian Kursk, Voronezh, and Orel gubernias, as well as the Moscow and Kaluga gubernias. By that indicator, the Kharkiv gubernia was far ahead of such regions as Kyiv and Katerynoslav.[55] The total number of migrants from the gubernias of Left-Bank Ukraine (Poltava, Katerynoslav) and, in part, from the Right Bank (the Kyiv and Podilia gubernias) was substantially smaller.

Third in number in Kharkiv, after Russians and Ukrainians, were Jews, who began to arrive from the Polish and Ukrainian historical regions. In the late nineteenth century, the Jewish population of Kharkiv grew at a much faster rate than the general population: in 1867, according to figures compiled by Aleksandr Rittikh, there was a total of 906 Jews of both sexes in Kharkiv; by 1879 their numbers had grown to 5,194;[56] and the census of 1897 gave a total of 9,848, or 5.7 percent of the city's population.[57] Of Ukraine's largest cities, Kharkiv had the smallest Jewish population, as compared with Kyiv (12.1 percent), Lviv (about 30 percent), or Odesa (32.6 percent).[58]

Aside from Russians, Ukrainians, and Jews, there were Poles and Germans living in Kharkiv. At the end of the nineteenth century, Poles numbered 3,969 (up to 3.3 percent) and Germans 2,353 (about 1.4 percent).[59] Representatives of other peoples, among whom one could encounter migrants from various countries and regions of Europe and Asia (particularly the French, Armenians, and Tatars), were insignificant in absolute numbers. It remains to be added that members of the various ethnic groups living in Kharkiv were represented unequally in its social structure. Ethnic Ukrainians turned out to be a minority in almost all spheres of employment, beginning with servants and carters and ending with highly qualified professionals as well as intelligentsia and business elites.[60] In that regard, Kharkiv was no exception to other large cities on Ukrainian ethnic territory, where Ukrainians remained a minority tied more to traditional than to modern society.

In the view of contemporaries, Ukrainians living in Kharkiv in the mid-nineteenth century acquired a lasting reputation as "turncoats" (*perevertni*)—an ethnically mixed type of population differing both from "pure" Ukrainians/Little Russians and from "pure" Russians/Great Russians. The Russian Slavophile Ivan Aksakov, visiting Kharkiv in 1854, noted that the population was "rabble, urban, civilized, spoiled Little Russians, spoiled Great Russians."[61] Similar descriptions and self-descriptions of inhabitants of the Ukrainian-Russian borderland were widespread in this historical period of the city and region.

"The population of Kharkiv," wrote a contemporary of Aksakov in 1856,

> constitutes a mixture of the Russian and Little Russian tribes. The gentry and officials are half from one and half from the other tribe; the merchants are almost all Russians and the eldest in their families or single, or they have gone no farther than their fathers in resettling from the Great Russian gubernias, mainly those of Kaluga, Tula, and Moscow; half the city dwellers are Russian, from the same gubernias as the merchants; on the other hand, four-fifths of the tradesmen and peasants are Little Russians. Hence, if one takes the population as a whole and examines the mores, customs, and mainly the language of Kharkivites, it turns out that neither of the main elements, Russian or

> Little Russian, is distinguishing or dominant, and as for language, a further peculiarity will present itself, that just as the dialect of the local Little Russians is not the genuine one of that tribe, so the dialect of the local Russians cannot be called pure and correct.[62]

There is hardly anything new in principle to be discovered in the foregoing testimonies concerning the specifics of the Ukrainian-Russian borderland as compared with notions about the Russification of the Sloboda region already widespread in the nineteenth century. These observations attest further to the partiality of such opinions. Behind the new waves of Russian migrants, it was somehow not always apparent that acculturation in Kharkiv was turning out to be a bilateral and multilateral process (if other ethnic groups are taken into account). Moreover, Russians were also somewhat influenced by Ukrainians and adopted certain features of the local population's everyday culture.

The Ukrainian historians Dmytro Bahalii and Dmytro Miller, considering the reasons for the "Russianization" of Kharkiv in the nineteenth century in ethnocultural and socioeconomic terms (the constant influx of Russians; the limited capacity of Little Russians, as compared with Great Russians, to engage in commerce and enterprise; the inexperience of Sloboda residents in urban life, and so on), still operated with the terminology of "all-Russian" culture, maintaining that it was precisely that type of culture (and not Great Russian culture) that was produced by the city's educational institutions, and that it was precisely all-Russian and not ethnic Great Russian culture that "overawed the local inhabitants and rendered them submissive."[63]

The Kharkiv "turncoats" represented the so-called native population of the city: it was impossible in short order to acquire certain traits of the culture of their closest neighbors and pass on some of their own to them. And yet the city's residents already possessed something of a common local identity. Convincing evidence of this may be seen in the reaction of Kharkivites to the influx of the thousands of migrants who came to the city at the turn of the twentieth century from various gubernias and regions of the empire.

"Under the influence of the unceasing oscillation of inflow and outflow," complained the Kharkiv *Statisticheskii listok* (Statistical leaflet) in 1884,

> the unmoving aborigines who once founded the city ... are being forced out everywhere. The city is being left without tradition; it is turning into a caravanserai on the beaten path, a place for notarial transactions, for medical assistance on a colossal scale, for all kinds of riffraff—for judicial investigations ... for speculation of every kind.... The population that would hold Kharkiv itself dear is constantly growing scarce.[64]

Slightly more than two decades later, Dmytro Bahalii and Dmytro Miller expressed apprehension that uncultured elements, penetrating in large numbers, will undoubtedly dilute the cultured stratum of citizens and bring their primordial rusticity into the city, and that will inevitably be reflected in dwellings, in the way of life and morals, and in public services, especially if the new arrivals are given the opportunity to influence them not only indirectly but directly as well. Of course, they will be in no condition to assimilate the cultured citizens, but the difference between them will be all the more stark, and there will be all the more scope for class struggle and class hostility.[65]

As we see, both quotations reproduce the nativist reaction of citizens to the influx of people from other towns and from the country. This reaction, fraught with fears of losing historical traditions and the urban cultural milieu, does not contain appeals for a united front of "us" against "them" or, even less, for prohibiting new migrants from coming into the city. The mass of new arrivals, who were basically migrants from the central gubernias of Russia proper, is defined by the authors of these quotations mainly by reference to their sociocultural and not their ethnic characteristics.

## Urban Space

Kharkiv's new urban space took shape according to new socioeconomic tendencies in the Russian Empire. The Kharkiv railway station, built in 1870 and reconstructed in 1896–1901, was long one of the city's major sights, a symbol of its unceasing progress and prosperity, impressing many of the passengers who made their way through it. An early twentieth-century traveler artlessly shared his impressions as follows: "In Kharkiv I was greatly impressed by the beautiful new railway station and its lavish architecture. In the first-class hall there are two large wall clocks supported by statues of muses; the walls and ceilings are decorated with signs of the zodiac and emblems of the Kharkiv gubernia and local railways. The abundance of light, cleanliness and tidiness, and huge dimensions of the building make a great impression."[66]

More than a decade later, he was echoed by Reverend N. Nikolaev, an Orthodox priest, who was traveling through Ukraine: "In Kharkiv, the arriving traveler is impressed first and foremost by the vast railway station, magnificent within and without, with molded and painted ceilings and walls. Hundreds of people arrive and depart, like living lava. Indeed, we have not seen such a station in the capitals, and Kharkivites say that as yet there is none to rival it in Russia."[67] It is worth noting that the author of those lines was echoed about fifteen years later by "Father Fedor," a literary figure of some repute in the satirical *Twelve Chairs* by the Odesa writers Ilf and Petrov, who would also "pass" that way. A monument to this comical adventurer was erected recently on the platform of the Kharkiv railway station.

The railway station transformed the peripheral Katerynoslav Street into a thoroughfare. The imposing banks that proudly occupied all of St. Nicholas Square, across from the building of the Assembly of the Nobility, transformed the city's historic center, where they still remain intact under different names. The local Russian merchant dynasties, immortalized by the Russian dramatist Aleksandr Ostrovsky, were joined by financial magnates of the new generation. Among them were the Ukrainians Aleksei/Oleksii Alchevsky and Ivan Vernadsky.

New quarters appeared in Kharkiv: industrial and working-class on the outskirts, elite in the center and adjoining streets, and hovels near the markets. Kharkiv experienced a major industrial and construction boom in the brief period between 1905 and 1914, when, in the words of a contemporary, it "turned from a large but quiet city of merchants and bureaucrats living a patriarchal life in small separate households into a truly contemporary big city with advanced capital activity, with large factories and workshops, with the centralization of all civic life, with economic levels at extreme odds, and an increasing struggle for existence."[68]

The consolidation of public space was conducive to the appearance of a new infrastructure of Kharkiv's economic and communications network: running water (1881), horse-drawn trams (1882), telephone lines (1888), and streetcars (1906). Kharkiv further consolidated its reputation as a major center of teaching and sci-

**Figure 4.2.** Former Land Bank in Kharkiv (1899), architect Aleksei Beketov. © Volodymyr Kravchenko, 2008.

ence in the late nineteenth and early twentieth centuries, when new institutions of higher learning were added to the university: veterinary (1873) and technological (1885) institutes, as well as specialized secondary educational institutions, all kinds of courses of study, and institutions of public education. As a result, there was a steady rise of literacy in the city: if in 1866 the literacy rate was about 36 percent, by 1897 it exceeded 52 percent.[69] However, statistics show that the Orthodox population of Kharkiv (with a literacy rate of about 50 percent) lagged significantly behind observant Jews (67 percent), Catholics (75 percent), and Protestants (89 percent).[70]

The appearance of all kinds of reference works, calendars, indexes, and city guidebooks describing and marking Kharkiv's cultural space may be considered another indication of the city's swiftly developing cultural milieu. The end of the nineteenth century even saw the publication of a humorous guide to Kharkiv written in verse—evidence of a certain maturity of local urban identity. But the fundamental two-volume *History of the City of Kharkiv over Its 250 Years of Existence* (1905-12) by Dmytro Bahalii and Dmytro Miller, unrivaled in scope anywhere in Ukraine, may of course be considered a weightier assertion of Kharkiv's claim to urban status.

Finally, local journalism was also creating Kharkiv's new civic space: the newspapers *Khar'kovskie gubernskie vedomosti* (Kharkiv gubernia news), *Iuzhnyi krai* (Southern land), *Khar'kov, Khar'kovskii listok* (Kharkiv leaflet), and many others, including special departmental publications and journals of various kinds, such as humorous ones. It should be emphasized that unlike such Russian cities as Pskov, Nizhnii Novgorod, Orenburg, and Irkutsk, where the press of the capitals was unquestionably dominant, Kharkiv could rival the Moscow and St. Petersburg papers with its own daily periodical publication, *Iuzhnyi krai*, published in a press run of 100,000 copies and distributed far beyond the boundaries of the Kharkiv gubernia throughout the southern regions of empire.[71] In that regard, *Iuzhnyi krai* continued the traditions of early nineteenth-century Kharkiv journalism.

## The Ukrainian Movement

The transformation of Kharkiv into a city of the modern industrial type and the consolidation of its sociocultural space created a milieu conducive to the reception and dissemination of ideas and concepts of modern nationalism in local society, even though it was limited mainly to the sociocultural space of the modernized enclaves of that society. Ukrainian national discourse developed mainly in the intellectual milieu associated with the local university. Its representatives were individuals who had come from various historical regions of Ukraine, above all the Sloboda region, the former Hetmanate, and Southern Russia. It was they who formed the quasi-legal Ukrainian association (*hromada*) in Kharkiv, which inaugurated its existence with initiatives to publish literature "for the people" in the Ukrainian language associated with the spiritual leaders of the Ukrainian national movement—Taras Shevchenko, Mykola Kostomarov, Panteleimon Kulish—and with discussions about Ukrainian literature.[72]

The Ukrainian national movement in post-reform Kharkiv progressed rapidly from the antiquarian to the organizational and, even more, to the political stage at the beginning of the twentieth century. But this was no orderly progression from one stage to another. A distinctive feature of the movement was its syncretism. It existed in two main forms, ethnocultural and sociopolitical, which were based, respectively, on the Little Russian and Ukrainian versions of national identity.[73] Those articulating the Little Russian version confined themselves to the official imperial doctrine of a "triune Slavo-Rossian nation" embracing Great Russians, Little Russians, and White Russians beneath the Orthodox umbrella and Russian-language high culture. Their rivals proclaimed their cultural and political distinction from imperial Russia on the basis of language and social radicalism.

The members of the Ukrainian *hromada* in Kharkiv were not marginal figures in the cultural, social, and economic life of the city. Notable among them, in the words of Professor Mykola Sumtsov, were solid, influential, and even rich people whose voices sounded "extraordinarily authoritative" in the local milieu and beyond.[74] In this regard, it suffices to recall the names of the Alchevsky and Vernadsky families of millionaire bankers, the scholars and pedagogues Yefimenko, the artist Serhii Vasylkivsky, the dramatist Marko Kropyvnytsky, and representatives of the university professoriate: the historian Dmytro Bahalii in addition to the philologists Oleksandr Potebnia and Mykola Sumtsov. It is interesting that all these people were not Kharkiv-born: they came to the city from different regions at various times.

Those Ukrainians who limited their activity to Little Russian discourse, not going beyond the national doctrine professed by the autocratic regime, presented no threat to the latter and could feel at peace in the ethnocultural space of "Little Russianism," availing themselves of the ambiguous national semantics of "Russianness" and even "Ukrainianness," which combined ethnic elements with regional ones. The ambiguity of Ukrainian semantics was artfully employed, for example, by Dmytro Bahalii as he defended himself against political charges of "Ukrainophilism" and showed that his dissertation on the colonization of Sloboda Ukraine corresponded fully to the official understanding of "nationality."[75] The same ambiguity of official discourse made it possible to develop certain elements of Little Russian culture within all-Russian bounds.

Practically all representatives of the older generation of the Ukrainian intelligentsia in Kharkiv took part in the activity of all-Russian cultural organizations or parties, most often under the slogans of cultural populism and love of their "small" motherland. They accepted Mykola Kostomarov's views on "two Russian nationalities," according to which a niche was reserved for "home use" of the Ukrainian language, while the sphere of "high" culture was reserved for Russian. In practice, the activity of Ukrainian "cultural figures" in Russian public space was made possible by the indeterminacy and ambiguity of "Russianism."

From the moment of its appearance, the Ukrainian language–based movement in Kharkiv felt its isolation in local society. A fateful role in that circumstance was played by the narrowness of the Ukrainian intellectuals' ideological program, as they placed their main emphasis on the symbolic aspects of Ukrainian folk culture, with language as their central concern. Not surprisingly, the Ukrainian language, deprived of conditions for unhampered functioning and dissemination in society, found modern urban cultural space uncongenial. Hence the lamenting and complaining characteristic of many early members of the Ukrainian *hromada* in Kharkiv about the steady decline of the Ukrainian language and indifference toward it on the part of educated social strata.

In what was perhaps the first public indication of its existence—an open letter to "Galician youth" published in 1862—the Kharkiv Ukrainian association gave a generally cheerless picture of the state of Ukrainian culture in Kharkiv: "if, five years or so ago, it had somehow come into your heads to send a letter to Kharkiv and call out: well, where are true Ukrainians to be found here? Speak up! It's hardly likely that anyone would have responded."[76] The authors of the letter went on to complain about the Ukrainian clergy, which had become alien to its people and was guilty of Russification and the moral degradation of its people, and to lament that "we, the educated Ukrainian gentry, will soon have been trailing behind Moscow for more than a century."[77]

If this picture is compared with the image of Kharkiv and region created through the efforts of Vasilii Karazin, Hryhorii Kvitka, and many of their contemporaries, then there is clearly a huge abyss between them. In all likelihood, Kvitka would have been astounded to find that two decades after the publication of his article about "Ukrainians" there were almost none of them left in Kharkiv. As noted earlier, at the turn of the twentieth century there was a greater percentage of ethnic Ukrainians in Kharkiv than in Kyiv or Lviv, to say nothing of Odesa, and fewer Russians than in Kyiv. But the imagined reality, multiplied by tradition and populist sentiments, proved stronger than statistics. Most likely, Kvitka would have been offended to hear that the local clergy, renowned, in his opinion, for its learning and morality, was in no condition to teach its flock anything decent. Finally, it would hardly have occurred to him to complain that the Ukrainian gentry had been trailing behind Moscow for more than a century, since Kvitka himself, as an all-Russian noble and descendant of Cossack officers, was positively disposed to the integration of the Sloboda region into the empire.

These contrasting descriptions, separated by about two decades, indicate a radical revaluation of former symbols and values associated with social estate, locality, and old regionalism in the new Ukrainian national discourse. Unlike the regional discourse of the early nineteenth century, which presented Kharkiv in the role of a metropolis advancing impetuously together with Odesa and Moscow, progressing in status from the periphery to the center, the new Ukrainian national discourse depicted Kharkiv as peripheral, not the capital of national life, and thereby lowered its social and cultural status.

In many ways, the negative attitude toward Kharkiv in local circles of the Ukrainian intelligentsia was influenced by conservative tradition going back to Hryhorii Skovoroda that counterposed the moral "superiority" of rural life to the "city of sin." This is apparent, for example, in the work of the Ukrainian-language Kharkiv poet Yakiv Shchoholiv in the 1840s. It may be assumed that the composer Petro Sokalsky, a native of the region, was guided by similar motives when in his frank correspondence with Grigorii Danilevsky he referred to Kharkiv as a "deliberate scoundrel."[78]

Kharkiv, being in fact, and not just in the imagination of local patriots, one of the most dynamic cities of the new industrial type, at first fitted poorly into the cultural space delineated by Ukrainian ethnopopulist discourse. Nevertheless, the Ukrainian intellectual "conquest" of Kharkiv proceeded much faster than its "conquest" by the local peasantry. In many ways, this is to be explained by the composition of the Ukrainian national movement in the late nineteenth and early twentieth centuries.

With the beginning of the era of mass politics and political nationalism, the situation in the Ukrainian national movement started to change, but the culmination of that process was still a long way off. The divergence between the moderate culturally oriented Ukrainians and those who were politically oriented or radical nationalists became even more pronounced. A leading exemplar of the moderates was the prominent scholar and civil-society activist Dmytro Bahalii, a professor of Kharkiv University, who represented the so-called *oblast* (regional) current in imperial historiography. Bahalii came to Kharkiv from Kyiv, already a conscious Ukrainian, a member of the Kyivan Old Hromada, and a student of Volodymyr Antonovych, intent on enlivening the "sleepy and rather inactive" Kharkiv "friends of the people," according to the expression of his older colleague, Professor Aleksandr/Oleksandr Kistiakovsky.[79]

Finding himself on the list of politically unreliable instructors at Kharkiv University in the mid-1880s, Bahalii was classified there as a *khokhloman*, not as a "Mazepite" or a "Ukrainian." That determined the relative ease with which he was able to rehabilitate himself in the eyes of the authorities: *khokhlomaniia* was associated with Little Russian love of folklore and peasant "folk roots" (*narodnost'*), not with Ukrainian political separatism or social radicalism, while in many respects the word *ukraina* retained its regional and not national significance.

Bahalii went on to take an active part in the life of the city and the empire in general, positioning himself as a Little Russian in Russian-speaking cultural space and limiting himself to cultural activity. For this he was subjected to severe criticism by Ukrainian national activists or even excluded by them from the category of "conscious Ukrainians." In the eyes of Russian nationalists, however, according to Sergei Shchegolev's pamphlet directory, Bahalii was still, along with Mykola Sumtsov, a prominent representative of the Ukrainian national movement in Kharkiv.

At the same time, Bahalii, professing the values of civil society and popular education, was counted as a member of "all-Russian" liberal-democratic society, which was oriented toward sociopolitical and educational considerations rather than ethnic ones. In this case, Bahalii's declared multiple identities on the personal level were nonetheless a result of political conditions, forced conformity, and opportunism, not the hybrid premodern identities characteristic of such figures as Hryhorii Kvitka and Vasilii Karazin.

The Ukrainian nationalists in Kharkiv were presented by the local lawyer Mykola Mikhnovsky and the new generation of Ukrainian student youth.[80] Mikhnovsky came to Kharkiv from Kyiv in 1899, becoming a prominent member of local society and one of the few ardent advocates of Ukrainian political independence. According to Yurii Kollard, one of the Ukrainian student activists, "it was Mikhnovsky who was largely responsible for the total break of our Kharkiv youth with Ukrainophilia and ethnographism, showing us a clear path toward revolutionary Ukrainian nationalism through radical democratism."[81]

Mikhnovsky became known as the author of the political manifesto *Samostiina Ukraïna* (Independent Ukraine). As an early ideologist of Ukrainian independence, he contributed substantially to the creation of the Revolutionary Ukrainian Party (RUP) in Kharkiv in 1900, which developed under the leadership of the former Kyiv students Dmytro Antonovych and Mykhailo Rusov. In 1902 Mikhnovsky assisted in organizing the Ukraine's People's Party, which was based on radical Ukrainian nationalism. Despite his many other political and cultural activities, Kharkiv did not became a main center of the Ukrainian movement. Instead, the new generation of the Ukrainian intelligentsia inherited "strong hostility" to Kharkiv as a Russified city.

The eminent Ukrainian composer Mykola Lysenko, replying in a letter of 1903 to a female correspondent who had asked why he avoided Kharkiv on his concert tours, wrote the following:

> I don't know how to respond to your question of why I avoid Kharkiv on my southern concert tours. Is it because it stands at the "dead end" of my artistic "journey," or did it seem to me that Ukrainian music and my work in it would not be received there? Who knows? I can't figure it out myself. I was once a greater patriot of Kharkiv when I did not live as a conscious Ukrainian, but when I went there from Kyiv after many years, I was struck by the depersonalization of Ukrainian nationality in the city: always, instead of Little Russians, I kept meeting Muscovite merchants and salespeople. With great pain in my heart, I did not see or

hear the Ukrainian people in Kharkiv, nor did I see Ukrainian society; everything there is effaced and trampled by the Muscovite spirit, Muscovite tastes. Well, everything is not ours, it's all foreign, not native.[82]

Similar motifs are clearly apparent in the words of the Ukrainian activist and patron Yevhen Chykalenko, who considered Kharkiv the most "Muscovized" of all Ukrainian cities,[83] and in the remarks of some of his contemporaries. In the final analysis, the positive image of a modern city of crossroads created by Vasilii Karazin took on the negative features in Ukrainian national discourse of a "dressing room" where people did not live but spent some time before going on to other "rooms" (that is, cities). Directly related to this was the new image of Kharkiv as Ukraine's "Moscow gate."[84]

## The Struggle for Kharkiv

The general direction of cultural policy in Kharkiv was determined, aside from the imperial bureaucracy and the Orthodox Church, by the city council, described by contemporaries as an institution consisting of "merchants and professors," and one that stood out against the background of other large cities of the Russian Empire because of its liberal character.[85] "Progressive" in its attitudes and political orientations, from the late nineteenth to the early twentieth century the elective organ of self-government in Kharkiv found itself in permanent conflict with the gubernia administration, which was appointed by the imperial center.

Michael Hamm, analyzing the politics of Kharkiv self-government, concluded that it was dominated by pragmatic considerations that obliged delegates to the city council to think more about the modernization of the civic economy, public services, and the development of education and culture than about national identity. The basic struggle in city council was waged not between Russian and Ukrainian nationalists but between progressives, who favored democratization, the rule of law, and basic civil liberties, and conservatives, who acted on the basis of official Orthodox imperial nationalism. In their polemics, these opponents exchanged conventional labels: progressives were accused of attempting to turn Kharkiv into Paris, while they replied in similar spirit that the conservatives ("rightists") were trying to bring "Odesa mores" to Kharkiv, meaning the Black Hundred movement and the militant Orthodox clericalism of the "southern Palmyra."[86]

From the late nineteenth century, civic self-government increasingly influenced the transformation of Kharkiv's cultural landscape. The details of the city council's cultural policy are most apparent in the toponymy and monuments[87] marking the new civic space, as well as in the names of civic institutions and community organizations, secondary educational institutions, schools, and scholarships named after individuals. The scope of that policy is attested by the fact that in 1894 alone the names of seventy-four streets, lanes, and other forms of Kharkiv's civic space were changed at the initiative of city council.

The Russian component of the city's cultural and civic life was quite fully reflected in the names of eminent cultural figures (Ivan Turgenev, Aleksandr Pushkin, Mikhail Lermontov, Vasilii Zhukovsky, Gavriil Derzhavin, Nikolai Nekrasov, Nikolai Chernyshevsky, Vsevolod Garshin, Petr Chaikovsky), military commanders (Petr Bagration, Mikhail Skobelev, Aleksandr Suvorov, Aleksandr Nevsky), administrators (Yevdokim Shcherbinin, Sergei Kokoshkin, Dmitrii Kropotkin), emperors (Alexander II), and geographic names (Urals, Tambov, Suzdal, Moscow, Belgorod).

Regional symbolism was no less if not more diversely reflected in the city's toponymy than that of Russia proper and represented by figures from local Slobodian history and culture such as Hryhorii Donets, Ivan Karkach, Tymofii Klochko, Hryhorii Skovoroda, Mykola Kostomarov, Vasilii Karazin, Hryhorii Kvitka, Leonard Girshman, and merchants such as Sergei Kostiurin, Vasilii Karpov, and Agrafena Goriainova. It may be considered a distinctive trait of local civic toponymy, reflecting the geographic location of the city of crossroads, that many streets were symbolically named after Ukrainian towns, including Sumy, Kharkiv, Poltava, Myrhorod, Sanzhary, Starobilsk, Zmiiv, Katerynoslav, and Sloviansk.

The Ukrainian intelligentsia of Kharkiv waged its battle for the city's cultural space under the banner of Taras Shevchenko. The struggle to immortalize the poet's name began in Kharkiv soon after his death in 1861 and was accompanied by a lively polemic in the local press concerning Shevchenko's intellectual and poetic legacy and his significance for posterity.[88] For the Ukrainian intelligentsia, Shevchenko was becoming a prophet of national renaissance. The Russian intelligentsia regarded him at best as a fighter against social injustice, and at worst as an exponent of national and social intolerance. Significantly, it was in the course of this polemic between Kharkiv intellectuals that the notion of Taras Shevchenko and Aleksandr Pushkin as opposing figures made its first appearance. This antithesis would find its continuation in the "monument war" to be discussed later.

The first Shevchenko monument in Ukraine was erected in the garden of the Alchevsky home in 1899, although it soon had to be taken down at the demand of the police. In 1907 the question of immortalizing Shevchenko's memory was raised in city council and met with sympathy. Finally, on the eve of the semicentennial of Shevchenko's death in 1911, four members of the Kharkiv city council, Ivan Kulynych, Mykola Mikhnovsky, Vasyl' Ponomarenko, and Mykola Sumtsov, raised the question again and obtained a positive decision.

On 4 March 1911 the Kharkiv city council adopted a resolution with several provisions: to place a portrait of Shevchenko in the Kharkiv Museum of Arts and Crafts; to name one of the city's main streets after him; to establish a Shevchenko Prize to be awarded annually by the Kharkiv Historical and Philological Society for the best works on Ukrainian history, literary history, and ethnography; and to establish a Shevchenko scholarship at Kharkiv Modern School no. 2. A new street on the outskirts of the city was named after the poet. It was also decided to erect a column in Ukrainian style with a depiction of the poet at the expense of city council, but the project proved impossible to realize.

The struggle "for" and "against" Shevchenko led representatives of the new generation of Ukrainian activists to counterpose the Ukrainian poet to a Russian national symbol, Aleksandr Pushkin. In the early twentieth century, the ideological and political struggle concerning monuments to each of them in Kharkiv came close to turning into a monument war. This time the initiative came from members of an illegal youth organization grouped around Mykola Mikhnovsky.

In 1904 members of the group made an unsuccessful attempt to blow up the Pushkin monument in Theater Square, in central Kharkiv, giving the authorities' refusal to permit the erection of a Shevchenko monument as the motive for their action.[89] The attempt failed for wholly technical reasons: the inexpert students failed to calculate the power of the explosive charge, so that the blast only shattered windows in the buildings closest to the monument. Such actions did far more significant damage to the image of the Ukrainian movement in the eyes of liberal Kharkiv society.

On the eve of World War I, Kharkiv witnessed the next round of the struggle between Ukrainian and Russian nationalists around the city's policy of memory. This time, discussions flared up around the name of the Ukrainian composer Mykola Lysenko, who died in 1919. The Ukrainian activist Mykola Mikhnovsky took the initiative to commemorate the composer by erecting a monument and a scholarship in his name.[90] Mikhnovsky's initiative was actively supported by a group of Ukrainian deputies who added two other names, Taras Shevchenko and Hryhorii Kvitka, to the list of prominent Ukrainians to be commemorated in Kharkiv. Their proposal, initially accepted by city council, met with opposition.

Nikolai von Ditmar, a well-known local businessman and member of the imperial State Council (*Gosudarstvennyi Sovet*), countered the Ukrainian project with the name of the famous Russian poet Mikhail Lermontov.[91] The subsequent debates between the opposing camps revealed a fundamental difference between them: when speaking of "the people," Mikhnovsky meant Ukrainians, while von Ditmar stressed openly that he recognized only the Russian people. The world war ended these debates but did not abate the growing political tension between ethnic Ukrainian and imperial Russian nationalists.

If Shevchenko could be regarded as a symbol of all-Ukrainian national culture seeking to gain civic space in Kharkiv at least in the symbolic sphere, it was Vasilii Karazin who became the most significant symbol of regional identity. Public discussion of him had begun in Kharkiv in the 1860s, when documents from the personal archive of the Slobodian educator, his observations scattered in publications difficult of access, as well as articles and memoirs about him began gradually to make their way into public circulation.

In many respects, the local cult of Karazin began to develop thanks to the efforts of his son Filadelf, who had exclusive access to his father's archive and published certain documents from that collection. Owing to the influence of Aleksandr Herzen, liberal society saw in Karazin the archetype of a westernizing intellectual unappreciated in his lifetime who had advised tsars on the "correct" development of Russia. Conservative Slavophiles, in their turn, found a good deal in his creative legacy that was consonant with their views. Patriotically inclined enthusiasts representing local society announced a campaign to raise funds for a Karazin monument in Kharkiv. As a result, his life and works took on symbolic significance, becoming one of the most influential components of the region's historical mythology.

To be sure, there was no lack of those wishing to delve into every conceivable rumor, legend, personal slight, mutual criticism, and praise that had accumulated around Karazin by recreating certain ambiguous episodes of his life and outlook. Such efforts were undertaken in particular by Osyp Bodiansky, Grigorii Danilevsky, Petr Lavrovsky, the Karazin biographers Yakov Abramov, Nikolai Tikhii, and several other scholars. As a result, the traditional regional assessment of Karazin developed through the study of local history joined with the liberal approach, managing to prevail and produce an almost ideal image of a selfless public figure, an ardent patriot of his land, a provincial scholar unappreciated in life, a liberal in disfavor who called for progressive reforms but suffered defeat in his struggle with the tsarist bureaucracy. As further developments showed, however, the public at large did not want to stand aside from the pundit controversy.

As the twentieth century began and the centennial of Kharkiv University approached, with the domestic political situation deteriorating sharply and a democratic revolution brewing in the empire, the name of Vasilii Karazin became central to a polemic that flared up in 1905 between liberal and conservative circles of the Kharkiv University professoriate. The immediate occasion for the polemic was an anonymous pamphlet under the eloquent title *Karazin, the Sham Founder of Kharkiv University, or a Story of How a Historian Can Make an Elephant Out of a Fly.*

The author of the pamphlet, whose name still remains unknown, attempted to cast doubt on the image of Karazin created by liberal and regional historiography, calling it a legend produced by juggling historical facts. Karazin is presented here as a "notorious charlatan and schemer" capable of nothing more than exaggerating his utterly modest merits and appropriating the thoughts and ideas of others, a man who had acquired a dubious reputation as a willing informer given to unscrupulous methods, and the like. That image would gain new life in the Kharkiv press a century later, in the early 2000s.

Although similar charges had also been made against Karazin by certain liberals, in this case they were supported by extreme right-wing university historians belonging to Black Hundred circles of Russian society.[92] But it was their opponents who triumphed. The erection of a monument to Karazin in Kharkiv in 1907 definitively sanctioned and symbolized his inclusion in the pantheon of eminent historical figures of the city and region. A supplement to the monument was the publication in 1910 of the first and, to date, the only collection of Karazin's works, letters, and papers, edited by Dmytro Bahalii. By then Karazin's avowal of love for his small motherland, Ukraine, which appeared on the pedestal of the monument, had managed to lose its purely local content and take on a distinct national significance.

By the eve of World War I, the Ukrainian national element of Kharkiv's cultural landscape had already become clearly apparent in the mosaic of city names: Cossack, Haidamaka, Taras Shevchenko. At the same time, there was an effort in Kharkiv's urban architecture to create a Ukrainian style. Its most prominent incarnation was the building of the Kharkiv School of Art, opened in 1912. The war prevented the realization of other "Ukrainian" projects debated in city council, especially monuments to the Ukrainian composer Mykola Lysenko and to the dramatist and artist Marko Kropyvnytsky.

Generally speaking, during the period of industrialization Kharkiv's architecture and public monuments featured movements that dominated the city's social and political life and reflected the tastes of the local administration, as well as those of the rising class of entrepreneurs.[93] If the neo-Russian Byzantine style dominates the architecture of Orthodox churches of the period, reflecting the general character of central imperial policy, then in secular architecture, both private and corporate, one sees eclecticism, most often devoid of any ethnocultural basis and more characteristic of a city imitating available models but offering nothing original.

## Regional "Ukrainization"

The success or failure of every variant of national development enumerated above was dependent in many ways on the extent to which it could adapt regional tradition. The traditions of regional historical narrative established in the late eighteenth and early nineteenth centuries were continued at Kharkiv University under the influence of democratic, populist, and Ukrainian national paradigms. The philologist Mykola Sumtsov and the historian Dmytro Bahalii, both professors at Kharkiv University, were considered the leaders of that process. The credit for creating an academic regional historical narrative at the turn of the twentieth century belongs mainly to Bahalii.[94]

The historian devoted more than a hundred specialized works to the Sloboda region, including articles, collections, monographs, and archeographic publications in which, for the first time, all the most important periods and episodes associated with the settlement, socioeconomic development, and cultural life of the region, mainly from the sixteenth to the nineteenth century, found reflection. His works included monographs of capital importance and documentary collections devoted to the historical geography of the region, the history of Kharkiv University, the biography and work of the philosopher Hryhorii Skovoroda and the educator Vasilii Karazin, and the one-of-a-kind two-volume *History of the City of Kharkiv over Its 250 Years of Existence*, written in collaboration with his student and colleague Dmytro Miller.

A historiographic analysis of Bahalii's publications on these subjects is beyond the scope of the present work. It can only be noted that the historian, like his teacher, Volodymyr Antonovych, professed the need to study the history of Ukraine region by region and represented in his work the so-called populist current in imperial Russian historiography, which stood in ideological liberal-democratic opposition to the statist juridical school. That did not prevent Bahalii from experiencing the substantial influence of the conceptions of Sergei Soloviev and Vasilii Kliuchevsky, who sought to explain many particular features of the Russian historical process by the settlement or, in the terminology of that day, the colonization of the country. Bahalii was inclined to consider colonization the basic fact of Ukrainian history.

Bahalii presented the history of Ukraine's settlement by means of a compromise formula, in the spirit of Mykola Kostomarov, based on the interaction of two streams, Great Russian and Little Russian, united by a common "cultural goal." "Their interaction was extremely useful and beneficial—one complemented the other."[95] In this regard, Bahalii followed the tradition of the regional historical narrative, which included the history of ethnic Russians and Ukrainians. Nevertheless, he drew a clear dividing line between Russian and Ukrainian colonization, considering the former to have been led by the state by means of military service and the latter a popular movement initiated "from below." Clearly, all his sympathies were with the latter.

This thesis aroused polemics during Bahalii's lifetime and drew objections from eminent Russian authors, first and foremost Vasilii Kliuchevsky, stung in their own national preferences. In imperial Russian discourse of the time, popular peasant colonization was regarded as the fundamental marker of national territory. In his *Obzor istorii russkoi kolonizatsii* (Survey history of Russian colonization), Matvei Liubavsky assessed the "consolidation of one territory or another by the Russian state in relation to the achievements of Russian colonization, first and foremost by the peasantry."[96] Some Russian publicists expressed the same opinion. But the guardians of the doctrine of official nationality did not regard comparative descriptions of Little Russians and Great Russians in Bahalii's works as politically subversive in themselves.

The title of Bahalii's doctoral dissertation, "Sketches in the History of Colonization and Life on the Steppe Frontier of the Muscovite State," which he defended successfully at Moscow University in 1887, sounded perfectly loyal, thereby drawing sarcastic comments from Mykhailo Drahomanov, who accused Bahalii of political conformism. At the time, few noted that the title itself contradicted the existing administrative and political organization of the empire, as it revived the boundaries of the historical Sloboda region, which had been significantly reduced in size during its integration into the empire.

Cautiously correcting the imperial grand narrative from a populist viewpoint, Bahalii came out openly at the same time against gentry historians of the region, who in their time had lovingly developed the myth of the noble origins of their ancestors, the first colonists. In Bahalii's opinion, such claims had to be considered groundless, as the overwhelming majority of Sloboda officers traced their origins to rank-and-file Cossacks. In his interpretation of the settlement and integration of the region into the empire, Bahalii held to anti-elitist conceptions, accusing the Cossack upper stratum of enserfing the Cossack and peasant commoners and taking over their lands. In that regard he followed his older contemporary, the historian of Little Russia Oleksandr Lazarevsky.

While rejecting the gentry narrative and the centralist interpretation of local history, Bahalii made creative use of the constructive element in those versions, the idea of progress—the discourse of modernization that was closely associated in the consciousness of local intellectuals of the early nineteenth century with integration, Russification, and the progressive reforms of the enlightened government. In Bahalii's work, however, that regional discourse of modernization was reinterpreted to favor the ideas and values of civil society over those of officialdom and promote efforts to decentralize the autocratic empire. The spirit of his writing was thus one of opposition to government policy.

The basic emphasis in Bahalii's work was not on politics or on the heroics of Cossackdom, lamenting its erstwhile glory or focusing on victimization in the national past. He turned first and foremost to the study of socioeconomic problems, questions of science and culture, as well as the traditions of civil society, especially problems of university autonomy and urban self-government and, finally, to the biographies of socially active local figures. As for chronology, Bahalii concentrated on the modern and recent history of the Sloboda region, following on the one hand the idea of the commonality of regional interests with regard to the center and, on the other, the idea of the historical continuity and "organic" link between the Sloboda region and Cossack Little Russia.

That is why, in his narrative, Bahalii sought to integrate the most notable representatives of community and cultural life—patriots of their region—regardless of their origin or the language in which they wrote. By taking this approach, he managed to include in the Ukrainian national and historical narrative those individuals and institutions whose "Ukrainianness" in the nineteenth century was of an entirely local, territorial character, above all Vasilii Karazin, Kharkiv University, and the sociocultural milieu created by the university.

Bahalii's discussion of the founding of Kharkiv University is instructive enough. His predecessors, especially Nikolai Lavrovsky, denied the "historical necessity" of the appearance of a university in Kharkiv, attributing it exclusively to Karazin's personal initiative and energy. A contemporary of Bahalii, the Polish scholar Ludwik

Janowski, showed convincingly that the idea of opening a university in Kharkiv could not be regarded as the direct result of the development of local cultural life, as it was in a state of profound somnolence at the time. In Janowski's opinion, the appearance of the university had no organic connection with the historical development of the Sloboda region and was in fact a break with tradition, not a reflection of the social and cultural evolution of local society.[97]

Nevertheless, Bahalii, arguing in some instances against facts available to him, came forward with a substantiation of the "organicism" of Kharkiv University—its association with the local cultural milieu. This allowed him to link the appearance of a university in Kharkiv not so much with governmental initiative as with elements of local civil society—the philosopher Hryhorii Skovoroda, the enlightened gentry elite of the region, urban self-government, and even particular social estates—the peasants and citizens who had supported the university project with their donations.

Bahalii sought not merely to reproduce and, all the more, to glorify the Ukrainian historical tradition: he attempted to integrate it into contemporary reality and bring it into accord with his own time. Striking in that regard is his attitude to a polemic concerning the entrepreneurial "aptitudes" of ethnic Russians and Ukrainians, of which Ivan Pereverzev had written back in the late eighteenth century. Bahalii attempted to prove that the stereotypical image of the Ukrainian—sleepy, lazy, and little given to enterprise, leaving all large-scale commerce to the more energetic Russian merchants—was not borne out by the facts. "It is usually accepted to think," he wrote, "that all ... market trade was in the hands of the Great Russian merchants, as the Little Russians were completely incapable of such activity. But this proposition requires some qualifications and explanations. Merchants from other towns settled for permanent residence only in Kharkiv and Sumy."[98] In other towns of the region, apparently, trade was in the hands of local entrepreneurs.

A most important achievement of Bahalii as a Ukrainian historian of the Sloboda region was his introduction of a whole series of subjects and personalities representing the region's cultural tradition into the arsenal of national historiography. These were, first and foremost, the life and work of Hryhorii Skovoroda, Vasilii Karazin, Petro Hulak-Artemovsky, and Grigorii Danilevsky, as well as the history of Kharkiv University and the periodicals and literature associated with it. As a result, Kharkiv was integrated into the new Ukrainian grand narrative in fairly respectable fashion, wholly compatible with regional tradition, as the capital of the Ukrainian national "renaissance," not the "Moscow gate" opening the way to the sacralized territory of the nation to the "foreigner."

Bahalii managed to synthesize within the framework of the Ukrainian national paradigm almost all the basic features of local regional discourse: modernization, the *antemurale*, progress, the supposedly always immanent inclination of Slobodians toward the sciences and education, ethnocultural Ukrainian-Russian dualism—all but the contradictions of the Sloboda region and Little Russiia. Bahalii affirmed the view that the region's identity was predominantly Ukrainian but did not deny or exclude from his narrative the Russian component, which had been present from the outset.

Even so, the new regional narrative created by Bahalii, which covered developments down to 1917, remained part of the "all-Russian" historical narrative, featuring populism and enlightenment. The collections of historical studies of the Sloboda region published by Bahalii at the beginning of the twentieth century appeared under the series title *Sketches from Russian History*. Thus, it is worth emphasizing that Bahalii's basic works on the history of the region, written during the imperial period, were published in Russian. These were evidently the circumstances that aroused doubts during Bahalii's lifetime about his belonging to Ukrainian national historiography.[99]

After the February Revolution, which put an end to the autocracy and opened the way for the democratic restructuring of the Russian Empire, Bahalii wrote his works exclusively in Ukrainian. The result of his many years of research was the first synthetic work on the history of Sloboda Ukraine, published in the Ukrainian language in 1918, which openly asserted that the region belonged to the national and historical space of Ukraine as a whole, although, as will be pointed out in the following chapter, Bahalii's treatment differed in substantial respects from the interpretation of the region's history proposed by Mykhailo Hrushevsky.

Bahalii was not the only creator of a Ukrainian national version of the history of the Sloboda region. His colleagues and students, most notably Dmytro Miller and Viktor Barvinsky, were companions and supporters in that process. A notable contribution to the creation of a Ukrainian image of the region was made by the philologist Mykola Sumtsov, who devoted many works to the study of the everyday life, folklore, and literature of Sloboda Ukraine. A synthesis of his research on the subject was a generalizing Ukrainian-language work of popular history entitled *Slobozhany* (Slobodians), published in Kharkiv in 1918 and still unique of its kind. To be sure, Sumtsov's *Slobodians* looked like nationally conscious Ukrainians, while Kvitka's "Ukrainians" remained regional "Slobodians."

It was not only professional scholars who took an active part in the "Ukrainization" of the past and present of the Sloboda region, but also writers and artists who produced striking, emotionally tinged works in their genre. The most memorable markers of the Ukrainian Sloboda region were landscape sketches devoted to the steppe, gravemounds, rivers, and depictions of Cossack warriors. In particular, the work of the aforementioned Ukrainian-language poet Yakiv Shchoholiv,[100] replete with steppe motifs, includes colorful evocations of Cossacks, reapers, beekeepers, fishermen, and wagoners. The collections of poetry that he published had familiar titles—*The Vorskla River* and *The Sloboda Region*—and synthesized motifs of the steppe landscape with nostalgia for the glorious Cossack past.

The work of a close friend of Bahalii's, the painter Serhii Vasylkivsky, also created a Ukrainian national image of the Sloboda region in significant measure. He painted a great many canvases depicting the landscape of the region, as well as paintings on historical themes delineating the expanse of the steppe with the help of the Cossack marker (*Cossack in the Steppe, Zaporozhian at His Post, Cossack Picket*), while watercolor portraits of Hryhorii Skovoroda provided a cultural reference. In the spirit of Ukrainian national historiography, he produced a typical rendering of a scene in which Peter I visits the Kharkiv fortress: the tall tsar is shown standing on its incline in such a way that he finds himself below the sullen Cossack officers in the foreground. It suffices to compare this painting with a canvas on the same subject by the Russian artist Viktor Vikhtinsky, in which Peter I towers above the officers listening deferentially to his directions, to appreciate the difference in principle between the two interpretations.[101]

Thanks to the efforts of Ukrainian intellectuals in Kharkiv, the history of the Sloboda region attained high status in the Ukrainian national historical narrative of the early twentieth century. Kharkiv was regaining its reputation as the cultural capital not only of a region but now of the whole Ukrainian national renaissance. This reputation was sanctioned by the actual creator of Ukrainian national historiography, Mykhailo Hrushevsky, and his followers and supporters.

Local history, with its pantheon of celebrities and famous sites, mainly of the most recent, university period, became an object of special study for Hrushevsky's brother, Oleksandr, also a historian, and underwent substantial "Ukrainization." Not only were Skovoroda and Karazin integrated into the Ukrainian national historical narrative, but so were all local Kharkiv periodical publications of the early nineteenth century (including those published in Russian), to say nothing of the scholarly and literary works of the Kharkiv Romantics, headed by Izmail Sreznevsky, and all authors of Ukrainian-language works living in Kharkiv in recent times.

Compared with the populist, democratic variant of the regional historical narrative represented by the works of Ukrainian historians, its official, imperial version looked much poorer. It was represented by the *History of the Kharkiv Gentry*, published in 1855 by Lev Illiashevich,[102] written in the spirit of the official ideology prevailing in the times of Nicholas I, as well as by descriptions of the martial feats of the "Sloboda regiments" by various authors. Russian nationalists could put up nothing to rival the new, professional historiography of the Sloboda region, which successfully combined Ukrainian national components with regional and liberal all-Russian ones. That historiography, stressing ideas of democratic self-government and social initiative in addition to criticizing the gentry and the bureaucracy, aroused ferocious criticism from the "right," which hopelessly lost the symbolic struggle for Kharkiv and the Sloboda region. Even Karazin and Kvitka, whose conservative spirit and feelings of loyalty to the tsarist regime were shared by representatives of the early twentieth-century "rightists," turned out to be practically monopolized by the Ukrainian liberal-democratic historians.

A public presentation of the Ukrainian image of the Sloboda region occurred in 1902 in conjunction with the XII Archaeological Congress in Kharkiv. Preparations for the congress were accompanied by an extensive press campaign and an appeal to numerous local enthusiasts to collect the historical and cultural legacy of the region. The basic result of the congress, at which a group of Ukrainian bandurists led by Hnat Khotkevych gave a performance, was the erection of an ethnographic museum in the city whose many exhibits attested to the predominance of Ukrainian culture in the everyday life of the region.

The "Ukrainization" of regional history coincided in time with the return of the Slobodian and Ukrainian lexicon to the public space of early twentieth-century Kharkiv and environs. The title of the first Ukrainian-language newspaper to appear in Kharkiv in 1906 in connection with the weakening of the ban on the Ukrainian language was Mikhnovsky's *Slobozhanshchyna* (The Sloboda region). The Ukrainian-language newspaper *Snip* (Sheaf), published in Kharkiv in 1912 also under the editorship of Mikhnovsky, represented the region as Sloboda Ukraine, with Kharkiv figuring as its capital and as the "Ukrainian Athens." In this case, there is no doubt that the "Ukrainian" terminology was meant in a national sense. In 1912, on the eve of World War I, the journal *Ukrainskii vestnik* (Ukrainian herald) was revived in Kharkiv, although for a brief period. Three years later, the journal *Slobodsko-Ukrainskii starozhil* (The Sloboda Ukraine old-timer) began its brief existence.[103]

The Ukrainian members of the Kharkiv city council, coming forward in 1911 with a program to immortalize the memory of Taras Shevchenko, formulated the Ukrainian national image of Kharkiv as follows: "The city of Kharkiv, located on the territory of the Ukrainian people and settled in significant part, if not in the majority, by the Ukrainian tribe, can and should participate most ardently in honoring the great poet, the luminary of the Ukrainian people."[104]

However, if we return to the newspaper *Snip* and its editorial, then it becomes apparent that along with "Sloboda Ukraine" symbolism it makes active use of the theme of the "Wild Field" (*Dyke pole*), or virgin soil, returning Sloboda Ukraine to its primordial geographic meaning:

> Again we have the Wild Field before us. Again, creative work is required. Thus we must cultivate the Wild Field anew and prepare the ground for the flowering of national genius ... this ground is organically, elementally Ukrainian, so that on that ground there grew a whole generation of Ukrainian writers with [Hryhorii] Kvitka at their head in the early nineteenth century and with [Oleksandr] Oles in the early twentieth century.[105]

However, as was natural for the borderland, the semantics of "Sloboda Ukraine" with its "Wild Field" showed their primal ambivalence in this instance as well. It was not only representatives of the Ukrainian national movement but also their implacable enemies, the Russian nationalists, who resorted to that motif. Thus, Professor Andrei Viazigin of Kharkiv University, one of the leaders of the Russian Congress, declared: "There is no separatism in Sloboda Ukraine ... individual voices that are sometimes raised in such a direction cannot be regarded as the voice of the whole region. No, the ancient Polovtsian steppe is not contemplating and does not want separation!"[106]

These words demonstrate, of course, not only the obvious fact that the phrases "Sloboda Ukraine" and "the steppe," which had denoted a frontier dangerous to human life more than two hundred years previously, were now being used to assert the political stability of the region. The very resort to "borderland" terminology leaves the impression that on the eve of World War I, which sharpened the perception of space and boundaries in society, the Kharkiv region began to recover the liminal status developed in the course of its history, turning into a borderland first in the symbolic and then in the literal sense of the word. But into the borderland of what, exactly? That question would have to be answered in the nearest future.

The processes of modernization, which transformed the socioeconomic and cultural space of the Russian Empire, brought new dimensions into the symbolic geography of Sloboda Ukraine but did not definitively eliminate the previous boundaries between regions developed in the course of history. The identification of the Sloboda region as part of Southern Russia did not completely coincide with the identification of Kharkiv as part of Little Russia. The former identification was oriented more toward spatial, geographic, and economic characteristics and the latter toward ethnocultural ones. But it is very difficult to assign priority to one or the other.

The foregoing also applies to the conclusion about the Ukrainian lands' definitive loss of frontier status in the nineteenth century and their integration into the historical core of Russia.[107] This is true only to the extent that "Little Russians" might have been called "Rusians" (inhabitants of Rus') in the traditional, archaic conception of "Rusianism." Yes, they might have, but with certain qualifications reflecting the remaining distance between "Great Russian" and "Little Russian" regions. The internal cultural borderland in a "backward" and primarily agrarian country remained heterogeneous: not only was it not disappearing under the influence of modernization, but it may have acquired additional resources for development.

Kharkiv on the eve of World War I and the February Revolution of 1917 did not cease to be an arena of conflicting identities, one of which was Ukrainian national identity. Assessed by its level of influence in the city and region, however, it yielded considerably not only to Russian identity in its premodern (imperial/confessional) and modern (ethnocultural/political) versions, but also to "South Russian" (economic and spatial/geographic) identity. In a few years, the struggle between them would advance to a new level of opposition.

The "South Russian" geographic localization of Kharkiv and Ukrainian nationalism at the turn of the twentieth century may be considered expressions of the general phenomenon of modernity. In principle, however, neither of them could claim a leading place in the hierarchy of various types of identity in the borderland. The dynamics of the Kharkiv region's development in the Russian Empire placed it among the most developed regions as compared not only with the western lands of the empire but also with the central regions of Russia proper. It can therefore be said that the southern regional identity of the Kharkiv region was not the result of lagging behind and weakness but, on the contrary, of the accelerated pace of modernization in the Russian Empire. It is another matter that the economic and national phenomena of modernity had little in common on the regional level.

Ukrainian intellectuals in their turn, engaged in the creation of a new national and cultural space, drew a boundary with Russia based no longer on a "Little Russian" or "Slobodian" but on a "Ukrainian" symbolic foundation. Consequently, the name "Ukraine" began to migrate from the Sloboda region to the former Little Russia, which was becoming the national heartland. Contrariwise, the name "Little Russia," becoming extended to Kharkiv and the Sloboda region, theoretically promoted the region's inclusion in the project of a "big" Russian nation in which the differences between Great Russia and Little Russia would become insignificant.

And so the new "Ukraine," changing places with the new "Little Russia," did not surmount the barrier that divided them. However, taking account of the specifics of nation-building in Ukraine, which lacked a political center, and in Russia, which tolerated regional ethnocultural particularities, the tandem of the Sloboda region and Little Russia could easily navigate the channel between them, shifting from a Russian borderland to a Ukrainian national one and back again, while remaining unscathed in the process. Depending on political conjuncture, the Sloboda region could be either an ally or an opponent of "Ukraine" or "Russia."

For the reasons noted, from the end of the nineteenth century the activity of Ukrainian "culturalists" in Kharkiv began to come under increasing criticism from Russian and Ukrainian nationalists alike, and the results of their activity were sometimes judged from diametrically opposite positions, most often according to the paradigm of a glass half full or half empty. In the view of the conservative Russian publicist Sergei Shchegolev, Kharkiv was a hotbed of Ukrainian nationalism.[108] In the comments of Ukrainian activists, Kharkiv "culturalists" came off at best as unreliable "Little Russian fellow travelers" intimidated by the government.

The Little Russian component of "Russianism" continued to predominate over the Ukrainian national segment in all spheres of the city's social, cultural, and political life thanks above all to its ambivalence and inclusive character, which made it simultaneously compatible with notions of Russianism and Ukrainianism alike. Consequently, when it came to nationality, Kharkiv held to its accustomed borderland status, maintaining the mutable heterogeneous character of a cultural contact zone.

The talented St. Petersburg critic Petr Pilsky, who visited Kharkiv in 1916, managed to feel and reflect the situation subtly on the eve of the empire's downfall. He wrote:

Kharkiv stands on black earth and expands into the steppe, and that is why it gets rich so easily and finds it so hard to become poor. It is Little Russian but also Great Russian, and the Great Russians try with all their might to speak like true and authentic *khokhly*, while the Little Russians add the ending *-ov* to their surnames and are not averse to passing even for Great Russians, although their songs disdain the *moskal'* and constitute a hymn to Ukraine alone and to Ukrainian style alone. Kharkiv passes almost for a Little Russian center among all, but in order to get a Little Russian skirt and a cloth decorated with a pattern, or a fine piece of embroidery, you need to get a ticket and go to another city entirely. That is the city of the learned, the intelligentsia, and books, but it has only three newspapers, for it pays attention only to foreign newspapers and supports their retail distribution, but the Little Russian, he buys the *Russkoe slovo* [Russian word] and the Petrograd *Kopeika* [Copeck], which are by no means intended for Little Russians and by no means for the intelligentsia.[109]

All this gave the author a basis for the witty conclusion that Kharkiv

is the most interesting city that you could possibly see: unexpected, contradictory, and strange.... There are various cities in Russia: smart and stupid, chaste and depraved, beautiful and ugly, old and young. But in Russia there is only one city of indefinition. That city is Kharkiv. ... Kharkiv knows neither rivers nor mountains nor hills nor dales, for it has little hills, little rivers, little dales—all small and, again, all undefined. Typicality is not a Kharkiv trait, for everything is worn down, lessened, reduced, and it seems that the whole suit worn by that mystical being has been taken from someone else's shoulders.[110]

## Notes

1. Fedir Turchenko and Halyna Turchenko, *Pivdenna Ukraïna: Modernizatsiia, svitova viina, revoliutsiia (kinets' XIX st.–1921)* (Kyiv: Heneza, 2003), 62–63.
2. Vitalii Sarbei, *Istoriia Ukraïny v dozhovtnevii bil'shovyts'kii presi* (Kyiv: Naukova Dumka, 1986), 84–93, 136–42.
3. R. E. Jones, "Ukrainian Grain and the Russian Market in the Late Eighteenth and Early Nineteenth Centuries," in *Ukrainian Economic History: Interpretive Essays*, ed. Iwan Koropeckyj (Cambridge, MA: Harvard Ukrainian Research Institute, 1991), 227.
4. Alfred J. Rieber, "The Debate over the Southern Line: Economic Integration or National Security?" *Journal of Ukrainian Studies*, nos. 1–2 (2004): 371–98.
5. Alexei Miller, "Russia's Ukrainian Policy before 1917," in *The Emergence of Ukraine: Self-Determination, Occupation, and War in Ukraine, 1917–1922*, ed. Wolfram Dornik et al. (Edmonton: Canadian Institute of Ukrainian Studies Press, 2015), 298–320, here 304–5.
6. *Kievskaia starina*, no. 5 (1903): 290–91; Valentyna Shandra, *Heneral-hubernatorstva v Ukraïni, XIX–pochatok XX st.* (Kyiv: NASU Institute of Ukrainian History, 2005), 218–29.

7. Hiroaki Kuromiya, *Freedom and Terror in the Donbass: A Ukrainian-Russian Borderland, 1870s–1990s* (Cambridge: Cambridge University Press, 1998).
8. Gerald Surh, "Ekaterinoslav City in 1905: Workers, Jews, and Violence," *International Labor and Working-Class History* 64 (Fall 2003): 139–66, here 140.
9. Petr Fomin, *Kratkii ocherk istorii s"ezdov gornopromyshlennikov Iuga Rossii* (Kharkiv: Zilberberg & Sons, 1908).
10. Dmitrii Bagalei and Dmitrii Miller, *Istoriia goroda Khar'kova za 250 let ego sushchestvovaniia*, 2 vols. (Kharkiv: City Press, 1993), 2: 248.
11. Bagalei and Miller, *Istoriia goroda Khar'kova*, 2: 230.
12. Rex A. Wade, "Ukrainian Nationalism and 'Soviet Power': Kharkiv, 1917," in *Ukrainian Past, Ukrainian Present: Selected Papers from the 4th World Congress for Soviet and East European Studies, Harrogate, 1990*, ed. Bohdan Krawchenko (New York: St. Martin's Press, 1992), 70–83.
13. Alchevsky's financial-industrial "empire" collapsed and, as the official version goes, he died by suicide in 1901. After his death, the small railway station of Yurievskoe was renamed Alchevskoe in his honor. Alchevskoe, with a population of more than one hundred thousand, is now an important railway node on the territory of the self-proclaimed and Russian-controlled "Luhansk People's Republic."
14. Turchenko and Turchenko, *Pivdenna Ukraïna*, 33.
15. "During the nineteenth century Ukrainian lands acquired the designation 'Little Russia' and were no longer considered a frontier but part of the core of the empire, distinguishable from Russia proper only by the dialect and curious folklore of its peasants." Michael Hamm, ed., *The City in Late Imperial Russia: Papers from a Meeting of the American Association for the Advancement of Slavic Studies, Held in Kansas City, MO, Oct. 1983* (Bloomington: Indiana University Press, 1986), 175.
16. A. Ia. Gusev, *Khar'kov: ego proshloe i nastoiashchee. Istoricheskii spravochnik-putevoditel'* (Kharkiv, 1902); *Khar'kov: putevoditel' dlia turistov*, 3rd ed. (Kharkiv, 1915), 36, 39; P. S. Kallikh, *Ukazatel' ulits goroda Khar'kova v alfavitnom poriadke...* (Kharkiv, 1908).
17. Konstantin P. Shchelkov, *Istoricheskaia khronologiia Khar'kovskoi gubernii*, 2nd ed. (repr. of 1882 publication) (Kharkiv: Muzei Mis'koï Sadyby, 2007).
18. Konstantin Beliaev and Andrei Krasniashchikh, eds., *Khar'kov v zerkale mirovoi literatury* (Kharkiv: Folio, 2007), 65.
19. Turchenko and Turchenko, *Pivdenna Ukraïna*, 66–67.
20. Konstantin P. Mikhal'chuk, *Otkrytoe pis'mo k A. N. Pypinu po povodu ego statei v "Vestnike Evropy" o spore mezhdu iuzhanami i severianami (k istorii otnoshenii k ukrainstvu predstavitelei progressivnoi chasti russkogo obrazovannogo obshchestva)* (Kyiv, 1909).
21. Aleksei I. Miller, *"Ukrainskii vopros" v politike vlastei i russkom obshchestvennom mnenii (vtoraia polovina XIX veka)* (St. Petersburg: Aleteya, 2000), 10.
22. Panteleimon Kulish, *Zapiski o Iuzhnoi Rusi*, 2 vols. (Kyiv, 1856, repr. 1994).
23. Ivan Lysiak-Rudnyts'kyi, *Istorychni ese*, 2 vols. (Kyiv: Osnovy, 1994), 1: 338.
24. Leonid Gorizontov, "Novye zemli imperii v zerkale kul'turnykh traditsii: Novorossiia G. P. Danilevskogo," in *Landshafty kul'tury. Slavianskii Mir* (Moscow: Progress-Traditsiia, 2007), 140–64.
25. Grigorii P. Danilevskii, *Ukrainskaia Starina. Materialy dla istorii ukrainskoi literatury i narodnogo obrazovaniia* (Kharkiv, 1866).
26. Grigorii P. Danilevskii, *Iz Ukrainy: Skazki i povesti*, vol. 2, *Povesti i ocherki* (St. Petersburg, 1860), 129.
27. Danilevskii, *Iz Ukrainy*, 78.
28. *Rossiia. Polnoe geograficheskoe opisanie nashego otechestva* (St. Petersburg, 1903), vol. 3: 63; *Illustrated Description of the Russian Empire; Embracing its Geographical Features, Political Divisions, Principal Cities and Towns, Population, Classes, Government, Resources, Commerce, Antiquities, Religion, Progress in Education, Literature, Art, and Science, Manners*

*and Customs, Historic Summary, etc., from the Latest and the Most Authentic Sources, by Robert Sears, Embellished with Numerous Engravings, and Maps of European and Asiatic Russia* (New York: Robert Sears, 1855), 119–21.
29. Ivan Sergeevich Aksakov v ego pis'makh, pt. 1, vol. 3, *Pis'ma 1851–1860, Poezdka v Malorossiiu* etc. (Moscow, 1892), 165; S. S. Evseenko, *Pod iasnym nebom Malorossii (putevye zametki i nabliudeniia)* (Moscow, 1901).
30. Annette Meakin, "Kharkiv," *Naukovi zapysky kafedry ukraïnoznavstva*, vol. 1 (1994): 40–47.
31. Liudmila Czhizhikova, *Russko-ukrainskoe pogranich'e. Istoriia i sud'by traditsionno-bytovoi kul'tury (XIX – XX veka)* (Moscow: Nauka, 1988), 38.
32. *Khar'kovskii kalendar' na 1912 god* (Kharkiv, 1911), 31.
33. Bagalei and Miller, *Istoriia goroda Khar'kova*, 2: 130–31.
34. *Istoriia goroda Khar'kova*, 2: 130–31.
35. Turchenko and Turchenko, *Pivdenna Ukraïna*, 37.
36. Andrei N. Krasnov, "Po russkomu Iugu," *Novoe delo*, no. 7 (1902): 38, 49, 55.
37. Aleksandr Rittikh, "Ėtnograficheskii ocherk Khar'kovskoi gubernii," reprint from *Khar'kovskie gubernskie vedomosti*, no. 170 (1880).
38. Petr Ivanov, *Zhizn' i pover'ia krest'ian Kupianskogo uezda Khar'kovskoi gubernii*, 2nd ed. (Kharkiv: Maidan, 2007), 5.
39. Paul Robert Magocsi, *The Roots of Ukrainian Nationalism: Galicia as Ukraine's Piedmont* (Toronto: University of Toronto Press, 2002), 62.
40. Igor' Omel'ianchuk, "Ukrainskii i pol'skii voprosy v kontekste ėtnopoliticheskoi sostavliaiushchei ideologii konservativno-monarkhicheskikh partii Rossii nachala XX veka," *Slavianovedenie*, no. 5 (2006): 11.
41. Ihor Mykhailyn, *Narys istoriï zhurnalistyky Kharkivs'koï huberniï, 1812–1917* (Kharkiv: Koloryt, 2007), 200.
42. *Iuzhnyi krai*, no. 114 (5 January 1889).
43. Igor' Omel'ianchuk, *Chernosotennoe dvizhenie na territorii Ukrainy (1904–1914)* (Kyiv, 2000).
44. Dmytro Chornyi, *Kharkiv pochatku XX stolittia: istoriia mista, doli liudei* (Kharkiv, 1995), 82.
45. V. I. Popik, *Politicheskaia bor'ba na Ukraine vokrug vyborov v III Gosudarstvennuiu Dumu* (Kyiv: Naukova Dumka, 1989), 78.
46. A. Voronov, "Vospominaniia byvshego studenta Khar'kovskogo universiteta 60-kh godov," *Russkaia starina* 154 (1913): 580.
47. Khristina Alchevskaia, *Peredumannoe i perezhitoe. Dnevniki, pis'ma, vospominaniia* (Moscow: I. D. Sytin, 1912), 456–57.
48. Michael F. Hamm, "Khar'kov's Progressive Duma, 1910–1914: A Study in Russian Municipal Reform," *Slavic Review* 40, no. 1 (1981): 17–36, here 21.
49. Lysiak-Rudnyts'kyi, *Istorychni ese*, 1: 8.
50. *Sovremennoe khoziaistvo goroda Khar'kova* (1910–1913), vol. 1–2 (1914), 2.
51. Hamm, ed., *The City in Late Imperial Russia*, 3.
52. *Pervaia vseobshchaia perepis' naseleniia Rossiiskoi imperii*, vol. 47 (St. Petersburg, 1904), 44–45.
53. Patricia Herlihy, "Ukrainian Cities in the Nineteenth Century," in *Rethinking Ukrainian History*, ed. Ivan L. Rudnytsky with the assistance of John-Paul Himka (Edmonton: CIUS Press, 1981), 144, 148.
54. Volodymyr Liubchenko, "Etnosotsial'nyi sklad mis'koho naselennia ukraïns'kykh huberniï: sproba veryfikatsiï danykh perepysu 1897 roku," in *Vid muriv do bul'variv: tvorennia modernoho mista v Ukraïni (kinets' XVIII–pochatok XX st.)*, ed. Oleksandr Reient (Kyiv: NAN Ukraïny, 2019), 188–228.
55. S. Kramer, "Ocherk revolutsionnogo rabochego dvizheniia v Khar'kove v 1905 godu," in *1905 god v Khar'kove* (Kharkiv, 1925), 9.

56. Rittikh, *Ėtnograficheskii ocherk*, 14.
57. The figure was 6.2 percent, according to Liubchenko, "Etnosotsial'nyi sklad," 204.
58. Herlihy, "Ukrainian Cities," 144.
59. *Pervaia vseobshchaia perepis'*, 1–3.
60. Bagalei and Miller, *Istoriia goroda Khar'kova*, 2: 132–33.
61. Ivan Aksakov, *Pis'ma k rodnym (1854–1856)* (Moscow: Nauka, 1994), 296–98.
62. Bagalei and Miller, *Istoriia goroda Khar'kova*, 2: 131.
63. *Istoriia goroda Khar'kova*, 2: 131.
64. *Istoriia goroda Khar'kova*, 2: 121.
65. *Istoriia goroda Khar'kova*, 2: 179, 121; Hamm, "Khar'kov's Progressive Duma," 21.
66. D. Sviatskii, "Ėkskursiia v samyi iuzhnyi gorod Rossii – Lenkoran'," *Zhivaia Rossiia* 2, no. 99 (1902): 569.
67. N. Nikolaev, "Na otdykhe (putevye vospominaniia iz zapisnoi knizhki sviashchennika)," *Strannik*, August-September (1914): 20–21.
68. Valerii Taliev, ed., *Priroda i naselenie Slobodskoi Ukrainy. Khar'kovskaia guberniia. Posobie po narodovedeniiu* (Kharkiv: Soiuz, 1918).
69. Bagalei and Miller, *Istoriia goroda Khar'kova*, 2: 778.
70. *Istoriia goroda Khar'kova*, 2: 779.
71. Mykhailyn, *Narys istoriï*, 86–103.
72. Fedir Turchenko, "'Kharkivs'kyi proekt' Mykoly Mikhnovs'koho," *Naukovi pratsi istorychnoho fakul'tetu Zaporiz'koho derzhavnoho universytetu*, 2002, vyp. 15: 7–35; Oleksandr Suproniuk, "Kharkivs'ka hromada naprykintsi 1862 roku," *Kyïvs'ka starovyna*, no. 2 (1998): 178–91.
73. Volodymyr Kravchenko, *The Ukrainian-Russian Borderland: History versus Geography* (Montreal, Kingston, London, and Chicago: McGill-Queen's University Press, 2022), 77–78.
74. Nikolai Sumtsov, "Khar'kov i Shevchenko," *Vestnik Khar'kovskogo istoriko-filologicheskogo obshchestva*, no. 1 (1911): 6.
75. Vladimir Kravchenko, *D. I. Bagalei: nauchnaia i obshchestvenno-politicheskaia deiatel'nost'* (Kharkiv: Osnova, 1990).
76. Suproniuk, "Kharkivs'ka hromada," 180.
77. "Kharkivs'ka hromada," 184.
78. *Kievskaia starina*, no. 4 (1903): 59.
79. Kravchenko, *D. I. Bagalei*, 18.
80. Turchenko, "'Kharkivs'kyi proekt' Mykoly Mikhnovs'koho," 7–35; Osyp Hermaize, *Narysy z istoriï revoliutsiinoho rukhu na Ukraïni*, vol. 1, *Revoliutsiina Ukraïns'ka Partiia (RUP)* (Kharkiv, 1926).
81. Quoted in Turchenko, "'Kharkivs'kyi proekt' Mykoly Mikhnovs'koho," 9.
82. T. V. L-aia, "Vospominaniia o N. V. Lysenko odnoi iz ego uchenits po Kievskomu institutu blagorodnykh devits," *Vestnik Khar'kovskogo istoriko-filologicheskogo obshchestva*, no. 3 (1913): 51.
83. Volodymyr Masliichuk, *Provintsiia na perekhresti kul'tur: Doslidzhennia z istoriï Slobids'koï Ukraïny XVII–XIX st.* (Kharkiv: Kharkiv Private Museum of the City Estate, 2007), 357.
84. Masliichuk, *Provintsiia na perekhresti kul'tur*.
85. Bagalei and Miller, *Istoria goroda Khar'kova*, 2; Hamm, "Khar'kov's Progressive Duma"; Aleksandr Golovko and Aleksandr Iarmysh, *"Sdelal, chto mog...": Khar'kovskii gorodskoi golova Aleksandr Konstantinovich Pogorelko* (Kharkiv: Osnova, 1998).
86. Hamm, "Khar'kov's Progressive Duma," 23.
87. Svetlana Zhuravleva, "K voprosu o toponimicheskoi politike Khar'kovskoi dumy v kontse XIX veka," *Aktual'ni problemy vitchyznianoï ta vsesvitn'oï istoriï*, no. 3 (1998): 75–79.
88. Vasilii Mova (Limanskii), *Iz literaturnogo nalediia* (Krasnodar, 1999), 35–95.

89. Serhii Naumov, "'Zamakh' na pam'iatnyk O. S. Pushkinu v Kharkovi (1904)," *Skhid-Zakhid*, no. 1 (1998): 120.
90. Anton Bondarev, "Nikolai Lysenko: Strasti po pamiatniku," *Nakipelo*, 19 September 2017 https://nakipelo.ua/nikolaj-lysenko-strasti-po-pamyatniku/.
91. Bondarev, "Nikolai Lysenko."
92. Andrei Viazigin, "Neskol'ko slov o V. N. Karazine," in idem, *V tumane smutnykh dnei* (Kharkiv, 1908), 310–22.
93. S. A. Shubovich, "Istoricheskie aspekty transformatsii planirovochnoi struktury Kieva, Khar'kova i Odessy v XIX–nachale XX veka," *Izvestiia vuzov stroitel'stva i arkhitektury*, no. 2 (1985): 54–58.
94. Volodymyr Kravchenko, "D. I. Bahalii v svitli i tini svoieï 'Avtobiohrafiï,'" in D. I. Bahalii, *Vybrani tvory u shesty tomakh*, vol. 1 (Kharkiv, 1999), 9–56.
95. Dmitrii Bagalei, *Ocherki iz istorii kolonizatsii i byta stepnoi okrainy Moskovskogo gosudarstva* (Moscow: Obshchestvo Istorii i drevnostei, 1987), 11; idem, *Ocherki iz russkoi istorii*, 2 vols. (Kharkiv, 1913), 2: 228.
96. Anatolii Remnev, "'Vdvinut' Rossiiu v Sibir': imperiia i russkaia kolonizatsiia vtoroi poloviny XIX–nachala XX veka," in *Novaia imperskaia istoriia postsovetskogo prostranstva*, ed. Il'ia Gerasimov et al. (Kazan: Ab Imperio, 2004), 227.
97. Janowski, *Uniwersytet Charkowski*, 45–46.
98. Dmitrii Bagalei, *Opyt istorii Khar'kovskogo universiteta (po neizdannym materialam)*, 2 vols. (Kharkiv: Kharkiv University Press, 1893–98), 1: 16.
99. Osyp Hermaize, "Ukraïns'ka istorychna nauka za ostannie desiatylittia," in *Studiï z istoriï Ukraïny naukovo-doslidchoï katedry istoriï Ukraïny v Kyïvi*, vol. 2 (1929), xiii.
100. Iakiv Shchoholiv, *Tvory. Povnyi zbirnyk z iliustratsiiamy* (Kyiv: Rukh, 1919).
101. Sergei Potrashkov, *Khar'kovskie polki: Tri veka istorii* (Kharkiv: Oko, 1998), 22.
102. Lev Illiashevich, *Kratkii ocherk istorii Khar'kovskogo dvorianstva* (Kharkiv: M. Zil'berberg, 1885).
103. Mykhailyn, *Narys istoriï*, 288.
104. Holovko and Iarmysh, "Sdelal, chto mog," 99.
105. Mykhailyn, *Narys istoriï*, 300.
106. Omel'ianchuk, "Ukrainskii i pol'skii voprosy," 17.
107. Hamm, ed., *The City in Late Imperial Russia*, 175.
108. Sergei Shchegolev, *Ukrainskoe dvizhenie kak sovremennyi ėtap iuzhnorusskogo separatizma* (Kyiv, 1912).
109. Originally published in the journal *Probuzhdenie* in 1916 under the title "Liki gorodov: Khar'kov"; repr. in *Sloboda*, no. 11 (1992), https://nik191-1.ucoz.ru/blog/liki_gorodov_kharkov/2016-10-10-2509.
110. "Liki gorodov."

CHAPTER 5

# To the "First Capital" and Back

World War I did not change the "indefinitive" image of Kharkiv. It only "shifted" the city and region closer to the western borderlands of the Russian Empire, which turned into an arena of bloody conflict. Some important industrial enterprises evacuated from Poland and the Baltic region were transferred to Kharkiv. They included the New-Aleksandrian agricultural institute in Puławy, the electromechanical plant of the General Electric Company (*Vseobshchaia kompaniia elektrichestva*), a local branch of the German *Allgemeine Elektricitäts Gesellschaft* (AEG), and a bicycle factory from Riga, along with their service personnel. In 1917 the Latvian workers would play a notable role on the Soviet side in the struggle for political power in Kharkiv.

A total of some 45,000 refugees found themselves in Kharkiv.[1] Tens of thousands of men mobilized for the front and wounded there were brought to Kharkiv for medical attention. The de facto abolition of the Pale of Jewish settlement, which allowed Jews to migrate to large cities in eastern Ukraine and central Russia, also contributed to the growth of Kharkiv's urban population. As a result, it increased to some 288,000 by the end of 1917; counting the suburbs, the figure was close to 363,000.[2]

The growth of industry and the proliferation of contacts with wartime allies considerably broadened Kharkiv's relations with the outside world. A Persian consulate, already established there by the early 1890s, was subsequently raised in status to a general consulate. A French vice-consulate appeared in 1900 and a German consulate in 1905. During World War I, there were general consulates of Belgium, Great Britain, the United States, Sweden, Italy, and Persia in the city. All these countries were interested in the production of Kharkiv's industrial enterprises filling orders for military equipment, especially the technologically advanced factories evacuated to Kharkiv from Riga and Warsaw. They produced strategically important matériel for the imperial army and navy and contributed enormously to the development of the city's military-industrial potential.[3] All this substantially increased the role of Kharkiv during the dissolution of the Russian Empire in 1917–20.

## 1917–1920: Into the Whirlpool

The war triggered seismic changes in Europe's geopolitical landscape, particularly in its eastern borderlands. The imperial Russian colossus began to crack along its national, social, and regional fault lines. For all the seeming novelty of the geopolitical and cultural reconfiguration of the Russian Empire in the course of the Civil War, the historian sometimes finds it hard to avoid the impression that previous historical patterns were resurfacing as a result of the deep sociopolitical, economic, and cultural fracturing of Ukrainian territory, especially during the comparatively brief four-year interval between the fall of the Russian Empire and the formation of the USSR. The changes experienced by the Kharkiv region between 1917 and 1920 may be compared in scale only to the geopolitical cataclysms that shook Cossack Ukraine in the mid-seventeenth century.

Very soon, however, the course of change resumed its accustomed pattern. Fragments and symbols of the old states and nations were reshuffled into a new combination. Kharkiv's twentieth century developed within the new political framework of the Soviet Union, which nevertheless retained features of the old empire. The century was marked by numerous changes in the administrative status of the city and region, shaped by competing influences from Kyiv and Moscow in the ambiguous political and cultural environment of the Ukrainian-Russian borderland.

For Kharkiv, the abolition of tsarism in 1917 meant first and foremost its transformation into an arena of fierce political struggle between parties and associations of diverse orientations—imperial, national, and democratic. Each of them contributed in its own way to the kaleidoscopic changes of Kharkiv's political landscape, which was inescapably drawn into the maelstrom of civil war. In 1917 Kharkiv's political life developed mainly under the influence of all-Russian parties and movements. But the transformation of the historical Ukrainian-Russian borderland into a Ukrainian national border region was already underway. It presented the local population with the problem of making an exclusive choice.

The future of Kharkiv and region depended less on the local political situation than on developments in Petrograd and Kyiv, especially on negotiations between the leaders of the Ukrainian national movement (the Central Rada) and the Provisional Government of Russia concerning the status of Ukraine as part of a future democratic Russian Federation. In May 1917 the two parties found the territorial problem a stumbling block, revealing different conceptions of "Ukraine" and "Russia" as perceived by the center and province of the former empire.

The Russian Provisional Government agreed to consider the gubernias of Kyiv, Poltava, Chernihiv (in part), Volhynia, and Podilia Ukrainian. Such a "Ukraine" coincided neither with the administrative territory of the former Little Russia, which had embraced only the Poltava and Chernihiv gubernias, nor with the Little Russian General-Governorship, which had also included the former Sloboda Ukraine, not even the "Little Russia" reimagined on the basis of ethnicity. In other words, "Ukraine" as imagined by the new Russian government was a product of improvisation with no historical or cultural basis other than the changing political situation. Despite such conceptual anarchy, Russian society showed rare unanimity in its attitude to the Ukrainian question. None of the Russian democratic parties, to say nothing of the conservatives, was prepared to recognize Ukraine's right to political autonomy.

The Ukrainian leaders had a different vision of their national territory and borders. They included the Kharkiv gubernia in Ukrainian political space on the basis of its history. The activization of Ukrainian national organizations in the city of Kharkiv and its gubernia was accompanied by extensive use of the old Sloboda Ukraine symbolism, now endowed with new national content. The Ukrainian gubernia convention, which met in Kharkiv on 15 April 1917, elected the Kharkiv Gubernia Ukrainian Council. That body, renamed the Council of Sloboda Ukraine at the end of September 1917, formulated its task as "instituting the autonomy of Ukraine in the Sloboda region."[4] One can only imagine how odd such a verbal collocation would have appeared to inhabitants of the Sloboda Ukraine gubernia in the late eighteenth and early nineteenth centuries.

Sloboda Ukraine symbolism also accompanied every step toward the institutionalization of the Ukrainian national movement in Kharkiv. Thus, in July 1917 the well-known artist Serhii Vasylkivsky established the Museum of the Sloboda Region Society with a donation of more than six hundred of his own Ukrainian landscape paintings, as well as a collection of weapons and Ukrainian national costume. The State Museum of Sloboda Ukraine was later established in Kharkiv on the basis of those artifacts. In the regional narratives elaborated by leading intellectuals of the local Ukrainian community and published in 1918, Kharkiv figured as the historical capital of Sloboda Ukraine. The region's historical narrative was represented by Bahalii's *History of Sloboda Ukraine* and the ethnographic one by Sumtsov's *Slobodians*. They were supplemented by the textbook *Priroda i naselenie Slobodskoi Ukrainy* (The nature and population of Sloboda Ukraine), edited by Professor Vitalii Taliev and intended for the Russian-speaking population of the city and region.

Looking ahead, it is worth noting that Ukrainian political leaders had different visions of "Sloboda Ukraine." When the newly established national government began to organize its military formations, it distinguished some of them with Sloboda regional markers: the *haidamaka kish* (literally, "encampment") of Sloboda Ukraine was headed by none other than Symon Petliura.[5] However, a reader turning to the administrative division of Ukrainian state territory elaborated by Mykhailo Hrushevsky and adopted by the Central Rada in 1918 would have been surprised to see Kharkiv excluded from the Sloboda Ukraine "land," which was subordinate to the jurisdiction of the city of Sumy.[6]

The Ukrainian national narrative of Kharkiv and the Sloboda region was contradicted by the Russian regional narrative of Southern Russia. The Union of

Southern Russians opposed the principle of Ukrainian self-determination with the slogan of local territorial self-government within the framework of so-called Southern Rus'—a territory delineated mainly on an economic basis in the form of a "land of coal mines, rich mineral deposits," well-developed agriculture, and "marvelous harbors on the Black Sea." That is how the territory was described in a special memorandum addressed by professors of the Kyiv Polytechnical Institute to the Provisional Government in early August 1917.[7]

It was no accident that the long-serving head of the Kharkiv-based Union of the Mining Industry of Southern Russia, the local entrepreneur Nikolai von Ditmar, played an active role in the opposition to the Central Rada. He came out against the inclusion of the Kharkiv, Katerynoslav, Kherson, and Tavriia gubernias in an autonomous Ukraine, as those were the basic territories of the union's economic activity. Curiously, von Ditmar referred to all those gubernias as the Kharkiv region, thereby assigning the leading role in it to Kharkiv rather than any other gubernia town.

Aside from Russian entrepreneurs and members of the intelligentsia, who thought mainly in economic terms when addressing the issue, the most consistent and implacable institutional opponent of Ukrainian national self-determination was the Russian Orthodox Church (ROC). The global cataclysms marking the inception of the new era had no effect on its ideology and policy. The leadership of the ROC continued with all its might to support the principle of the unity of Holy Rus', identifying the concept of Russianism with that of Orthodoxy. At the same time, the Orthodox hierarchs recognized the existence of Little Russia as the local ethnocultural branch of the "all-Russian" Orthodox people (*narod*). For them, Little Russia was the true Ukraine as opposed to the hostile Western-oriented and Catholic-inspired Ukraine seeking national independence. These aspects of the ROC's ideology are sometimes obscured by confusing terminology that does not distinguish "Little Russia" from "Ukraine."

The first political battles for Kharkiv brought victory to the Russian Socialist Revolutionaries and Constitutional Democrats. In the elections to Kharkiv city council, held on 9 July 1917, the Socialist Revolutionaries won fifty-four seats (with 37,548 votes, or 46.4 percent), the Constitutional Democrats sixteen (10,942 votes, or 13.5 percent), the Mensheviks thirteen (9,345 votes, or 11.6 percent), and the Bolsheviks eleven (7,521 votes, or 9.3 percent).[8] However, in the elections of November 1917 to the All-Russian Constitutional Assembly, it was the Bolsheviks' turn to celebrate, as they won 27.8 percent of the vote, slightly surpassing the Constitutional Democrats (25.2 percent), while the Russian Socialist Revolutionaries took third place with 12.7 percent.[9]

The political battles that accompanied the gradual fragmentation of the former Russian Empire revealed a growing gap between Kharkiv and its region. While the former remained oriented toward Petrograd, the latter was already turning to Kyiv. The Kharkiv Provincial Peasants' Congress voted for Ukrainian national-territorial autonomy in May 1917 and recognized the Ukrainian Central Rada as the country's legitimate authority in August.[10] In the Kharkiv electoral district, the Ukrainian and Russian Socialist Revolutionaries won a convincing victory in November 1917, jointly obtaining almost 73 percent of the vote, while the Bolsheviks took second place with only 10.5 percent, and the Constitutional Democrats trailed with 5.3 percent.[11]

The results posted by Ukrainian political parties in the city of Kharkiv paled in comparison. In the elections to Kharkiv city council, the Ukrainian Social Democratic Labor Party obtained only 1,437 votes and the Ukrainian Democratic Bloc 1,045 votes.[12] The incumbent mayor and greatest historian of the Sloboda Ukraine region, Professor Dmytro Bahalii, who ran as a candidate for the Ukrainian Democratic Bloc, was not initially elected to the new city council, since he claimed only the fifth "unelectable" place in the bloc's party list. It was only the renunciation of seats by politicians first on the list that allowed Bahalii and his younger ally, the Ukrainian intellectual Hnat Khotkevych, to enter city council as members. The episode clearly revealed the difficulties facing the Ukrainian movement in Kharkiv and very graphically indicated the orientation of most local voters toward democratic Russia rather than little-known Ukraine.

Despite its electoral defeat, the Ukrainian intelligentsia of Kharkiv worked actively to complete what Miroslav Hroch terms the second stage of national movements, solving problems of a cultural and organizational nature. In that field, Ukrainian activists enjoyed a much more favorable reception from local society than in the political sphere, thanks not least to their first opportunity to discuss the prospects of Ukrainian autonomy openly in the local press. And so in 1917 Kharkiv city council adopted a resolution to open Ukrainian schools in the city at the beginning of the new school year. A meeting of the Kharkiv chapter of the Ukrainian Prosvita (Enlightenment) Society, chaired by Mykola Sumtsov and Dmytro Bahalii, was held on 1 September 1917. The Ukrainian community of Kharkiv planned to establish a people's university of Ukrainian studies and the first Ukrainian secondary school in the region.

Accordingly, standing Ukrainian language and Ukrainian studies courses, with emphasis on Ukrainian history, were instituted for teachers. A manual of self-instruction in the Ukrainian language made its belated appearance in Kharkiv in 1917, well over a century after the publication of a similar work of self-instruction in Russian, issued specifically for local Ukrainians in 1788.[13] The Ukrainian courses were inaugurated with a lecture by Dmytro Bahalii under the eloquent title "Kharkiv as a Ukrainian City," which later saw print as a chapter of his *Istoriia Slobids'koï Ukraïny* (History of Sloboda Ukraine)—the first synthetic history of the region written in the Ukrainian language and intended for use as a school textbook. The Bolshevik seizure of power in Petrograd, as well as events in Kharkiv itself, made it impossible to implement the adoption of the textbook as widely as the authorities had planned.

The communist coup of October 1917 gave the Central Rada an opportunity to proclaim its rule over the disputed territories, as well as over some districts of the Kursk and Voronezh gubernias inhabited mainly by ethnic Ukrainians. Finding itself between the hammer of communist Russia and the sickle of the Ukrainian People's Republic (UPR), on 2 December 1917 Kharkiv city council adopted a resolution on joining the UPR as a constituent part of the Russian Democratic Republic, acknowledging the rule of the UPR General Secretariat.[14] The Academic Council of Kharkiv University made the same choice, expressing its protest against the communist seizure of power and affirming its support for the Central Rada.[15]

In the new circumstances, the Russian-speaking intelligentsia of Kharkiv calmly accepted the political reality, as evidenced in a book on the Sloboda region prepared by several Kharkiv University specialists under the guidance of Professor Valerii Taliev. Its introduction included the following statement:

> A new life is dawning for the population of Ukraine and of the Sloboda region in particular. A broad expanse, not bound by the imposition of political shackles, is opening up for its creative and productive activity. But this requires knowledge of one's land, its nature, its positive and negative aspects. Old Russian history was scarcely conducive to independent activity, and knowledge of one's motherland was utterly neglected. There should be none of that now.[16]

The author of those words was in fact adopting the concept of the "small motherland," popular in the Russian Empire in the late nineteenth and early twentieth centuries, which was regarded as one of the basic means of arousing patriotism and love for the "great Fatherland." One can only speculate as to how the authors imagined that fatherland, although, given the ongoing civil war and the fragmentation of the cultural space of the former Russian Empire, local and regional identity often took precedence over national identity. Nevertheless, the book may be considered significant mainly because its authors assigned the Kharkiv region, under the name of the Sloboda region, to Ukraine, inspired as they were by its prospects of democratic development and its rejection of the archaic imperial legacy.

Kharkiv society was now confronted with a dilemma for which it was by no means prepared—that of choosing loyalty either to Ukraine or to Russia. That dilemma was significantly modified by the principle of "dual loyalty" toward the autonomous (Kyiv) and all-Russian (Moscow/Petrograd) political centers. Very soon, however, under the influence of external factors, that system of political relations between province and center was replaced by a new one. Kharkiv did not manage to remain equidistant from the two basic contending parties, Ukraine and Russia. It may be assumed that the shifting compromise position of urban society, which was striving to avoid a worsening of the situation and reconcile the implacable opponents, favored the party that showed the greater will to power.

In early December 1917 the Bolsheviks, less numerous and popular but much more determined than the other parties, managed to seize power in Kharkiv.[17] That is how Kharkiv unexpectedly found itself in the role of capital of Soviet Ukraine after a hastily arranged congress of soviets and military revolutionary committees of Ukraine, protected by Bolshevik military formations. The Central Executive Committee of Soviets of Ukraine elected by the congress formed a government, the People's Secretariat, and declared its support for the communist government in Petrograd, simultaneously announcing the overthrow of the Central Rada. Those events were preceded by a declaration of the Soviet government of Russia under the eloquent title "Manifesto to the Ukrainian People with Ultimate Demands to the Ukrainian Rada," written by Vladimir Lenin in the spirit of opposing "good" people to a "bad" government—a rhetorical device that remains in the arsenal of the Russian government to the present day.

The choice of Kharkiv as capital of Ukraine was dictated not only by the particular political conjuncture but also by geographic, economic, and political considerations. Kharkiv was the most convenient railway junction for transit between the center of the former empire and its best industrially developed region, located in the south of the former empire. Moreover, Kharkiv had already played the role of regional communist party center since mid-July 1917, when the organizational center of the Donets-Kryvyi Rih oblast party organization, the strongest Bolshevik organization on Ukrainian territory, had been transferred there from Katerynoslav.[18] But the very organizational structure of the Russian Social Democratic Labor Party (Bolshevik), which included, along with the Donets-Kryvyi Rih and "southern" units, the oblast organization of the Southwestern Land with its center in Kyiv, leads to the conclusion that at the time the Bolsheviks did not yet conceive of Ukraine as a single national territory.

The attitude of the communist leadership to the nationality question in general and to the Ukrainian question in particular remained ambiguous. The moderate section of the Bolshevik party leadership was prepared for compromise, although it preferred the principle of political rather than national self-determination. The radicals insisted that nations were archaic in principle and proclaimed the exclusive need for territorial and economic self-determination. On the symbolic level, these disagreements were reflected in a confrontation between "Ukrainian" and "South Russian" markers of regional identity. From this angle, the arrival at the *southern* railway station in Kharkiv of the "*northern*" flying squad from Petrograd under the command of Rudolf Sivers to assist the local Bolsheviks took on a surprisingly clear symbolic meaning.

At the beginning of February 1918, Kharkiv was again proclaimed a capital, this time of the Donets-Kryvyi Rih Republic, which had expropriated the Kharkiv and Katerynoslav gubernias, as well as the industrial districts of the Don Cossack Host, which had joined them and were supposed to be incorporated into Soviet Russia. The Southern Oblast Soviet of the People's Economy (*Iuzhnyi oblastnoi*

*Sovet narodnogo khoziaistva*) became the chief economic agency of the republic. The press organ of the Kharkiv Soviet of Workers' and Soldiers' Deputies of the Donets-Kryvyi Rih Basin was titled *Izvestiia Iuga* (Southern news). Thus, the communists elevated Kharkiv to the role of administrative and political center of the economic region of Southern Russia in the very same way as Nikolai von Ditmar, the representative of large-scale capital, had done the previous year.

On 20 March 1918 *Izvestiia Iuga* proclaimed: "Inasmuch as Ukraine has separated from Soviet Russia, that is its own affair. We are not following it.... The cry should be heard around the world that the Donets proletarian does not consider himself part of the Ukrainian state."[19] The oblast committee of soviets declared that "the soviets of the Donets Basin are taking part in the joint development of public activity with the soviets of all southern Russia—Ukraine and the Don-Kuban-Terek district."[20] In this case, as we see, the concept of "southern Russia" turned out to be much broader than that of the official Sloboda Ukraine gubernia of the late eighteenth and early nineteenth centuries.

The Donets communists proclaimed their renunciation of the principle of national self-determination in general and its replacement by territorial and economic self-determination. At the Fourth Oblast Congress of Soviets of Workers' and Soldiers' Deputies of the Donets-Kryvyi Rih Oblast, held on 27–30 January 1918, the following theses were announced:

> With the development of the socialist revolution, as the means of production are socialized and the main branches of industry nationalized in the free federation of Soviet republics of Russia, the division of republics increasingly will and should proceed according to the principle of the particular features of this or that region in economic terms.... The Donets and Kryvyi Rih basins, as a region that already has a definite economic face of its own, should have its own bodies of economic and political self-government, the sole ruling bodies that organize political, economic, and cultural law and order in the Soviet republic.[21]

It may be assumed that the regional identity of the Donbas took shape long before 1917 and was conditioned above all by the particular features of its economic development in the modernizing expanse of Southern Russia. But this did not mean that in the given case the economic components of regional identity crowded out all others under the influence of international communist ideology. The officially recognized Russian "nationality" (*narodnost'*), along with the corresponding type of identity, further sharpened by conditions of civil war and the secularization of "Holy Rus'" in reaction to the proclamation of Ukrainian statehood, was turning out to be more influential than regional identity after all.

The Donbas is shown on a poster of the period as the "heart of Russia" with veins carrying its lifeblood to all the major cities of the land. Ukraine as such does not appear on the poster at all. The militant anti-Ukrainian position of the Donbas communists allowed them to declare as separatists even those of their party comrades who came out in favor of establishing Soviet Ukraine on a national rather than an economic basis, even though the latter, in their turn, were not preparing to separate from Russia and basically bent their efforts toward its transformation.

The political organization of Southern Russia proposed by the moderate Ukrainian national communist Mykola Skrypnyk called in particular for the establishment of Donets-Kryvyi Rih autonomy within a "South Russian Ukrainian Republic as part of an All-Russian Federation of Soviet Republics."[22] Deliberately or not, Skrypnyk loaded his proposal with contradictory symbols in order to combine the regional principle of "Southern Russianness" with the Ukrainian national principle. This compromise proved as unacceptable to the radical communists as to Ukrainian and Russian nationalists.

Curiously, no one taking part in the politics of the time cast doubt on the role of Kharkiv as the regional center, no matter what political configuration the region assumed. In any case, the expulsion of the Bolshevik armies from Ukraine and the coming to power of Hetman Pavlo Skoropadsky in April 1918 again brought to the fore the problem of separating Ukraine from Russia on the basis of nationality. By that time the Donets-Kryvyi Rih Republic had managed to dissolve itself unobtrusively on the Don. Kharkiv briefly became a border city and a prime destination for those who managed to escape communist-ruled Russia.

The occupation of Kharkiv by German military forces showed that Germany recognized Ukraine within the ethnic boundaries declared in the Central Rada's Third Universal of 1917. The German military presence delineated Ukraine's northern borders more clearly. In order to lend them greater political legitimacy, Hetman Skoropadsky's government began negotiations with the communist government of Russia in 1918. It became apparent very quickly, however, that the two parties were using different criteria to define the territories in question. The ethnic principle was fundamental for the Ukrainian side, while the Russian side declared the need for territorial self-determination.

The de facto line of demarcation between Ukraine and Russia began at Kupiansk in the Kharkiv region, proceeded along the territory of present-day Belgorod oblast, and ended in Surazh in the Orel gubernia. The Ukrainian side maintained its right to ten districts of the Voronezh, Kursk, and Orel gubernias, as well as four districts of the Chernihiv gubernia and one-third of the Don Cossack oblast. Russia, for its part, advanced claims to considerable territories in the Chernihiv, Kharkiv, and Katerynoslav regions that would deprive Ukraine of 85 percent of Donets coal resources.

Ukraine's border negotiations with the government of the Almighty Don Cossack Host proved no less complicated, as the Ukrainian side asserted its right to Taganrog oblast, while the Don Cossack government claimed Luhansk and the Starobilsk district of the Kharkiv gubernia. Unlike the aforementioned negotiations, however, these were concluded successfully.[23] It is worth noting that when the communist leadership created a new Donetsk gubernia in 1919–20, the Starobilsk district was incorporated into it, as were parts of the Izium and Kupiansk districts of the Kharkiv gubernia.

The bone of contention in this dispute of "Slavs with one another" was possession of the industrial and mineral region of Southern Russia. That region became the major battlefield of 1919–20: Denikin's White Army, advancing against the Bolsheviks from the Cossack regions of the Don and Kuban and known officially as the Armed Forces of Southern Russia, essentially remained within the region, halting in the vicinity of Kursk and Orel—cities that had once marked Ukraine's ethnic border with Russia. But these defenders of "Holy Russia" were confused as to the identity of the region they were trying to control. In one version of the administrative division of "South Russia" elaborated by the renowned Russian scholar Aleksandr Bilimovich, Kharkiv and its region is defined as the center of "Left-Bank Little Russia"; in another version, it figures as the center of the "mining and industrial" region.[24]

In the final analysis, political conditions determined the identification and perception of Ukrainian regions of the Russian Empire that had again become borderlands. The present-day Japanese scholar Yoshiro Ikeda has indicated a curious proof of this. Officials of the central party apparatus in Moscow, which became the new capital of Russia, considered in the autumn of 1919 that the Donbas and the Katerynoslav and Kharkiv regions belonged to the Ukrainian and not the Russian periphery. Although, in Ikeda's opinion, "Ukraine" was perceived by the Moscow communists in strictly territorial rather than ethnic terms,[25] it may be concluded that Kharkiv, as seen from Moscow, lay outside the boundary of the Russian heartland, as had been the case during the settlement of the steppe borderland in the mid-seventeenth century.

The testimonies of contemporaries and the perceptions of memoirists reflected the kaleidoscopic change of images of Kharkiv in various periods of the Civil War. For the writer Aleksei Tolstoy, who described events during the Hetmanate of 1918, Kharkiv was a city of the borderland and periphery conquered by external forces of some kind; its image was defined by the feverish commercial activity of adventurers and speculators of every description feasting in times of famine against the background of a Ukrainian operetta stage set.

Tolstoy wrote:

> Columns of German soldiers in steel helmets walked the streets heavily, waddling. Descendants of ancient Ukrainian lineages in red Caucasian fur hats raced along the streets in smart cabs. A multitude of dealers thrown up by the war, in blue cheviot suits, crowded together in coffeehouses, making money out of the air, incessantly driving wagons of aspirin, castor oil, and lubricating oils from one end of Ukraine to the other. At dusk the peeling doors of cafes and movie houses were

lit by mercury street lamps. Music thundered from the city garden, and on the bank of the Neticha River, overgrown with duckweed, frogs and toads swarmed, called, and croaked; twelve fevers wound in foggy broken files.[26]

A committed Denikinite officer, the publicist Boris Suvorin, viewed Kharkiv with different eyes in the summer of 1919, bursting out against Kharkiv philistines with a tirade reminiscent of lines written by Petro Sokalsky to Grigorii Danilevsky in the 1860s and quoted in the preceding chapter. Suvorin complained: "but how hypocritical is the city of Kharkiv. Especially its well-to-do strata. Completely incapable of sacrifice or achievement; profound indifference to ideas of a higher order, to everything outside the sphere of private interests."[27]

True, this impression is contradicted by the testimony of others who served in the ranks with Suvorin and recalled the enthusiasm with which Kharkivites, at least those in the middle and upper urban strata, greeted Denikin's forces. All in all, however, the figure of a Kharkiv resident greeting Bolsheviks with a red flag and Whites with the imperial tricolor may be considered perfectly natural for a border town that kept changing hands and had become an arena of conflict between the main political forces struggling for power: Russian communists, Russian imperialists, and Ukrainian nationalists of various stripes.

Compared with the ephemeral Soviet "republics" of New Russia, Tavriia, and the Donets-Kryvyi Rih Basin, as well as the efforts of large and small peoples of the former Russian Empire to achieve national self-determination, Kharkiv showed no tendency toward regional political autonomism or separatism of its own. By that time the contending political projects that drew Kharkiv into their orbits—imperial, communist, Ukrainian national, and southern regional in its different variants—had long made any potential project of Sloboda Ukraine autonomy irrelevant. There was no political, cultural, symbolic, or institutional basis for it.

The few community organizations surviving in the city that came forward with political declarations during the Civil War did not touch on the problem of regional autonomy. For example, the first regional congress of cooperatives, held in Kharkiv on 19–21 May 1919, established the Council of Kharkiv Oblast Cooperative Congresses, adopted a number of resolutions on questions of domestic and foreign policy, and expressed itself particularly in favor of a review of the Brest-Litovsk peace treaty of 1918 and a federation of Ukraine with Russia. None of the documents adopted at the congress mentioned the problem of special status for Kharkiv or its region.

The final victory of the Russian communists and their seizure of Kharkiv at the end of 1919 raised the city to the status of capital once again. This time it became the capital of Soviet Ukraine. The Bolsheviks, led by Vladimir Lenin, turned out to be the only political force in post-imperial Russia prepared to recognize, at least partially, the national status of Ukraine. The city fell "slightly short" of becoming the capital of the Terrestrial Globe, whose "chairman," Velimir Khlebnikov, was then, by happy coincidence, residing in Kharkiv. In all other cases, Kharkiv residents perfectly confirmed Philip Ther's observation that

> the population of the borderland in the age of nationalism had to find various strategies to cope with the compulsion to be unambiguous. The first ideal type (in the Weberian sense) was to join one of the competing national movements, the second one to resist and to establish regional movements, the third one to retreat into the private sphere and to keep a distance from political activities in general, including the competing nationalisms.[28]

## An Experimental Capital

The communist government of Russia chose Kharkiv as the capital of Soviet Ukraine under the influence of a whole host of factors, among which military and political considerations were unquestionably fundamental. The situation in Ukraine at the beginning of 1920 was still indefinite. The communist experiment with the economy was failing once again. The Crimea had not been taken, Nestor Makhno's insurgent army was rising again in the south, and Polish and Ukrainian forces were preparing for a campaign in the west. In May 1920 they briefly managed to take Kyiv.

Under these conditions Kharkiv, thanks above all to its strategic significance as a railway hub and its closeness to Moscow, became the basic center for Soviet forces behind the lines of the southwestern front, as well as a bridgehead for an advance toward the Crimea. Analogies with the late seventeenth and early eighteenth centuries, when Kharkiv became the primary base for Russian armies advancing toward the Crimea, while risky, may be appropriate. It was this very military-strategic role of Kharkiv in the final stage of the Civil War that was intended to be memorialized in the form of a gigantic Soviet diorama showing the storming and capture of Perekop by forces under the command of Mikhail Frunze in 1920.

The symbolic role played by Kharkiv during the years of civil war also made the new masters of the country favor it over Kyiv as a capital. By that time, Kyiv had gained a reputation as the basic center of the Ukrainian national movement, hostile to communists and supporters of "Russia, one and indivisible" alike. Kharkiv, on the other hand, had been the capital not only of Soviet Ukraine but also of the Donets-Kryvyi Rih Republic and therefore aroused no hostile associations either for orthodox communists, who rejected nationality in principle, or for Russian imperial nationalists, who denied the right of existence to one nation only, the Ukrainian.

Finally, given the significant modernizing component of communist ideology and policy, which remained vital in the 1920s, Kharkiv, thanks to its industrial potential, its considerable Russian-speaking factory proletariat, and its status as transit and administrative hub of the Donets-Kryvyi Rih industrial and mineral basin, was much better suited for the role of avant-garde experimental proletarian capital of Ukraine than the more traditional Kyiv.[29] It remained to be decided of what, precisely, Kharkiv was being proclaimed the capital.

In the 1920s the successive division of territory between the Soviet republics of Ukraine and Russia was accompanied by debates no less fervent than those under previous political regimes.[30] Until then, the border between the Ukrainian SSR and the Russian SFSR had been defined by the treaty of 1919, under which more than 1.5 million ethnic Ukrainians turned out to be residing outside Ukrainian territory. Given wartime conditions and the shifting situation at the front, that border was temporary. Now, with the communist regime becoming stabilized and adopting a policy of local "indigenization," discussions revived about borders between Soviet republics. They basically concerned the districts of the Kursk and Voronezh gubernias settled by ethnic Ukrainians.

It is telling that in the course of negotiations on disputed questions both sides were guided by the ethnographic principle.[31] For example, the Russian side, arguing its unwillingness to concede the disputed territories, cited the residents' use of Russian as a lingua franca and their employment of traditional "Little Russian" and "Great Russian" terminology.[32] By that time the term *khokhol*, often used as an informal name and self-designation of Ukrainians in the Ukrainian-Russian borderland in the late eighteenth and early nineteenth centuries, had taken on a pejorative character. Oleksandr Dovzhenko, the famous Soviet Ukrainian film director and writer, left an interesting testimony to this fact when he talked to residents of the Russian part of the former Sloboda Ukraine during World War II. One of them informed him that "the Ukrainians are over there, in Kharkiv and Poltava oblasts, but here, they are not Ukrainians. They are *khokhols*."[33] It may be assumed that in Kharkiv oblast, Dovzhenko could have been similarly assured that the "real" Ukrainians were living even farther away.

In order to substantiate the Ukrainian identity of the local population, the Soviet Ukrainian government had recourse to the assistance of experts—the most eminent professional historians in the republic, Dmytro Bahalii and Mykhailo Hrushevsky. Both took part in drafting a document titled "On the External Borders of the Ukrainian SSR," which the Ukrainian side presented for consideration to the USSR Central Executive Committee in 1924.[34] As expected, both scholars concluded that the disputed territories belonged to Ukraine, but, curiously enough, each of them defined the Ukrainian-Russian border in different terms. For Bahalii, it was the "northern" border, which generally conformed to Kharkiv's customary "north–south" system of geographic coordinates, while for Hrushevsky it was the "eastern" border.[35]

On the basis of the experts' conclusions, the Soviet Ukrainian government expected to incorporate several districts of the Kursk and Voronezh gubernias inhabited mainly by ethnic Ukrainians into the Ukrainian SSR. Although the special commission of the USSR Central Executive Committee that examined the project agreed to base its work on the ethnographic principle and partly acknowledged the justice of the Ukrainian side's proposals, consideration of the question of territorial division was accompanied by stormy exchanges and mutual accusations, showing that even in the communist camp the achievement of internationalism was still far off.

It is apparent at first glance that ethnic terms did not become the sole or defining ones in shaping the policy of the Soviet center toward Ukraine. They were paralleled by the economic principle in the administrative division of Soviet territory. Thus, the administrative reform of 1925 reflected a struggle between the USSR *Gosplan* and the Ukrainian party and government leadership. *Gosplan* intended to divide Ukraine into two economic regions: southwestern (primarily agricultural), with its center in Kyiv, and southern (mining and industrial), with its center in Kharkiv.[36] Essentially, this approach reproduced the old imperial Russian system for dealing with Ukrainian territory.

A leading Russian expert, Professor Ivan Aleksandrov, the author of the Dnieper Hydroelectric Station project, defended the division of Ukraine on the basis of economic criteria in 1921. He substantiated his view as follows: "Our position on the creation of autonomous regions at present is based on the completely new principle of the expedient division of the state on a rational economic basis, and not on the remains of lost sovereign rights."[37] In effect, the central planning agencies of Soviet Russia tried to restore the integrity of Southern Russia as an economic region, thereby ignoring the principle of Ukraine's national self-determination.

This aroused opposition on the part of the Ukrainian leadership of the day, exactly as seven years earlier it had opposed the ideas and projects put forward by the leaders of the Donets-Kryvyi Rih Republic in 1918. The Ukrainian government found support on the part of Vladimir Lenin, who agreed for political reasons to regard Ukraine as a single economic region. In that case, the national principle triumphed over the economic one. The government of Ukraine, admitting no thought of dividing the republic, carried out its administrative reform contrary to the wishes of *Gosplan*.

That circumstance in turn made it necessary to divide the economic region of Southern Russia. Part of it went to Russia and was institutionalized as the so-called southeastern oblast, with its center in Rostov, taking over the disputed territories of Taganrog and adjoining lands. In time, the southern marker disappeared completely from the name of that region, which became part of the North Caucasus *krai* (national minority region). Those developments notwithstanding, Kharkiv and Ukraine, at least the Left Bank of Ukraine, known as Little Russia since the late eighteenth century, were associated in the Soviet center with Southern Russia, as before.

Contemporaries well understood such a dialectic of geographic symbols. Accordingly, during the discussion of the first five-year plan, when it came to the choice of location for the development of the Soviet military-industrial complex, some members of the party leadership came out against choosing Ukraine, giving political reasons for their position. Hryhorii Petrovsky, who then chaired the All-Ukrainian Central Executive Committee, opposed such an approach and declared, to laughter from the audience, that in order to avoid accusations of national exclusivism, industry should indeed be developed primarily in the south.[38] Those present perfectly understood his deliberate pun: if "Ukraine" remained politically unreliable, then its territory, in its more accustomed guise of Southern Russia, lost its borderland status, as it were, and aroused no suspicions. Once again, the combination of geographic and national terms played out its dialectic in the former borderland of the Muscovite state—a dialectic that representatives of the local elite had exploited, not without success, in the course of their homeland's history.

The administrative transformations of the territory of the Ukrainian SSR in the 1920s also affected the Kharkiv region, repeatedly changing its extent and configuration. Thus, in 1920, with the creation of the Donetsk gubernia, Starobilsk was added to it, as were parts of the Izium and Kupiansk districts. The new administrative reform of 1925 reduced the territory of the Kharkiv *okruh* (district), part of which was assigned to the Poltava *okruh*. Later, on 27 February 1932, in connection with the enhancement of the centralized administrative system, the Kharkiv oblast was created, consisting of seventy-eight districts (*raiony*, sing. *raion*) directly subordinate to the oblast center. In 1939 the raions were enlarged and their number reduced to thirty-three.[39] But the administrative experiments conducted in the Kharkiv region during the first years of Soviet rule made no significant changes to the symbolic geography of Kharkiv, which was elevated to the status of national capital.

For the capital of the region, now the Soviet Ukrainian capital, the 1920s–30s became a period of fairly rapid and dynamic growth. Until the early 1920s the territory of Kharkiv remained comparatively small; then it began to expand quickly and, thanks to extensive construction, by 1923 it had already grown to 119 square kilometers. A year later it reached 140 square kilometers, exceeding its prerevolutionary size more than four and a half times and incorporating a considerable part of the outlying suburbs. In 1939 the size of Kharkiv was almost 288 square kilometers.[40]

In 1920 the population of Kharkiv was almost 270,000.[41] By 1925 it had increased to 373,414. According to the all-Union census of 1926, the population of Kharkiv was 415,400, almost 25 percent more than in 1923. The increase was due mainly to migration, first and foremost from the Kharkiv region and from adjacent Ukrainian and Russian regions. The rate of growth then slowed somewhat, only to make another jump in the late 1920s and early 1930s, during the period of forced industrialization. As a result, Kharkiv, with a population of 521,000, became the second most populous city in Ukraine, not far behind Kyiv. The all-Union census of 1937 reported a figure of 759,000.[42] Thus, the city's population was approximately three times greater than in the early 1920s.

After the Civil War, the ethnosocial structure of Kharkiv's population did not change in principle: as before, Russians held first place (136,466, or 51 percent of the city's population), exceeding the Ukrainian SSR average by more than five times; those officially identified as Ukrainians were almost two and a half times fewer in number than Russians (57,366, or 21 percent); and there were almost as many Jews as before (55,474, or 20.5 percent).[43] The notable increase of Kharkiv's Jewish population was due to the abolition of the Pale of Settlement, the upheavals of World War I and the Civil War, and the city's attainment of the status of capital of the republic.

This last circumstance, in turn, promoted an increase in the number of Ukrainians and a decrease in the number of Russians in Kharkiv. According to the census of 1923, ethnic Ukrainians constituted a majority in the city (119,407, or 38.5 percent), pushing Russians down to second place (107,172, or 34.5 percent), while the number of Jews increased slightly (to 64,533, or 20.8 percent). The total population of Kharkiv increased by 40,340 in those three years, while the number of Ukrainians grew by 42,041.

The considerable rise in the number of ethnic Ukrainians and the simultaneous decrease in the number of Russians (more than 21 percent) was not due to ethnic cleansing or a demographic catastrophe. The true reason was a change of national self-identification: many of those who, following established practice, had given their nationality as Russian in 1920 now changed it to Ukrainian. This was relatively easy to do, as party officials, implementing the policy of Ukrainization, did not regard the Russian population of Kharkiv as a national minority. The secularization of cultural and sociopolitical life in the country, which broke the traditional identification of "Russian" with "Orthodox," undoubtedly contributed its mite to the process.

The process of Kharkiv's ethnic Ukrainization continued, regardless of sharp turns in the communist regime's domestic policy. Thus, according to the all-Union census of 1926, the number of Ukrainians in the capital of the republic was 160,138 (38.6 percent), while Russians numbered 154,448 (37.2 percent), and Jews 81,130 (19.5 percent).[44] By 1939 the number of Ukrainians had grown to 403,606 (48.5 percent), while the totals of ethnic Russians (274,173, or 32.9 percent) and Jews (130,250, or 15.6 percent) continued to decline.

The majority status of Ukrainian residents in Kharkiv by no means influenced the city's primarily Russian-speaking character. The number of Kharkivites giving Russian as their mother tongue, regardless of the "achievements" of Ukrainization, exaggerated by Soviet propaganda, or its "horrors," as registered by public opinion, remained relatively stable. In 1926, 64.2 percent of the city's residents gave Russian as their mother tongue, decreasing slightly to 63.8 percent in 1939, while the corresponding figures for Ukrainian were 23.8 percent in 1926 and 31.5 percent in 1939.[45]

While Kharkiv was the capital of the Ukrainian SSR, its cultural space and image underwent cardinal changes. From an Orthodox commercial, gentry, and university town, it became—not for long, to be sure—the "capital of the Ukrainian proletariat," the incarnation of the socialist utopianism of the industrial era, with its constructivist architectural style and new generation of Ukrainian intelligentsia. Those intellectuals sought to combine Ukrainian nationalist ideas with communist ones, concluding, in the words of Mykola Khvyliovy's well-known pamphlet, with a new version of modern Ukrainian Europeanism under the slogan "Away from Moscow!" The "national communist" generation, largely annihilated by Stalin in the 1930s, became in its turn a symbol of the advance of the Ukrainian national movement in the twentieth century and its attainment of the mature, concluding stage of its development.

Kharkiv's new cultural space began to appear in outline as early as 1919, when the city started renaming its central streets and squares. Among the new names were those of Karl Liebknecht (previously Sumy Street), Rosa Luxemburg (previously Paul Square), Moises (Yakov) Tevelev (previously Nicholas Square), Yakov Sverdlov (formerly Catherine Street), and Georgii Plekhanov (formerly Petynka), as well as other leaders of the world proletariat and heroes in the struggle for its brilliant future, including those of local origin or sphere of activity. Outdoing all competitors in the latter group was the leader of the Donetsk communists, Fedor Sergeev (Artem), whose name, following his romantic life and death in the early 1920s, was immortalized with a monument in Kharkiv and bestowed not only on a street, the All-Ukrainian Social Museum, the Communist University, and a library club, but also on Sviati Hory (Holy Hills) on the Donets River. Added to these and other names in the 1920s were those of luminaries of the French Revolution, Soviet military commanders, "Red" professional corporations, dates of this or that event in the history of the Communist Party, and the like.

Although the historical center of Kharkiv underwent the symbolic renaming of its streets, it was not destroyed. The Bolsheviks turned their attention instead to the suburbs, thereby establishing a basis for city planning, which would soon become universal throughout east central Europe.[46] According to the new models, distinctive enclaves were created in urban space, shaped according to ideological templates—so-called socialist townlets embodying postulates of collectivism, the merging of industrial production with everyday life, functionality, and so on. In Kharkiv, that policy began with the construction of a new "proletarian" center, built in record time in the northern quarter of the city as a counterweight to the old "merchant-gentry" center, and continued with the transformation of the suburbs into industrial and residential quarters grouped around factories and plants.

The new Soviet center of Kharkiv was intended to embody signs of the coming era. That conception was therefore based on the ideas of modernization, progress, and the "bright future of all humanity," but not Ukrainization, which was seen as a temporary concession to the "burden of the past." The new center of Kharkiv was a gigantic open space, surrounded by a complex of office and residential buildings, known as Dzerzhinsky Square (now Svoboda [Liberty] Square) and advertised as

**Figure 5.1.** *Derzhprom*, the first Soviet skyscraper (1925–28), architects Serhii Serafimov, Samuil Kravets, Mark Felger, © Volodymyr Kravchenko, 2021.

the largest square in Europe. It was there, in 1926–28, that the Gosprom (State Industry) Building was erected, becoming the symbol of Soviet modernization and celebrated as perhaps the first "Soviet skyscraper," evoking an "American" image of Kharkiv. Theodore Dreiser describes the Gosprom as "a great new gray stone building of eight or ten stories, which looked as though it had been taken out of New York and set down here in the snow plains."[47]

The so-called workers' settlements that arose on the southwestern edge of Kharkiv along with large factories, and even the huge residential massif of the so-called socialist townlet built around the gigantic Kharkiv tractor factory, may be considered incarnations of socialist utopia in the spirit of Tommaso Campanella's "City of the Sun." The rectilinear structure of the new residential buildings, designed in avant-garde style, was subordinate to the idea of practical utility and a collective way of life. Communal residences, buildings of iron, glass, and concrete formed the new face of Kharkiv, eclectically combining ideas of classicism, communism, Ukrainian nationalism, and modernization.

The monument to Taras Shevchenko was supposed to serve as a reminder of the capital's all-Ukrainian status. True, it was erected not in the city center and not in place of the Pushkin monument that Ukrainian nationalists had sought to destroy at the beginning of the twentieth century but in the university park in place of a

**Figure 5.2.** Monument to Taras Shevchenko, 1935, sculptor Matvei Manizer, © Volodymyr Kravchenko, 2008.

monument to Vasilii Karazin. Ironically enough, the monument was raised just as Kharkiv was again demoted from capital to oblast center. Fortunately, Karazin did not suffer as a result, and the name of Taras Shevchenko, immortalized in the monument, did, after all, become one of the most recognizable markers of Ukrainian Kharkiv, as if to put an end to the polemics about the poet that had burst out in the local press in the early 1860s. Karazin, by contrast, was not fortunate enough to make his way immediately into the pantheon of historical figures considered worthy of incarnating if not the Soviet then at least the Ukrainian character of the proletarian capital.

Even after Karazin's death, his fate continued to be associated with that of his brainchild. Kharkiv University, like all other imperial universities on Ukrainian territory, found itself in a past that was considered unnecessary for the communist future. In the early 1920s Kharkiv University ceased to exist, divided as it was into a whole series of specialized independent institutes or academies, including the Academy of Theoretical Sciences, which gave the name Free Academy to the former University Street. And so the very name of the university was stricken from the urban cultural landscape.

Curiously, the struggle against the old university briefly united communist ideologues with Ukrainian nationalists. For the former, the university system was part of class-ridden autocratic Russia, dominated by its police and bureaucracy, and thus hopelessly antiquated, having outlived its time.[48] They countered the image of the "temple of knowledge" with that of the "productive enterprise," whose functions were strictly utilitarian. For the latter, universities acted above all as centers and transmitters of the imperial policy of Russification, institutions for the cultural colonization of Ukraine. It was, indeed, the fleeting coincidence of communist and nationalist positions that led to the temporary abolition of the university system on the territory of Soviet Ukraine in the 1920s and early 1930s.

A different fate awaited the philosopher Hryhorii Skovoroda. In the early nineteenth century, he had symbolized the local cultural specifics of the Sloboda region. Later on, he became an all-Ukrainian national symbol. Skovoroda entered Soviet Kharkiv with the rank of officially recognized "progressive" representative of Ukrainian national tradition. The bicentennial of this "philosopher of the people" was celebrated at the end of December 1922 with a ceremonial session at the Comrade Artem Social Museum. Skovoroda's name was bestowed on literacy courses and on the Museum of Sloboda Ukraine, and Dmytro Bahalii's monograph about him, recognized with a special scholarly prize, was published in 1926 at state expense.

Along with Skovoroda, Hryhorii Kvitka-Osnov'ianenko, Oleksandr Potebnia, and Serhii Vasylkivsky entered Soviet Ukrainian culture as symbols of Ukrainian Kharkiv of the preceding era. The historical, ethnographic, and artistic sections of the Hryhorii Skovoroda Museum of Sloboda Ukraine, respectively, were named after them. This continued the process, now on a new institutional level and in a new Soviet version, of integrating the region into Ukrainian national discourse. It is hard to say in this regard to what extent such a task could have been accomplished with the assistance of old civil society institutions—the Kharkiv Historico-Philological Society or the Kharkiv Literacy Society, which did not manage to survive the Civil War.

Regardless of the constant influx and increase of Ukrainians in Kharkiv, which allowed them once again to constitute a majority of its population, as had been the case at the city's founding; regardless of the official policy of Ukrainization and the expansion of the sphere of usage of the Ukrainian language, various generations of Ukrainian intellectuals found it hard to conceive of Kharkiv in the role of national capital. Unfortunately, the intellectual schism in Ukrainian society, relatively speaking, between supporters of Ukrainian Kyiv and Soviet Ukrainian Kharkiv has not yet been studied as an independent scholarly problem on the same level of analysis as the cultural opposition between Moscow and St. Petersburg.[49] Consequently, in the present work it is characterized only by means of particular observations.

Thus, the well-known Ukrainian literary scholar Serhii Yefremov, an academician of the All-Ukrainian Academy of Sciences and a committed opponent of communism, made the following diary entry after his return from Kharkiv to Kyiv on 4 August 1925: "I have returned from Kharkiv. . . . A city of liars and speculators, overblown reputations, arrogance and ignorance, idlers and chatterers. Every city has its soul, so to speak, only in Kharkiv it is not to be seen. A poor little copy of Asiatic Moscow, but outsize pretensions. I spent three days there and am very glad that I managed to break out of this hell."[50]

The younger generation of Ukrainian intellectuals, already associated with the Soviet system, partly inherited a dislike of the new capital from its predecessors. The lines of the Ukrainian national communist Mykola Khvyliovy are laced with deadly irony: "a stinking industrial city, great but not grand—it has forgotten its Slobodian birth, forgotten the Sloboda regiments, and has not created the American fable: the buildings did not reach the sky—fine, it now hides bloody legends for hundreds of ages in its back alleys."[51] His contemporary Pavlo Tychyna cried out: "Kharkiv, Kharkiv, where is your visage? / To whom do you call? / You're enmired in a slimy myriad of years, / You're dark as night."[52]

Nevertheless, that generation had already set out, as George Shevelov put it, on the intellectual "conquest" of Kharkiv, making use of it to transform Ukrainian anti-urban discourse and integrate the city into a renewed national narrative.[53] Mykhailo Klokov (pseud. Mykhailo Dolengo), comparing Kharkiv with Kyiv, stressed the youth of the new capital first and foremost, its "unbuttoned" openness to innovation, its headlong rush into the future and modern urbanism as compared with Kyivan orderliness, predictability, and intellectual refinement, marked with a permanent "rustic brand."[54]

The young Ukrainian writer Hryhorii Kostiuk entered into a polemic with Pavlo Tychyna, demonstrating his attachment to the Ukrainian historical myth of Kharkiv cultivated by the Kharkiv intelligentsia at the beginning of the twentieth century:

> The thought occurred to me: am I really going to a city without a visage? Is it really "as dark as night"? No, this is some ambiguous

hyperbole on the part of Pavlo Hryhorovych. And Skovoroda? And Karazin? And Kharkiv University, the first university in Ukraine? And Kvitka-Osnov'ianenko, the one to whom Shevchenko himself bared his soul: "It's hard, father, to live with enemies!" And the Kharkiv school of Romantics, and many, many more "Ands"? Is this not Kharkiv? Is this not its visage?[55]

The symbolic geography of the Ukrainian society of that time also found its reflection on the level of public presentations—in particular, during the almost simultaneous anniversary ceremonies on the occasion of the sixtieth birthday of Mykhailo Hrushevsky, a leader of the Ukrainian national movement and founder of Ukrainian national historiography, who was then living in Kyiv, and the seventieth birthday of Dmytro Bahalii, the greatest historian of the Sloboda region, who had been associated with Kharkiv for most of his life. As perceived by Hryhorii Kostiuk, a representative of the younger generation of the Ukrainian intelligentsia, those were two different anniversaries, one of which, in Kyiv, turned into a manifestation of national scholarship and culture, while the other, in Kharkiv, was strictly limited to a scholarly, academic occasion marked by a formal, official atmosphere.

Divergences in the assessment and perception of the two leaders of Ukrainian academic historiography of the time, Hrushevsky and Bahalii, were not accidental and found confirmation in the approaches they had formulated toward evaluating the role and significance of the Kharkiv/Sloboda region in Ukrainian history. Until 1917, a tendency toward intellectual rapprochement had been observed between the two historians, associated with the integration of the regional Slobodian historical narrative into the Ukrainian national one and with the recognition of Kharkiv's leading role in Ukrainian national development during the early nineteenth century. After the defeat of the Ukrainian national-democratic revolution of 1917–20, the attitude toward the Sloboda region in the Ukrainian national narrative began to change.

Hrushevsky deepened Bahalii's predominantly populist thesis concerning the differences in principle between Russian and Ukrainian colonization of the territory and modified it in a national spirit. Naturally, given that approach, Hrushevsky gave preference to the Ukrainian colonizing stream and evaluated it quite optimistically,[56] comparing the settlement of the southeastern steppe territories, as had Grigorii Danilevsky, to the domestication of the New World. At the same time, Hrushevsky understood the very fact of Ukrainian eastward resettlement to the Russian steppe borderland in terms of the national "statist" paradigm and gave it a generally negative assessment, considering that Ukrainian emigration to the east had been more harmful than beneficial to the successful continuation of the war and the consolidation of the Cossack state.

Bahalii, preparing a new version of his monograph on the settlement of the Sloboda region for print, entered into an open polemic with Hrushevsky on the nature of that process, expressing himself in the spirit that, as it were, the basic motives that had brought the migrants to the steppe borderland in the mid-seventeenth century had been socioeconomic and not national. To be sure, this comment of Bahalii's must be evaluated in relation to the political campaign that was developing against him and his efforts to conform to the official Soviet historiographic canon, whose exponent was still considered to be Mikhail Pokrovsky. Bahalii took a moderate approach to interpreting the early colonization of the Sloboda Ukraine region by presenting it in terms of cooperation between Ukrainian and Russian participants. Bahalii's school was closer in that regard to official Soviet Ukrainian discourse, which was then in the stage of conceptualization and subsequent transformation into an ideological scholarly canon.

It is interesting to note that, in spite of their differences of opinion, both leading Ukrainian historians reached conclusions about the Ukrainian identity of the Sloboda region that provoked objections from Russian historians. The Voronezh scholar Sergei Vvedensky, who published an article in 1925 "On the Ukrainian Population within the Boundaries of the Voronezh Gubernia (With Regard to the Historical Briefs of Academicians Bahalii and Hrushevsky)," maintained that the territory of the Voronezh region "had wholly belonged to the core areas domesticated by the Great Russian tribe and had never constituted a neutral belt belonging to no one or disputed by any two ethnographic entities whatever."[57] Matvei Liubavsky, who explored the history of Russian colonization, refused to take account of the Ukrainian national interpretation of the settlement of the Sloboda region and assigned the principal role in that process to the Russian state. Indirect evidence of the popularity of the views expressed by these Russian historians on the problem of the historical allegiance of the Ukrainian-Russian borderland may be found in a publication on the economic geography of Ukraine that saw print in Moscow in 1928 in the series "Economic Geography of the USSR."[58]

Nevertheless, it must be noted that in the 1920s part of the Soviet Russian intelligentsia took a generally benevolent attitude toward Kharkiv in the role of Ukrainian capital. They did so, at least, until the nationality policy of the Soviet regime again began to be defined by imperial Russian nationalism. It was thanks to Kharkiv in particular that the Soviet Russian intelligentsia discovered the world of the Ukrainian language and culture, regarding it now as an ally, and not as an insidious competitor in the struggle for world hegemony produced by murky Austro-German or Polish or Roman Catholic circles. For those arriving from Russia, it was Kharkiv in particular that symbolized, as it had done more than a century earlier, the transition from Russia proper to Ukrainian cultural space, which was marked by the language difference.

Marietta Shaginian described her impressions of Kharkiv as follows: "The delight of Ukrainian speech can be grasped only in Ukraine. ... I, a sinner, first felt the language when from the wall newspaper of the huge Kharkiv electromechanical factory—the KhEMZ ... my own Russian words looked back at me in Ukrainian."⁵⁹ The verses of Nikolai Aseev continue that motif: "The new city stretched out / In the former speech of peasants– / Opening up and rustling / In the soft Ukrainian language."⁶⁰

In Soviet literature of the 1920s, Kharkiv was most often depicted and perceived as a model contemporary city associated with the new industrial era, striving toward the bright future. Kharkiv's "Ukrainian" and "capital" air itself became part of modernizing Soviet discourse. Vladimir Maiakovsky wrote: "And I see— capital after capital / Grows from the immeasurable strength of the Union; / Where ravens hovered, above the carrion of cawings, / Bandaged in the dressings of railways / Ukrainian Kharkiv hums like a capital, / Alive, working, iron-and-concrete."⁶¹

The local area studies narrative developed in the same direction at that time, creating a new symbolic space for the city of Kharkiv as the center of revolutionary activities. In numerous guidebooks, popular outline histories of the city and its suburbs, lists of recommended excursions in the city, and even textbooks in the area studies genre, Kharkiv was pictured as new, unknown, and waiting to be discovered, an industrial giant whose hands were streets, which breathed factory smoke, and so on.

It is hard to say what role Kharkiv's proximity to the Donbas played in all this, but there is no doubt that its cultural and political influence was felt quite clearly in the life of the capital and in the country as a whole, especially as the domestic situation worsened. In 1931, when the Kharkiv party organization began another propaganda campaign against intellectuals, the neopopulist rhetoric of "paying back the debt to the Donbas" figured prominently in it, and owing to that rhetoric even the Ukrainian Academy of Sciences was soon proclaimed a "cultural Donbas."⁶²

In the early years of Soviet rule, Kharkiv benefited from the innovative potential built up in the preceding decades, during the period of rapid development of the South Russian economic region. That reserve of durability sufficed only for a brief period. The policy of communist experimentation yielded very soon to one of return to the traditions of Russian imperial statism and its cultural legacy, which clearly proved impossible to shed with the methods adopted by the new regime.

## From the "First" to the "Second" Capital

In the late 1920s and early 1930s, when the communist experiment with the market and national culture was discontinued, and the Soviet Union—a prototype for the whole new world—went back to being a new version of the Russian Empire, the capital of Ukraine left Kharkiv and returned to Kyiv. The first public announcement of the decision to effect that transfer was issued on 21 January 1934 at the ninth session of the Twelfth Congress of the Communist Party (Bolshevik) of Ukraine. Serhy Yekelchyk thinks that the initiative came directly from Stalin and took many responsible party functionaries in Ukraine by surprise.⁶³

The motives officially put forward for moving the capital were as follows: it would confound the plans of the fascist and Petliurite-White agents, in whose strategy Kyiv held first place; it was necessary to bring the capital closer to the largest agricultural regions of the Right Bank in order to proletarianize and industrialize them; it was necessary to accelerate the development of national culture and Bolshevik Ukrainization on the basis of industrialization and collectivization; and, finally, Kyiv was in and of itself the "natural geographic center" of Ukraine.[64]

What the official version did not say about the change of capital was that it was being transferred from one border, Russo-Ukrainian, to another, Ukrainian-Polish. According to Yekelchyk, the basic reason for the transfer was political, and it was associated with the international situation of the mid-1930s, as well as with the defeat of Ukrainian national communism, the abandonment of Ukrainization, and the increasing scope of purges in Ukrainian society.[65] Kyiv was positioned as an "impregnable front-line fortress." It is another matter that, along with external borders, internal ones played no less significant a role in the Soviet Union. In 1937, according to a resolution of the USSR Central Executive Committee, the Poltava region was separated from Kharkiv oblast, becoming the basis for the creation of the Poltava oblast. The administrative boundary between the historical Sloboda region and Little Russia, or the former Hetmanate, was thus restored. Kharkiv again found itself at the edge of Ukrainian national territory.

At the same time, Kharkiv became politically closer to the Russian/Soviet capitals. Kharkiv had managed to attain third place, after Moscow and Leningrad, in the new hierarchy of Soviet cities, established according to degree of restriction of ordinary citizens' rights and freedoms. In the middle of that system, which resembled a number of concentric circles expanding on the map from center to periphery, were cities in which it was hardest of all to obtain the right of permanent residence and work. Until the outbreak of World War II, they were headed by Moscow, Leningrad, and Kharkiv. Those were precisely the cities to which the passport system, introduced by a Soviet government resolution of 31 December 1932, pertained in the first instance. The same trio headed the list of so-called forbidden Soviet cities, where "undesirable" Soviet citizens could not obtain a residence permit. In that regard at least, Kharkiv found itself in the "core" area of the Soviet Union, just as before the October Revolution of 1917 it had belonged to the Orthodox core of the Russian Empire.

In the 1930s Kharkiv played the role of Ukrainian "capital" of state terror, the arena of political show trials of the top Soviet scholarly and party hierarchy and, finally, the site where a new weapon of mass destruction—the man-made famine (Holodomor) that encompassed the Soviet part of Ukraine in 1932–33—was employed.[66] It appears that Kharkiv and Kyiv oblasts—the two "capital" oblasts of Ukraine—were those most affected by the Holodomor. That can hardly have been an accident, since the neighboring Chernihiv oblast was treated much more favorably and had much lower losses. It is worth mentioning that according to present-day Russian scholars, Ukrainians appear to have been the nationality most affected by the man-made famine in the border region between Belgorod and Kharkiv oblasts.[67] The Holodomor was directly associated with the official reversal of the Ukrainization policy, which led to national reidentification of the borderland population. As a result, the number of Ukrainians in the border region decreased approximately by three-quarters.

All information related to the human catastrophe became a state secret. When the next paroxysm of Soviet-produced famine occurred in 1936–37, Kharkiv's stores were full of bread in order to deceive foreign visitors. Tens of thousands of Soviet and non-Soviet citizens passed through the prisons and interrogation "isolators" of the city. To put it briefly, these were places of destruction of human "material left over from the previous era" and judged unfit for the "bright future."

Like Katyn of sorrowful memory, Kharkiv became a place of mass annihilation of Polish military servicemen taken prisoner when Stalin's USSR, along with Nazi Germany, attacked Poland in 1939. In Kharkiv, where the forest park now stands, Polish officers were shot on the eve of Germany's invasion of the Soviet Union. Later, a guest house for KGB personnel would be built on the site of the mass executions. But that somber image of a city of repression either remained unknown to the public at large or was afterward forced out of the sphere of collective historical memory of Soviet citizens, coming to light only, and then only briefly, during the disintegration of the Soviet Union.

The official aspect of Soviet Kharkiv was represented, as before the October Revolution of 1917, by industrial enterprise, education, and scholarship. In those sectors at least, the communists strove to maintain continuity with the preceding era. Kharkiv's industrial potential attained third place in the USSR after that of Moscow and Leningrad, mainly because of the rapidly developing military-industrial complex. Huge new machine-building enterprises appeared in the 1930s, especially the Kharkiv tractor factory, considered one of the largest in the world, the Kharkiv machine-tool plant, the Kharkiv turbogenerator plant (the largest in Europe, according to contemporaries), and a number of others. At the same time, Kharkiv became a center of basic contemporary scientific research serving the defense industry and represented by the physicists Lev Landau, Aleksandr Akhiezer, Abram Ioffe, Anton Valter, the tank designer Aleksandr Morozov, and other scientists.

Enterprises of so-called Union subordination, directly linked to Moscow and not to Kyiv, looked like standard parts of the Soviet hierarchy, and not of Ukrainian space, from the moment of their appearance. They were the most powerful organizational enclaves of Soviet Russian uniformity, conforming to the strategic goal of producing the new Soviet man. It was no accident that Russian and Russian-speaking workers and officials of Kharkiv's large industrial enterprises remained practically untouched by the official policy of Ukrainization. The number of people "freed" from the obligation of learning the Ukrainian language in Soviet Ukrainian educational institutions increased constantly.

The "great leap" in Soviet economic policy was accompanied by the "great retreat" in Soviet ideology, which turned away from avant-garde experimental values to more traditional imperial ones. "Soviet" increasingly became incarnate as "Russian," which in turn closely resembled the concept of the "all-Russian people" as developed in the Russian Empire in the 1830s and defined by the formula "Orthodoxy, autocracy, *narodnost'*." Orthodoxy, for its part, temporarily gave place to another equally all-embracing civil religion—communism; autocracy might well be said never to have disappeared from Russian political practice; and *narodnost'*, beginning in the mid-1930s, was modified into the doctrine of the "friendship of peoples" under Russian leadership, replacing the policy of "indigenization" and assigning the leading role to Russian culture in the multinational "family of Soviet peoples."

Ironically enough, the new course of the Soviet leadership found its visible incarnation in the rebirth of so striking a symbol of pre-Soviet Kharkiv as the university. That took place almost at the same time as Kharkiv lost its status as capital. Publications on the history of Kharkiv University, which appeared in the Soviet Ukrainian press in connection with the school's by no means "round" 130th anniversary in 1935, were characterized first and foremost by the aspiration to reestablish historical continuity. By no accident whatever, the first Soviet synthetic publication on the subject contains no hint that in the 1920s and early 1930s Kharkiv University did not actually exist at all.[68]

Accidentally or not, but definitely after the annexation of Western Ukraine, along with Lviv and its university (whose history, even if one begins it with 1784, still turns out older than that of Kharkiv University), to the Ukrainian SSR in 1940, the tag "oldest in Ukraine" began to be applied to Kharkiv University. Moreover, practically all official publications dedicated to the "not round" (130th and 140th) anniversaries of Kharkiv University placed it in Ukrainian national symbolic space. After World War II the treatment of the university's history would undergo substantial change.

The cultural landscape of Kharkiv also changed during the Stalin era. In 1936 more than 480 of the city's streets and lanes were renamed on government orders. About one-third of those names, reflecting the processes of industrialization, militarization, and ideologization of Soviet social and cultural life, survived until 2014. In 1937–38 Railway Station Square was named after Lazar Kaganovich, as was the old city's Zhuravlivka quarter; Fish Street became Beria Street; Dostoevsky Street was renamed after Nikolai Yezhov; and present-day Smithy Street after Semen Budenny. Moscow Avenue was deemed worthy of being named after Stalin himself, to whom a huge monument appeared at the entrance to Dzerzhinsky Square in the very center of town.

## World War II

During World War II, Kharkiv again found itself in the role of a frontier town.[69] The Soviet poet Abram Katsnelson, describing the retreat of Soviet forces in 1941, speaks of Kharkiv as "the last boundary of Ukraine."[70] After the occupation of the city and its region by the Nazi forces and their Italian, Romanian, and Hungarian allies on 25 October 1941, it was near the front line. Interestingly, Nazi German ideologists, confronted with the rich cultural treasures "discovered" by the occupying forces in the city's museum and art collections, organized a public exhibition of such artifacts in order to prove the region's European identity. Oskar Weindnagel, a representative of Alfred Rosenberg's headquarters, even proclaimed eastern Ukraine an "East European *antemurale*."[71] That did not save Kharkiv from disaster or shield its inhabitants from mass terror and extermination.

At the end of 1941, Kharkiv had a population of 457,000, slightly more than one-third of the prewar total.[72] During the Nazi occupation of 1941–43, Kharkiv lost between 226,000 and 260,000 citizens, who either died or left the city for various reasons, voluntarily or not.[73] Kharkiv also lost about 70 percent of its industrial potential; its infrastructure was almost totally destroyed. The Nazis were completely indifferent to the civil population, which was left on the brink of starvation, with no food supply or medical assistance. No wonder the inhabitants remained generally hostile toward the occupiers.

Among those who were anti-Soviet, the Organization of Ukrainian Nationalists was perhaps the most influential force. It was divided into mutually antagonistic factions led by Andrii Melnyk and Stepan Bandera. There were also anti-Soviets among the local intelligentsia.[74] Their main institution, Prosvita (Enlightenment Society), became the most important center of Ukrainian cultural activities. The toponymic commission, organized by Prosvita and headed by Professor Vasyl' Dubrovsky, began to rename Kharkiv streets as early as 1941. As a result, in 1942 alone, 483 streets were renamed. Their pre-Soviet, politically neutral names were usually reinstated. Thus, Lavrentii Beria Street became Fish (Rybna) Street; Karl Liebknecht Street became Sumy Street; Lenin Avenue became New Avenue, and so on. Some names reflected the city's occupied status; thus, for example, Dzerzhinsky Plaza was renamed German Army Plaza.[75]

During the war, Kharkiv changed hands as the front line advanced and retreated until the city was finally liberated by Soviet forces of the Steppe Front on 23 August 1943. Notable in this regard is an official Soviet attempt to "award" Kharkiv the title of "second capital"—a term apparently first used in an order issued by Supreme Commander Joseph Stalin in connection with the liberation of the city. The formula "city of the second salute" appeared immediately in Soviet literary fiction[76] (first in that category was neighboring Belgorod). But neither designation lasted in the former "first capital" or took root in the consciousness of Kharkivites themselves. The reason was most probably that Kharkiv's ambitions and standing in the Soviet Union did not allow it to be satisfied with a secondary role, especially in tandem with provincial Belgorod.

Nor was Kharkiv officially recognized as a hero city, like Kyiv and Odesa. Given the major failures of the Red Army at Kharkiv, passed over in silence by Soviet propaganda, there was no longer any hope of that.[77] The city's wartime reputation was elevated only in part by symbolic actions associated with its liberation by Soviet forces. Thus, Kharkiv became the site of the first public trial of Nazis in history in 1943, before the world-famous Nuremberg trials.[78] A programmatic article featuring the slogan of the "reunification" of all ethnic Ukrainian lands, prepared by the highly placed Soviet Ukrainian writer Oleksandr Korniichuk, was published in Kharkiv. These actions did not elevate Kharkiv to the rank of a hero city, but they initiated the creation of its heroic Soviet narrative based on Resistance and Liberation paradigms.

In the cultural policy of the Soviet leadership, the late 1940s and early 1950s were marked by an intensification of xenophobia, anti-Semitism, imperialist and nationalist attitudes.[79] There is every reason to see this as a consequence of the spiritual inertia of the war era, when the authorities used not so much Soviet as religious and nationalist symbols of the Russian Empire to mobilize the population. In Kharkiv especially, this wartime shift was reflected in yet another toponymic "change of signposts" as the "internationalism" of the initial period of Soviet rule unexpectedly began to look like "cosmopolitanism" in the late 1940s and early 1950s. The period was marked by a reversion to pre-Soviet names of the city's streets and squares. At the end of 1945 the old names of Sumy Street (formerly Karl Liebknecht Street), Saddlery Street (formerly Klara Zetkin Street), University Street (formerly Free Academy Street), and Lowland Lane (formerly Jean Marat Lane) were restored, as were some others.

Kharkiv's pre-Soviet cultural tradition began returning to Soviet public space immediately after World War II in connection with the rampage of official Russian nationalism in the USSR. An iconic figure of the time was the eminent Kharkiv educator and initiator of the founding of Kharkiv University, Vasilii Karazin, who was given a pass into the ranks of "progressives"—public figures and eminent scholars acceptable to Soviet man. Of course, this automatically made Karazin one of the public figures opposed to the tsarist regime and calling for incipient bourgeois reforms, a talented, innovative scholar unappreciated in his lifetime, like Ivan Michurin or Konstantin Tsiolkovsky.

It was not only Karazin's credentials as a man of the Enlightenment that were welcomed in postwar Soviet culture but also the conservative, anti-Western and imperial, messianic features of his worldview. In the climate of struggle against "rootless cosmopolitans" and "truckling" to the West, those qualities restored him to the status of "Ukrainian Lomonosov," consonant with the official cult of Lomonosov in Soviet literature. Similar parallels had been made as early as the mid-nineteenth century by Grigorii Danilevsky, a native of the Kharkiv region and a well-known writer, historian, and public figure.

A brochure about Karazin by the Kharkiv historian Anton Sliusarsky, published in 1952,[80] contains the standard set of clichés that made possible not only the "rehabilitation" but also the mythologization of Karazin in official Soviet discourse. There he was depicted as a "self-sacrificing fighter on the field of enlightenment, a talented representative of advanced gentry society,"[81] a fighter against despotism and serfdom, and the like. With certain stylistic corrections, such rhetoric still largely defines the character not only of popular or fictional but also of scholarly literature devoted to Karazin.

It is noteworthy that such characterizations were offered mainly by Soviet Ukrainian authors and were somewhat balanced by another viewpoint critical of Karazin, which was associated with the liberal tradition in historical studies of the Decembrists and Aleksandr Pushkin cultivated in the Soviet Russian capitals. In the works of Vasilii Bazanov, Karazin figured as an informer against the Decembrists and Pushkin, a reactionary and serf owner close in outlook to official circles of the Russian Empire.[82] Such a treatment of Karazin's personality and views could not, of course, rival the popularity of the aforementioned characterization. Nevertheless, it enjoyed a perfectly official existence, so to speak, in Soviet humanities scholarship, although it was later corrected somewhat and made more balanced with the aid of the metaphor of Karazin's "contradictory" personality.

After World War II, significant changes were made in the treatment of the history of Kharkiv University. In the 1930s, the university was not so much reborn as fashioned anew in a semiotic and cultural space different from the pre-Soviet one, under severe pressure from propaganda of the idea of socialist construction, industrialization, and militarization. The new image of Kharkiv University under its previous name was initially defined by the phraseology of the 1920s, with its utilitarian emphasis on production, likening the university to an industrial enterprise, factory, or combine for the mass production of cadres for the economy.[83] Closer to the war and immediately after its conclusion, under the influence of the militarization of culture and society, the university ever more frequently took on the image of a "citadel" or "fortress."

In the postwar years, however, the university narrative also began to undergo metamorphoses strange at first glance: in it, along with "smithy," not very distant from "factory," or with "flag officer," evidently standing idly by the "citadel," and other familiar metaphors, expressions such as "temple of learning" began to appear, and then, probably influenced by the subject of the cosmos, solar symbols such as "solar temple," "solar palace," and "solar home." Thus, in the university narrative, which reflected changes in official policy as the country "approached communism," a rapprochement became possible not only between Lenin's "palaces and hovels" but also between Bazarov's "temple and workshop."

At the same time, the compromise between Soviet and Ukrainian national tradition in the university's historical narrative proved short-lived. As early as its first "round" (150th) anniversary since the pre-Soviet period, in 1955, the university's Ukrainian identity began imperceptibly to give way to other markers associated with territory and industry. It suffices to compare two anniversary articles by the rector of Kharkiv University, Professor Ivan Bulankin, published in 1945 and 1955 respectively. The title of the first article is "Kharkiv University—the Home of Ukrainian Scholarship and Culture,"[84] while that of the second is already different: "The Oldest University in Ukraine."[85] That tendency would become even more apparent with the celebration of the of the 175th anniversary of Kharkiv University in 1980, when it was awarded the Order of the Friendship of Peoples, and the epithet "Ukrainian" disappeared completely from the titles of publications devoted to that event.

The late 1950s saw the beginning of the official rehabilitation of Dmytro Bahalii in Soviet historiography. The process was inconsistent: some of the historian's works published after 1917 remained classified as long as the Soviet authorities considered his public reputation dubious. The public reinstatement of the traditional name "Sloboda Ukraine" to the principal subject of Bahalii's scholarly work was doubtless the most significant change. It was made possible by the official celebration in 1954 of the tercentenary of the Treaty of Pereiaslav, which brought Ukraine under a Russian protectorate. In official discourse, "Sloboda Ukraine" became the embodiment of "eternal" Russo-Ukrainian friendship.[86]

The history of the settlement of the Sloboda region, its historical geography and socioeconomic history, the life and work of Vasilii Karazin, and the history of Kharkiv University and the city of Kharkiv began to be studied by Kharkiv authors, of whom Professor Anton Sliusarsky was the most prominent.[87] A new Soviet historical narrative of the former Sloboda region and, in particular, of the city of Kharkiv began to be created with the active participation of local scholars who took part in the huge project of compiling a multivolume history of cities and villages of the Ukrainian SSR in the 1960s.

In spite of the official rhetoric, Sloboda Ukraine remained an ambiguous object of study precisely because of its entangled Russo-Ukrainian history. Along with a complex of half-forgotten texts, the discussions among historians of the late nineteenth and early twentieth centuries about the proportional relations of Russian and Ukrainian colonization of the territory gradually began to return to Soviet scholarly space. The Soviet Russian scholar Vladimir Zagorovsky explored the history of Sloboda Ukraine from the perspective of the Russian state's southward progress and the success of Russian popular colonization. He accused Dmytro Bahalii of demeaning "the creative powers and aptitudes of the Russian people."[88]

The Soviet Ukrainian historian Anton Sliusarsky acknowledged that the Russian state had played the leading, organizing role in the colonization of the southern borderlands but found it possible to repeat Bahalii's well-known thesis that, contrary to Russian colonists, "the Ukrainian people ... migrated to the Sloboda region by themselves," that is, voluntarily.⁸⁹ Evidently, for the Ukrainian author, the Sloboda region belonged to Ukrainian national territory conceived in the class-based and populist terms of official historiography.

The earliest history of the region written in this period turned out to be less controversial, if only at first glance. In postwar Soviet literature one can find topics and symbols that reconstruct images of the Kharkiv region as the "Wild Steppe" and the ancient Rus' borderland as, for example, in the poetic lines of Konstantin Kuzminsky: "And the Kharkiv River grows more shallow / The polecat goes boldly into the water / In the Wild Steppe the Cuman stars / Burn out in their own way"; "Khan Asana or Osenia / Built the town of Sharukhan / And then he became Cheshuev / After the death of Sharuk."⁹⁰ Mykhailo Hetmanets, a Kharkiv scholar, undertook to establish that it was precisely the Kharkiv region in which the events described in the *Tale of Igor's Campaign* had taken place.⁹¹

It proved much more difficult to combine the principles of communist internationalism with the growing ideological influence of Russian nationalism on the Soviet *nomenklatura* of the postwar period. After Stalin's death, policy differences in the Soviet leadership between, relatively speaking, "Leninists" and "Stalinists" began to become more apparent: the former continued to orient themselves toward the modernizing components of Soviet ideology and the latter toward its nationalist (Russian imperial) components.⁹² The first group remained Soviet "westernizers" and reformers, while the second gravitated toward the "Slavophiles" and traditionalism. The constant "shifts of party line" at a time when the party was no longer looking forward so confidently to the communist future brought the problem of historical continuity to the fore: arguments about the future gradually turned into arguments about the past.

### *New/Old Tradition*

The renunciation of Stalinism created an ever-growing need to legitimize the political regime established by the new generation of the Soviet party establishment in the second half of the twentieth century. The basic role in that process was assigned to the two fundamental historical myths of the Soviet period: the "Great October Socialist Revolution" and the "Great Patriotic War." Both made a deep impression on the cultural and symbolic space of Kharkiv, remaining there until recently.

The partial de-Stalinization that began in the USSR with the coming to power of Nikita Khrushchev made itself apparent primarily through the removal of Stalinist symbols from the city's landscape—the numerous monuments, busts, portraits, and names of the Leader and those of his comrades who had escaped the firing squad. After the Khrushchev leadership replaced that of Stalin, Stalin Avenue was again named Moscow Avenue, and the giant Stalin monument on Dzerzhinsky Square at Sumy Street was soon removed. Given, however, that "sacred sites do not remain empty," Stalinist places of memory quickly began to be filled with equally omnipresent, all-penetrating, and obligatory Leninist ones. The award of an Order of Lenin to Kharkiv oblast in 1958 for its achievements in the development of agriculture was also meant to promote the "Leninization" of its social space, including that of the oblast center.

The erection of a giant Lenin monument in the new center of Kharkiv on Dzerzhinsky Square in 1963 was officially dedicated to the forty-sixth anniversary of the October Revolution, obviously not a round number. More in keeping with official Soviet calendar celebrations was a second Lenin monument erected on the territory of the Kharkiv Lenin Order of Lenin Polytechnical Institute in 1967. The triple repetition of the Leader's name in that connection resoundingly emphasized its sacral character for every Soviet citizen. The total number of Lenin monuments erected in the Kharkiv region during the years of Soviet rule soon reached 118,[93] while the number of busts, portraits, and other depictions, not to speak of the rituals associated with them, very soon became countless and beyond rational comprehension.

The policy of returning to "Leninist sources" as a counterweight to Stalin's "perversion" of them was graphically illustrated by the numerous monuments to "Leninists" that heavily dotted Kharkiv's public space: Sergo Ordzhonikidze (1956), Sergei Kirov (1957), Yakov Sverdlov (1958), Stanislav Kosior (1966). This practice continued after the fall of Khrushchev, with the palm passing to Feliks Dzerzhinsky, the supreme patron of the Soviet "organs," deemed worthy of two monuments at once (1970, 1975) and a few dozen memorial plaques, including one on the establishment closest to his memory (1977). Indeed, even the Communist Party official Pavel Postyshev, who had perished in the depths of that very institution, did not remain unremembered and was deemed worthy of a monument in 1977, seemingly personifying the dialectics of party policy.

While Kharkiv's new center was awarded a monument to the Leader, the old center found itself obliged to take on the fundamental burden of the Revolution. The monument to the fighters of the Revolution, erected there in 1957 with an eternal flame in front of it, looked fairly modest and, thanks to its apt position on the square at the edge of the old city's height, it became the choice pilgrimage site for newlyweds. In 1975, however, a pompous monument personifying the proclamation of Soviet rule in Ukraine wedged its way into the ensemble on the city's former main square. The square itself, previously named for the local Bolshevik Moises (Yakov) Tevelev, was accordingly renamed Soviet Ukraine Square—sonorous but awkward as a reference in everyday speech.

The historical mythology of the Great Patriotic War very soon caught up with and overtook that of the Great October, especially after Leonid Brezhnev came to power. It was created by tens of thousands of authors whose works, printed in large quantities, topped a billion copies; the war took first place as a subject of films and plays; it was marked annually with mass rituals and celebrations; even more, it enjoyed the support not only of the party state but of society itself. Against the background of the monumental evils of the Stalin regime—and, let us add, the spread of corruption under Brezhnev—the mythology of the Great Victory appeared to be perhaps the only argument in favor of the Soviet system.[94]

From the moment of its appearance, the subject of the Great Patriotic War took on a sacral, quasi-religious character, becoming, like the Great October, an important component of Soviet civil religion. The graves of fallen Soviet soldiers were turned into ritual sites of worship. Monuments to heroes and victims of the war were usually erected on sites where Orthodox churches and chapels had formerly stood.[95] The religious character of places of worship preserving the memory of the recent war was emphasized by the official rhetoric associated with them, sounding distinctly in reports about the newly erected monuments: "land that has become a temple," "imperishable memory," "sacred place," "thrice-holy names," and the like.[96]

In total, some twelve hundred memorials, monuments, memorial plaques, and specialized museums dedicated to wartime events were established on the territory of Kharkiv oblast. In the oblast center, their intensive construction began, evidently, in the latter half of the 1950s. As noted earlier, Kharkiv was not judged worthy in official Soviet mythology of the laurels bestowed on Kyiv, Moscow, Odesa, Sevastopol, and other hero cities. Accordingly, in the monumental propaganda and toponymy associated with the wartime period of its history, it was not heroic defense of the city but the discourse of resistance and liberation that took pride of place.

The myth of a massive underground and partisan movement on Ukrainian territory began to be created at an accelerated pace with the direct support of Nikita Khrushchev. In Kharkiv itself, prominence was given to participants in the city's underground resistance headed by Ivan Bakulin, who was posthumously awarded the status of Hero of the Soviet Union in the mid-1960s. Monuments were erected in their honor and memorial plaques placed. The particular emphasis on resistance by the Young Communist League that accompanied the memorialization was of course a tribute to the mythology of the "Young Guard" created by Aleksandr Fadeev. In 1958 a gallery of Young Communist League heroes appeared in central Kharkiv and, later, a gallery of Young Guard heroes next to Secondary School 116. A monument to partisans and underground fighters of the Kharkiv region was erected in 1978.

But the theme of liberation, prioritized in cultural policy by the Kharkiv authorities in the years of "stagnation," proved much more popular than that of "partisan and underground resistance." Numerous names of Soviet military commanders, military units and formations, soldiers and officers of the Soviet Army who had taken part in the liberation of the city in August 1943 figured in Kharkiv's cultural landscape, memorialized in the names of streets and subway stations, monuments and memorial plaques, as well as Pioneer and Young Communist League chapters. The most visible symbols of the Soviet historical mythology of the Great Patriotic War in Kharkiv were the huge memorial complex of Glory on the outskirts of the city, in the forest park (1977), and the pompous monument to the Soldier-Liberator erected in 1981 on August 23 Street.

Kharkiv's postwar history made no significant changes in its generally established image of the Ukrainian proletarian capital, center of scholarship and education, heavy industry, transport hub, city of labor, city of scholars, proletarians, and students. The city gained clandestine fame as the Soviet military-industrial center of advanced technology associated with atomic experiments, tank construction, and systems for cosmic and military rockets. Kharkiv's research centers and industrial enterprises associated with defense were administered directly from Moscow and had little to do with Kyiv, the capital of the republic.[97]

The informal shadow image of postwar Kharkiv was also defined by its inclusion in common Soviet intellectual space, shaped mainly by Moscow, by the artistic and literary tastes of its intelligentsia, the nonconformist culture of the new generation, the dissident movement, underground commercial activity, and the "black" market, which flourished thanks to Kharkiv's transport connections and the constant presence of large numbers of students from many countries in its institutions of higher education. But those pages of the city's history have not yet been written. Some of them are depicted quite vividly in Eduard Limonov's autobiographical Anthony Burgess–like *Kharkiv Trilogy*, with its hoodlums, outrageous slums, and cynical bohemia.

In relation to Kyiv, the capital of Soviet Ukraine, Kharkiv always maintained a certain cultural distance, mindful of its recent past as capital and traditionally modeling itself in the image and likeness of Moscow and Leningrad. There are no grounds to speak of a virtual Kharkiv–Kyiv axis like the one that arose after World War II, in the opinion of Roman Szporluk, between Lviv and Kyiv.[98] The mutual relations and stature of the two largest cities of Soviet Ukraine allowed David Hooson, for example, to compare them with two Italian metropolises, correspondingly, Milan and Rome.[99] By that time, however, Kharkiv's symbolic potential no longer sufficed for it to compete seriously with Kyiv for the role of capital of Ukraine.

The loss of capital status did not pass without consequences for Kharkiv. The city's architectural appearance lost its principal characteristic—the spirit of innovation and experiment.[100] New urban construction in Kharkiv, unlike that of the 1920s and early 1930s, was dominated by typicality, standardization, and mass character. In Kharkiv's history, the "Typical Thirties" were rendered cheerlessly incarnate in the bedroom communities of Pavlove Pole, Novi Domy, and Saltivka, with their utter standardization and economical asceticism. The rout of the "Sixtiers" generation completed the downfall of Soviet Ukrainian culture, which had been sinking into the mire of provincialism and conventional optimism. Kharkiv declined steadily as Ukraine's center of innovation and figured ever more often in the role of intellectual donor to the Soviet capitals.

Cultural Russification remained a constant of Soviet policy. Never before, perhaps, had the city and region been under such pressure to become part of the Russian cultural and linguistic "nucleus." The result of that policy was a steady decline in the proportion of ethnic Ukrainians in Kharkiv oblast, from 82.2 percent in 1959 to 63.1 percent in 1989.[101] In Kharkiv, Ukrainians constituted about 47 percent of its population in 1959, while their numbers in Lviv and Kyiv attained 60 percent.[102] At the same time, there was a corresponding increase in the number of Russians in Kharkiv, from 17.2 to 33.4 percent. The number of Ukrainian-language schools decreased from 71.8 percent in the 1951/52 school year to 27.9 percent in the 1985/86 school year.[103]

In terms of mental geography, in the postwar decades Kharkiv remained at the intersection of two competing discourses: Russian southern, associated with centralizing tendencies in the policy of the Union center, and Ukrainian national, reflecting the officially permitted national component of Soviet reality. Both discourses led a satisfactory existence throughout Soviet history, coming to the surface of social reality only in periods when the domestic political situation deteriorated.

A constant reminder of Kharkiv's southern orientation was the southern railway line passing through the city, along with its southern—and main—railway station. Reminders of Kharkiv's ties with the Donbas were not only the enterprises that continued to work for the mining industry (the Miner's Light Factory and the Mining Institute, which offered higher education in the subject) but also *Yuzhgiproshakht*, the State Institute for Designing Mines and Ore Concentration Plants. The Great Patriotic War had added yet another southern marker to the city, *Yuzhkabel* (Southern Cable), serving the needs of the southern fronts.

A reminder that the *Yug* (South) never actually disappeared from the practice of the central Soviet planning agencies is a resolution adopted on 10 August 1945 by the office of the Kharkiv Oblast Committee of the All-Union Communist Party (Bolshevik). According to that document, the office, carrying out the directions of the USSR *Gosplan*, had determined in particular that "the basic direction of industrial development in the Kharkiv region should be the increase of production ... of equipment for the Donbas coal industry and southern metallurgy."[104]

A preliminary and selective analysis, making no claim to comprehensiveness, of titles and subjects of scholarly historical literature about the region of Southern Russia issued by the central publishing houses of the USSR allows one to assume that in and of itself the region continued to hold its place in official discourse, although it maintained its territorial indeterminacy and inconsistency of geographic terminology applied to it. In the titles of applicable publications of various years, including those published after the incorporation of the Crimea into the Ukrainian SSR in 1954, one finds, for example, the terms "South of Russia," "New Russia," "northern Black Sea littoral," and "Southern Ukraine" for one and the same territory.[105]

It is no less curious that Western specialists, not bound by the conventions of Soviet censorship or a unified normative terminology, considered it possible to speak as before, for instance, of some integral economic region within a radius of about six hundred miles around Kharkiv, coinciding approximately with the pre-Soviet territory of Southern Russia. The aforementioned David Hooson wrote of the common economic interests of residents of that conditional region and their growing dissatisfaction with the policy of the center, while R. B. Adams simply divided Ukrainian territory into two regions, one centered in Kharkiv, the other in Kyiv, which essentially reproduced the Southern Russia and the Southwestern Land of imperial Russia.[106]

Nevertheless, Kharkiv did not remain in the symbolic geographic space of Southern Russia. It shifted to the northeast, which meant that the city was located in the national space of Ukraine. In Soviet geographic and area studies publications of the late twentieth century, Kharkiv is depicted as the "main economic and cultural center of the Northeast [of Ukraine], with a population of 1.2 million, yielding only to Kyiv in number of residents."[107] The Kharkiv regional center of the Academy of Sciences of the Ukrainian SSR was designated northeastern (and still retains that designation today). It is worth mentioning in this regard that the Russian city of Rostov underwent a similar evolution in its time, becoming the center of the southeastern oblast in 1924 but soon shifting to the territory of the North Caucasus *krai*. Today it would appear that Rostov is pretending to the role of capital of Southern Russia in the new configuration of that region.[108]

Thus, in the Soviet period Kharkiv formally established itself in Ukrainian national and administrative political space. More precisely, as it turned out, Kharkiv had never left that space. The Soviet Russian poet Samuil Marshak confirmed the existence of an ethnocultural boundary between Ukraine and Russia extending approximately where it had been delineated by Russian and foreign travelers in the early nineteenth century: "What his kin and country are / You won't grasp from his speech. / He'll say now *ishchu*, now *shukaiu* ["I search" in Russian and Ukrainian] / And after *liubliu*, then *kokhaiu* ["I love" in Russian and Ukrainian] / Now *zhyto*, now *rozh'* he'll pronounce. ["Rye" in Ukrainian and Russian] / If you please, between the oblasts of Kursk / And Kharkiv, that's how they speak."[109]

An unexpected confirmation of this poetic observation appeared in the years of Soviet perestroika (restructuring) in a book by the Soviet scholar Liudmila Chizhikova on the ethnic Russo-Ukrainian borderland.[110] For the first time since the implementation of the policy of Soviet internationalism and the "friendship of peoples," that work confirmed the inconsequential degree of assimilation of Russians and Ukrainians living side by side for centuries in the Kharkiv region, as well as the existence of an ethnocultural boundary between the peoples first in line for transformation into a "united historical community of peoples."

As the nationality policy of the Soviet leadership continued to evolve, Kharkiv remained part of the Russo-Ukrainian cultural borderland. Taken as a whole, the "short" twentieth century showed that despite the dramatic changes in the political and cultural life of the peoples of Eastern Europe, the geopolitical coordinates in which the history of the region and its center, Kharkiv, had developed remained practically unchanged: they localized the city between "Ukraine proper" and "Russia proper." Kharkiv's periodic gain and loss of capital, supraregional status and its related return to the condition of borderland may perhaps be regarded as the most notable confirmation of that thesis.

The region's symbolic markers, beginning with its name, show remarkable durability and resistance to political change. The traditional symbols of specific features of local culture—Hryhorii Skovoroda, Kharkiv University, Vasilii Karazin, the Ukrainian intellectual heritage of the nineteenth and early twentieth centuries—were not eliminated but supplemented by new ones: Gosprom, the "socialist city" of the 1920s and early 1930s, the symbolism of the Ukrainian "Executed Renaissance," schools of scholarly thought, and so on. In time, however, the features of Kharkiv's official Ukrainianism—several Ukrainian-language newspapers, schools, university chairs, a drama theater—increasingly took on the appearance of decorations, and the memory of the Ukrainian national communism of the 1920s was marginalized.

At the same time, Soviet historical mythology, Russification, and, supremely important, the totalist character of Soviet propaganda, in which several generations of Soviet people were brought up, actively involved the city and region in the common Soviet cultural and linguistic space. Perhaps the basic role in that process was played by the modernizing component of Soviet policy. Kharkiv oriented itself toward the capitals, Moscow and Leningrad. Western ideas and cultural values penetrated almost exclusively in Russian versions. All that could not fail to leave its mark on the most recent, post-Soviet history of Kharkiv, which is the subject of the next chapter.

## Notes

1. A. V. Gutovskii, *Zhilishchnyi vopros v Khar'kove* (Kharkiv, 1918), 12; Mikhail Kurman and Ivan Lebedinskii, *Naselenie bol'shogo sotsialisticheskogo goroda* (Moscow: Statistika, 1968), 19.
2. *Dannye predvaritel'nogo podscheta odnodnevnoi perepisi goroda Khar'kova i ego prigorodov 31 dekabria 1917 goda* (n.p., n.d.), 9.
3. Dmitrii Chernyi, "Khar'kov v gody Pervoi mirovoi voiny i revoliutsii," in *Goroda imperii v gody Velikoi voiny i revoliutsii: Sbornik statei*, eds. Aleksei Miller and Dmitrii Chernyi (St. Petersburg: Nestor-istoriia, 2017), 318–48, here 332–34.
4. Vladyslav Verstiuk, Victor Horobets', and Oleksii P. Tolochko, *Ukraïns'ki proekty v Rosiis'kii imperiï: Narysy*, vol. 1 of *Ukraïna i Rosiia v istorychnii retrospektyvi*, 3 vols, ed. Valerii Smolii (Kyiv: Naukova Dumka, 2004), 1: 420.
5. Nataliia Polons'ka-Vasylenko, *Istoriia Ukraïny* (Munich, 1976), 479.
6. Mariia F. Dmytriienko, "Administratyvno-terytorial'nyi ustrii ukraïns'kykh zemel': istoriia, proekty, real'nist' (XIX–pochatok XX st.)," *Problemy istoriï Ukraïny XIX–pochatku XX st.*, no. 6 (2003): 105–24, here 120.
7. Verstiuk, Horobets', and Tolochko, *Ukraïns'ki proekty v Rosiis'kii imperiï*, 1: 442–43.
8. Chernyi, "Khar'kov v gody," 329.
9. "Khar'kov v gody," 329.
10. Steven L. Guthier, "The Popular Base of Ukrainian Nationalism in 1917," *Slavic Review* 38, no. 1 (1979): 30–47, here 33–34.

11. L. M. Spirin, *Rossiia. 1917 god. Iz istorii bor'by politicheskikh partii* (Moscow: Nauka, 1987), 319–20.
12. *Izvestiia Khar'kovskoi gorodskoi dumy*, nos. 4–5 (1917): xx.
13. Sylvie Archaimbault and Serhii Wakoulenko, *Ivan Pereverzev et ses "Préceptes de la rectitude grammaticale russe... à l'usage des Ukrainiens" (1782)* (Paris, 2010).
14. *Iuzhnyi krai*, 3 December 1917.
15. V. Savva, "Khar'kovskii universitet na sluzhbe naroda," *Zhizn' Rossii*, 17 January 1918.
16. Valerii Taliev, ed., *Priroda i naselenie Slobodskoi Ukrainy. Khar'kovskaia gubernia. Posobie po narodovedeniiu* (Kharkiv: Soiuz, 1918), 3.
17. Rex A. Wade, "Ukrainian Nationalism and 'Soviet Power': Kharkiv, 1917," in *Ukrainian Past, Ukrainian Present: Selected Papers from the 4th World Congress for Soviet and East European Studies, Harrogate, 1990*, ed. Bohdan Krawchenko (New York: St. Martin's Press, 1992), 70–83.
18. *Ocherki istorii Khar'kovskoi oblastnoi partiinoi organizatsii* (Kharkiv: Prapor, 1980), 118.
19. Dmitrii Kornilov, "Obrazovanie Donetsko-Krivorozhskoi Respubliki," *Donetskii Kriazh*, 19 February 1998, http://www.lookdon.by.ru/about/don_republic.htm.
20. Valerii Soldatenko, "Donetsko-Krivorozhskaia Respublika: illiuzii i praktika natsional'nogo nigilizma," *Zerkalo nedeli*, 4–10 December 2004.
21. Soldatenko, "Donetsko-Krivorozhskaia Respublika."
22. "Donetsko-Krivorozhskaia Respublika."
23. Vasyl' Boiechko, Oksana Hanzha, and Borys Zakharchuk, *Kordony Ukraïny: istorychna retrospektyva ta suchasnyi stan* (Kyiv: Osnovy, 1994), 30–31.
24. Dmytriienko, "Administratyvno-terytorial'nyi ustrii," 122.
25. Ikeda Ioshiro, "The Reintegration of the Russian Empire and the Bolshevik Views of Russia: The Case of the Moscow Party Organization," *Acta Slavica Iaponica*, vol. 22 (2005): 134.
26. Konstantin Beliaev and Andrei Krasniashchikh, *Khar'kov v zerkale mirovoi literatury* (Kharkiv: Folio, 2007), 308.
27. S. Volin, "Denikinshchina," in *1917 god v Khar'kove* (Kharkiv: DVU, 1927), 17.
28. Philip Ther, "Caught in Between: Border Regions in Modern Europe," in *Shatterzone of Empires: Coexistence and Violence in the German, Habsburg, Russian, and Ottoman Borderlands*, eds. Omer Bartov and Eric D. Weitz (Bloomington: Indiana University Press, 2013), 485–502, here 486.
29. Stanislav Kul'chyts'kyi, "Poshuky stolytsi radians'koï Ukraïny," *Rozbudova derzhavy*, no. 4 (1997): 50–54.
30. Boiechko, Hanzha, and Zakharchuk, *Kordony Ukraïny*, 50–61; Elena Borisenok, "Ukraina i Rossiia: spor o granitsakh v 1920-e gody," in *Regiony i granitsy Ukrainy v istoricheskoi retrospektive* (Moscow: Institut slavianovedeniia RAN, 2005), 205–37; I. Sluzhyns'ka, "Formuvannia ukraïns'ko-rosiis'koho kordonu: dyskusiï i politychni rishennia 20-kh rokiv XX st.," *Rehional'na istoriia Ukraïny*, no. 7 (2013): 115–24.
31. Boiechko, Hanzha, and Zakharchuk, *Kordony Ukraïny*, 54.
32. *Kordony Ukraïny*, 55.
33. Vladyslav Hrynevych et al., *Radians'kyi proekt dlia Ukraïny*, vol. 2 of *Ukraïna i Rosiia v istorychnii retrospektyvi*, 3 vols., ed. Valerii Smolii (Kyiv: Naukova Dumka, 2004), 382.
34. Boiechko, Hanzha, and Zakharchuk, *Kordony Ukraïny*, 52; Iaroslava Vermenych, *Teoretyko-metodolohichni problemy istorychnoï rehionalistyky v Ukraïni* (Kyiv, 2003), 328.
35. Borisenok, "Ukraina i Rossiia," 216–17.
36. Francis Hirsch, "State and Evolution: Ethnographic Knowledge, Economic Expediency, and the Making of the USSR, 1917–1924," in *Russian Empire: Space, People, Power, 1700–1930*, 139–68.
37. Vladyslav Hrynevych et al., *Radians'kyi proekt*, 44.
38. *Radians'kyi proekt*, 52– 53.

39. *Istoria gorodov i sel Ukrainskoi SSR v 26 tomakh: Khar'kovskaia oblast'* (Kyiv: Naukova Dumka, 1976), 48.
40. *Statistika Ukrainy, seriia 1, Demografiia* 1, no. 5 (1922): 12.
41. *Vsesoiuznyi perepys liudnosti 1926 roku*, vol. 12 (Moscow, 1929), 311.
42. *Vsesoiuznaia perepis' naseleniia 1937 goda: Kratkie itogi* (Moscow, 1991), 66.
43. Chernyi, "Khar'kov v gody," 323.
44. Rinat V. Sharibzhanov, "Natsiona'lni menshyny Kharkova v 20–30-ti roky XX stolittia," Candidate of Sciences diss., Kharkiv University, 2007, 57.
45. Sharibzhanov, "Natsional'ni," 59, 63–64.
46. Kiril Stanilov, ed., *The Post-Socialist City: Urban Form and Space Transformations in Central and Eastern Europe after Socialism* (e-book, 2007).
47. Thomas P. Riggio and James L. W. West III, eds., *Dreiser's Russian Diary* (Philadelphia: University of Pennsylvania Press, 1996), 220.
48. Serhii Posokhov, *Obrazy universytetiv Rosiis'koï imperiï druhoï polovyny XIX–pochatku XX stolittia v publitsystytsi ta istoriohrafiï* (Kharkiv: Kharkiv State University, 2006), 118.
49. Mykhailo Dolengo, "Kyïv ta Kharkiv – literaturni vzaiemovidnoshennia," *Chervonyi shliakh*, nos. 6–7 (1923): 151–57. Cf. Olga Gritsai and Herman van der Wusten, "Moscow and St. Petersburg, a Sequence of Capitals, a Tale of Two Cities," *Geo-Journal* 51, nos. 1–2 (2000): 33–45.
50. Serhii Iefremov, *Shchodennyky, 1923–1929* (Kyiv, 1997), 262.
51. Iurii Sherekh, *Porohy i zaporizhzhia: literatura, mystetstvo, ideolohiï*, vol. 1 (Kharkiv, 1998), 479.
52. Sherekh, *Porohy i zaporizhzhia*, 480.
53. *Porohy i zaporizhzhia*, 480.
54. Dolengo, "Kyïv," 151–57.
55. Hryhorii Kostiuk, *Zustrichi i proshchannia* (Kyiv and New York, 1997), xx.
56. Mykhailo Hrushevs'kyi, *Istoriia Ukraïny-Rusy*, vol. 8, pt. 2, 2nd ed. (Kyiv, 1922), 42, 58.
57. Borisenok, "Ukraina i Rossiia," 219.
58. V. S. Klupt, ed., *SSSR po raionam: Ukraina* (Moscow and Leningrad, 1928), 10, 17–18, 21, 162.
59. Grigorii Gel'dfanbein, *General i ad"iutant: rasskazy o pisateliakh* (Kharkiv: Prapor, 1966).
60. Gel'dfanbein, *General i ad"iutant*.
61. Beliaev and Krasniashchikh, eds., *Khar'kov v zerkale mirovoi literatury*.
62. Nataliia Polons'ka-Vasylenko, *Ukraïns'ka Akademiia Nauk: Narys istoriï* (Kyiv, 1993), 12, 137.
63. Serhy Yekelchyk, "The Making of a 'Proletarian Capital': Patterns of Stalinist Social Policy in Kiev in the Mid-1930s," *Europe-Asia Studies* 50, no. 7 (1998): 1233.
64. *Sotsialistychna Kharkivshchyna*, 23 June 1934.
65. Yekelchyk, "The Making of a 'Proletarian Capital,'" 1229.
66. Oleh Wolowyna et al., "Regional Variations of 1932–34 Famine Losses in Ukraine," *Canadian Studies in Population* 43, nos. 3–4 (2016): 175–202.
67. V. V. Bublikov, "Otvet opponentu," *Ėtnograficheskoe obozrenie*, no. 6 (2016): 85–91, here 88.
68. *Korotki narysy z istoriï Kharkivs'koho derzhuniversytetu imeni O. M. Hor'koho: Iuvileine vydannia, 1805–1940* (Kharkiv, 1940).
69. Anatolii Skorobohatov, *Kharkiv u chasy nimets'koï okupatsiï (1941–1943)* (Kharkiv: Prapor, 2004).
70. Volodymyr P. Kopychko and Iurii H. Kopychko, eds., *Kharkiv'iany: Poema pro misto v tsytatakh poetychnykh tvoriv* (Kharkiv: Slobozhanshchyna, 2007), 84.
71. N. Kashevarova, "Obhruntuvannia istorychnykh prav na ukraïns'ki terytoriï v ideolohichnii doktryni natsyzmu: Promova hauptainzats-fiurera Oskara Vendnahelia na vidkrytti istoryko-arkheolohichnoï vystavky u Kharkovi 1 lystopada 1942 r." *Arkhivy Ukraïny*, nos. 1–3 (2005): 221–32.

72. Skorobohatov, *Kharkiv*, 19.
73. *Kharkiv*, 326.
74. *Kharkiv*, 211–21; Arkadii Liubchenko, *Shchodennyk* (Lviv and New York: Marian Kots', 1999); Oleksandr Semenenko, *Kharkiv, Kharkiv...* (Kharkiv and New York: Berezil' and Marian Kots', 1992); Iurii Shevel'ov, *Ia, mene, meni... (i dovkruhy). Spohady*, vol. 1, *v Ukraïni* (Kharkiv: Folio, 2015).
75. Skorobohatov, *Kharkiv*, 197–98.
76. Grigorii Okladnoi, "Khar'kov – vtoraia stolitsa Sovetskoi Ukrainy," *Krasnoe znamia*, 20 August 1949; *Kharkiv'iany: Poema*, 106.
77. David M. Glantz, *Kharkov 1942: Anatomy of a Military Disaster* (Rockville Centre, NY: Sarpedon, 1998).
78. Greg Dawson, *Judgment before Nuremberg: The Holocaust in the Ukraine and the First Nazi War Crimes Trial* (New York: Pegasus Books, 2012).
79. Kevin M. F. Platt and David Brandenberger, eds., *Russian History and Literature as Stalinist Propaganda* (Madison: University of Wisconsin Press, 2006).
80. Anton G. Sliusarskii, *Vasilii Nazarovich Karazin: uchenyi i obshchestvennyi deiatel', 1773–1842* (Kharkiv: Kharkivs'ke knyzhkove vydavnytstvo, 1952).
81. Sliusarskii, *Vasilii Nazarovich Karazin*, 28, 31.
82. V. G. Bazanov, *Vol'noe obshchestvo liubitelei rossiiskoi slovesnosti* (Petrozavodsk, 1949); idem, *Uchenaia Respublika* (Moscow and Leningrad, 1964).
83. Posokhov, *Obrazy universytetiv*, 120.
84. Ivan Bulankin, "Kharkivs'kyi universytet," *Sotsialistychna Kharkivshchyna*, 3 October 1945.
85. Ivan Bulankin, "Naistarishyi na Ukraïni...," *Sotsialistychna Kharkivshchyna*, 29 January 1955.
86. Tatiana Zhurzhenko, *Borderlands into Bordered Lands: Geopolitics of Identity in Post-Soviet Ukraine* (Stuttgart: Ibidem Verlag, 2010): 191–206.
87. Anton H. Sliusars'kyi, *Slobids'ka Ukraïna: Istorychnyi narys XVII–XVIII st.* (Kharkiv: Kharkivs'ke Knyzhkovo-Hazetne Vydavnytstvo, 1954); idem, *Sotsial'no-ėkonomicheskoe razvitie Slobozhanshchiny XVII–XVIII vv.* (Kharkiv: Kharkivs'ke Knyzhkove Vydavnytstvo, 1964).
88. Vladimir Zagorovskii, *Belgorodskaia cherta* (Voronezh: Voronezh University Press, 1969), 22; idem, *Iziumskaia cherta* (Voronezh: Voronezh University Press, 1980), 9, 11.
89. Sliusars'kyi, *Slobids'ka Ukraïna*, 52.
90. K. K. Kuzminskii and G. L. Kovalev, *Antologiia noveishei russkoi poėzii u Goluboi Laguny*, 5 vols. (1980), vol. 3-a, http://b-bbib.narod.ru/tom3a/cont_3a.htm.
91. Mikhail F. Getmanets, *Taina reki Kaialy: "Slovo o polku Igoreve,"* 2nd ed. (Kharkiv: Izd. Khar'kovskogo universiteta, 1989).
92. Yitzhak M. Brudny, *Reinventing Russia: Russian Nationalism and the Soviet State, 1953–1991* (Cambridge, MA: Harvard University Press, 1999); Simon Cosgrove, *Russian Nationalism and the Politics of Soviet Literature: The Case of "Nash Sovremennik," 1981–91* (London: Palgrave Macmillan, 2004), 9–16.
93. Valentyna Kornilova et al., "Memorial'ni doshky – kul'turno-istorychna pam'iat' Kharkova," *VIII Vseukraïns'ka konferentsiia "Istorychne kraieznavstvo i kul'tura,"* pt. 2 (Kyiv and Kharkiv, 1997), 293.
94. Vladyslav Hrynevych, "Mit viiny ta viina mitiv," *Krytyka*, no. 5 (2005).
95. N. Konradova and A. Ryleeva, "Geroi i zhertvy. Memorialy Velikoi Otechestvennoi," http://www.nz-online.ru/print.phtml?aid=30011389.
96. *Pamiatniki istorii i kul'tury Khar'kovskoi oblasti: Bibliograficheskii ukazatel'* (Kharkiv: Oblastnaia biblioteka, 1985), 63–64, 87, 115.
97. Anatol Lieven, *Ukraine and Russia: A Fraternal Rivalry* (Washington, DC, 1999), 100.
98. Roman Szporluk, *Russia, Ukraine, and the Breakup of the Soviet Union* (Stanford: Hoover Institution Press, 2000), 158.

99. Szporluk, *Russia*, 95, 157.
100. Iurii Ia. Barabash, "Ėtnokul'turnoe pogranich'e: kontseptual'nyi, tipologicheskii i situativnyi aspekty (chuzhoe-inoe-svoe). Stat'ia vtoraia: Kharkiv, Donbass – ėtno-lingvokul'turnoe pogranich'e," *Studia Litterarum*, no. 2 (2020): 286–321, here 302.
101. Peter W. Rogers, "A Study of Identity Change in the Eastern Borderlands of Ukraine" (PhD diss., University of Birmingham, 2005).
102. Szporluk, *Russia*, 149.
103. Rogers, "A Study of Identity Change."
104. *Ocherki istorii Khar'kovskoi oblastnoi partiinoi organizatsii*, 359.
105. G. D. Bakulev, *Chernaia metallurgiia Iuga Rossii* (Moscow: Metallurgizdat, 1953); Sergei Zhebelev, *Severnoe Prichernomor'e antichnoi ėpokhi* (Moscow: AN SSSR, 1953); V. M. Kabuzan and K. G. Beskrovnyi, *Zaselenie Novorossii: Ekaterinoslavskoi i Khersonskoi gubernii v XVIII–pervoi polovine XIX veka* (Moscow: Nauka, 1976); Elena I. Druzhinina, *Iuzhnaia Ukraina v period krizisa feodalizma: 1825–1860 gg.* (Moscow: Nauka, 1981).
106. Szporluk, *Russia*, 96, 157.
107. *Sovetskii Soiuz: Geograficheskoe opisanie v 22 tomakh. Ukraina. Raiony* (Moscow: Mysl', 1969), 21.
108. O. I. Vendina and V. A. Kolosov, "Gde nakhoditsia stolitsa Iuga Rossii," *Politiia*, no. 1 (2004): 7–15.
109. *Khar'kov v zerkale mirovoi literatury*, 249.
110. Liudmila Czhizhikova, *Russko-ukrainskoe pogranich'e. Istoriia i sud'by traditsionno-bytovoi kul'tury (XIX–XX veka)* (Moscow: Nauka, 1988).

## CHAPTER 6
# Post-Soviet Borderland

The "engaged observer" is not always able to distinguish the agony of the old Soviet world from efforts to preserve or reform it or create something new out of its fragments. From today's perspective, all these trends were reflected in the series of events intended to dissociate Ukraine from its Soviet past, which, in turn, was entangled with the imperial legacy of Rus'/Russia.[1] Those events began with the formal dissolution of the Soviet Union in 1991 and were followed by the Orange Revolution of 2004 and the Revolution of Dignity in 2014. The historical Ukrainian-Russian borderland became an arena of competing identity discourses articulated by post-Soviet political regimes on both sides of the border. Kharkiv's economic and cultural potential, as well as its strategic location, made the local elite influential political players in post-Soviet Ukraine. In this chapter I shall concentrate on the identity politics promoted by the Kharkiv authorities from 1991 to 2010, when Viktor Yanukovych came to power.[2]

## Borderland

After the declaration of Ukrainian independence, Kharkiv reverted to the status of a border town, as had repeatedly been the case in its history. The international border between Ukraine and Russia passed only slightly more than forty kilometers north of Kharkiv. From the very beginning of its existence, that border began to take on various, sometimes contradictory, political and cultural meanings reflecting the balance of forces on the political landscape of the new state. The lines of political fracture along which the Soviet Union began to disintegrate in the late 1980s and early 1990s coincided with the boundaries of the Soviet republics, which remained intact for some time.

The weakness of the legitimizing functions of those boundaries was exposed as the two largest successors to the Soviet Union engaged in national reidentification. Both Ukraine and Russia strove to nationalize their common historical legacy and divide its symbolic space. Their nation-state building proceeded in divergent directions. Kyiv was faced with the task of consolidating the borderland, incorporating it into national space, and imparting symbolic significance to the new international border. Moscow, on the contrary, sought to minimize the divisive function of the border and make it as inconspicuous or "transparent" as possible. In this competition Russia, oriented toward the past, appeared to be significantly ahead of Ukraine in the search for a new national consensus.

As the Soviet Union dissolved, the local population on both sides of the Russo-Ukrainian border engaged in a process of national reidentification. After 1991, many ethnic Ukrainians in the Belgorod and Voronezh oblasts of Russia decided to identify themselves as Russians. For example, the percentage of Ukrainians in the Rovenki district of Belgorod oblast decreased from 20.5 percent in 2002 to 6.9 percent in 2010.[3] The number of settlements with a predominantly Ukrainian population in the same oblast declined from seventy-five in 1989 to two in 2010.

On the Ukrainian side, the process of de-Sovietization began before the dissolution of the Soviet Union under ideological influences different from those in Russia. The first priorities were those of reestablishing historical truth, filling in the "blank spots" of the Soviet past, and uncovering the crimes of the communist regime characteristic of that era. That wave led to the initial renaming of Kharkiv's streets and squares, beginning with the central square, named after Feliks Dzerzhinsky and now styled Liberty (Svoboda) Square. Dzerzhinsky Street met the same fate, though under Orthodox symbolism: it reverted to the name of Myrrh-Bearing Street, as in the days of the Russian Empire.

The local factor also significantly influenced changes in the city's toponymy. Thus, the riverside street, which bore the name of Stalin's postwar ideologue, Andrei Zhdanov, was renamed Kharkiv Street, while Eighth Congress of Soviets Street was renamed in honor of the local poet Boris Chichibabin, who had a reputation as a dissident. It may seem strange that the fate of odious Soviet symbols was shared by the Russian "revolutionary democrat" Aleksandr Herzen, canonized by Soviet propaganda, but the street named in his honor was now renamed after Bondarenko, a Kharkiv astronaut who died in a rocket test flight.

After 1991, it seemed that the history of relations between the Russian Provisional Government and the Ukrainian Central Rada of 1917 was being repeated. Less than two days after the declaration of Ukrainian political independence, the new Russian government, then still democratic, came forward with an enumeration of its territorial claims against its neighbor, accusing the Ukrainian authorities of "separatism."[4] Russia claimed the Crimea, the Donbas, the Odesa oblast, and all of so-called New Russia—the most important and economically advanced parts of Ukraine. Until recently, however, the delineation of the Belgorod and Kharkiv oblast sections of the Ukrainian-Russian border was accompanied by symbolic not military struggle.

Kharkiv played an important role in Moscow's strategy of keeping Ukraine within the Russian sphere of influence. A council (*sobor*) of Ukraine-based bishops of the Russian Orthodox Church (the only officially sanctioned church in Soviet times) was convened there on 27 May 1992. It prevented the defection of the formerly autocephalous Ukrainian Orthodox Church from Moscow, reestablishing a supreme Orthodox hierarchy loyal to Russia in Ukraine. The new institution was christened the Ukrainian Orthodox Church of the Moscow Patriarchate. As a result, post-Soviet Kharkiv found itself reincorporated into Russian-dominated religious and cultural space.

In Kharkiv itself, as in all other large cities and regions of Ukraine, power remained in the hands of the Soviet party and economic *nomenklatura*. At the level of Kharkiv oblast it was represented by Oleksandr Maselsky (1936–1996), who headed the oblast from 1985, while in the city executive authority was held by Yevgenii Kushnarev, a member of the so-called Democratic Platform of the CPSU. Conflicts between the oblast and city authorities accompanying the redefinition of their spheres of influence turned out to be non-antagonistic, as the theory of scientific communism would lead one to expect. They were settled very quickly in joint efforts to privatize "ownerless" and, it must be admitted, considerable state, party, and trade union property. At first, when it came to the formulation and execution of cultural policy, the local authorities left the initiative to the center.

The cultural policy that sought to integrate Kharkiv oblast into Ukrainian national space initially employed names and symbols drawn from the Soviet Ukrainian arsenal. As in the other regions of Ukraine, they included Cossack markers, which were most familiar to the public. Accordingly, monuments were erected in the oblast: in the town of Barvinkove to its founder, the Cossack Barvinok (1992), and in Merefa to the legendary *kish* otaman of the Zaporozhian Sich, Ivan Sirko (1993), who had owned property there.

Curiously, Ukrainian Cossack symbolism barely touched the urban space of Kharkiv itself. True, in the early 1990s a granite stela appeared not far from the Mykola Lysenko Kharkiv Academic Theater of Opera and Ballet, its appearance distantly suggesting that of a mounted Cossack. This was evidently meant to call up associations with the heroic past of the borderland steppe region, the struggle of the Sloboda settlers with the Tatars, and the like, but after a while the stela disappeared without notice, ceding its place to a depiction of the Archangel Michael.

To mark the urban landscape of Kharkiv, the local authorities turned much more often to the names of Ukrainian intellectuals of various historical periods who were significant for the Kharkiv region, had been adapted to the Soviet historical narrative at one time or another, and were therefore more acceptable to the local political and cultural elites. Thus, in the early 1990s, several individuals were symbolically recognized on the cultural map of the city and region. Some of them came from the imperial era: the poet Pavlo Hrabovsky (1990), the philosopher Hryhorii Skovoroda (1992), and the writer Hryhorii Kvitka (1993). Other individuals were associated with the Soviet 1920s: the drama director Les Kurbas (1993), the poet Vasyl' Ellan-Blakytny (1994), and the writer and publicist Mykola Khvyliovy (1995).

The first "enclaves of counter-memories" to mark the city's cultural landscape, as Tatiana Zhurzhenko has called them, emerged in the pantheon located in the Youth Park (Molodizhnyi Park) and the Ukrainian-Polish Memorial to Victims of Totalitarianism.[5] The pantheon, erected owing to the initiative of local civil society activists in a former recreation zone, was established on territory where victims of the Holodomor and political terror had been secretly buried during the Soviet period. The memorial was built by the state authorities. Both sites remained marginal in Kharkiv's public space.

The political regionalism that managed to assert itself after the period of Soviet perestroika became influential in the dispute between Kyiv and Moscow. The regional projects that arose in various parts of the former Ukrainian SSR represented a rather motley political spectrum divided in their attitude to the Ukrainian political center as well as to the Soviet and Russian imperial legacies. Ghosts of history began returning to the contemporary world: the Soviet Donets-Kryvyi Rih Republic (the Donbas), imperial New Russia (Odesa), Habsburg Eastern Galicia (Lviv), and, finally, Carpathian Rus' (Uzhhorod). In the latter instance, the movement for regional autonomy took on a more distinct ethnocultural character, finding a basis in Rusyn ideology.

Kharkiv cultural regionalism was conducted under the banner of Sloboda Ukraine. The Sloboda "brand" immediately gained wide popularity, defining the city's symbolic landscape in such features as the titles of nine newspapers ranging from the oblast daily *Slobids'kyi krai* (Sloboda territory) to a new city paper, *Sloboda*, the name of a Ukrainian cultural center (*Slobozhanshchyna*), an elite residential complex, a popular brand of beer, and an expensive restaurant. The list could be extended. As a result, more than 90 percent of current names associated with the "Sloboda" nomenclature are concentrated in Kharkiv and oblast.[6]

Tatiana Zhurzhenko rightly notes that in post-Soviet Ukraine the term "Sloboda region" "can be filled with various messages to legitimize different interests."[7] It has been exploited by various actors bearing "hybrid and mixed identities combining some elements of Ukrainian and Russian culture, Orthodox belief, and Soviet symbols."[8] The national version of the "Sloboda Ukraine" discourse was promoted by reissuing the publications of the most important pre-Soviet authorities on the region, Dmytro Bahalii (*History of Sloboda Ukraine*) and Mykola Sumtsov (*Slobozhany*), which became available to a broad readership. They signaled the return of the Ukrainian national paradigm to the interpretation of the Kharkiv region's history.

Nevertheless, Kharkiv did not avoid the temptation of emphasizing its local rather than Ukrainian national identity, although it appeared in the distinctive form of an intellectual curiosity little noticed against the background of the stormy political debates and deepening economic crisis of the early 1990s. In 1992 Gennadii Zgursky, then a lecturer at the Kharkiv State Institute (Academy) of Culture, made the first attempt since the days of Hryhorii Kvitka to formulate a program of local ethnocultural regionalism. Since the text of his article, under the title "Malorosiians, Ukrainians, or. . . ?," was issued in an ephemeral publication that is difficult to access, it hardly attracted the attention of the general public, and I shall permit myself to dwell on it in some detail.

Zgursky formulated his conception of the prospects for the development of Sloboda regional culture as follows: "One would think that Slobodians should attempt to conceive of themselves as an entity not identical to another entity, Russian or Ukrainian, and become aware of their ethnocultural uniqueness. We should more clearly delineate the borders of our region, which do not coincide with administrative or economic/geographic boundaries."[9] In that regard, Zgursky drew a distinction between the historical regions of the Left Bank (former Hetmanate) and the Sloboda Ukraine region, going on to exclude the territory of the Donbas from the latter.

The author strove to substantiate the necessity and possibility of making the Sloboda Ukrainian vernacular (*surzhyk*) normative, to formulate its grammatical regularities, unify its phonetic particularities, and bring it into a broader literary and social context. Perhaps, speculated Zgursky, elementary school classes should be established with the "local language" as the medium of instruction, and works of literature should be translated into the "vernacular." It is telling that in his search for examples of such activity, the author adverted to the experience of the Transcarpathian Rusyns.

Analyzing this text, one may assume that from the outset the author limited himself to an exclusively intellectual rather than a political provocation. Such an assumption finds support in the fact that Zgursky himself found it necessary to make a public renunciation of any political parallels, as well as in the attitude of the political forces striving for power in the region, none of which seriously considered a program of ethnocultural institutionalization of Sloboda cultural regionalism either in the early 1990s or later. The regional preferences of the local elite found their expression in a manner somewhat different from the one that presented itself to Zgursky.

On the political map of Ukraine, Kharkiv oblast, together with those of Donetsk, Luhansk, Dnipropetrovsk, Zaporizhia, and several other oblasts of southern and, in part, central Ukraine, positioned itself in an imagined "eastern" region distinguished by a high level of urbanization, industrial development, concentration of Russian and Russian-speaking population, and degree of the latter's involvement in the project of producing a "Soviet people." Geographically, this region distantly resembled the Southern Russia of the early twentieth century, but with no distinct ethnocultural identity other than Ukrainian. Politically, Ukrainian borderland elites tried to imitate their Russian counterparts in many ways, especially by taking advantage of their privileged position to enrich themselves.

The transformation of the socialist economy into a market economy made a notable impression on the sociocultural landscape of the city. First and foremost, one cannot fail to note the deurbanization of Kharkiv, which was characteristic of the early 1990s. Perhaps its most striking manifestations were the many spontaneous markets and shopping arcades that appeared directly on sidewalks. That scene also included passersby hauling large checked bags with treasures of some kind on homemade carts, as well as domestic animals—goats and even cows grazing within fifteen minutes' walk from the center of town, and packs of friendly stray dogs. Kharkiv architecture of the period was limited to so-called "small forms" that adapted buildings of the Soviet period to the needs of enterprises and organizations engaged in "small business." Not until the end of the twentieth century did investors with the means to erect new buildings appear in the city.[10]

The deep economic crisis accompanying the disintegration of the USSR notably weakened the economic and thus the political influence of Kharkiv, most of all in connection with the fall of the giant military-industrial complex, the mechanical engineering sector, basic scientific research, and the city's potential as a transit hub. The psychological complex of a certain weakening that resulted from the collapse of the previous system of political relations between center and oblasts; the widespread complaints about the provincialization of Kharkiv; its steady decline; the new political center's expressions of underestimation, outright contempt, and similar attitudes were characteristic not only of Kharkiv but of other large Ukrainian cities.[11]

The response of the "electorate" to the new economic, political, and cultural realities was one of increasing nostalgia for the Soviet period and growing attraction to parties and movements whose slogans synthesized communist rhetoric with religious eschatology, closer in style to the beginning of the twentieth century than to its end. No less a role in the political attitudes of Ukrainian electors was played by pro-Russian sympathies diligently intensified by Russian mass media. As a result, the brief burst of democratic enthusiasm during the perestroika period quickly yielded to the tendencies just described, making post-Soviet society even more susceptible to the archaic social patterns and values inherited from the past.[12]

## Soviet Afterlife

In the presidential elections of 1994, it was Leonid Kuchma, a representative of the Dnipropetrovsk party and economic *nomenklatura*, who gained a majority of votes in Kharkiv oblast. In the 1994 elections to the Verkhovna Rada, twenty-five deputies were elected from Kharkiv oblast, slightly more than a third of whom (nine deputies) represented communist, socialist, or pro-Russian forces. But most deputies from the city and oblast tried to look like "pragmatists," resembling the new Ukrainian president, having concentrated the material and political resources of the region in their hands. They could no more be haunted by the specter of communism than by the specter of nationalism, which had managed by then to reveal its immaterial substance. The new regime's policy was favorable to regionalization and strengthening the influence of local elites.

In this regard, Kharkiv and oblast did not differ in any way from other large cities and regions of Ukraine. Clear attributes of the patrimonial model of mutual relations in the milieu of the local elite were to be found, for example, in the cult of Oleksandr Maselsky, the long-term Soviet leader of Kharkiv oblast. He headed the oblast until his death in 1996, creating conditions for the smooth transition of many of his cronies, relatives, and close friends to the neofeudal/oligarchic model of "wild" capitalism.[13]

An apologetic biography of Maselsky, written by a former comrade of his in party and all-Union affairs, was published in Kharkiv, as was a volume of memoirs contributed by representatives of his "close circle," who compared the former head of Kharkiv oblast with Peter I and vied with one another in calling him "father," "master," "people's governor," and "son of the Sloboda region."[14] In the interpretation of Vasilii Salygin, a political pupil of Maselsky's who also headed the Kharkiv oblast council, it turned out that his boss's local patriotism took precedence over his public service as an official of independent Ukraine.

In significance and scale, the cult of Maselsky can perhaps be compared only to the cult of Yevgenii Kushnarev, a representative of the younger generation of the Soviet local party *nomenklatura* during the perestroika period. He became head of the administration of President Leonid Kuchma, mayor of Kharkiv, and Maselsky's successor as head of the Kharkiv oblast state administration. Kushnarev died under mysterious circumstances while hunting in Kharkiv oblast in 2007. His cult manifested itself in efforts to rename Kharkiv's central Sumy Street in his honor. The "Sumy" name, which had outlasted even Soviet experiments, was considered no less a historic symbol of the city than De Ribas Street in Odesa or Khreshchatyk in Kyiv.

It is telling that the names of Maselsky and Kushnarev quickly found their way into the regional historical narrative, promptly prepared by historians of the Hryhorii Skovoroda Kharkiv National Pedagogical Institute. A relevant passage of this "ethnography textbook," titled *Kharkiv, My Small Motherland*, presents a narrative not lacking in drama about the "talented leadership" of Maselsky and Kushnarev, who had helped to "save the Sloboda region from decline and fall" while "Yeltsin's" Russia sought to bring Ukraine "to its knees" by means of economic pressure.[15] But an analysis of the crypto-Soviet intellectual stereotypes reliably protecting the subconscious of the authors of such a text is not one of the tasks that the present author has set for himself.

Against this background, the policy of restoring historical continuity with the recent Soviet era, which the regional elite began to implement after the election of Kuchma as president of Ukraine in 1994, seemed perfectly logical. It was symbolic that Kharkiv oblast, marking its seventieth anniversary with an official ceremony, united elements of the imperial and Soviet eras in its coat of arms, supplementing the horn of plenty with a depiction of a factory gear and a "peaceful" atom along with a book—the "source of knowledge"—and a sheaf of grain.

The presidency of Leonid Kuchma (1994–2004) was marked by a veritable explosion of Kharkiv and region's symbolic public space, which began actively to be filled with the names of Soviet party, Young Communist League, and trade union figures, members of various ranks of the economic *nomenklatura*, military commanders, sportsmen, as well as scholarly and cultural figures. They were all united by regional origin or activity.

The policy of "reconciliation" with the Soviet past at the local level was reflected, for example, at the ceremonial unveilings of plaques in memory of the first secretaries of the Central Committee of the Communist Party Petro Shelest (1996) and Volodymyr Ivashko (2002). Memorialized along with them were the names of the Soviet scientific designers Aleksandr Ivchenko and Mikhail Koshkin, the scholars Nikolai Barabashov, Dmitrii Volkov, and Lev Palatnyk, the artist Sergei Besedin, the sculptor Dmytro Klebanov, the builder Vasyl' Liapin, the trade union leader Oleksii Katerynchuk, the transport director Valentyn Vedernikov, the director of the Malyshev Plant Oleg Soich, the surgeon Vladimir Zaitsev, the anatomist Vladimir Vorobiev, the art historian Valerii Eisenstadt, the poet Robert Tretiakov, and others.

The Soviet component of contemporary regional discourse was constantly stocked with the historical mythology of the Great Patriotic War, which gained a special place in Kyiv's cultural policy in the times of Leonid Kuchma and was fully supported on the local level. Symbolic reflections of Soviet memory of the war included a memorial complex in honor of the soldiers of the rifle platoon led by Petr Shironin (1995, village of Taranivka, Zmiiv raion, Kharkiv oblast), a monument to Ivan Kozhedub in Kharkiv (1995), and monuments and memorial plaques to soldiers and officers who died in the Barvinkove-Kharkiv operation of 1942 (1997), as well as to the heroes of student battalions, participants in the Kharkiv communist underground resistance, heroes of the tank corps, and the trial of fascists in 1943.

The historical mythology of the Great Patriotic War, which has a special place in the cultural policy of the Russian leadership, is taking on a sacral character under the patronage of the Russian Orthodox Church. An illustration of that policy in the Kharkiv region may be seen, for example, in the Konev Heights memorial complex, erected in honor of the Soviet marshal commanding the troops who liberated Kharkiv from the Nazis in 1943. In 2003 an Orthodox chapel appeared beside the monument to the Soviet military commander. A similar example was the proposal to build an Orthodox chapel in place of the gallery of Soviet heroes of the underground resistance in the historical center of Kharkiv.

The traditional selection of national historical symbols demonstrating the allegiance of the city and region to Ukrainian national space also was not forgotten by the local leadership. At their initiative, monuments were erected at various times: to Bohdan Khmelnytsky (on oblast territory in 1995), to Taras Shevchenko (also on oblast territory in 2001), to the historian of the Zaporozhian Cossacks Dmytro Yavornytsky (in Kharkiv oblast in 1998), and to Ukrainian bandurists and *lira* players who fell victim to Stalinist persecution (in central Kharkiv in 1997). A memorial plaque to the early twentieth-century ideologue of Ukrainian nationalism Mykola Mikhnovsky was placed in the historical center of Kharkiv.

With the change of political regime in Ukraine, "Sloboda" terminology began to take on a somewhat different significance than it had had in the period of Soviet perestroika. If it had been used earlier basically to emphasize the Ukrainian national identity of the Kharkiv region, the concept of the Sloboda region now began to be employed more often in order to substantiate the policy of drawing Ukraine closer to Russia and emphasizing traditional transregional Russo-Ukrainian ties.[16]

In the "Regional Complex Program for the Socioeconomic Development of Kharkiv Oblast to 2010" prepared at the initiative of the then head of the local oblast state administration, Oleg Demin, the Kharkiv region was positioned as the basis of the "broad historico-cultural and geographic region of Sloboda Ukraine," consisting of adjoining oblasts of Russia and Ukraine, with the Kharkiv city depicted as the mediator between them.[17] The image of Kharkiv as a mediator between Ukraine and Russia, a place of intensive Ukrainian-Russian contacts and, at the same time, a site for the "meeting of various peoples and cultures," something of a model of interethnic toleration and dialogue, was actively disseminated in regional and national public space from the late 1990s. During the parliamentary elections of 2002 and the presidential elections of 2004, Kharkiv even tested the image of "capital of Ukrainian-Russian cooperation," becoming a place of nonperiodic meetings of leaders and community representatives of the two neighboring states.[18]

In general, this image of a Kharkiv as a link between Ukraine and Russia, summoned to become something of an alternative to the political tension between them, a space for dialogue and, at the same time, a region self-sufficient in economic and cultural potential, fully satisfied the interests of the incumbent regional elite, which consolidated its position during the Kuchma presidency and continued to orient itself mainly toward Russia. The various projects of cooperation with neighboring Russian regions elaborated by the local authorities did not diverge in principle from the policy of Kyiv.

On 27 January 1995 the governments of Ukraine and Russia signed an agreement on cooperation between border oblasts, concretized by means of agreements on cultural, scientific, and educational cooperation, joint use and conservation of water resources, environmental protection, and other matters.[19] In February 2001 a joint Program of Interregional and Border Cooperation between Ukraine and Russia was adopted for the period 2001–7, including support for the idea of Euroregions. The leadership of Kharkiv and Belgorod oblasts was particularly active in that regard, initiating the development of a projected "Sloboda" Euroregion.[20]

For the substantiation of that project, they employed the concept of the Sloboda region as one that had developed in the course of history and whose territory did not coincide with the new state borders between Ukraine and Russia. To a certain degree, the appearance of that project may be seen as expressing a negative reaction on the part of local elites to the transformation of the Ukrainian-Russian borderland into a political border. Curiously enough, in preparing the document its authors based themselves on the historical memorandum on the Ukrainian-Russian border written by Dmytro Bahalii in the 1920s at the behest of the Soviet Ukrainian government for precisely the opposite purpose—to divide the territory of Ukraine and Russia on the ethnographic principle.

In its treatment of the "Sloboda" Euroregion, the Kharkiv administration appealed mainly to European experience and emphasized the economic and ecological prospects of borderland cooperation, proceeding simultaneously from the premise that in the following decades Ukraine would remain in the zone of Russia's political influence. That feature of the project was also accented in its sections on national culture and the humanities, which employed the rhetoric of a "common cultural and information space" and a "single process of historical development." As far as may be judged from an article by Aleksei Kiriukhin, a representative of the Kharkiv oblast administration, the authors of the Ukrainian draft proceeded from the prospect of "turning the [state] border into a 'gray' frontal zone,"[21] that is, orienting themselves toward minimizing the influence of the border in the region.

In the final analysis, the Russian participants in the project aspired to the same goal, although they employed somewhat different rhetoric. It was based not so much on historical and pragmatic considerations or, even less, European analogues, as on Russian neoimperial nationalism reverting to its intellectual sources—the concept of a "Slavic-Rus' people" discussed in previous chapters. Its leitmotif is the idea of the "indissoluble cultural unity of the Slavic peoples, traditions, way of life, character, thinking, and mutual attraction of our peoples' contemporary cultures."[22] Essentially the same way of thinking characterizes the Russian authors of the concept of "economic Slavic studies," who substantiated their ideas with the aid of the "integrationist" rhetoric of Vladimir Putin, then premier of Russia.

Tatiana Zhurzhenko has noted that one of the meetings of the heads of government of Russia, Ukraine, and Belarus with leaders of oblast state administrations and businessmen of border oblasts in October 2002 was called an Assembly of Slavic Peoples, and the newspaper of the Council of Border Oblasts, published for some reason in Kursk, began to be titled *Slavianka*. In the framework of cross-border cooperation in the humanities, a special Boian (Bard) prize was established for those who contributed to "preserving the spiritual space of the peoples of the Slavic world."[23] There was no need to speculate whether that world included, for example, Poles, Czechs, or Croats. The "Slavic" world in Russian interpretation was coterminous with the Orthodox world.

No less symbolic was the initiative of the Belgorod oblast leadership to establish an Orthodox theological academy on the site of the Prokhorovka memorial center, where one of the greatest tank battles of World War II had taken place in 1943. It was to train military chaplains for the armies of both countries who would provide a spiritual basis for their "Slavic unity," taking the place of the former communist political instructors who had done the same thing in principle during the years of Soviet rule. All these examples confirm Aleksandr Libman's conclusion about the Russocentric essence of the absolute majority of integrationist projects that have arisen and continued to arise in post-Soviet space.[24]

To be sure, one should not ignore the different approaches of the Ukrainian and Russian sides in conceiving the "Sloboda" Euroregion. The difference derived not only from concrete political considerations and doctrines to be implemented by the leaderships of the participating countries. A much more substantial obstacle to the realization of the project was lack of unity between the participants with regard to the content and nature of their cooperation; moreover, ideological priorities were hardly an adequate substitute for economic motivation on the part of small and medium business on both sides of the border. To what extent the initiators and participants of the "Euroregion" project were prepared to observe European standards and values in actual practice has never been discussed.

## The Historical Narrative

In parallel and in connection with the formation of the new cultural space of the city and region, a new regional historical narrative was actively being created. From the end of the last century, one could observe a true boom of local historical studies in Kharkiv and region encompassing not only the academic milieu but also broad strata of society. Dozens if not hundreds of new publications reflected growing interest in the local past among enthusiasts of various kinds: writers, journalists, heads of large departments and enterprises, community organizations, and the like. There was particular interest in the history of the territory on the part of local politicians, who themselves took an active part in creating the new regional historical narrative. Regional historical studies became a subject taught in schools and higher educational institutions, which led to the publication of textbooks, programs, and study aids for learners. In the historical literature about the region, however, the clash of national discourses very quickly became no less apparent than in the various cultural strategies implemented by representatives of the competing political forces.[25]

The regional historical narrative developed under the influence of the official normative discourse shaped by Ukrainian academic historiography. Its representatives strove to integrate local material into a new version of Ukrainian history, which was being created within the framework of the nation-state school of historical writing. The allegiance of the Sloboda region to Ukraine was most often established, in the spirit of Bahalii, with references to historical discontinuity in the life of the "autochthonous" Ukrainian population of the region, as well as to the priority of Ukrainians in the process of its colonization in modern times.

The combination of those two arguments in support of the "prevailing" historical right of ethnic Ukrainians to the Sloboda region was reflected in textbooks on the history of Kharkiv and region prepared by historians of the local pedagogical university. The basic markers of the region's Ukrainian identity in their textbooks are Cossackdom, the university, and the status of Kharkiv as capital of Soviet Ukraine, personified respectively by Ivan Sirko, Hryhorii Skovoroda, Vasilii Karazin, and Hryhorii Kvitka, as well as Oleksandr Potebnia, Dmytro Bahalii, Mykola Sumtsov, Mykola Mikhnovsky, and, finally, by the generation of intellectuals of the 1920s, which received the name "Executed Renaissance" in national tradition: Mykola Khvyliovy, Les Kurbas, and other contemporaries of theirs. Accordingly, Kharkiv is most often described as the "spiritual" or "cultural" capital of the Ukrainian national renaissance, although in Ukrainian national historical discourse the status reserved for Kharkiv is, after all, that of the second and not the first capital of Ukraine.

Local historians sought not only to renew the historiographic tradition that had been interrupted for some time but also to promote the right of "their" region to a more prestigious place in the new Ukrainian grand narrative, expressing dissatisfaction with the normative academic canon created without their participation. Philologists, for instance, focused attention on the existence of a particular Slobodian period in the development of the Ukrainian literary language; historians attempted to make the city's past "more ancient" or enrich the new interpretation of its history with a greater diversity of subjects.[26]

In 1996 the idea was raised in the academic milieu of establishing a regional museum and writing a new history of the region. Perhaps the most prominent aspect of this proposal was the claim that the eastern region had been underestimated as compared to the western region and the Right and Left Banks of Ukraine. Curiously enough, perhaps for the first time in local historiographic tradition Kharkiv's claim to the role of regional leader was supported by means of "eastern," not only "Slobodian" or, even less, "southern," symbolism, as had earlier been the case.

The conceptual substantiation of the new regional project fared worse: of the problems identified as priority items (questions of the colonization of the region, especially its Ukrainian-Russian aspects; the military history of imperial times; the history of military formations, both Ukrainian and Russian, on the territory of the region during the Civil War; suppressed issues of the Great Patriotic War in the years 1941–43), perhaps only a reference to the genesis of the enigmatic "Slobodian mentality" gave some idea of what might be specific in a regional version of Slobodian history as compared with Ukrainian national or Russian neoimperial narratives.

Significantly, the Soviet past did not figure at all in the list of priorities put forward by those advocating a new regional museum: not a word was said in the proposal about the crimes of the Soviet regime, although on the cusp of the 1980s and 1990s the subject had been prominent enough in local historical publications. Passing over the issue in silence corresponded in general terms to the policy of "reconciliation" with the Soviet legacy enacted by the local and central political leadership of Ukraine alike.

Conceptual narrowmindedness on the one hand and the quality of available cadres on the other were the basic reasons for the failure of the collaborative Ukrainian-Russian project to publish a new version of the history of the Sloboda region undertaken with the support of the Kharkiv oblast state administration.[27] The politically correct principle of equal representation of Kharkiv and Belgorod historians in the team of authors proved unable to endow the project with academic respectability or even to protect its text from outright compilation.[28]

## In Search of Alternatives

From the early 1990s on, Kharkiv political elites were striving to consolidate power and strengthen their position in relations with the national center. They created a new civic organization, the Society of Kharkivites, theoretically uniting all those with some relation to Kharkiv who maintained allegiance to the city regardless of nationality, but practically organizing a group of politicians, officials, and businessmen to lobby for local interests in the capital. The twenty-third session of Kharkiv city council confirmed the statute of the territorial community and adopted regulations concerning the flag, awards, and official city holidays. In 1995 the city's old imperial Russian coat of arms, in the form of a horn of plenty and a caduceus, was restored to it.

On the occasion of Kharkiv's 350th anniversary, many new works were published about various aspects of its history. The local authorities sponsored scholarly projects on the city's history, initiating a reprint of the capital work of Dmytro Bahalii and Dmytro Miller, as well as the writing of a collective monograph on the twentieth-century history of Kharkiv.[29] The contemporary version of the city's history differs from the one prepared at the beginning of the twentieth century to the same degree as the city's administration at the time of writing differed from the old, pre-Soviet one. Bahalii and Miller strove to demonstrate the potential and effectiveness of civil society as compared with state bureaucracy. In post-Soviet times, it would appear, the authors of works on that subject are preoccupied first and foremost with problems of national, cultural, and political identity.

The aforementioned Yevgenii Kushnarev, who organized the reprint of Bahalii and Miller's book in 1993, supplied it with his own introduction, in which the priority of local identity over national was openly postulated: the author argued the necessity of "special" legal status for Kharkiv, and his emotionally charged declaration of loyalty to the city ("my native, wonderful city, worthy of eternal love") contrasted strikingly with his cursory mention of the "young" state, which was not even identified by name.[30]

The first decade of the twenty-first century saw the publication of a good many new works, including monographs, devoted to various aspects of the history of Kharkiv University, which celebrated its two-hundredth anniversary in 2005. The conferment of the name of Vasilii Karazin, who initiated the founding of Kharkiv University, on that institution should be considered symbolic. In conjunction with the renaming, the Karazin monument was also transferred to the university's main entrance, emphasizing the institution's association first and foremost with local historic and cultural tradition. On the other hand, the personality of Karazin himself was still treated ambiguously, as before, provoking vigorous scholarly and public debate.

The Russian intellectual segment of Kharkiv society had mixed feelings about Ukrainian nation-state building. These people had to find a way of coming to terms with the new political and cultural environment, which was unfamiliar to many of them. A local journalist, Kevork Kevorkian, the founder of the *Pervaia stolitsa* (First capital) TV channel, attempted to create a new variant of the regional historical discourse as opposed to the Ukrainian national one. In 1995 he published a collection of publicistic articles intended for a mass readership under the title *Pervaia stolitsa*.[31] Kevorkian's television programs and publications give some idea of Russian-speaking citizens' attitude toward the ongoing "Ukrainian project."

The collection, which looks like a distinctive guidebook to Kharkiv, is identified as a "teaching aid": historical sketches are devoted to the city's streets, squares, and quarters. A new image of the city takes shape as re-discovered pages of its past, made up of various components of regional, Russian imperial, and Soviet historiography, are presented to the reader. If in the 1920s the basic idea inspiring Kharkiv authors of such compilations was faith in education, progress, and a brilliant future, then at the beginning of the twenty-first century such attitudes give way to skepticism and nostalgia for the past.

Kevorkian makes use (whether consciously or not is another question) not only of the archetype of the "loyal" Sloboda elite, which opposed "traitors"—hetmans and Zaporozhian Cossacks—but also of many stereotypes and clichés created by Russian/Soviet propaganda in its struggle against Ukrainian nationalism. In using such material, Kevorkian does not distinguish particular currents and political regimes that arose as the Ukrainian national movement developed. For him, they are all "birds of a feather," from Mazepa to Petliura and local Ukrainian nationalists who were identified with the Nazis.[32] Kevorkian's basic motive appears to be an aspiration to reproduce the "golden age" of Kharkiv, which is limited, in the author's opinion, to the period of the Russian Empire. This was perhaps the author's main reason for depicting the brief occupation of Kharkiv by Denikin's White Army in 1919 as an "idyll."[33]

Kevorkian interprets the Soviet past selectively, unlike the Ukrainian past. For example, he condemns the crimes of the Soviet regime in the Civil War and Stalin's repressive measures but extols Kharkiv's status as capital at every opportunity, whether the reference is to the Donetsk-Kryvyi Rih Republic or to Soviet Ukraine. While making use of the mythology of the "first capital," Kevorkian does not accept the Soviet policy of Ukrainization, depicting it with metaphors more characteristic of Stalin-era persecution ("merciless purges"). It is readily apparent that the "horrors" of Ukrainization are nothing more than the present-day phobias of the author, who reproduces the oral tradition of historical memory handed down by Russian-speaking Kharkiv intellectuals of the 1920s.

Kevorkian's "installation" of Soviet motifs about the "first capital" into contemporary regional discourse is apparently due to his belonging to the generation formed by Soviet adventure classics of the 1920s—the novels *The Twelve Chairs* and *The Golden Calf* by Ilf and Petrov. To the best of my knowledge, it was precisely at Kevorkian's initiative that Kharkiv's symbolic space came to include the bronze images, derived from films, of characters from *The Twelve Chairs*—Father Fedor at the southern railway station and Ostap Bender and Ellochka the Cannibal in the city center.

To be fair, however, let us note that unlike the Denikinites, the author does not strike Ukrainian symbols of Kharkiv's past out of his text. He even includes critical remarks directed against anonymous Russian chauvinists while accepting representative symbols of Ukrainian identity canonized in the Soviet period: Taras Shevchenko, Hryhorii Kvitka, Borys Hrinchenko, Lesia Ukrainka, and even (an influence of perestroika) Mykola Khvyliovy. But these symbols look like mere decoration on the walls of the city, which, as the author imagines, might reclaim its capital status by becoming the "shadow capital ... of all Russian-speaking Ukraine."[34]

The second edition of *Pervaia stolitsa*, which saw print in 1999, attests to a certain evolution of the author's views. If in the first edition the symbolic struggle against Ukrainian national discourse was largely defined by the democratic traditions of the perestroika period, in the second edition that struggle begins to take on the distinct flavor of Russian neoimperial nationalism with ethnic overtones. For example, an article entitled "The Fate of the City," written in 1995, is now generously laden with pseudo-scholarly outbursts in the spirit of Lev Gumilev about "two super-ethnoses," western and eastern, living in Ukraine, remarks on the harmful effects of the Ukrainian Catholic (Uniate) Church and the traditions of struggle against it in the Sloboda region, on Little Russia and Little Russians, and, finally, on the Slavic unity of Ukraine and Russia as well as other familiar aspects of new/old imperial tradition that continues to attract the Russian and Russian-speaking intelligentsia. It is no wonder, then, that the author found it impossible to come to terms with Ukrainian nation-state building and emigrated to the Crimea after its annexation by Russia in 2014.

The Soviet background of many authors of contemporary works on the history of Kharkiv and oblast becomes even more obvious when they address the subject of interethnic, above all Ukrainian-Russian, relations. In such works, Ukrainian national discourse is opposed by multinational discourse, which has much in common with the Soviet doctrine of the "friendship of peoples." Its influence is apparent, for example, in the publication *Khar'kov mnogonatsional'nyi* (Multinational Kharkiv), prepared with the support of the Kharkiv oblast and city administration. It describes local community and cultural organizations of so-called national minorities belonging to the Association of National Cultural Societies of Ukraine, emphasizing their "contributions" to Kharkiv's cultural life but saying not a word about the Ukrainians and Russians who make up most of the city's population.[35]

Conceptions of the particular nature of Ukrainian-Russian relations (in their Soviet or imperial Russian versions) have also left their imprint on many other publications devoted to the city's history. Thus, for Ivan Saratov, Kharkiv's past is defined by the metaphor of "Ukrainian-Russian friendship" and joint resistance of the two "fraternal peoples" to the traditionally "alien" Tatars and Poles. Such conceptions probably also inspired the authors of the opera *Da budet grad* (Let there be hail), composed for Kharkiv's 350th anniversary in 2004: in the finale, Russian and Ukrainian settlers had to sing a hymn to the city of Kharkiv in both languages.

## The 350th Anniversary of Kharkiv

Post-Soviet eclecticism, combining selected elements of Soviet, imperial Russian, and Ukrainian national discourses, found its reflection in public representations of Kharkiv's history. The most notable event in that series was the ceremonial observance in 2004 of the 350th anniversary of the city's founding. A profusion of metaphors produced by various discourses at different times was employed in preparations for the event: here one could find the "first capital," the "Athens of the Sloboda region," and the Soviet image of the "city of labor." In general, however, the anniversary celebrations of 2004 reflected the growing influence of pro-Russian discourse on the city's life. The 350th anniversary of Kharkiv passed under the sign of the strengthening of Ukrainian-Russian "brotherhood."

As part of the celebrations, the local authorities erected a monument on one of the city's central streets to the mythical founder of Kharkiv, the Cossack Kharko, produced by the Soviet Russian sculptor Zurab Tsereteli. Although this was the first statue of a mounted rider in the city's history, it does not appear to have caused any particular excitement among Kharkivites, although it managed to attract undue public attention to painstakingly fashioned anatomical details of the noble animal that are usually concealed with fig leaves on ancient statues. The statue is located in a virtual space created by contradictory symbols. The Cossack Kharko is shown solemnly entering the city via Lenin Avenue, heading toward Liberty Square, with the cupolas of the newly built Russian Orthodox Church of the Moscow Patriarchate behind his back.[36]

No less eloquent evidence of the ideological eclecticism marking the anniversary celebrations was the placement in Kharkiv's new historical center of a bust of the first imperial vicegerent of the Sloboda region, Count Yevdokim Shcherbinin. In the Ukrainian historical narrative, he is considered to have been the "gravedigger" of the autonomy of the Ukrainian Sloboda Cossack regiments. At the same time, a monument was erected in Kharkiv to Prince Aleksandr Nevsky of Novgorod, Russia, for whom no better place could be found than a psychiatric clinic far from the city center.

Long before the anniversary celebrations of 2004, the Ukrainian national historical paradigm in its Kharkiv version took on a different resonance than it had in central Ukraine. It was reformulated in the context of "organic" continuity with the Soviet past, not in the tradition of "a thousand years of Ukrainian statehood." Thus, for a monumental architectural project—the creation of a monument to the tenth anniversary of the proclamation of Ukrainian statehood in 2001—the symbol chosen was that of a ten-year-old girl, fully corresponding to the notions of the local elite concerning the origins and history of the independent Ukrainian state.

The monument was erected in the center of Rosa Luxemburg Square, cut off from sidewalks by streams of traffic on all sides and thus unapproachable. It took on the depressing aspect of a dead spot of collective memory from the very beginning, isolated in its own space and unwanted by the community. Thus, activists of Ukrainian national organizations preferred to hold their events in the space around the Taras Shevchenko monument, erected in the Soviet period and incarnating the doctrine of national communism, which had ceased to be relevant. No wonder the monument to the tenth anniversary of Ukrainian statehood lasted only ten years and was removed in 2011.

The city's historic central square, called Soviet since 1977, was given a new name, Constitution Square, for the tenth anniversary of Ukrainian independence. The name referred contemporaries to the Ukrainian Constitution, which the Verkhovna Rada in Kyiv had produced with great labor in 1996. But the "Soviet" name remained on the subway station beneath Constitution Square, consigned to the underground. The monument to fighters for Soviet rule, erected in 1975, also remained in place, awaiting the next wave of decommunization.

Finally, Liberty Square, which remains the principal barometer of the city's political and cultural life to this day, took on a rather distinctive appearance. It combined the ideas of the communist avant-garde of the 1920s, incarnated in the Gosprom architectural ensemble, with neoclassicism in the monument to Vasilii Karazin, situated alongside a building in Stalinist Empire style, not far from a monument to Vladimir Lenin, his hand pointing either to the bust of Count Shcherbinin or to the building of the oblast state administration (the former party oblast committee). In fact, Kharkiv's central square remained practically untouched by Ukrainian national symbolism, unless one counts the orphan granite stone with a sign announcing that a monument honoring the rebirth of Ukrainian statehood would be erected in its place. From time to time the huge space of Liberty Square was filled with market stands, gaming booths, sand sculptures, or political gatherings, depending on the season and the political conjuncture.

The giant statue of Lenin towering above Liberty Square once led Catherine Wanner to make a somber association with Tiananmen Square in Beijing, which entered recent history with the Chinese leadership's brutal crushing of student demonstrations. For her, statues of Lenin in Ukraine were traditional gathering places for anti-reformist, anti-Ukrainian, pro-Soviet political agitators.[37] Not surprisingly, the very sight of the monument led her to recall William Faulkner's dictum: "The past is never dead. It's not even past."

A decade later, however, Catherine Wanner would most probably have turned not to Faulkner but to Leon Trotsky, the frenzied herald of world revolution, when seeking the closest analog to Kharkiv's Lenin. In 2004 it was in fact the democratic forces of Ukrainian "Orangeists," inclined toward reform, who gathered around the statue of the chief of the world proletariat, while their pro-Soviet and pro-Russian "white-and-blue" opponents arranged themselves nearer to the building of the former oblast committee of the CPSU.

## At the Crossroads of the "Orange Revolution"

The reaction of Kharkiv's party, economic, and cultural elites to the Ukrainian nation-state project has been largely muted by the political weakness and unsureness of the Ukrainian political center on the one hand and by the absence of civil society on the other. Efforts on the part of the center to change the balance of forces in its favor, or even the threat of such a development, could potentially mobilize the regional elites and strengthen centrifugal or even separatist attitudes. An example of such a turn of events was the "Orange Revolution" of 2004.[38]

Kharkiv, under the leadership of Yevgenii Kushnarev, was assigned a special role in realizing a project of so-called southeastern autonomy meant to involve the most industrially developed Russian-speaking oblasts of Ukraine, including the Crimea, the Black Sea littoral, and the Donbas. A conference of representatives of Ukraine's southern and eastern oblasts, intended to legitimize the political autonomy project, was supposed to take place in Kharkiv. In essence, this was an attempt at the political institutionalization of the region previously known as Southern Russia. But something went wrong.

The conference took place on 28 November 2004, not in Kharkiv but in the peripheral town of Severodonetsk in Luhansk oblast. Thus, the second attempt since the Donets-Kryvyi Rih Republic of 1918 to create a counterweight to Ukrainian national statehood in the form of regional autonomy, with its capital in Kharkiv, came to grief. Perhaps the divergent interests of those involved in the project played a role in this fiasco. Differences between the historical regional discourses of Kharkiv and Donetsk, which took shape in the years preceding the Orange Revolution, are worth attention in this regard. To compare them, I have basically drawn on the mass media: the Kharkiv oblast newspaper *Slobids'kyi krai* (Sloboda land) and the Donetsk newspaper *Donetskii kriazh* (Donets ridge).

In the Kharkiv publication, materials on Ukrainian history are generally presented in the spirit of the Soviet paradigm of the "friendship of peoples," with the traditional accompanying rhetoric intended to emphasize, on the one hand, the special "fraternal" nature of Ukrainian-Russian relations, the "sacred" character of the Great Patriotic War, and, on the other, a view close to the official one with regard to Ukrainian Cossackdom, the Holodomor, and traditional Ukrainian folklore. Moreover, the regional discourse is most often reflected in the rhetoric of the "first capital."

In the newspaper *Donetskii kriazh*, the attitude to Ukrainian history, above all to its nation-state paradigm, is much more aggressive, close to contemporary Russian propaganda, making extensive use of anti-Western, pan-Slavic, and Orthodox rhetoric. The authors of articles were inclined to integrate regional identity into imperial "all-Russian" rather than Ukrainian national discourse; moreover, curious efforts to endow the Donbas with the status of a Russian heartland through the "expropriation" of the Khazar ("Rusian") kaganate[39] were paralleled with glorification of the Donets-Kryvyi Rih Republic. The revival of its legacy was accompanied by particular rituals and symbols, including an annual ceremony at the monument to Artem, the leader of the local communists, honoring the red-blue-black flag accepted as the standard of the Donbas region.

It is hard to imagine that political regionalism in Ukraine emerged without the Kremlin's assistance. The post-Soviet Russian elites never accepted Ukrainian independence. Long before 2014, they contemplated such ideas as the administrative federalization of Ukraine or the secession of its southern and eastern oblasts in order to form a Moscow-friendly buffer state, Novorossiia (New Russia), including the Crimea, Odesa, and Transnistria.[40] Russian intellectuals, in turn, were prepared to contribute to the fragmentation of Ukraine by means of a reinvented Little Russian identity.[41] The growing aggressiveness of the Russian attitude toward Ukraine was entwined with a more vigorous "nationalization" of the Russian-Ukrainian borderland. That policy may be illustrated with the example of Belgorod, the Russian border city with perhaps the closest historical connections to Kharkiv.

The post-Soviet symbolism of Belgorod derives directly from the mythology of the Battle of Poltava (1709), in which the Belgorod infantry regiment particularly distinguished itself and was awarded a standard in 1712 depicting a lion rampant, the symbol of defeated Sweden, and a soaring eagle—the symbol of victorious Russia. The present-day coat of arms of Belgorod, adopted in 1999, reproduces the earliest version of the battle standard of the Belgorod infantry regiment but does not include elements of the town's Soviet coat of arms—oak branches, ears of wheat, and halves of cogwheels.[42]

With the coming to power of Vladimir Putin and the new leadership of the town, a more decisive move was made in local historical policy to renounce Soviet tradition in favor of the Russian imperial and Orthodox heritage. In 2004 a wave of renaming engulfed several streets and squares of Belgorod, including central ones. As a result, Communist Street began to be called Transfiguration Street, Revolution Square became Synod Square, Vorovsky Street received the name of Prince Trubetskoi, Kirov Street was renamed after the Belgorod regiment, and only Lenin Avenue became nonpolitical Civic Avenue.[43]

The politics and rhetoric of the Russian Orthodox Church in Belgorod and oblast also looked far more aggressive than in Kharkiv. The leadership of the Belgorod and Starooskolsk eparchy of the ROC stubbornly defends the notion of its great antiquity, tracing it back to the era of Kyivan Rus' and substantiating the need for active missionary activity on the resurgent southern steppe fringe of Russia with the help of the now traditional "borderland" rhetoric.[44] It is no accident that a twenty-foot-high monument to Saint Prince Vladimir (Ukr. Volodymyr), the Christianizer of Rus', was erected at the top of Kharkiv Mount in Belgorod in 1998, and that visitors approaching Belgorod along the Kharkiv highway are welcomed with an Orthodox chapel in the new university complex. In recent years the educational and cultural space of the Belgorod region has been transformed ever more palpably by Orthodox symbols and rhetoric.[45]

All this indicates that Belgorod has distanced itself much more from the Soviet mythology of the "city of the first salute" than has Kharkiv from its depiction as the "city of labor" or Donetsk from the image of the city of "miners' glory." Belgorod was trying on the mantel of a missionary frontline city, as it was several hundred years ago. In light of recent events, it is worth noting that as early as 2006 governor Yevgenii Savchenko of Belgorod ordered the start of preparations for a defensive war against an unnamed potential enemy, which was immediately "decoded" by ordinary Russian citizens as an "Orange Ukraine."[46]

Returning to the political events of 2004 in Kharkiv, it should be emphasized that the bitter information war proved unable to shake the preference of Kharkiv voters for seeking a "golden mean," in this case between the extremes of post-Soviet Russian nationalism and Soviet discourses of identity. Kushnarev was shot dead in suspicious circumstances while hunting along the border between Kharkiv and Donetsk oblasts. His political successors reached a compromise with Kyiv, which neutralized the impetus for regional autonomy, for some time at least.

The results of the 2004 presidential elections showed the Kharkiv region in a middle position between the Sumy, Poltava, and Kirovohrad oblasts of Left-Bank

Ukraine, won by Viktor Yushchenko, and the Donbas and the Crimea, where Viktor Yanukovych gained overwhelming support (81–94 percent). By that indicator, Kharkiv oblast, where Yanukovych won 68.1 percent of the vote, was closest to the oblasts of Zaporizhia (70.1 percent), Mykolaiv (67.1 percent), and Odesa (66.6 percent),[47] confirming the conclusions of contemporary observers about the differences in regional identity between inhabitants of the Kharkiv region and the Donbas.[48]

## Polarization

Subsequent events produced no significant changes in the balance of political forces in eastern Ukraine. As a result of elections to the Verkhovna Rada in 2006, the Party of Regions won an unconditional victory, gaining 51.7 percent of the vote in Kharkiv oblast, while the Bloc of Yulia Tymoshenko, taking second place, had to content itself with 12.7 percent, and the pro-presidential bloc Nasha Ukraina ("Our Ukraine") took 5.9 percent.[49] In elections to local government, the Party of Regions also took first place, gaining fifty-four seats (39.97 percent) in city council and eighty-three seats (38.85 percent) in oblast council.[50] As a result of the Orange Revolution of 2004, the places of the party and economic *nomenklatura* of the Soviet period were taken by representatives of business who had begun their climb to the heights of power in the years of perestroika and the initial "wild" capitalism.

A local businessman, Arsen Avakov, associated with the family clan of Viktor Yushchenko in Kharkiv by political interests, was appointed by the new president to head Kharkiv oblast. At the same time, Mikhail Dobkin, also a local businessman representing the Party of Regions, was elected mayor of Kharkiv, and the oblast council was headed by his party colleague Vasilii Salygin, a "bird of Maselsky's nest" soon replaced by a less odious comrade. A fierce conflict developed immediately between the city authorities and the oblast administration not only over the successive repartition of property but also because of political and even ideological opposition.

In the history of Kharkiv there has probably been no previous city leadership that managed, in somewhat more than two years in power, to give rise to so many political scandals as to become notorious far beyond Ukraine, thanks above all to the World Wide Web. Nevertheless, the efforts of competing business and political elites to oust that leadership by means of early elections or lawsuits proved fruitless. They shattered against the passivity of voters, especially those who had actively supported Yanukovych during the Orange Revolution of 2004 and felt deeply disappointed after the accession to power of Viktor Yushchenko. One more reserve element of stability enjoyed by the city leadership was not only and not so much the local population's reputation for passivity as the further degradation of its level of political culture—a factor that perpetually escaped notice in sociological surveys.

The discreditation of practically all state institutions in the eyes of society at large could not fail to influence the attitude of voters toward local authority. Thus, in a sociological survey of 20 March 2008, 7.6 percent of participants expressed full confidence in Mikhail Dobkin, 16.4 percent partial confidence, and 39.6 percent no confidence. The head of the oblast administration, Arsen Avakov, inspired full confidence in 8.7 percent of participants, relative confidence in 15.6 percent, partial confidence in 26.8 percent, and no confidence in 18.3 percent.[51] But those attitudes had hardly profound influence on political life in the city and oblast.

The Orange Revolution of 2004 polarized Ukrainian society. The inertia of political confrontation along the east–west line that had permeated the presidential elections found its continuation in the cultural policy of local political elites. If the leader of the oblast administration followed the official line intended to realize the Ukrainian nation-state project and held in some measure to the democratic traditions of the Soviet perestroika period, then the policy of the Kharkiv city leadership was defined by confrontation with Kyiv, demonstrative support for the foreign policy of the Kremlin, and further utilization of nostalgia for the Soviet period.

## Memory Politics

The politics of memory practiced by the Kharkiv authorities at that time was opposed to the official policy of the Ukrainian leadership, which shifted its priorities from the Cossack period, as in the early 1990s, to the recent past. The ideology of imperial Russian nationalism was actively employed, for example, by the Natalia Vitrenko Bloc, the Russian Bloc, and the Eurasian Youth Bloc. But their influence was not to be compared with that of the Russian Orthodox Church, which had revived the practice of identifying the concept of "Russian" with that of "Orthodox" and considered the Kharkiv region an organic element of a single "Russian" historico-cultural space. A reminder of the thoroughly political character of that space was the active participation of priests of the ROC in the presidential elections of 2004 on the side of the pro-Russian candidate.

The basic role of integrating the regions into Ukrainian national space was now assigned to the symbolism of the Holodomor of 1932–33, which the Verkhovna Rada of Ukraine recognized as genocide against the Ukrainian people. The city and oblast authorities differed in particular on memorializing the victims of the Holodomor.[52] As Tatiana Zhurzhenko puts it, "the official narrative of the Holodomor as a genocide and the corresponding memory regime have been contested, renegotiated, and modified on the regional level, through the conflicts and the bargaining of local political actors."[53]

While the "Orange" deputies in the oblast leadership insisted on erecting a monument to the victims of the tragedy in the Youth Park in the center of town, where a wooden cross had already been placed through community efforts during the perestroika period to memorialize that page of history, their "Blue-and-White" political opponents found it necessary to situate the monument on oblast territory outside the city. It was finally decided to erect the memorial complex dedicated to the victims of the Holodomor on the ring road leading to Belgorod in Russia.

The treatment of the Holodomor as genocide against Ukrainians, accepted on the official level, provoked open rejection on the part of the Kharkiv city authorities. After furious debate, they agreed to build a memorial to the victims of Stalinism in Kharkiv only on condition that the word "genocide" in its name be changed to "victims of totalitarianism" and that the monument itself be placed not in the center of the city but on the outskirts, in Young Communist League Park. Since even this compromise decision (which, by the way, the oblast authorities did not support) produced a new battle over names, the city council deputies initially decided to rename the Young Communist League Park, calling it the Park of Memory.

In response, the new mayor of Kharkiv, Mikhail Dobkin, made the following declaration:

> If this is a monument against the part of history that is associated with the Soviet Union, that is one variant. If it is a monument to the victims of totalitarianism and the Holodomor, that is another variant. I respect the memory of all those people who perished at the time of those terrible events in Ukraine. But I am categorically opposed to the version that certain marginal political forces are trying to present, striking out all the good things that existed in the life of our state and were associated with the Soviet Union.[54]

The local authorities effectively countered President Yushchenko's policy of memory with the Russian neoimperial narrative of recent history. In November 2008 they organized a Russo-Ukrainian conference entitled "The Famine in the USSR in the 1930s: Historical and Political Interpretations." The event took place two days after President Yushchenko visited Kharkiv to unveil the memorial dedicated to Holodomor victims.[55]

Even greater confrontation was provoked in the city between the Russian "Great Patriotic War" and the Ukrainian "national resistance" of World War II narratives. The historical mythology of the Great Patriotic War was taking on a sacral character under the patronage of the Russian Orthodox Church. An illustration of that policy in the Kharkiv region may be seen, for example, in the Konev Heights memorial complex, erected in honor of the Soviet marshal commanding the troops who liberated Kharkiv from the Nazis in 1943. In 2003 an Orthodox chapel appeared beside the monument to the Soviet military commander. A similar example was the proposal to build an Orthodox chapel in place of the gallery of Soviet heroes of the underground resistance in the historical center of Kharkiv. A chapel built in a central section of the city and dedicated to St. Yevgenii, a soldier of the

Russian army who died in the most recent Russo-Chechen war, belongs to the same logical sequence.

President Viktor Yushchenko decided to rehabilitate the Ukrainian Insurgent Army (*Ukraïns'ka povstans'ka armiia*, UPA), which waged partisan warfare in the course of World War II against the communist USSR, armed Polish nationalist formations, and finally the German Reich. In return, the Kharkiv oblast council, most of which consisted of members of the Party of Regions, made a decision to take down all memorials dedicated to the UPA on the territory of the city and oblast and to revise all Ukrainian history textbooks in which UPA fighters were called heroes.[56] The decision was based on the grounds that, as one deputy put it, "the UPA has nothing to do with Kharkiv." None of the deputies of the Kharkiv oblast council who were political opponents of the Party of Regions took the risk of disputing that decision. One of the indirect results of their silence was the defacing of an UPA memorial sign in the Kharkiv Youth Park in December 2006 by members of the Eurasian Youth Union, an extremist Russian organization that rejected Ukrainian statehood.

The Kharkiv city authorities expressed demonstrative support for the Russian government in the conflict that flared up around the monument to the Soviet soldier-liberator in Tallinn in 2007. Mayor Mikhail Dobkin addressed the Estonian authorities at the time with a proposal to remove the monument and install it in Kharkiv. That initiative in turn was directly continued in an expression of political support for Russia in the Russo-Georgian war of 2008.

The local authorities aggressively promoted the Russian narrative of World War II under "anti-fascist" slogans. For example, in 2007 a conference took place in Kharkiv to commemorate the seventieth anniversary of the Molotov-Ribbentrop Pact. It concluded with the proclamation of an anti-Orange "anti-fascist" front.[57] Anti-fascist rhetoric became an ideological platform for a new political alliance of pro-Russian forces in Kharkiv. In September 2009 the city hosted a conference on "The Second World War: Lessons and Significance for Ukraine," where the convening of an Anti-Fascist Forum of Ukraine was announced.[58]

Symbolically, the co-chairs of the Forum were the Kharkiv people's deputy Dmytro Shentsev and Luhansk Oblast Council chair Valerii Holenko, who seemed to represent a new political alliance between Sloboda Ukraine and Donbas political elites. The conference was attended by the Kharkiv mayor, Mikhail Dobkin, as well as people's deputy Mykola Azarov (future prime minister of Ukraine) and representatives from various regions of Ukraine and Russia. At this time, Serhii Chernov, the chair of the Kharkiv Oblast Council, stressed that attempts to separate the history of Ukraine during the years of the Great Patriotic War from the history of the USSR are unacceptable. In sum, local Kharkiv policies of memory became increasingly congruent with the identity politics of the Kremlin even before Victor Yanukovych came to power in 2010.

Another example of the spiritual solidarity of Kharkiv's political elite with that of Russia is the widespread practice of wearing the so-called St. George ribbon, a new symbol of the Great Patriotic War that appeared in Russia and was introduced in Kharkiv by the administration of one of the city's private institutions of higher education in 2006. Mayor Dobkin did not conceal the underlying political significance of the St. George ribbon promotion, declaring on the eve of Victory Day celebrations in 2009 that "for me personally, the 'St. George ribbon' is, among other things, a reply to those who are now seeking to rewrite our history and praise the scoundrels who fought on the side of the fascists."[59]

In comparison with the Soviet and Russian post-Soviet versions of collective memory of the Great Patriotic War, all others appear to have been marginalized in Kharkiv's cultural space. Among them are memory of the Holocaust, honored in the Drobytskyi Yar memorial complex; memory of the "Kharkiv Katyn"—the Polish officers murdered en masse by the Soviet regime after the partition of Poland in 1939, to whom a memorial complex is dedicated in the forest park area; and the very concept of World War II, which was almost completely supplanted in the Kharkiv regional narrative by the paradigm of the Great Patriotic War. The same might be said about the Ukrainian mythology of the OUN-UPA, actively promoted by Victor Yushchenko. It appeared to be hostile not only to the Soviet but also to the regional Kharkiv mythology of the "Great Patriotic War."

Generally speaking, in the Soviet narrative Kharkiv occupied a much higher and more prestigious place than in the national Ukrainian narrative, for several reasons, including the "vastly superior" World War II–era T-34 tank, designed and built in Kharkiv; the first-ever trial of Nazi war criminals (1943); and, last but not least, the successful expulsion of the Nazis in 1943. It is no wonder that the Kharkiv local government brooked no compromise in rejecting attempts to include Kharkiv in the Ukrainian national narrative by using the historical symbols of the OUN-UPA.

Both Russian and Ukrainian national discourses had their representatives and adepts in Kharkiv society. On the mental map of increasing Russian nationalism, Kharkiv, along with the other southeastern Ukrainian oblasts, was located somewhere in the southern Russian borderland between "genuine Russian" Crimea and hostile, nationalist western Ukraine. These oblasts were only partially "sullied" by Ukrainian nationalism and could easily be "purified" by integrating them into the Russian spiritual and political realm. Kharkiv thus gradually acquired the imperial image of a border outpost in the *Dikoe Pole* (Wild field), cut off from its Russian homeland.

In local Russian discourse, Kharkiv figured as a border town considered to be situated, relatively speaking, on the Russian side of the former Belgorod Line of fortifications. Indeed, it was not even a town but a fortress on a hostile border—a heroic garrison choking in the stifling alien space of Ukrainian nationalism but not yielding and continuing its unequal struggle against a tireless and insidious enemy behind which stands the hypocritical and hostile West. This was combined with the Soviet image of the Brest fortress, a Soviet wartime western outpost that held a prominent place in the "Great Patriotic War" mythology.

As an example of such gloomy fantasies, one may cite the Kharkiv writer Stanislav Minakov, whose works reproduce the basic parameters of traditional Russian anti-Ukrainian discourse.[60] The poetry collection *Dikoe Pole* (Wild Field), compiled with his participation, which includes "Russian poets of Ukraine" and, for some reason, of Moscow as well, turns out to be a "greeting sent to the Russian reader from Ukrainian Russian Kharkiv, from Russian Ukraine." Minakov's "New Campaign Song of the Sloboda Regiments," probably written in the heat of the political confrontation of 2004, might well be endorsed by the most fanatical adepts of the Black Hundreds active a century ago if they were alive today.[61] The author did his best to establish Kharkiv's identity as a Russian city but, when his compatriots decided otherwise, emigrated to the real, not fictional "Russian world"—neighboring Belgorod.

In the Ukrainian national narrative, the representation of Kharkiv remained contradictory. Depending on the observer's perspective, Kharkiv could be named either the "cradle of the Ukrainian Renaissance" or the "capital of despair," "doomed city," and a victim of forcible Russification. The heroic component of national mythology was represented by Ukrainian Cossackdom, the local philosopher Hryhorii Skovoroda, the vanguard Kharkiv University and, obviously, the state-sponsored Ukrainization program during the brief period of national communism. The victimization of Kharkiv was accompanied in the Ukrainian narrative by such symbols of national suffering as Stalinist repressions and the Holodomor. In that regard, the Russian language and culture and the Soviet past were depicted as wholly external, imposed by Russia, "inorganic" components of the history and contemporary life of the city and region.[62] Xenophobic, Slavophile, or anti-Western overtones may sometimes be discerned in such stereotypical representations.

## The Regional Narrative

Borderland Kharkiv became gradually marginalized by both Ukrainian and Russian nationalist discourses. Predictably, the Ukrainian discourse provoked a reaction from the local Russian-speaking elites traditionally oriented toward Moscow. Theoretically, they could influence the Ukrainian agenda of nation-state building. In practice, however, they came up with their own regional discourse that combined Ukrainian, Russian, and Soviet myths and symbols. It was designed to overcome the crisis of Soviet identity and adapt to the changing political and sociocultural atmosphere. But the cultural policy of Kharkiv's Russian-speaking leadership had no independent regional component. To a significant degree, their policy seemed to reflect the neoimperial doctrine of the Russian political regime.

The intellectual legacy of the official Soviet "Friendship of Peoples" discourse, with its emphasis on special relations between Ukrainians and Russians, was finally replaced by the brand-new discourse of *Pervaia stolitsa* mentioned earlier. It was actively supported by the local authorities. None other than Mikhail Dobkin, mayor of Kharkiv and chief representative of the Party of Regions, who had become the major sponsor of a collection of scenarios under the title *The Unknown Kharkiv* compiled by Kevork Kevorkian, signed his name to the assertion that Kharkiv had been subjected for many years to "systematic humiliation" and had "systematically been deprived of the right to creative initiative" by the "state policy of suppressing the regions."[63]

And yet, in the midst of intellectual battles over history, regional historical discourse can act as something of a stabilizing factor, a distinct alternative opposed to the extremes of mutually exclusive nationalist paradigms. As an example of this, one may cite the project "Leading Kharkivites: Stars of the Sloboda Region," initiated toward the end of 2007 by the online newspaper *Glavnoe* (The lead), which was close to the Kharkiv oblast leadership. By means of an internet survey involving more than sixteen thousand residents of the city, a group of ten famous Kharkivites had been identified by the summer of 2009. It included mainly names of intellectuals, such as Hryhorii Skovoroda, Dmytro Bahalii, Ilia Repin, Ilia Mechnikov, Petro Hulak-Artemovsky, and Vladimir Vernadsky, as well as Leonid Bykov and Aleksei Beketov.[64]

For all the peculiarity of such a system of identifying the city's leading personalities, the majority of whom were not Kharkiv-born, the list reflected the conception held by participants in the project of Kharkiv as a city of scholars and creative figures, a cultural capital. Among the organizers' intentions were the creation of a Gallery of Famous Kharkivites in the city center and the production of new teaching, educational, and publishing programs to create a new intellectual discourse, or, in the words of Vladimir Chistilin, "a paradigm of Kharkiv, with its own stylistics, its own architecture, its own monuments," and its own mythology.[65]

## What Tongue Will Land You in Kyiv?

In the regionalization of Ukrainian political and cultural discourse, a particular role belongs to language. On the Ukrainian-Russian borderland, language is not only a means of communication but also an influential symbol associated with national, cultural, and even political identity. Of course, that symbol is not all-embracing. Contemporary scholars have reason to insist on distinguishing the sphere of everyday practice from that of the symbolic significance of a language: the use of one language in conversational practice does not at all mean rejection of the other as a symbolic marker of national identification.[66] One may speak Russian all one's life but advert to the Ukrainian language, or elements of it, at moments of imperative need to emphasize one's allegiance to the Ukrainian nation or ethnos. Clearly, the same applies to the Ukrainian language. For that very reason, a simple distinction between Russophones and Ukrainophones has proved inadequate for the identification of inhabitants of post-Soviet Ukraine: there were many shades of "Ukrainianness" embedded in the language practices of the borderland dwellers.[67]

Kharkiv remained a predominantly Russian-speaking city if one judges by the degree of prevalence of the Russian language in all social spheres. The Russian language and contemporary Russian mass culture have been also dominant in Kharkiv's information space. The Ukrainian language, having obtained the status of sole official language, was often used until recent times as a means of national identification. Since 1991 the sphere of its practical use has been expanding, to judge by numbers of students in Ukrainian-language schools, official documentation, radio and television, advertising, and the like. According to Margrethe Søvik, all this attests that the project of official linguistic Ukrainization was being accepted more calmly in Kharkiv than in the neighboring Donbas.[68]

Nevertheless, the language problem in Kharkiv remained politically and ideologically acute. It may be said that the struggle between politicians defending the interests of Russophones and Ukrainophones respectively has not slackened for a moment since the late 1980s and early 1990s and remained uncompromising in character. Each side expressed dissatisfaction with official policy on the question. In public debate on language, Russophones appealed to European norms and standards. Ukrainophones, in turn, more often called for official intervention in the spirit of affirmative action.

In 1996 Kharkiv city council decided to grant the Russian language official status as a second language within city limits. Although the decision was protested in the judicial system up to the Supreme Court, in March 2002 the city authorities organized a referendum on the question, obtaining the support of about 83 percent of voters. It is noteworthy that the question of the Russian language turned out to be directly associated with the granting of particular juridical status to Kharkiv within the state. In 2006, basing itself on official documents of the European Union, city council did after all grant the Russian language official status, and some time later it adopted a special program of support for the Russian language and culture. The question of the role and place of the Ukrainian language in Kharkiv received no particular attention in that regard.[69]

It is perfectly apparent that the struggle for language status was not so much practical as symbolic in character. The Ukrainian language, yielding to Russian in the sphere of communications, remained the basic instrument of Ukrainian national identification. The Russian language, functioning as a lingua franca in post-Soviet space, united bearers not of one but of several types of identity, including Russian proper, Soviet, local, and Ukrainian national, to name just a few. Each of them may play a different role in the process of Ukrainian nation-state building.

The mobilizing potential of the language problem was exploited with invariable success by the communists and pro-Russian parties. The banner of defense of the Russian language made it relatively easy to conceal the ideological rags on the corpulent bodies of the political elites that dominated the city and region. The center, for its part, did not see and was not seeking ways of using the cultural potential of the Russian language in its own interests. Nevertheless, as the events of the autumn of 2004 demonstrate, the slogan of defense of the Russian language could not in and of itself unite voters of different political orientations. In turn, appeals to struggle for the rights of the Ukrainian language had even less mobilizing potential in the region.

In practice, the language question in Kharkiv was not so acute as competing politicians were trying to make it. The bilingualism typical of a cultural borderland has arisen here spontaneously. The only theoretical alternative to the confrontation between Ukrainophones and Russophones might be the legitimization of so-called *surzhyk*, a conversational patois of Sloboda region Ukrainians that mixes the Russian and Ukrainian languages. Proposals of this kind were to be heard from time to time among Kharkiv politicians, and Metropolitan Nikodim of Kharkiv and Bohodukhiv (Moscow Patriarchate) even used *surzhyk* in his social and literary practice.

But *surzhyk* was hardly capable of playing anything more than a symbolic role, although the number of its speakers in the eastern oblasts generally exceeded that of Ukrainophones.[70] It can serve as a marker of regional identity, but in the cultural hierarchy of public opinion it holds one of the lowest places, remaining a symbol of all that is shoddy, second-rate, and marginal, even though it is recognizable and close to everyday life. Thus, any attempt to build a "high" culture on the basis of *surzhyk* can hardly be contemplated. *Surzhyk* remains a symbol of ambivalence in a regional zone of cultural contact, and in that regard it is closer to conversational Russian, with a particular "Kharkiv" accent, than to literary Ukrainian.

## Symbolic Orientations

To be sure, what has been discussed above does not exhaust the spectrum of political and cultural life in the post-Soviet megalopolis. In the social space between the bureaucracy, the oligarchy, and the passive "electorate," elements of civil society have managed to establish themselves, including, for example, the Kharkiv Human Rights Group, the Committee of Voters, individual scholarly, artistic, cultural, and humanitarian organizations, and even mass media. Unfortunately, their influence on the community, to say nothing of the politics of the city and region, was hardly noticeable until recently, and sources of financing for such organizations were mostly to be found outside Ukraine.

Nor was the city's cultural space wholly politicized. There were many neutral symbols that carried no political or ideological baggage. They included the now well-known figure of a fiddler on the roof of a downtown building; the provocatively styled monument to lovers on Beketova Street; the huge soccer ball on a playground in Taras Shevchenko Central City Park—something of a Hyde Park in the Soviet period, where endless discussions about soccer took place; and the projected symbolic delineation of the 50th parallel, which passes, *as became clear quite recently*, through Kharkiv.

As in other large cities of Ukraine, especially Kyiv and Odesa, there were quite a few people in Kharkiv for whom national or local identity contradicted European identity. Transnational types of identity were quite widespread among city residents.[71] Signs of contemporary transnational discourse may be found not only in garish advertisements promising some kind of "European" quality of goods and services, as well as in names of diverse establishments, but also in the presence of a growing number of migrants from various regions and countries of the world. The question to what extent the "capital of diversity"[72] is appreciated and utilized by representatives of the civic community; to what degree the mental and everyday structures of civic life in post-Soviet space are prepared for change and acceptance of new realities, remained open.

In recent years Kharkiv and region have gradually been taking on a more contemporary cultural and spatial identification than the one that arose in the Soviet period. The metaphor of the "friendship of peoples" is being replaced ever more often by that of a "crossroads" employed by Vasilii Karazin in his day.[73] It was also employed by the nameless author of a historical sketch of Kharkiv architecture, who wrote the following lines:

> Kharkiv ... is a great European crossroads. Civilizations and peoples, faiths and philosophies meet here and collide, enriching one another—the thrifty and efficient North with the ardent emotional South, the egocentric West with the East, which has come to believe in the transience of all things. Is there anyone who has not been and is not in Kharkiv today—Ukrainians and Russians, Jews and Germans, Karaites and Poles, Greeks and Armenians, Azerbaijanis and Tatars?[74]

In any case, the "crossroads" metaphor with reference to local history considerably expands the dimensions of the city and region, placing them in a broader sociocultural space than before—that of a globalizing world.

In the post-Soviet era, the symbolic geography of Kharkiv underwent certain changes but generally remained rather confused. The Kharkiv authors Rostyslav Melnykiv and Yurii Tsaplin wittily overcame the problems involved in the spatial identification of the region, entitling their article about the literary life of post-

Soviet Kharkiv the "northeastern region of the southwest."[75] After Ukraine became a state, Kharkiv did indeed manage to change its symbolic "northeastern" orientation of Soviet times to the less precise "eastern" one, renouncing—for the time being, at least—the southwestern and, almost certainly, the previous "southern" and "Little Russian" orientations.

Kharkiv's symbolic orientation toward the former capital of the Russian Empire, St. Petersburg, was still apparent in the local intellectual milieu, as before. It may be discovered, for example, in many literary works of Russian-language Kharkiv authors ("the Ukrainian Leningrad," "the Ukrainian Petersburg," the Lopan River as "Kharkiv's Neva," and so on). The accustomed echo of Kharkiv/Petersburg was heard, for example, in the name of the literary and artistic exhibition "First Capitals: Two Cities, Two Fates," dedicated to the 350th anniversary of Kharkiv and the 325th anniversary of St. Petersburg.

The growing "Ukrainocentrism" of Kharkiv might be indirectly attested by the fact that the piety toward Leningrad/St. Petersburg characteristic of the older generation of the Kharkiv intelligentsia may be considered lost among the younger generation. At least, a sociological survey of students at Kharkiv institutions of higher education carried out over several years by members of the Department of Ukrainian Studies at the Karazin National University of Kharkiv together with the Canadian Institute of Ukrainian Studies has shown that for young Kharkivites, Kyiv has become the most significant urban symbol. It was followed by Poltava and Donetsk, while the Russian capitals, including Moscow and St. Petersburg, were to be found at the end of the list of geographic preferences, neighboring with Lviv.[76]

The "capital complex" still exerted considerable influence on the image of Kharkiv. The French photographer Julien Goldstein, who visited the city in 2006, admitted to having been warned that Kharkiv treasured its reputation as a capital and maintained the characteristic "haughtiness" that supposedly distinguished it from other large cities of Ukraine visited by Goldstein. His travel impressions were strikingly formulated by Kharkiv journalists in a report entitled "Kharkiv the Skeptic, Lviv the Nationalist, Odesa the Pragmatist, and Kyiv the Democrat (A French View of Ukraine)."[77] Although it is unclear from the story whose metaphors these are, in my view they successfully reflect the perspective from which Kharkivites themselves look at their city. For the authors of the story, these cities are "four keys to the discovery and understanding of Ukraine." The appearance of Lviv on the list of cities with which Kharkiv is symbolically compared is significant indeed: traditionally, that list had included Kyiv and Odesa on the one side and Moscow and St. Petersburg on the other.

And yet, in the self-definition of contemporary Kharkivites one may find a direct link with motifs of modernity that inspired Hryhorii Kvitka, Vasilii Karazin, and Grigorii Danilevsky in their time. Most often, its social basis consists of representatives of the nascent "middle class." According to such an index as the proportion of small business in industrial production, Kharkiv oblast, with 10 percent, surpassed Donetsk oblast (approximately 4 percent) and Zaporizhia oblast (approximately 5 percent) more than twice. That is evidently the stratum cultivating notions of some particular entrepreneurship and pragmatism among Kharkivites, as well as their constant aspiration to economic liberty and marked inclination to engage in trade.[78] The liking of Kharkivites for risky entrepreneurship has already manifested itself in the city landscape with a sculptural depiction of perhaps the most popular Soviet adventurist, Ostap Bender, as well as his predecessor Pavel Ivanovich Chichikov, whose name is honored in that of a comfortable private hotel in the historic center of town, on Gogol Street.

The image of Kharkiv as a city of successful entrepreneurs, merchants, and tradesmen, innovators and high technology, and the capital of small business nevertheless has something of a compensatory character about it. The economically and politically weakened Kharkiv region yielded considerably to the Donbas in mineral reserves and concentration of capital in the hands of local oligarchs, as well as in volume of industrial production and share of national exports; its standing was closer to that of Zaporizhia oblast. Moreover, social identity, based on categories of "economic optimism," was considerably weakened by the consequences of the global economic crisis of 2008 and by the direct link between market orientation and national cultural identification in the consciousness of those residing in the region.[79]

In the ten to twelve years prior to 2010, commercialization had been influencing the urban landscape of Kharkiv ever more strongly. The most blatant signs of socioeconomic degradation of urban space in the early 1990s were gradually disappearing under the influence of a new type of architectural construction laden with "features of globalism in the minimalism of form against the background of broad technological capacities."[80] Supermarkets of competing commercial networks, which give the appearance of having sprung up simultaneously, have forced out spontaneous street markets practically everywhere (paradoxically, the sole exception is the city's central square). Other results of the building boom are residential skyscrapers in all parts of the city, office and banking centers, and numerous cafés and restaurants, even as the automobile fever of recent years fills those spaces with inevitable traffic jams.

The architectural constructions and sections of the city most saturated with Soviet ideology—the "socialist city" of the first five-year plans, the monumental Stalinist Empire style, the standard five-story residential buildings of the Khrushchev period, the "bedroom communities" of the Brezhnev years, as well as the central and local copies of the Moscow Kremlin with ubiquitous Lenin monuments and memorial plaques—have withstood marketization most strongly, leaving no space for architectural innovation.[81] When a French director of a new art film with

Emir Kusturica as a participant was seeking a location in 2008 to represent the Moscow of Stalin's times, he found it in the center of Kharkiv on the former Dzerzhinsky Square, now Liberty Square. When the popular rock group Queen toured Ukraine and looked for a concert site in Kharkiv, they found it on Liberty Square, formerly Dzerzhinsky Square.

It was perfectly obvious that the Soviet legacy remained an influential factor in the city's political, social, and cultural space. Nostalgia for the recent Soviet past was apparent not only among the older generation but also among young people, and it was no less prevalent in the new political and business elites than among the vast majority of people impoverished as a result of the unfair repartition of resources. In November 2008 almost half the surveyed residents of Kharkiv evaluated the seventy years of the existence of the USSR as a "period of stability, [good] life prospects, and prosperity for workers," 15.3 percent called it a "period of a totalitarian regime with hard consequences for many peoples," 14.2 percent described it as a "contradictory period of realization of enticing ideas of socialism by severe methods," another 18.7 percent had difficulty in responding, and 5.1 percent preferred a different formulation.[82]

These figures may be considered something of an interim report on the political development of a society that had undergone more than one shock in the process of Ukraine's gradual development into a full-fledged nation-state. At the same time, components of Soviet identity remaining in the consciousness of a considerable part of the population opened the way to their transformation in the Russian as well as Ukrainian national reidentification,[83] especially as post-Soviet Ukrainian political space lacks a contemporary left-wing social-democratic component. Neither outright populism nor ochlocratic slogans nor Orthodox-Slavic fundamentalism can make up for its absence. The latter was openly at odds not only with Ukrainian national identity but also with European transnational identity.

It was the protracted agony of the Soviet identity that made the Ukrainian-Russian border both stable and undefined, not only as a geographic but also as a symbolic reality.[84] The demarcation of the Ukrainian-Russian border had been the stumbling block in Ukraine's relations with Russia, which regards the borders within the Commonwealth of Independent States as its "internal" boundaries and seeks in every possible way to prevent them from becoming "real." But that was only part of the truth. The influence of the Soviet component of local identity can be explained in part by the former's deep roots in the Slavic-Orthodox imperial tradition, which survived the Soviet experiment and manifested itself differently in various segments of the Ukrainian-Russian borderland.

**Figure 6.1.** Monument to fighters of the "Great October Socialist Revolution" of 1917 (1976), sculptors V. I. Agibalov, Y. I. Ryk, and M. F. Ovsiankin. Dismantled in 2011; replaced by monument to Ukrainian Independence in 2012 (see figure 6.2.), © Volodymyr Kravchenko, 2008.

**Figure 6.2.** Monument to Ukrainian Independence, sculptors Oleksandr Ridny and Hanna Ivanova, 2012, © Volodymyr Kravchenko, 2015.

**Figure 6.3.** Gallery and memorial steles honoring Soviet Komsomol members engaged in anti-Nazi resistance during World War II, © Wikimedia Commons.

**Figure 6.4.** Church of the Myrrhbearers in Kharkiv belonging to the Orthodox Church (Moscow Patriarchate). It replaced competing Soviet and Ukrainian national symbols, © Volodymyr Kravchenko, 2021.

## Notes

1. Stephen Kotkin and Mark R. Beissinger, eds., *Historical Legacies of Communism in Russia and Eastern Europe* (New York: Cambridge University Press, 2014).
2. Margrethe B. Søvik, *Support, Resistance, and Pragmatism: An Examination of Motivation in Language Policy in Kharkiv, Ukraine* (Stockholm: Stockholm University Press, 2008); Peter W. Rodgers, *Nation, Region, and History in Post-Communist Transitions: Identity Politics in Ukraine, 1991–2006* (Stuttgart: Ibidem Verlag, 2008); Tatiana Zhurzhenko, *Borderlands into Bordered Lands: Geopolitics of Identity in Post-Soviet Ukraine* (Stuttgart: Ibidem Verlag, 2010).
3. V. V. Bublikov, "Transformatsiia ètnicheskogo sostava naseleniia Belgorodchiny v otrazhenii ètnograficheskikh kart," *Ètnograficheskoe obozrenie*, no. 6 (2016): 72–81, here 80.
4. Roman Solchanyk, "The Politics of State Building: Centre-Periphery Relations in Post-Soviet Ukraine," *Europe-Asia Studies* 46, no. 1 (1994): 22, 47.
5. Tatiana Zhurzhenko, "Memory Wars in Post-Soviet Kharkiv," in *Civic Education and Democratisation in the Eastern Partnership Countries*, ed. Dieter Segert (Bonn: Bundeszentrale für politische Bildung, 2016), 102–22, here 107.
6. Anatoliy Melnychuck, Oleksiy Gnatiuk, and Mariia Rastvorova, "Use of Territorial Identity Markers in Geographical Researches," *Scientific Annals of "Alexandru Ioan Cuza" University of Iaşi* 60, no. 1 (2014), s. IIc, Geography Series (2014): 167.
7. Zhurzhenko, *Borderlands*, 222.
8. *Borderlands*, 234–35.
9. Gennadii Zgurskii, "Malorossy, Ukraintsy, ili. . . ?," *Kontekst: kul'turno-prosvetitel'skii zhurnal*, no. 1 (1992): 9–12.
10. S. Chechel'nitskii, ed., *Arhitektory Khar'kova* (Kharkiv, 2008), 24.
11. Tanya Richardson, *Kaleidoscopic Odessa: History and Place in Contemporary Ukraine* (Toronto, Buffalo, and London: University of Toronto Press, 2008), 18.
12. Hans van Zon, "Political Culture and Neo-Patrimonialism under Leonid Kuchma," *Problems of Post-Communism* 52, no. 5 (2005): 12–22; Vladimir Shlapentokh, *Contemporary Russia as a Feudal Society: A New Perspective on the Post-Soviet Era* (New York: Palgrave Macmillan, 2007); Mykola Riabchuk, *Zona vidchuzhennnia: ukraïns'ka oligarkhiia mizh Skhodom i Zakhodom* (Kyiv, 2004).
13. Ivan M. Kulinych, *Hubernator* (Kharkiv: Maidan, 1997), 219–20.
14. *"Hospodar – ioho zvaly u narodi. . ."* (Kharkiv: Folio, 2006), 5, 9–10, 240.
15. *Kharkiv – moia mala bat'kivshchyna: Navchal'nyi posibnyk z narodoznavstva* (Kharkiv, 2003), 30.
16. Tatiana Zhurzhenko, "Ukraïns'ko-rosiis'kyi kordon iak kul'turnyi i politychnyi konstrukt," in *Ukraïns'ko-rosiis'ke porubizhzhia: formuvannia sotsial'noho ta kul'turnoho prostoru v istoriï ta suchasnii politytsi* (Kyiv, 2003), 9–17, here 16.
17. *Rehional'na prohrama sotsial'no-ekonomichnoho rozvytku Kharkivs'koï oblasti do 2010 roku* (Kharkiv, 1999).
18. Ray Taras, Olga Filippova, and Natalia Pobeda, "Ukraine's Transnationals, Far-away Locals and Xenophobes: The Prospects for Europeanness," *Europe-Asia Studies* 56, no. 6 (2004): 844.
19. Oleksii Kiriukhin, "Formuvannia transkordonnykh evrorehioniv: chy ie perspektyva dlia Slobozhanshchyny?" in *Ukraïns'ko-rosiis'ke porubizhzhia: formuvannia sotsial'noho ta kul'turnoho prostoru v istoriï ta suchasnii politytsi* (Kyiv, 2003), 39.
20. Tatiana Zhurzhenko, "Cross-Border Cooperation and Transformation of Regional Identities in the Ukrainian-Russian Borderlands: Towards a Euroregion 'Slobozhanshchyna'?" *Nationalities Papers* 32, no. 1 (2004): 207–32; no. 2 (2004): 497–514.
21. Kiriukhin, "Formuvannia," 41–43.
22. http://www.nbuv.gov.uaarticlescrimea200558.pdf.

23. Zhurzhenko, "Ukraïns'ko-rosiis'kyi kordon," 14–15.
24. A. Libman, "Regionalisation and Regionalism in the Post-Soviet Space: Current Status and Implications for Institutional Development," *Europe-Asia Studies* 59, no. 3 (2007): 402.
25. Peter Rodgers, "'Compliance or Contradiction?' Teaching 'History' in the 'New' Ukraine: A View from Ukraine's Eastern Borderlands," *Europe-Asia Studies* 59, no. 3 (2007): 503–19.
26. *Kharkiv – moia mala bat'kivshchyna*, 59–60; Boris Shramko and Valentin Skirda, *Rozhdenie Khar'kova* (Kharkiv, 2004). Fortunately, local historians managed to avoid the embarrassment that befell their colleagues from Belgorod, whose authorities celebrated their city's quadricentennial in 1993 but solemnly proclaimed its millennium in 1995.
27. V. I. Torkatiuk and O. L. Sydorenko, eds., *Istoriia Slobids'koï Ukraïny: Navchal'nyi posibnyk z narodoznavstva ta kraieznavstva* (Kharkiv: Osnova, 1998).
28. Torkatiuk and Sydorenko, *Istoriia Slobids'koï Ukraïny*, 3, 366.
29. Oleksandr Iarmysh and Serhii Posokhov, eds., *Istoriia mista Kharkova XX stolittia* (Kharkiv: Folio, 2004).
30. Ievhen Kushnariov, "Peredmova," in Bagalei and Miller, *Istoriia goroda Khar'kova*, 1: 1–2.
31. Konstantin E. Kevorkian, *Pervaia stolitsa* (Kharkov: Pervaia stolitsa, 1995); 2nd ed. (Kharkiv: Folio, 1999); 3rd ed. (Kharkiv: Folio, 2002).
32. Kevorkian, *Pervaia stolitsa* (1995), 79.
33. *Pervaia stolitsa* (1995), 99.
34. Kevorkian, *Pervaia stolitsa* (1999), 210.
35. *Khar'kov mnogonatsional'nyi* (Kharkiv: Vostochno-regional'nyi tsentr gumanitarno-obrazovatel'nykh initsiativ, 2004).
36. Lenin Avenue was renamed Science Avenue in 2015.
37. Catherine Wanner, *Burden of Dreams: History and Identity in Post-Soviet Ukraine* (University Park: Pennsylvania State University Press, 1998), 81.
38. Andrew Wilson, *Ukraine's Orange Revolution* (New Haven, CT: Yale University Press, 2005).
39. A. Ivanov, "Rus' poshla iz Donbassa," *Donetskii kriazh*, 2 July 2004.
40. Dmitri Trenin, *Post-Imperium: A Eurasian Story* (Washington, DC: Carnegie Endowment for International Peace, 2011), 57, 100.
41. Oleg Nemenskii, "'Nedoukraintsy' ili novyi narod? Al'ternativy samoopredeleniia Iugo-Vostoka Ukrainy," *Russkii zhurnal*, 29 December 2004, http://old.russ.ru/culture/2004 1229_nem-pr.html; see also Oleg Nemenskii, "Modeli iuzhnorusskogo natsionalizma na Ukraine," *Voprosy natsionalizma* 2, no. 18 (2014): 20–31.
42. http://www.calend.ru/cityday/807/.
43. http://www. bitugin.narod.ru/statyi/history/pereimen.htm.
44. http://www.patriarchia.ru/db/text/31098.html.
45. http://www.hrono.ru/metodika/msimvol_ru.html; http://www.ipkps.bsu.edu.ru/source/kafedra/history/nauka/chernoval.doc.
46. See Viktor Filippov, "Belgorod gotovitsia k voine s Ukrainoi," *Izvestiia*, 30 June 2006, http://izvestia.ru/news/315046.
47. Ralph S. Clem and Peter R. Craumer, "Orange, Blue and White, and Blonde: The Electoral Geography of Ukraine's 2006 and 2007 Rada Elections," *Eurasian Geography and Economics* 49, no. 2 (2008): 134.
48. Roman Solchanyk, *Ukraine and Russia* (Lanham, MD: Rowman & Littlefield, 2001), 141; M. Lewicka and A. Foland, "Terytorial'na identychnist' u Pol'shchi ta Ukraïni: rehional'ni vidminnosti," in *L'viv i Donets'k: sotsial'ni identychnosti v suchasnii Ukraïni* (*Ukraina Moderna*, special issue, 2007): 290, 292, 295–96.
49. Clem and Craumer, "Orange, Blue," 134.
50. Filip Dykan, "Bytva za Kharkiv," *Dzerkalo tyzhnia*, no. 12, 1–7 April 2006.
51. http://news.mediaport.info/society/2008/50670.shtml.
52. Tatiana Zhurzhenko, "'Capital of Despair': Holodomor Memory and Political Conflicts in

Kharkiv after the Orange Revolution," *East European Politics and Societies* 25, no. 3 (2011): 597–639.
53. Zhurzhenko, "'Capital of Despair.'"
54. http://news.mediaport.info/city/2007/42734.shtml.
55. Zhurzhenko, "Memory Wars," 106.
56. http://news.mediaport.info/city/2007/43079.shtml.
57. Zhurzhenko, "Memory Wars," 106.
58. Volodymyr Kravchenko, "Kharkiv: The Past Lives On," *The Soviet and Post-Soviet Review* 64, no. 3 (2019): 324–51.
59. *Khar'kovskie izvestiia*, 25 April 2009, http://www.izv.kharkov.ua/index.php?editionID=201&menuID=1941&newsID=5285.
60. Stanislav Minakov, "Khar'kov: priznaki zhizni," *Znamia*, no. 5 (2001), https://znamlit.ru/publication.php?id=1437.
61. Stanislav Minakov, "Novaia pokhodnaia pesnia slobodskikh polkov," in *Kharkiv'iany: Poema pro misto v tsytatakh poetychnykh tvoriv*, eds. V. P. Kopychko and Iu. H. Kopychko (Kharkiv, 2007), 363–64.
62. *Holos Ukraïny*, 30 April 2008, http://www.golos.com.ua/rus/article/189841.
63. *Neizvestnyi Khar'kov*, ed. O. Iu. Adam (Kharkiv: Frunze, 2000), 3.
64. http://maydan.tv/articles/a128.
65. http://maydan.tv/articles/a88.
66. Laada Bilaniuk, *Contested Tongues: Language Politics and Cultural Correction in Ukraine* (Ithaca, NY: Cornell University Press, 2005).
67. Søvik, *Support, Resistance, and Pragmatism*, 307.
68. *Support, Resistance, and Pragmatism*, 99.
69. *Support, Resistance, and Pragmatism*, 99.
70. Amelie Constant, Martin Kahanec, and Klaus F. Zimmermann, "The Russian-Ukrainian Political Divide," *Eastern European Economics* 49, no. 6 (2011): 97–109.
71. Taras, Filippova, and Pobeda, "Ukraine's Transnationals," 835–52.
72. Blér Rubl' (Blair Ruble), *Kapital rozmaïtosti: Transnatsional'ni mihranty u Monreali, Vashinhtoni ta Kyevi* (Kyiv, 2007).
73. Volodymyr Masliichuk, *Provintsiia na perekhresti kul'tur: Doslidzhennia z istoriï Slobids'koï Ukraïny XVII–XIX st.* (Kharkiv: Kharkiv Private Museum of the City Estate, 2007).
74. *Arkhitektory Khar'kova*, ed. S. Chechel'nitskii (Kharkiv, 2008), 4.
75. Rostyslav Mel'nykiv and Iurii Saplin, "Severo-vostok iugo-zapada (o sovremennoi khar'kovskoi literature)," *Novoe literaturnoe obozrenie*, no. 3 (85) (2007): 263–88.
76. Helinada Hrinchenko et al., "Natsional'no-kul'turna identychnist' meshkantsia 'kontaktnoï zony' (za materialamy anketuvannia studentiv-pershokursnykiv mista Kharkova)," *Skhid-Zakhid* 8 (2006): 161–84.
77. http://news.mediaport.info/.
78. Antonina Maznytsia, "Malyi i serednii biznes – vizytna kartka Kharkivshchyny: kozhen pratsiuiuchyi – pidpryiemets'," *Dzerkalo tyzhnia*, no. 25 (2003), http://www.zn.kiev.ua/ie/show/450/39185/.
79. S. Makeev and A. Patrakov, "Regional'naia spetsyfika sotsiokul'turnykh razlichii v Ukraine," *Sotsiologiia: teoriia, metody, marketing*, no. 3 (2004): 122–23.
80. Makeev and Patrakov, "Regional'naia."
81. Vladimir Kaganskii, "Sovetskoe prostranstvo – nashe nasledstvo," *Russkii zhurnal*, 20 August (2004), www.russ.ru/culture/20040820_kag.html.
82. "Chto 7 noiabria dla zhitelei Kharkova? – sotsopros," *Media-Port-Novosti*, 7 November 2008, http://www.mediaport.ua/.
83. Viktoriia Sereda, "Regional Historical Identities and Memory," in *L'viv i Donets'k: sotsial'ni identychnosti v suchasnii Ukraïni* (*Ukraina Moderna*, special issue, 2007), 200.
84. Zhurzhenko, "Ukraïns'ko-rosiis'kyi kordon," 9–17.

# CHAPTER 7

# The Front Line

Strictly speaking, this chapter should have been the shortest. Not because the author had little to say for lack of facts. On the contrary, one might sooner speak of difficulties caused by a surfeit of facts and lack of appropriate historical distance from the events described. And yet, even today, after thirty years of Ukrainian independence, no rational observer would venture to predict the future of the country, which is desperately trying to redesign its national and geopolitical identities. In this chapter I shall dwell on the dramatic reversals of fortune in the political and cultural life of Kharkiv and its oblast from the coming to power of Viktor Yanukovych in 2010 to the Russo-Ukrainian war that began in 2014 and is still going on.

Until 2010 the Ukrainian ship of state followed an erratic course, veering either away from or alongside the political coastline of the former USSR. If I am not mistaken, sailing of this kind is known as cabotage, but in this case it was done "without wheel or sails."[1] With the election of Viktor Yanukovych, a native of the Donbas, Ukraine's most Sovietized and criminalized region, it seemed that Ukrainian society, especially in the eastern and southern borderlands of the state, had finally attained the stability and predictability for which many longed. The ruling authorities, particularly as compared to their predecessors, looked consolidated and decisive as never before. The democratic camp of Ukrainian society, by contrast, was demoralized by the effects of the five-year rule of the "Orange coalition."

The victory of Viktor Yanukovych over his predecessor in the presidential office, Viktor Yushchenko, was triumphant for the former and humiliating for the latter. In the 2010 presidential elections, Yanukovych won more than 50 percent of the vote in Kharkiv oblast and more than 40 percent in the city of Kharkiv, which was almost twice the total obtained by his nearest rival in the first round, Serhii Tihipko.[2] Those favoring Viktor Yushchenko managed to obtain only 1.4 percent of the vote in all of Kharkiv oblast.

The results of the presidential elections promptly influenced elections to local government institutions toward the end of 2010. They were marked by unprecedented administrative interference and clouded by countless infractions that could not fail to influence the results of the voting.³ And the results produced a shocking victory for the Party of Regions in the elections to the Kharkiv oblast council, where it won 95 of the 136 seats; its nearest rival, the *Batkivshchyna* (Fatherland) Party of Yulia Tymoshenko, won no more than 16 seats. The Kyivan authorities appointed Mikhail Dobkin to head the oblast, while his partner in business and politics, Hennadii Kernes, became mayor of Kharkiv after an unconvincing victory at the polls.

The local Kharkiv elite made haste to declare its support for the new authorities even before the local elections. A collective open letter signed by many Kharkiv directors, rectors (headed by Vil' Bakirov, the rector of the Karazin National University of Kharkiv), entrepreneurs, and politicians, published in the summer of 2010, was intended to manifest the political loyalty of local "party and economic activists." Imbued with the Soviet rhetoric of "stability" and "establishing order," as well as the standard wishes of future success in a selfless endeavor for the common good,⁴ it was undoubtedly more comprehensible to a mass audience than the Kyivan authorities' incessant vacillation between European values and ethnic nationalism.

The Soviet system of values manifested by the Kharkiv elite included not only the sacralization of rule but also uncompromising struggle against political opponents. In any event, the punishment meted out by the Yanukovych regime to its competitors aroused no mass protest in Kharkiv. Yulia Tymoshenko, who had been preparing to don the mantle of opposition leader, was imprisoned in a Kharkiv jail, and her associate Arsen Avakov, having lost the mayoral election to Hennadii Kernes, was compelled to emigrate. He only managed to return to Ukraine in 2012, protected by his status of newly elected deputy to the Supreme Rada. Yulia Tymoshenko was not released until the Revolution of Dignity in 2014.

In the words of Serhii Zhadan, a well-known Ukrainian-language writer and community activist in Kharkiv, the city found itself "on the front line of a new domestic and foreign policy."⁵ Tatiana Zhurzhenko has described the new political regime as an "authoritarian backlash,"⁶ while Oleksii Vedrov identifies it as an "effective power vertical," having in mind the "nonconflictual tandem of Dobkin-Kernes, who ruled the oblast and the city," with the power structures of both city and oblast fully subordinated to them.⁷

There was in fact nothing new in this model. It was based on the principles of the late Soviet "administrative command system," which combined populist rhetoric with authoritarianism. A relatively new addition to it was the de facto legalization of mafia-style business, which was controlled by representatives of the power structures in league with the mob. Local society, used to a patrimonial model of political culture, did not have far to look for examples: they had been successfully tested in neighboring Russia.

The ideological basis for such a model was also exported to Ukraine from Russia. The local establishment marched toward the future under the banners of

Slavo-Orthodox fundamentalism and the cult of the Great Victory in World War II. Hennadii Kernes, "a charismatic politician and Jewish gangster"[8] who ruled the city for a decade as mayor and rejoiced in an unprecedented degree of support from Kharkivites, may be considered the most striking symbol of such a policy in Kharkiv.

Undoubtedly it was all these factors that compelled the aforementioned Serhii Zhadan to declare that "the myth of a scientific and cultural capital, of a city of students and industrial giants, cultivated by generations of Kharkivites" had hardly stood the test of time.[9] Its place was taken by a traditional mythology whose elements may be found in the official hymn of Kharkiv oblast, adopted in 2010. Its text includes mentions of the "Sloboda region," which has Cossack roots and is under the protection of the Orthodox icon of the Mother of God traditionally associated with Ozeriany in Kharkiv oblast. Freedom and prosperity also figure in the hymn, but there is no direct mention of Ukraine, which is only hinted at in a reference to the "yellow and blue colors of the state flag."[10]

The Ukrainian language of the hymn pales somewhat, given the adoption in 2012 of a language law (known as the Kivalov-Kolesnychenko law), according to which six southeastern oblasts, including Kharkiv oblast, and nine city councils, including that of Kharkiv, gave Russian the official status of a regional language.[11] The Russian language became the main vehicle for communicating to Ukraine the new Russian identity discourse elaborated by the Kremlin. Neither the central nor the local authorities of Ukraine even considered the possibility of promoting Ukrainian identity by means of the Russian language or the Russian imperial heritage.

## The "Russian World"

The Little Russian component of local identity policy was well adapted to the discourse of the Russian World (*Russkii mir*), which became the basis of the policy adopted by Vladimir Putin's regime in the "near abroad." It was based on the idea of a triune Russian Orthodox people consisting of Great Russians, Little Russians, and Belarusians. This concept was not new but borrowed from the ideological legacy of the type of Russian imperial nationalism associated with the reactionary Black Hundred movement of the early twentieth century. In its revival at the beginning of the twenty-first century, this ideology was combined successfully with the historical legacy of Stalinism and the mythology of the Great Victory. The only unchanging element was the active role of the Russian Orthodox Church in the domestic and foreign policy of the Russian state.

Kharkiv's official identity policy may be said to have been purged of any hint of ambivalence. It was being radicalized, succumbing increasingly to the influence of contemporary Russian nationalist doctrine. As had previously been the case in

Kharkiv's history, the city was assigned a special role in the geopolitical doctrine of the "gathering of historical Russian lands" under Moscow.[12] After Viktor Yanukovych took office as president, the idea of the "Sloboda Ukraine Euroregion" fell out of favor. If Kharkiv's role had previously been defined by the Soviet paradigm of the "friendship of peoples" or the rhetoric of a bridge between "fraternal" peoples," those symbols were now replaced by the idea of Kharkiv as the "capital of Russian culture" *in* Ukraine. That idea was proclaimed in 2010 at a Russo-Ukrainian conference on the Treaty of Pereiaslav (1654), which was attended by representatives of the Kharkiv Oblast State Administration. Kharkiv was thus turning into the main gateway of Russian influence in Ukraine.

Particularly symbolic of the city's new role was the Kharkiv Pact or Kharkiv Accords, which became fundamental to the further development of Ukraine's relations with Russia. This bilateral Russo-Ukrainian agreement, signed in Kharkiv on 21 April 2010, extended Russia's lease of its military naval base at Sevastopol in the Crimea for twenty-five years beyond its original expiry date of 2017. In exchange, Ukraine was granted a reduction in the price of Russian natural gas. According to a Ukrainian expert, Admiral Ihor Kabanenko, "This was a heavy blow to Ukraine's strategic national interests, while Russia's Navy, made up of many warships, aircraft, marines, reconnaissance and support units, could now be deployed on Ukrainian territory for a long period of time just as, under the original lease agreement, it was supposed to begin withdrawing from the Crimea."[13] The agreement was decried by the Ukrainian political opposition to the Yanukovych regime as a "new Treaty of Pereiaslav," a reference to a fateful meeting in 1654 at which Ukraine's Cossack leader, Bohdan Khmelnytsky, submitted to the protection of the Muscovite tsar.

Following the visit of senior Russian political leaders to Kharkiv, it was time for a representative of the Orthodox hierarchy to follow suit. A "pastoral visit" to Donetsk and Kharkiv by Kirill, Patriarch of Moscow and All Russia, in 2011 was formally timed to coincide with the sixtieth birthday of Metropolitan Ilarion of Donetsk and Mariupol and the ninetieth birthday of Metropolitan Nikodim of Kharkiv and Bohodukhiv. In fact, it was part of the Kremlin's political agenda. On the eve of the patriarch's visit yet another Orthodox marker, a monument to St. Tatiana, was unveiled in the underground passage beneath Liberty Square leading to Kharkiv National University.

Kirill presided over a liturgy in Liberty Square on 8 May, the day before the official state holiday marking the "Great Victory over Fascism." According to the symbolic organization of space accepted by the Orthodox Church, Patriarch Kirill would have had to speak facing the monument to Lenin, whose hand, extended from above, would have pointed toward him. In placing the stand for the liturgy, the organizers were constrained to disregard tradition. In the course of planning, none of the city and oblast leaders ventured to address the question of moving the monument to another location. In any other section of the city, however, that could have been done much more easily.

The ceremony was attended by Russia's ambassador to Ukraine Mikhail Zurabov; Ukraine's deputy prime minister Viktor Tykhonov; the mayor of Kharkiv Hennadii Kernes; the head of the Kharkiv regional state administration Mikhail Dobkin; and the head of the Kharkiv oblast council Serhii Chernov. Patriarch Kirill also took part in a wreath-laying ceremony at the Memorial of Glory in Kharkiv, warning against devaluing the memory of the "Great Patriotic War"[14] by emphasizing the historical unity of Russia, Ukraine, Belarus, and Moldova.

The Russian borderland city of Belgorod was assigned the role of "Russian outpost of Russo-Ukrainian friendship," evoking memories of the Belgorod military line of fortifications erected in the seventeenth century.[15] On 1–2 May 2010 a regional chapter of the World Russian People's Council (*Vsemirnyi russkii narodnyi sobor*), created under the aegis of the Russian Orthodox Church to promote the doctrine of the Russian World around the globe, was formally established in Belgorod. Among the honored guests attending this assembly, besides Patriarch Kirill, the minister of culture of the Russian Federation Aleksandr A. Avdeev, and the governor of Belgorod oblast Yevgenii Savchenko, was the head of Kharkiv oblast Mikhail Dobkin. No statement was released about his role at the assembly, but it was probably no accident that shortly afterward the Russian government announced its intention to establish five offices of the Russian World in Kharkiv to propagate the Kremlin's geopolitical doctrine.[16] Even without those offices there would have been no lack of individuals willing to pave the way for the advent of Russia, beginning with communists and Orthodox priests and ending with corrupt representatives of power structures.

Dozens of Russian and pro-Russian organizations existed legally in Kharkiv, ranging from cultural and religious bodies to sports and paramilitary associations.[17] Among them were Triune Rus' (*Rus' triedinaia*), the Russian Assembly (*Russkoe Veche*), Cossack organizations, and even a branch of the Black Hundred Union of the Russian People (*Soiuz Russkogo Naroda*).[18] Beginning in 2008, activists of the latter organization initiated a series of measures designed to incorporate Kharkiv into the symbolic space of the Russian World, including prayer services, cross-bearing processions, and the erection of crosses and memorial monuments. Through their efforts, a heroic cult of the White Guard began to be resurrected in the Kharkiv region, drawing a response from part of the local intelligentsia. In 2011, not far from Kharkiv, in the village of Kochetok in the Chuhuiv district (raion), a cross was ceremonially raised to the memory of Denikinites who died in battle attempting to take Kharkiv in 1919.[19] The cross was placed beside an Orthodox church with the blessing of Metropolitan Nikodim of Kharkiv and Bohodukhiv.

The most ominous pro-Russian organization in Kharkiv was the paramilitary sports club *Oplot* (Bastion), established by the former policeman Yevgenii Zhilin. The official purpose of *Oplot* was to assist the families of deceased policemen, but it was actually intended to support the policy of integrating the borderland into the Russian sphere of influence and do the dirty work of powerful Kharkiv businessmen. According to Taras Kuzio, *Oplot* was the most aggressive of the paramilitary pro-Russian vigilante groups.[20] Without the direct or indirect support of the local authorities, that organization could hardly have established a ramified network of businesses as well as informational and judicial structures in such a short time, to say nothing of recruiting several hundred (if not several thousand) trained fighters who later joined the army of the Donetsk separatists.

## *The Russian Discourse of "Southeastern Ukraine"*

The history of the Sloboda region underwent gradual de-Ukrainization in Russian national discourse. In 2011 historians from Belgorod National University quickly prepared a new regional narrative for publication in the form of a student textbook entitled *The History of the Sloboda and Belgorod Regions*.[21] It was issued at the initiative and under the patronage of the oblast governor Yevgenii Savchenko, with the participation of some Kharkiv historians. In general, this methodologically eclectic text is an interesting illustration of the direction in which current Russian historiography is evolving under the influence of neoimperial nationalist doctrine.

As we see, the word "Ukraine" does not appear in the title of this book. The Sloboda region is presented in the text as an age-old element of the Russian state and historical Orthodox space. According to one of the authors, "The whole history of the Belgorod and Sloboda regions was marked by marvelous signs of divine grace."[22] With regard to the ethnic identity of the inhabitants of the Sloboda region, however, the Russian authors take different approaches. One approach is clearly influenced by the Soviet paradigm of the "friendship of peoples," according to which Russians and Ukrainians are different but "fraternal" ethnicities. Another is based on the old imperial/Orthodox ideologeme of the triune Russian people, consisting of Russians, Ukrainians, and Belarusians. Finally, a third echoes Lev Gumilev's doctrine of passionary ethnicities, which is fashionable in Russia. All of them are meant to denationalize the Ukrainian population of the Russian borderland.

Some of the authors engage in regional fragmentation of Ukrainian ethnicity, from which (to take one example) a distinct sub-ethnos of *khokhly* is artificially split off because it supposedly has a language, mentality, and culture of its own.[23] Others imagine a new Sloboda nation of up to five million people. It supposedly consists of various ethnicities and, curiously enough, bears a distinct resemblance to the "single historical community—the Soviet people."[24] A nineteenth-century Ukrainian poet from Kharkiv, Yakiv Shchoholiv, is presented as an example of this Sloboda nation.

These ideas were creatively adopted and disseminated by some Kharkiv authors. For example, a conference entitled "510 Years of Unity" was organized in Kharkiv on 19 December 2013 by the Russian nationalist organization Triune Rus' with the participation of the Russian consulate general and the video channel *Pervaia stolitsa* (First capital), headed by the aforementioned Konstantin Kevorkian, who was then a deputy of Kharkiv city council.[25] The keynote address was given by Vladimir Alekseev, a deputy of the Kharkiv oblast council and former deputy of the Supreme Rada of Ukraine. Reflected in his remarks were basic clichés of Russian propaganda that denied the existence of a distinct Ukrainian people, propagated the notion of a separate "Sloboda sub-ethnos," and revised the boundaries of the Ukrainian state.

Alekseev asserted that

> in social consciousness, Ukraine is understood as the territory of the Ukrainian SSR and its current successor. According to the decision of the Pereiaslav Council [of 1654], however, it was the lands controlled by Hetman Bohdan-Zinovii Khmelnytsky that entered the corpus of the Russian state, and they were only 10–12 percent of the territory of today's Ukraine—part of the territories of present-day Poltava, Sumy, Kyiv, and Chernihiv oblasts. All the rest of Ukrainian territory is, without exaggeration, the fruit of the victories of Russian arms, the art of Russian diplomacy and, as the saying goes, gifts of the 'elder brother' presented in the Soviet period of the history of the homeland.[26]

The author enumerates these "gifts" in the following passage:

> Nor should we forget that the Donetsk-Kryvyi Rih Republic was liquidated thanks to V[ladimir] Lenin, as a result of which the industrial regions of the Donbas and the lands along the Dnipro became part of Ukraine: the Bolsheviks understood that without a proletariat, agrarian Ukraine would find itself in great difficulty. J[oseph] Stalin, as is well known, "presented" Galicia, Volhynia, Transcarpathia, and Northern Bukovyna to the Ukrainian SSR, and N[ikita] Khrushchev sliced off the Crimea as well.[27]

Clearly, by Alekseev's logic, the Kharkiv region was also "presented" to Ukraine by the Bolsheviks in 1917–18. In the course of this territory's historical existence, "there were in fact three attempts on the part of the West to tear the Kharkiv region away from the Russian World, to drive the Russian language and culture out of that region, and such actions were always initiated under foreign patronage, plunging Kharkivites into the abyss of misfortune and privation. And they invariably ended in failure."[28]

I have not cited this fragment of an address by a Russian nationalist, Ukrainian by citizenship, accidentally. First, his text literally coincides with one that appeared on a Russian literary portal in 2014 but was signed by a different author, one Vladimir Bugar.[29] Second, the basic theses of this text, which somehow has different authors, find their reflection in the article of yet another "historian," although it appeared seven years after Bugar's publication. The name of this author was unknown among professional historians, although it was better known outside their milieu.

He is Vladimir Putin, the author of an article on the "unassimilable and inseparable" identity of Ukrainians and Russians published on the site of the president of Russia in 2021.³⁰ It contains everything that appears in the texts of his numerous predecessors, beginning with Petr Valuev, with the obvious exception of the "Sloboda region sub-ethnos," which is doubtless hard to descry from the Kremlin towers. The question remains whether all these texts actually have a single source or whether the ideas of Orthodox imperial nationalism have so pervaded Russian society as to encompass all its social strata, "from lord to servant."

The basic priority of the post-Soviet local authorities in Kharkiv and oblast has always been to privatize resources. Under the new regime that priority has expressed itself in somewhat more civilized forms than at the start of the thieving 1990s, but its content has not changed in principle. The symbolic capital of the Soviet legacy was exchanged for new capital formed under the influence of competing Russian and Ukrainian discourses of national identity. Privatization, both legal and illegal, was accompanied by changes in the cultural landscape of the city.

One of the most significant Soviet-era monuments, dedicated to fighters for Soviet rule and erected in 1977 on Constitution Square in the historical center of the city, may serve as an example.³¹ This monument (popularly known by the ironic designation of "five men coming out of a pawnshop") was moved from its location in 2012 during preparations for the European football tournament under the pretext of renovating the city center. It was to be relocated to one of the city's industrial quarters. Protests raised by communists did not prevent the move, perhaps because the authorities simultaneously removed a monument to Ukrainian independence, erected in 2001, from a neighboring square (dedicated to Rosa Luxemburg). That removal also aroused no protests from the citizenry, as the monument in honor of Ukrainian independence would now take the place of the one to fighters for Soviet rule. But there was a catch: it would do so not in its original form but in a new one.

The new independence monument became known officially as "Flying Ukraine." It represents the figure of a winged woman, similar to the ancient Greek goddess Nike, holding a branch of laurel and flying over the globe. According to former president Viktor Yanukovych, who officially unveiled it in 2012, "the monument symbolizes our fathers' long-standing hope for freedom; our centuries-long striving for independence. At the same time, it symbolizes the aspiration and will of present-day Ukrainians to strive for new achievements and victories."³² But it would be hard for any observer to interpret the meaning of the monument in this way, as its design contains no recognizable Ukrainian national symbols at all. Instead, its style bears a striking resemblance to a statue of Jesus Christ atop a globe that stands a couple of hundred meters away, hidden in the courtyard of the Holy Protection Monastery of the Russian Orthodox Church.

Another example of post-Soviet iconoclasm is the story of Glory Way (*Aleia Slavy*), which commemorated Komsomol underground heroes of the Great Patriotic War. Located in the city center alongside Kharkiv's most popular recreation area, known as Mirror Stream (*Dzerkal'nyi strumin'*), this monument was long targeted by the new administration. In 2013 the monument was destroyed, and a huge Russian Orthodox church was built at the end of Glory Way. The protests of citizens were ignored. Ukrainian nationalists had earlier attempted to mark this corner with a memorial stone in honor of the heroes of Kruty, a symbol of the Ukrainian National Revolution of 1917-20. The stone toppled in 2007 and was not replaced. Thus, Soviet symbolism of the Great Patriotic War was reinvented in the spirit of the new Russian mythology of the Great Victory and, as such, appeared to be compatible with the new imperial/Orthodox discourse.

As noted in the preceding chapter, the Kharkiv authorities actively employed "anti-fascist" discourse in their struggle against Ukrainian nationalism, beginning in the years immediately following the Orange Revolution of 2004. With the coming to power of the Dobkin-Kernes tandem, that discourse gained even stronger support at every level. It stigmatized "any form of Ukrainian nationalism as 'fascism' and reduce[d] any anti-Soviet activity to 'collaboration with the Nazis.' Starting in late 2013, this 'anti-fascist' discourse proved to be an especially powerful instrument of anti-Ukrainian mobilization."[33]

In 2013 there was even a military parade in Kharkiv in honor of Victory Day, 9 May—something that citizens probably had not seen since the end of World War II itself. There was a mass installation of memorial plaques on 117 buildings in which Heroes of the Soviet Union had lived. By contrast, the issue of installing a plaque in memory of a Kharkivite, the well-known Ukrainian philologist and Columbia University professor Yurii (George) Shevelov, gave rise to a battle royal. The Kharkiv city administration initially gave permission to install the plaque toward the end of 2013 but soon reversed its decision. The basis for this was an accusation of collaborationism against Shevelov, as he had worked with the newspaper *Nova Ukraïna* (New Ukraine), published in Kharkiv during the war with the permission of the German occupation authorities. A plaque installed by Ukrainian activists two days before the official inauguration was smashed and taken down by individuals acting on behalf of the local administration. This action produced a wave of protest far beyond the borders of Ukraine. Following the events of 2014, the Kharkiv Administrative Court of Appeal confirmed that the plaque had been installed legally and gave permission for its replacement, but that has not been carried out to date.

The fact that Kharkiv's symbolic space has become a political bargaining chip is also attested by a similar story involving a plaque in honor of Yosyp Slipy, a major archbishop of the Ukrainian Greek Catholic Church and a cardinal of the Catholic Church. Compared with the case of Shevelov, that of Slipy offered much greater scope for accusations of collaborationism. After the war that was the basic charge leading to his incarceration in Soviet labor camps and prisons, including the Kharkiv transfer prison, for eighteen years. A memorial plaque in his honor was installed in Kharkiv in 2005 during a convention of the Ukrainian World Congress. It was vandalized by persons unknown in 2008, replaced, and vandalized again in 2010. Nevertheless, when Mayor Andrii Sadovy of Lviv visited Kharkiv in early 2011, the plaque was reinstalled with the permission of the civic authorities. Communist protests were no obstacle to this.

The public space of Kharkiv was by no means a constant battleground between competing symbols of identity. It repeatedly gave way to the pressure of commercialization, which imprinted it with the aesthetic tastes of the "new Russians"—a particular category of nouveaux riches often associated with the criminal milieu. Liberty Square, which has been mentioned repeatedly in this book and will be mentioned again, most often became the location of periodic markets or amusements and attractions of every kind.[34] To the accompaniment of a loudspeaker and television screen mounted on an old Kharkiv hotel, one kitschy diversion succeeded another: chambers of comedy or horror, carousels and skating rinks, tents with goods of every description, Russian *matrioshkas* (nesting dolls), Easter eggs, and sand sculptures. It seemed that on a square meant to incarnate the idea of modernity, the old Kharkiv bazaar of the times of Kvitka and Hulak-Artemovsky was coming back to life.

Commercialization totally changed the cultural landscape of the two most popular places of recreation in Kharkiv, Gorky Park and Shevchenko Park. In May 2010 Kharkiv city council approved the building of a highway cutting through Gorky Park, which involved the felling of hundreds of trees and opened up the zone of recreation to the prospective construction of high-priced apartment buildings. According to the calculations of the Pechenihy ecological group, more than 1,500 trees were cut down in order to clear a path for the highway, although the figure announced had been 503. The monument honoring the proletarian writer for whom the park had been named was of course taken down, this time with no protest of any kind. It was replaced with the image of a squirrel. No less eloquent was the transformation of Shevchenko Park, where a plethora of commercial structures made their appearance along with a fountain in the form of a moving orchestra of monkeys that may be considered one of the most striking examples of the new cultural style of the former proletarian capital.

Commercial bacchanalia, not ideology, seemed to be the factor that united the demoralized Kharkiv opposition. It was led not by political parties but by sprouts of civil society.[35] A group of activists established the Green Front to protect the recreational zone of Gorky Park and was joined by other organizations. Among them were quite a few participants in the Orange Revolution of 2004, both left- and right-wing, Russian-speaking and Ukrainian-speaking. A small tent city, supported by local residents, sprang up in the park. Kharkiv mountain climbers nested in the trees to prevent them from being cut down. Flash mobs in Kyiv and Lviv supported the protesters.

It proved impossible to prevent the commercial reconstruction of Gorky Park, which was effectively protected by *titushky* dressed in municipal uniforms. These were illegal formations of thugs actively employed by the local and central authorities against any form of opposition. Nevertheless, ecological protest rather quickly took on a political character. It exposed a shocking level of corruption enveloping not only the administration but also the law enforcement agencies, the police first and foremost, as shown by events involving the park. It also showed that neither the local nor the central authorities had a political strategy based on the priority of national interests, nor any room to maneuver between competing Ukrainian and Russian national projects and symbols. When forced to choose one side or the other, the regime quickly became bogged down in contradictions and susceptible to increasing Russian influence.[36]

As Peter Dickinson notes,

> Before the political crisis that erupted in the winter of 2013–14, Kharkiv appeared to be the ideal place to mount political opposition to Kyiv-based nationalism. The political leaders of the oblast (Mykhailo Dobkin) and city (Hennadii Kernes) were known to be loyal allies of Yanukovych and openly pro-Russian; they also maintained intensive contacts with their Russian counterparts, not only in Moscow but also in neighboring Belgorod and even in the more distant Chechen capital, Grozny. Their politics were becoming ever more compatible with the official Kremlin "Russian World" discourse and "Great Fatherland War" mythology.... No other Ukrainian city outside of Crimea looked to be quite as firmly rooted in the "Russian World."[37]

And that was exactly the place where the fate of Ukraine would be decided at the beginning of 2014.

## Turning Point 2014

### *Russian Discourses about Ukraine*

The Russian information campaign intended to federalize Ukraine was initially deployed to the accompaniment of the Revolution of Dignity in 2014, as the Yanukovych regime gradually lost control of the political situation in the capital and particular regions.[38] The campaign began under the slogan of the "Little Russianization" of Ukraine. At the beginning of 2014, Russian nationalist organizations in Sevastopol raised the prospect of establishing a "federative state of Little Russia oriented toward Russia" on the basis of the southeastern and central oblasts of Ukraine.[39]

Until then, the historical mythology of Sevastopol, which had the reputation of a hero city in Russo-Soviet discourse, had never been associated with "Little Russia." The significance of this unexpected escapade was revealed on 23 February, when the scandalous Russian politician Vladimir Zhirinovsky, speaking at a meeting of the Liberal Democratic Party of Russia, called for the formation of a new Little Russian state in the eastern oblasts of Ukraine, with its capital in Kharkiv.[40] Zhirinovsky also announced that units of Russian "volunteers" were already prepared for dispatch to Kharkiv to render assistance to the "fraternal people."

The use of "Little Russian" discourse to provide ideological justification of Russian aggression was short-lived. Its development was outpaced by events on the ground. After the annexation of the Crimea, Russian strategists decided to replace that discourse with a "New Russian" one. None other than President Vladimir Putin had recourse to history, announcing that the "southeastern" oblasts of Ukraine were in fact "New Russia," which the Bolsheviks had allegedly transferred to Soviet Ukraine, "God alone knows why."[41] Some Russian historians hastened to create a "New Russian" historical narrative in response to this political conjuncture,[42] but the "New Russia" discourse remained poorly conceptualized.[43]

It soon became apparent even to nationally committed Russian authors that the allegedly united Ukrainian southeast has a composite structure.[44] The Russian nationalist Oleg Nemensky found himself constrained to admit that the southern and eastern oblasts of Ukraine "have no particular self-awareness, no national thinking, and no local patriotic elites. They are simply territories insufficiently involved in the process of building a united Ukrainian nation."[45] Obviously, "New Russia" was never coterminous with the whole territory of "South Russia," even in its broad version. Kharkiv and the Sloboda region had never belonged to historical New Russia, but without Kharkiv, as Peter Dickinson points out, there would be no New Russia as Putin conceived it.[46] Curiously, Putin's propagandists did not make use of the well-known and nationally ambiguous "Sloboda" discourse in order to bring Kharkiv into the "Novorossiia geopolitical adventurism," as Marlene Laruelle calls it.[47]

Even more important was the nature of Putin's "New Russia" simulacrum, which bore only a superficial resemblance to the initial Russian imperial project under that name. The latter was a product of inclusive Enlightenment-era westernization, while the former became a manifestation of exclusive Russian nationalism in the spirit of Anton Denikin's White Army, also known as the Armed Forces of South Russia (*Vooruzhennye Sily Iuga Rossii*). It was no accident that the Russian ex-KGB officer Igor Girkin (alias Strelkov), one of the most active military commanders of pro-Russian separatists in the Donbas in 2014 and a fanatical nationalist, was known as a reenactor who reimagined and presented himself as an officer of the White Army.[48]

After the first salvos on Independence Square (Maidan) in Kyiv at the beginning of 2014, Kharkiv prepared to take over the functions of an alternate capital of Ukraine. With more than three thousand lawmakers of all levels of government gathered in Kharkiv from the southern and eastern oblasts of Ukraine, including Sevastopol and the Autonomous Republic of the Crimea, they awaited only the president and the speaker of the Supreme Rada of Ukraine, who were already hastening there from Kyiv. Russia was represented by the head of the Russian parliamentary commission on foreign affairs, Aleksei Pushkov, his counterpart in the Russian Federation Council, Mikhail Markelov, and the governors of Russian oblasts bordering Ukraine: Yevgenii Savchenko from Belgorod, Aleksandr Gordeev from Voronezh, and Nikolai Denin from Briansk. Russia's consul general in Kharkiv also attended the gathering as an "observer."

As they sought an ideological basis for their political and national federalism, the organizers of the gathering did not refer to any of the existing regional discourses (Little Russian, New Russian, or Slobodian). Instead, they found that basis in the Russian "Great Victory" discourse. The gathering represented a new political alliance, the Ukrainian Front, established by the Party of Regions slightly earlier, on 1 February 2014, in Kharkiv. It evoked associations with the Great Patriotic War discourse: in 1943 the Steppe Front of the Red Army under the command of General Ivan Konev, which liberated Kharkiv from the Nazis, was renamed the Second Ukrainian Front, and the Voronezh Front led by General Nikolai Vatutin was renamed the First Ukrainian Front. The enormous hall of the Kharkiv Sports Palace, where the gathering took place, was decorated with a symbol of "invented tradition," the St. George Ribbon, introduced by Putin's regime in Russia and accepted by pro-Russian institutions and movements in the "Near Abroad." Incidentally or not, the gathering took place on the eve of one of the most popular Soviet holidays, the Day of the Soviet Army and Navy (23 February).

The Ukrainian Front, led by "Private" Mikhail Dobkin and his associates, announced plans to liberate Ukraine from unspecified enemies in the tradition of their wartime forefathers. There was no need to identify those enemies, as every member of the new organization "knew" that they were Ukrainian nationalists. Kharkiv was to be the starting point for the "liberation" of all Ukraine from "Ukrainian fascism." To that end the organizers initiated the formation of military units recruited from members of *Oplot*, Russian Cossacks, Afghan War veterans, Russian state-sponsored bikers belonging to the "Night Wolves," and various quasi-sport clubs.[49] These units were expected to take control of all administrative buildings in the oblasts of "southeastern" Ukraine.

The Ukrainian president Viktor Yanukovych and his entourage flew to Kharkiv in two helicopters.[50] He was accompanied by Volodymyr Rybak, who chaired Ukraine's parliament, the Supreme Rada, and by Andrii Kliuiev, head of the Presidential Administration, along with twenty-one bodyguards.[51] Yanukovych's spokespersons tried to assure everyone that it was an ordinary trip by the president to meet his constituents. In fact, given the tense political atmosphere in Ukraine, such assurances sounded like a mockery of common sense, and Yanukovych's hasty departure from Kyiv for Kharkiv—that is, from the Ukrainian capital to its "rival capital" bordering on Russia—took on sinister connotations. Ukraine seemed to be reliving the political rift of the Orange Revolution of 2004 or perhaps even of 1917.[52] It was not clear at the time whether the organizers of the anti-Maidan "counteroffensive" were going to proclaim the independence of the southeastern region or stay within Ukrainian political space.

Yanukovych himself appeared to deliver the first heavy blow to the idea of southeastern political autonomy under a Russian protectorate. Having arrived in Kharkiv, he unexpectedly changed his plans. Instead of going to meet representatives of the Ukrainian Front and Russian emissaries on the afternoon of 22 February, his cortege headed for the airport. An hour later his two helicopters landed in Donetsk. After that Yanukovych, already stripped of his presidential prerogatives, fled to Russia and ended up in Rostov-on-the-Don. Many details of this Hollywood-like scenario still remain a mystery. There are various explanations of Yanukovych's erratic behavior, none of which seems convincing.[53] In all likelihood, the organizers of the Ukrainian Front were taken by surprise. And so, after the untimely conclusion of their meeting, none of its confused leaders even went to meet their supporters, who were waiting outside the Sports Palace.

"Both the city's Mayor and Governor were caught with their pants down" when the Revolution of Dignity (Euromaidan) succeeded in Kyiv.[54] Both of them hastily fled to Russia, presumably to Belgorod or Grozny, where they stayed for several days. But the duo realized very quickly that Kharkiv businessmen turned politicians were hardly likely to be of interest to anyone in the Kremlin in the role of political immigrants. Whatever their motives, Kernes and Dobkin returned to Ukraine, where they parted ways. Hennadii Kernes made a deal with the new authorities and remained mayor of Kharkiv until his death in 2020. Mikhail Dobkin decided to challenge the authorities and, after a brief arrest on charges of "inciting separatism," ran for the Ukrainian presidency in the election of 25 May 2014, obtaining about 3 percent of the vote.

At this point, the political standoff in Ukraine entered a phase of outright armed conflict between pro-Ukrainian and pro-Russian forces. The Russian leadership engaged the mechanism of annexation of Ukrainian territory, employing secret services and armed pro-Russian groupings financed by it. Thousands of so-called volunteers were brought to Kharkiv from Belgorod oblast and other Russian territories to mix with the local population and take initiatives in its name. According to Taras Kuzio, some of them were trained and paid by Russian military and intelligence agencies: "'Igor,' a vigilante in Kharkiv ... admitted to being paid by these Russian agents $40 per hour to beat up 'fascists.'"[55]

The aforementioned Arsen Avakov, formerly Ukraine's minister of internal affairs and an active participant in the Revolution of Dignity, has made public secret documents attesting to an operation planned in detail by Russian special services to seize Kharkiv and proclaim it a "people's republic" together with analogous "republics" in Odesa, Donetsk, and other cities in eastern Ukraine. The plan provided for the seizure of communications, strategic infrastructure, and mass media, as well as the employment of local collaborators and the physical elimination of representatives of the Ukrainian administration and military.[56] Notably, in the new Russian discourse, the old Soviet rhetoric of "friendship of peoples" was given short shrift in favor of the nationalist rhetoric of "gathering Russian (*russkie*) lands." Kharkiv played a very important role in changing the political and symbolic geography of the Russo-Ukrainian borderland.

The flight of Yanukovych and his supporters did not significantly change the political situation in Kharkiv, where the enthusiasm of Euromaidan activists proved premature. The city became a battleground between Ukrainian and Russian nationalists: the former were represented by the right-radical organizations Patriot of Ukraine (*Patriot Ukraïny*) and Right Sector (*Pravyi sektor*) and opposed by the much more numerous and better organized fighters of *Oplot*. At first the pro-Russian groups, twice as large as their Ukrainian counterparts, managed to seize the oblast administration building and declare a "Kharkiv People's Republic" in the spring of 2014. Their representatives, whose names were unfamiliar to the public at large, appealed for help to Viktor Yanukovych and the Russian government, but it was already obvious that their initiative lacked political leadership. It was the weakness of the Ukrainian authorities, not the strength of the pro-Russian separatists, that accounted for the short-lived success of the latter.

Local law enforcement officers appeared unreliable. Almost all the high-ranking officers of the police and the Security Service of Ukraine in Kharkiv were Kernes-Dobkin appointees. In addition, many members of the local riot police unit, Berkut, harbored anti-Maidan and openly pro-Russian feelings. They brazenly sabotaged the orders of the newly appointed interior minister, Arsen Avakov, and stood by passively as Russian nationalists beat and humiliated the Ukrainian Euromaidan activists and destroyed the premises of the local ATN television channel.[57] According to Yaroslav Hrytsak, "The pro-Russian sympathies of the local administrative and industrial elites were allegedly stronger here than anywhere else, including Donetsk."[58] The new Ukrainian authorities did not have reliable forces in Kharkiv other than a few hundred unarmed cadets at the Internal Forces Academy and individual police detachments that proved unable to hold off the mob and the separatists.

This time, however, Ukraine managed to avoid the scenario of 1917, when Kharkiv was declared the capital of Soviet Ukraine, while Kyiv became the capital of the Ukrainian People's Republic under the leadership of the Central Rada. Kharkiv was saved by a Jaguar special forces squad quartered in the village of Kalynivka near Vinnytsia, more than seven hundred kilometers from Kharkiv.[59] It must be acknowledged that the members of the Jaguar contingent, like the forces of other power structures, were enraged by the actions of the former political authorities, whom they blamed for making scapegoats of them. Relatives of the Jaguar force blocked its dispatch to Kharkiv for an hour and a half until they yielded to the persuasions of its commander, Yurii Allierov, and dispersed. In the end Jaguar followed orders and left for Kharkiv in a complement of two hundred men.

By that time the building of the Oblast State Administration had already been occupied by pro-Russian separatists. The authorities planned to retake it on the morning of 8 April with a force of four hundred to five hundred men, including local power structures, but the latter ignored orders. The operation, which lasted about twenty minutes, was therefore carried out by Jaguar alone. Kharkiv policemen and Berkut riot police appeared only after the operation ended but were immediately withdrawn at the first sign of possible conflict between them and the Jaguar contingent. The new Ukrainian government thus took control of the situation in Kharkiv.

Close to three hundred of the most active Kharkiv separatists were arrested. Most of them, according to Taras Kuzio, were members of *Oplot* and "volunteers" brought in from Russia. Armed formations of Ukrainian and Russian nationalists soon left Kharkiv to take up positions in the Donbas. The former created the well-known Azov battalion (later regiment), commanded by Oleksandr Biletsky, which distinguished itself in the liberation of the city of Mariupol,[60] while the latter formed an elite unit led by the self-styled prime minister Oleksandr Zakharchenko of the "Donetsk People's Republic."[61] *Oplot* fighters from Kharkiv played an active role in seizing the Donetsk city hall.

Kharkiv remained an arena of acute confrontation between pro-Russian and Ukrainian forces until approximately the beginning of 2015. Until then, a few dozen pro-Russian terrorist groups, one of which called itself the Kharkiv Partisans, were active in the city and oblast. They carried out dozens of acts of sabotage and murder in the Kharkiv region.[62] In April 2014 there was an attempt on the life of Mayor Hennadii Kernes, probably organized by members of *Oplot*. In the autumn of that year, a bomb injured eleven people at a Kharkiv pub belonging to an activist of the volunteer movement who was helping the Ukrainian Army.[63] In February 2015 four people were killed and nine wounded at the hands of pro-Russian terrorists during a pro-Ukrainian demonstration near the Kharkiv Sports Palace. The situation in Kharkiv was stabilized only after the Ukrainian authorities managed to consolidate their rule and the power structures finally began to show understanding of the need to protect national interests.

In the course of 2014–15, the "Russian Spring" in Kharkiv turned back into "Winter." The colors of the Russian flag became practically invisible in the city's symbolic landscape: more blue-and-yellow shades appeared in it than ever before, but the green color of the city council remained dominant. It is notable that the two main forces engaged in the battle for Kharkiv were represented by relatively small groups of activists numbering a few hundred on each side, while most city dwellers remained neutral or indifferent.[64] For them, being pro-Kharkiv or neutral turned out to be more important than being pro-Russian or even pro-Ukrainian.[65] According to recent sociological polls, Kharkiv was the city registering the greatest degree of satisfaction with living in one's hometown (close to 90 percent).[66]

## Sloboda Ukraine after 2014

After Russia's annexation of the Crimea, the eastern and southern regions of Ukraine underwent yet another political reconfiguration.[67] Some analysts have remarked on the disappearance of 'the Southeast' as a common designation of the Russo-Ukrainian border regions.[68] By contrast, a new "Central Ukraine" has begun to take shape between the eastern and western border regions.[69] Finally, the border city of Dnipro, the former Soviet Dnipropetrovsk and Russian imperial Katerynoslav, has acquired new political significance as a symbol of Ukrainian political loyalty and even a new "heart of Ukraine."[70] On the other hand, the former role of Donetsk as the Ukrainian regional center most opposed to official Kyiv was transferred not to Kharkiv but to Odesa, also for a short time.

To be sure, various regional discourses continue to articulate the ongoing symbolic struggle for the Ukrainian-Russian borderland. The self-proclaimed "Donetsk People's Republic," jammed between Ukraine and Russia, feverishly tried to find its own basis for identity. During the "Russian Spring," Donetsk, one of the most Sovietized Ukrainian cities, became the main citadel of Putin's reinvented "New Russia." But the "Confederation of New Russia," solemnly proclaimed in 2014, was quietly dissolved in the following year.[71]

On 5 February 2015 the separatist political entity declared itself the successor to the Donetsk-Kryvyi Rih Soviet Republic (DKR) and called on all other territories, including Kharkiv oblast, to join the "new federal state."[72] Not surprisingly, the main centers of the Ukrainian-Russian borderland, including Kharkiv, Dnipro (formerly Dnipropetrovsk), and Odesa, turned away. The disappearance of the Party of Regions in Ukraine deprived the regional elites of a political platform for joint action.[73] It would appear that none of the models of political autonomism offered to the Ukrainian border elites by Russian political technologists have proved viable in practice.

The idea of historical Little Russia (*Malorossiia*) appeared to be even more fantastic than that of the DKR. It lasted about twenty-four hours after Oleksandr Zakharchenko, the self-proclaimed leader of the "Donetsk People's Republic," announced the formation on 18 July 2017 of another "federal state" named "Little Russia," with its capital in Donetsk.[74] Nowadays, the "Little Russian" discourse seems as dead as Mr. Zakharchenko himself, who was assassinated in 2018. Instead, the Donetsk political leaders finally confirmed their desire to join Russia. It is still unclear what remains, if anything, of the local, Soviet, and Ukrainian identities of that territory.

### *The Sloboda Ukraine Regional Discourse*

"Sloboda Ukraine" discourse no longer fulfilled its main role of being an intermediary between Ukraine and Russia. It appeared to have been sidelined and marginalized, although the idea itself still existed on both sides of the border. On the Ukrainian side members of the Communist Party, banned in Ukraine, attempted to revive it. The leader of the Kharkiv communists, Alla Aleksandrovskaia, created a civic organization called *Slobozhanshchyna* (the Sloboda region) that intended to appeal to the government to grant the Kharkiv region special status under that name.[75] One of the sponsors of that project, whose details remained unknown, was to be the *Vidrodzhennia* (Rebirth) Party, under whose flag former members of the Party of Regions came together. But the project was stillborn. A meeting of its activists was dispersed by Ukrainian nationalists belonging to the Right Sector.

It would appear that the historical Sloboda Ukraine ceased to exist as a transborder region dotted with Ukrainian and Russian settlements.[76] Kharkiv oblast is firmly positioned in Ukrainian political space. At the same time, this space bears the vivid imprint of the Russo-Ukrainian border. Some sociologists consider it part of eastern Ukraine along with the Dnipro and Zaporizhia oblasts.[77] According to others, Kharkiv oblast stands apart from its neighbors.[78] On the political map, Kharkiv finds itself somewhere between Odesa and Dnipro. It would appear that the loyalty of Kharkiv oblast inhabitants to their locality has become strong enough to withstand comparison with their national loyalty.

For that reason, I can hardly agree with the conclusion that already before 2022, "the region of Kharkiv has turned into a fortress, with a defensive wall being built on the border with Russia."[79] Before that year, only 40 percent of the so-called European Wall, intended to present an impregnable barrier to Russian tanks and make visible the symbolic border between Europe and Russia, had been completed.[80] Its defensive and symbolic functions arouse skepticism. From my personal impression of crossing the border, it looked more like a desolate and neglected territory, at least from the Ukrainian side, than an impregnable fortress.

## *Economics*

The "hybrid" war with Russia and its Donbas proxies has again turned Kharkiv and oblast into a militarized borderland, as it was centuries ago. Kharkiv has lost a significant portion of its economic potential as a center of transportation, trade, and industry. The breaking of historical ties with Russia, toward which the local economy was mainly oriented, has been a painful blow to small and medium business. But industrial enterprises whose production was intended for the Russian market have also suffered losses. According to Tomasz Piechal, in 2014 industrial production value in Kharkiv oblast fell by 5.2 percent (the overall decline of production in Ukraine ran at the level of 10.1 percent) and amounted to US $4.6 billion.[81]

At the same time, for several reasons, Kharkivites managed to adapt quite quickly to the new conditions. The city's economy had never been dominated by oligarchic clans to such an extent as those, for example, of Donetsk or Dnipropetrovsk. Accordingly, it was less dependent on political conjuncture and more flexible than those economies. Local tycoons such as the banker and investor Oleksandr Yaroslavsky or the businessman and patron Oleksandr Feldman, who owns the Barabashovo Market, one of the largest on post-Soviet territory, used to emphasize their indifference to "big politics" and presented themselves as local patrons of sports and the arts.[82]

Kharkiv's military-industrial complex managed to find alternative markets elsewhere, mainly in Asia, Latin America, and Africa. Some of the largest factories obtained new state contracts and investments because of the war. This applied primarily to the Malyshev Tank Factory, which became famous in World War II for its production of the T-34 tank, and in the post-Soviet period for a new tank that, in an ironic twist, was given the same name as that of the most odious anti-Ukrainian organization—*Oplot*. As a result, the first signs of renewal became apparent in the Kharkiv economy as early as 2016.[83] One aspect of that process was the growth of service export, more than half of which consists of information technology and telecommunication services.[84]

Economic agreements with the European Union and the arrangement of nonvisa trips to Europe, even short-term ones, created more favorable conditions for Ukrainian labor migrants. Kharkiv obtained direct airline connections with cities in Poland, Germany, and Italy. Beginning in 2014, Poland replaced Russia as the main destination of Ukrainian labor migration.[85] On the other hand, Kharkiv became one of the principal cities of settlement for migrants from the war-torn Donbas. Over the years their numbers varied between 130,000 and 150,000, substantially influencing the labor market and retail prices in the oblast. The political views of the migrants, many of whom remained oriented toward Russia, also could not fail to influence general attitudes in the city and oblast.

## *The Political Landscape*

Neither the failure of the "Russian Spring" in Kharkiv nor the ongoing Russo-Ukrainian "hybrid" war significantly changed Kharkivites' traditional value system. As before, it was dominated by the typical borderland culture of conformity, most often manifested in ambivalence, indifference, and cultural hybridity. Significant numbers of Kharkivites, like residents of other eastern and southern Ukrainian cities, remain nostalgic about Soviet times.[86] Close to 40 percent of the inhabitants of Kharkiv oblast missed the USSR in 2018, a higher figure than the all-Ukrainian norm.[87] This nostalgia found expression in voting for politicians whose rhetoric recalled the Soviet style.

According to polls conducted by the Reitynh sociological group, those most nostalgic for the USSR voted for Yurii Boiko in the presidential elections of 2014.[88] He was the Kharkivites' favorite candidate for president of Ukraine that year, outpolling another opposition politician, the like-minded Vadim Rabinovich, by 2 percent.[89] Soviet nostalgia was accompanied by pro-Russian sympathies. According to Tatiana Zhurzhenko, in spite of the war on the Donbas, almost 80 percent of Kharkivites had a positive attitude toward Russia, as did slightly more than 70.2 percent toward the Russian leadership.[90] The number of those who harbored pro-Soviet and pro-Russian sympathies declined gradually but not substantially before 2022.

The elections of 2015 to the Kharkiv oblast legislature were won decisively by politicians representing the former Party of Regions, which had undergone some cosmetic reorganization.[91] In 2018 the successors to the Party of Regions, the pro-Russian political parties *Za Zhyttia* (For Life) and *Opoblok* (Opposition bloc), remained the most popular among Kharkivites.[92] However, recent presidential (2019) and parliamentary elections in Ukraine produced a hardly predictable political alternative to both the "Soviet/Russian" and the "Ukrainian national" discourses, which lost to a "third force" represented by Volodymyr Zelensky and his Servant of the People Party.

In the first round of the presidential elections in Kharkiv oblast, Zelensky took first place with 36.4 percent of the vote; Yurii Boiko, representing the Opposition Platform–For Life, came second with 26.6 percent; and Petro Poroshenko came third with 8.6 percent.[93] In the second round, on 21 April 2019, Zelensky took 86.88 percent of the vote in Kharkiv oblast to Poroshenko's 11.17 percent.[94] Such a result for an incumbent president could be compared at best, perhaps, to that of Viktor Yushchenko in 2010, when he lost disastrously to Viktor Yanukovych. In the elections to the Supreme Rada of Ukraine on 21 July 2019, the Servant of the People Party won with 42.72 percent of the vote,[95] surpassing its closest competitor, the pro-Russian Opposition Platform–For Life, led by the pro-Kremlin politician Viktor Medvedchuk, which received 26.6 percent.

Nevertheless, local politicians in Kharkiv mostly maintained their control over the city and region.[96] In elections to the Kharkiv oblast council on 25 October 2020, first place went to the Kernes Bloc–Successful Kharkiv! (38.33 percent); second place to the Opposition Platform–For Life (24.17 percent); third and fourth places were divided between the Servant of the People Party and the pro-presidential Svitlychna Bloc "Together!" (14.17 percent); and Poroshenko's European Solidarity received only 9.17 percent.[97] The elections to Kharkiv city council yielded similar results, with Kernes's party doing even better against the other parties and blocs.[98]

The structure of the Kharkiv region's political landscape remained as it had been at the time of the Revolution of Dignity in 2014. The achievement of a compromise between the leadership of the city and the oblast may be considered its main distinguishing feature. While the mayoralty of Kharkiv is elective, the head of the oblast is appointed by Kyiv, but as a rule the center's appointees look more to Kharkiv than to the national capital. As head of his administration, President Petro Poroshenko appointed the Kharkiv media magnate and president of the Jewish Confederation of Ukraine Borys Lozhkin, who held the post in 2014–16. He was replaced by another Kharkiv businessman and politician, Ihor Rainin, who served until 2019. After returning to Kharkiv that year, Rainin headed the Kharkiv oblast branch of the pro-Russian Opposition Platform–For Life. It may be recalled that Rainin's predecessor as head of the presidential administration, Yevgenii Kushnarev, followed a similar political trajectory.

Political observers found that Kharkiv and Odesa shared many similar features. Odesa enjoys the advantages of a port on the Black Sea. Kharkiv, for its part, is something of a port on dry land: its giant Barabashovo Market sells goods from the whole former USSR and neighboring countries. "Both cities generate significant income from their advantageous positions on key trade routes. Too often, these resources have been captured by corrupt local elites with alleged links to the criminal underworld who trade their loyalty to Kyiv in exchange for impunity to continue ripping off their hometowns for private gain."[99] The mayors of the two cities—the late Hennadii Kernes of Kharkiv and incumbent Hennadii Trukhanov of Odesa—not only shared a first name but were businessmen of dubious reputation; both maintained a similar political orientation and enjoyed tremendous support from their citizens.

Hennadii Kernes may be considered the most striking representative of the Kharkiv political elite since 2014. The failure of the "Russian Spring" in Kharkiv and an attempt on his life left Kernes an invalid but had no effect on his political career. On the contrary, it may be said that after 2014 his popularity increased: he handily won the 2015 municipal elections with 65.8 percent of the vote and firmly established himself as the most influential politician not only in Kharkiv but in the oblast as well. In 2018, 75 percent of Kharkivites endorsed his work.[100] No other Ukrainian politician attained such a positive rating at the time. Not surprisingly, Petro Poroshenko, then president of Ukraine, sought a political compromise with Kernes, but he proved too tough a nut to crack even for the new authorities.

Kernes had no political ambitions in the all-Ukrainian arena and was perfectly happy in the role of regional leader. He could therefore afford limited dissent from Kyiv's political line, such as refusing to recognize Russia as the aggressor in the continuing war in the Donbas.[101] Kernes's policy in the realm under his control became more careful than it had been in the times of Yanukovych but did not change substantially. As before, he held to a pro-Russian orientation and steered a course toward reconciliation with the Soviet legacy, as well as further clericalization and commercialization of Kharkiv's public space. It is another matter that holding to such a course in the first years after the victory of the Euromaidan was difficult, mainly because of the radicalization of Ukrainian nation-state building in confrontation with Moscow.

In Kharkiv "the war on communist monuments, which had previously been fought through presidential decrees and the courts, shifted onto the streets."[102] The main target of that war was the gigantic statue of Lenin on Liberty Square, which united both pro-Soviet and pro-Russian sympathizers.[103] After Ukrainian independence, repeated attempts were made to remove the statue, but every time they encountered resistance from local authorities and part of society.[104] In 2014

THE FRONT LINE | 275

**Figure 7.1.** Monument to Lenin, 1964, architect Aleksandr Sidorenko, erected in place of the monument to Stalin. The monument to Lenin was considered the largest in Ukraine. Dismantled in 2014. © Volodymyr Kravchenko, 2011.

**Figure 7.2.** In place of Lenin, what? A failed attempt to replace the monument to Lenin with Ukrainian Orthodox symbolism. © Volodymyr Kravchenko, 2015.

**Figure 7.3.** Overcoming history? Liberty Square. © Mikhail Protsenko, 2018.

the Lenin monument became an epicenter of violent clashes between Maidan and anti-Maidan partisans.[105]

In the autumn of 2014, the situation in Ukraine changed in favor of the new authorities. The Kharkiv police began to act more decisively with regard to pro-Russian separatists. On 27 September they dispersed a meeting of the Communist Party, illegal in Ukraine, that was being held in the center of town. Riding this wave, pro-Ukrainian forces organized a demonstration many thousand strong the following day that brought its participants to the Lenin monument. That same evening radical Ukrainian activists brought down the monument, which proved to be hollow inside and injured no one as it fell. The political resonance of this action, sanctioned by Kyiv after the fact, proved much stronger both in Ukraine and abroad.[106] In 2015 several more statues of Lenin and other communist leaders were toppled by Ukrainian activists.[107]

Mayor Kernes reacted with a public promise to restore the monument as soon as possible, but it is hard to say how sincere he was. In fact, the Kharkiv city fathers tacitly accepted reality and decided to replace the Lenin monument with a huge column crowned with an angel bearing an Orthodox cross. Consciously or not, they oriented themselves toward the precedent of 2012, when the local authorities removed the monument to fighters for Soviet rule on Constitution Square, replacing it with the baroque Nike. This time their action met with energetic protest from local civic activists, who prevented the "clericalization" of Ukraine's constructivist square. The civic authorities finally decided to avoid any symbolism and built a fountain there, putting an end to the issue.

### The "Great Victory" Discourse

Compared with the mythology of the Great October, which only a handful of communists were prepared to defend, that of the "Great Victory" in World War II proved much stronger, obtaining powerful support from the Russian side. It was this mythology that became one of the principal components of the local authorities' identity politics in the post-revolutionary era. A true war of symbols broke out around the monument to Georgii Zhukov, a principal Soviet military commander in World War II, and the avenue named after him. A cult of Zhukov developed in post-Soviet Russia and was exported to Ukraine. In Kharkiv, an avenue previously named after the sixtieth anniversary of the proclamation of the USSR was renamed in honor of Zhukov. A monument to him was erected on the same avenue in 2013.

In 2016 the name of the avenue was changed in memory of Petro Hryhorenko, a Soviet general turned dissident. The city council responded by reinstating Zhukov's name in June 2019. Ukrainian activists, for their part, reacted by removing the Zhukov monument, but the civic authorities reinstalled it the following month. In September 2019 the Kharkiv administrative court canceled the city council's decision and restored Petro Hryhorenko's name to the avenue. After losing all its appeals, the city council simply renamed the avenue again on 26 February 2020. The local administrative court again canceled this decision. The third round of this confrontation began in 2021, when Ihor Terekhov, Kharkiv's acting mayor and longtime associate of Hennadii Kernes, solemnly declared: "the monument to Marshal Zhukov stood, stands, and will stand in the city of Kharkiv. Marshal Zhukov Avenue existed, exists, and will exist in the city of Kharkiv. And our Victory Day is 9 May, not 8 May."[108]

By sticking to the identity policy of his former boss, Hennadii Kernes, in opposition to the Kyiv authorities, Terekhov clearly expected to secure the support of local voters in the mayoral elections of 2021. It is also clear that his rhetoric was sharply at odds with the attempt of the central authorities of Petro Poroshenko's day to replace the Soviet discourse of the "Great Patriotic War" with that of "World War II" as part of the pro-Western course of Ukraine's foreign policy. According to Western tradition, the victory over Nazism is celebrated annually on 8 May, while Russia demonstratively celebrates it on 9 May. This episode is also worth examining in the broader context of the policy of decommunization, which acquired the force of law in 2015.

## *Toponymics*

Since 2015 Kharkiv has undergone the third toponymic revolution in its recent history, in which 268 urban names were changed.[109] As a result, most Soviet and communist names and symbols disappeared from the city's space. This may be considered a very moderate revolution, as most municipal voters opposed it in principle or tried to hold to the principle of seeking the golden mean—the city's characteristic behavior throughout its history. Public debates over decommunization sometimes produced comic situations in which the old toponym remained intact but was recoded and endowed with a different meaning.

For example, Mikhail Kalinin Street, named after the Soviet state and party leader, was "renamed" after the aircraft engineer Konstantin Kalinin. Spartacus Lane began to trace its name not to the German communist Spartacus League of the early twentieth century but to the name of the leader of a slave revolt against the Roman Republic.[110] Local historians promptly "discovered" that the Soviet revolutionaries Mikhail Frunze and Feliks Dzerzhinsky had relatives with the same surnames, which allowed them to survive the "purge" of decommunization.

As for the new names, their selection was associated predominantly with local tradition. More than half the new names of streets and squares turned out, in fact, to be old ones associated with the imperial, pre-Soviet era.[111] A significant proportion of them refer to local parishes or spiritual symbols of the Russian Orthodox Church: Annunciation Street (formerly Karl Marx Street), Holy Spirit Street (formerly Proletarian Street), Myrrh-Bearers Street (formerly Soviet Commissars'

Council Street), and so on. In other words, Orthodox symbolism was restored in place of Soviet symbolism.

Ukrainian national symbols in the new names of Kharkiv streets were also usually chosen with an eye toward local history. They memorialize scholarly and cultural figures of the imperial or Soviet eras such as the Alchevskys (formerly Artem), Dmytro Bahalii (formerly Frunze), Petro Hulak-Artemovsky (former Red October), Dmytro Miller (formerly Pioneers), Les Serdiuk (formerly Army Commander Kork), Yevhen Pluzhnyk (formerly Rudnev), and so on.[112] Only a handful of the new names belong to the historical mythology of the Ukrainian National Revolution of 1917–20. The wartime mythology of the Organization of Ukrainian Nationalists and the Ukrainian Insurgent Army is not represented at all in the new toponymy. Along with these, to be sure, the new toponymy of Kharkiv reflects events associated with the Revolution of Dignity (2014) and the names of heroes of the Ukrainian-Russian war.

At the same time, numerous Soviet monuments and memorials erected to commemorate the "Great Patriotic War" mythology remain intact. The conflicts provoked by the Zhukov monument just discussed were played out alongside a new place of memory associated with the Revolution of Dignity. On Zhukov/Hryhorenko Avenue a memorial plaque was installed in 2016 at the site of a terrorist attack that took place on 22 February 2015, leading to the death of four citizens of Kharkiv who took part in a mass procession for the unity of Ukraine. The plaque has already been in place long enough to be vandalized.

The Kharkiv authorities have shown themselves much more favorable to Cossack symbolism, established since early times in local identity discourse. For example, there is a monument to the Cossack hetman Petro Sahaidachny originally installed in Sevastopol in 2008; after Russia's annexation of the Crimea, when the local authorities decided to destroy it, the monument was transferred to Kharkiv in 2014 at the personal request of Mayor Kernes. Another example of the cultivation of Cossack mythology in Kharkiv is a monument to the Cossack leader Ivan Sirko erected in the city's historic center in 2017 next to the historical museum. Interestingly, the idea was proposed in 2011 by local activists.[113]

## *Local Identity*

The city's local identity remained quite strong. In fact, according to a recent sociological survey, it seems more powerful than national identity.[114] Local residents respond with hostility to any hint of disparagement of the "first capital" mythology, as a recent example attests. The Kyiv philologist Vira Aheieva, seeking the reasons for the proclamation of Kharkiv as the capital of Ukraine in 1920, concluded that there was nothing behind this Bolshevik decision but the desire to "deprive the people of memory," since she considered Kharkiv catastrophically lacking in the symbolic and cultural capital befitting such status.[115] In her view, the transfer of the

Ukrainian capital from Kharkiv to Kyiv in 1934 was motivated first and foremost by the Bolsheviks' desire to consolidate their victory over a nation exhausted by the famine of 1933 and deprive the people of their historical memory once again.

Aheieva's article touched the Kharkiv readership to the quick, and it reacted promptly with an anonymous text written by one or several authors that was printed in the Kharkiv informational publication *Status Quo*.[116] The article asserted that Aheieva's essay was "insulting to Kharkivites and millions of their ancestors, who had done not a whit less than residents of Kyiv or other Ukrainian cities for the development of Ukraine." The author(s) of those lines were up in arms against Kyiv's capital snobbery, rising in defense of cities that "proudly, with their heads held high, bore the title of oblast centers."

Although the Kharkiv text is more fact-based than the Kyivan text, both echo the turbulent moods of the Revolution of Dignity. This is what makes them interesting material for the student of post-Maidan Ukraine. To simplify, it may be concluded that in this polemic, which does not appear to have been continued, the discourse of the "national capital" stands opposed to the discourse of "regional diversity" in Ukraine. From this viewpoint, the cultural texts just discussed scarcely differ from political manifestos.

In general, Kharkiv and oblast remain objects of intense Russian attention. According to Peter Dickinson, "Even without the support of imported insurgents from Russia itself, Kharkiv's pro-Russian camp has always been large, vocal, and influential."[117] Russian propaganda found not only eager listeners but also active disseminators of Russian cultural and political influence in the Russian Orthodox Church, to say nothing of propagandists paid by the Kremlin and political structures created by them, such as the Sharii Party. Former Kharkivites who emigrated to Russia after 2014—Konstantin Kevorkian, Konstantin Dolgov, Stanislav Minakov—were particularly active in promoting the Russian nationalist narrative.[118]

Kharkiv's characteristic ambivalence and distancing from extremes of any kind is typical of the borderland. In this vein, we note an insightful observation of the journalist Peter Pomerantsev:

> Kharkiv is not so much a place of bipolar dividing lines and "simmering historical resentment" as a do-as-you-please, disinterested mess of mini-movements. ... The population's political passivity and disinterest in real change that so infuriates pro-democracy activists also means it's hard to stir up strife: post-Soviet cynicism saved Kharkiv from Russia. But the fractured nature of life in Kharkiv also means a unified push for reforms is also impossible.[119]

Pomerantsev's observation and conclusions seem quite apposite, given the conditions taking shape after the disintegration of the USSR. But few could foresee that armed Russian aggression against Ukraine, which began with the annexation of the Crimea and part of the Donbas, would turn into full-scale war eight years later. That is what actually happened on the morning of 24 February 2022, when Russia began a rocket bombardment of the Ukrainian capital, Kyiv, and broke into Ukraine. This time, however, the Russian leadership was not after the mere annexation of new territory. Its goal had become the "final solution of the Ukrainian question," which the imperial elites had sought unsuccessfully to resolve for the past two centuries.

Quite a few Western analysts sought to evaluate the actions of the Russian leadership in terms of geopolitics and imperial ambitions. Among them were those who thoughtlessly echoed the Russian narrative's basic theses about the threat allegedly posed to Russia by NATO's eastward expansion. As the poet Tiutchev wrote, however, "the mind cannot grasp Russia." One of my colleagues in the historical profession, an ethnic Russian, was much closer to the truth when he confessed that, sitting in a cellar during the Russian bombardment, he kept pinching his hand to assure himself that present reality was not the product of a diseased imagination.

Those watching the face of the Russian dictator, twisted with hatred, as he announced the start of the "special military operation" on the territory of a neighboring sovereign state might well have had the same feeling. But the war cannot be attributed to a strategic error or a personal disorder of Putin's. The disease may be said to encompass almost all of Russian society, afflicted by some frenzied

**Figure 7.4.** The Ukrainian-Russian border before the Russian invasion. © Volodymyr Kravchenko, 2017.

anti-Ukrainian hysteria that many find incomprehensible. Hence the shocking brutality of the Russian troops, whose actions in Ukraine showed signs of genocide from the very beginning.

Under the pressure of Russian aggression, the Ukrainian-Russian borderland is quickly losing its ambivalence.[120] A process of national demarcation is taking place there. The front line has become today's de facto border between Ukraine and Russia. Dozens if not hundreds of thousands of Ukrainian citizens have been deported to Russia. It is not yet known how many of them come from the Kharkiv region, but here too they are counted in the thousands. More than ten million Ukrainian citizens have become refugees; of these, more than three million are now in Europe. This is the most massive migration since World War II. The symbolic extent of the "Russian World" is now coterminous with the internationally recognized borders of the Russian state, which is cordoning itself off from the outside world. By contrast, the "Huntington line," which supposedly divided east from west in Ukraine, is now practically invisible. The country's population is becoming Ukrainian regardless of language, place of residence, or religion.

Under the conditions of the current war, Kharkiv and its region are undergoing yet another change of political and symbolic orientations. As I write these lines, the Russians are occupying a considerable part of the Kharkiv region, including the towns of Kupiansk, Balakliia, Vovchansk, Izium, and Borova. They are all large raion centers, and Kupiansk is a strategically important railway junction located on the Oskil River. It has been turned into a logistic center for the Russian army, funneling human resources and armaments southward. In all, twenty-two of the fifty-six territorial communities in Kharkiv oblast are now in the Russian zone of occupation.[121] For the most part, the aggressor is exploiting Kharkiv oblast as a transit territory.

The city of Kharkiv is surrounded on three sides—north, east, and west. Russian artillery is systematically bombarding Kharkiv from the small town of Lyptsi located about twenty kilometers to the north. This is the town that both Russian and Ukrainian contemporaries identified as the marker of the Ukrainian-Russian ethnic boundary in the late eighteenth and early nineteenth centuries. Kharkiv is now being deliberately destroyed. More than 1,700 of its buildings have been ruined, along with much of its infrastructure, and between 565 and 725 civilians, including 30 children, have been killed.[122] These figures are incomplete, given the constant bombardment.

Perhaps I exaggerate in asserting that Kharkiv became a different city on 24 February 2022, but residents of Kharkiv themselves confirm that assumption. According to the Kharkiv historian Anton Bondarev, "probably no one in Kharkiv has done as much to promote Ukrainization as Putin with his destruction."[123] According to the testimony of Eduard Rubin, there are almost no "outsiders" remaining in the city: "those who, sitting in their kitchens, expressed feeble hopes of peaceful relations with the neighboring terrorist polity have seen the light and now crave

**Figure 7.5.** Russian missile near the Orthodox Church of the Assumption of the Theotokos in the old center of Kharkiv. © Andrii Marienko, used with permission.

**Figure 7.6.** Kharkiv oblast administration building after Russian bombardment, 1 March 2022. © Andrii Marienko, used with permission.

only victory, having broken off contacts with relatives on the other side."¹²⁴ Even so odious a politician as Mikhail Dobkin has experienced an identity crisis that led him to take holy orders. The current mayor, Ihor Terekhov, did not follow his predecessor's path and chose a patriotic pro-Ukrainian position instead.

Russia's annexation of the Crimea in 2014 and its "hybrid" war in the Donbas dealt a powerful blow to the Soviet historical legacy. It set off a wave of symbolic decommunization directed against the mythology of the "Great October Socialist Revolution" that resulted in the *Leninopad* (removal of monuments to Lenin). Russia's war of 2022 against Ukraine also struck another pillar of the Soviet legacy—the mythology of the "Great Patriotic War." Putin's Russia stressed the last word of the formula, turning Soviet discourse into the nationalist myth of the "Great Victory" that "could be repeated." In Ukraine, by contrast, the word "patriotic" took on a distinct national coloring.

The discourse of the "Ukrainian Patriotic War" is somewhat reminiscent of its Soviet counterpart. It has given rise to its own "hero cities," including Kharkiv. The city enjoyed no such status in Soviet times, but Kharkiv, destroyed by Russian rockets, called forth analogies with Stalingrad.¹²⁵ The song "Sinen'kii skromnyi platochek" (Modest little blue shawl), which spoke of the bombing of Kyiv by German airplanes on the morning of 22 June 1941, was popular during World War II. Given the new Ukrainian context, with *rashysty* taking the place of Nazis, it acquired a completely different resonance. Russian aggression came to resemble its Nazi predecessor even more when it claimed the life of the ninety-six-year-old Kharkivite Borys Romanchenko, vice president of the International Buchenwald-Dora Committee, who had survived the Nazi concentration camps of Buchenwald, Peenemünde, Dora, and Bergen-Belsen.¹²⁶ He was killed in his own apartment by a Russian bomb.

Under such conditions, changes in Kharkiv's symbolic landscape were inevitable. The Gogolian saga concerning the memorialization of the Soviet marshal Georgii Zhukov found its continuation on 17 April, when a special subunit of the Azov Battalion demolished the marshal's commemorative bust with lightning speed, leaving a Ukrainian national coat of arms with the inscription "Glory to Ukraine!" in its place. The commander of the subunit, Konstantin Nemichev, commented as follows: "Putin wanted true decommunization: now he's got it. Soon, like his idol, he will find himself on the dustheap of history."¹²⁷ Mayor Ihor Terekhov of Kharkiv declined comment on the subject. The Russian Investigative Committee, for its part, immediately opened a criminal case with reference to this "insult to the memory of defenders of the Fatherland."¹²⁸ The Kremlin, it would appear, has already decided to extend Russian legislation to Kharkiv.

Russian aggression has served to intensify the campaign of symbolic Ukrainization, which has now been extended not only to the Soviet but also to the Russian imperial legacy. Decommunization has produced derussification in its wake. Its beginning in Kharkiv may be dated to the Russian bombing of the city's historical center, where the most imposing buildings of the imperial era were located. Symbolically enough, a Russian rocket struck the building of the former *Rossiia* Insurance Company, which was renamed the Palace of Labor in Soviet times.[129] The building is still embellished with a sculpture titled "Russia Extends Protection to Subjugated Peoples."

A considerable group of representatives of the Kharkiv intelligentsia, including leading lights of science and culture, addressed an open letter to the municipal authorities calling for the initiation of a process to remove Russian toponymy from Kharkiv's civic space.[130] It was proposed in particular to change the names of all streets with Russian geographic references (notably Moscow Avenue), as well as names of Russian historical figures (Aleksandr Nevsky, Dmitrii Donskoi, et al.) and artists (Pushkin et al.). It became known that the monument to Pushkin was dismantled during the all-Ukrainian wave of "pushkinopad" at the end of 2022.

Kharkiv's local identity also suffered when the former Gorky Park and the premises of Kharkiv city council, both symbolic to city residents, were bombed by Russian forces. The city's famous Barabashovo Market was set on fire and heavily damaged by Russian rockets. Kharkiv's equally well-known Ecopark was badly damaged, and two members of its staff who looked after the animals died. Russian troops also damaged one of the buildings of Kharkiv University, new and old residential districts, children's playgrounds, and hospitals. According to Mayor Terekhov, the city will have to be rebuilt, but at present it is hard to say when and under what conditions that might become possible.

## Notes

1. Yaroslav Hrytsak, "On Sails and Gales, and Ships Driving in Various Directions: Post-Soviet Ukraine as a Test Case for the Meso-Area Concept," in *Emerging Meso-Areas in the Former Socialist Countries (Histories Revised or Improvised?)*, ed. Kimitaka Matsuzato (Sapporo: Slavic Research Center, Hokkaido University, 2005), 42–68.
2. *Glavnoe*, 18 January 2010, http://glavnoe.ua/news/n41765.
3. Ol'ha Miroshnyk, Oleksandr Romaniuk, and Ihor Polishchuk, *Mistsevi vybory 2010: Kharkivs'ka oblast'* (Kharkiv: Foundation of Local Democracy, 2010), http://fmd.kh.ua/publishing/mistsevi-vibori-2010-harkivs-ka-oblast.html.
4. Elena Sergeeva, "Izvestnye khar'kovchane publichno zaiavili o podderzhke M. Dobkina i G. Kernesa na vyborakh," *Gorodskoi dozor*, 5 June 2010, https://kharkov.dozor.ua/news/vlast/1070661.html.
5. Serhii Zhadan, "Problema Khar'kova," *Glavnoe*, 11 November 2010, http://glavnoe.ua/articles/a4306.
6. Tatiana Zhurzhenko, "Memory Wars in Post-Soviet Kharkiv," in *Civic Education and Democratisation in the Eastern Partnership Countries*, ed. Dieter Segert (Bonn: Bundeszentrale für politische Bildung, 2016), 102–22, here 106.
7. Oleksii Vedrov, "Park konfliktiv: borot'ba v parku Hor'kogo iak dzerkalo kharkivs'koho suspil'stva," *Spil'ne*, 6 September 2010, https://commons.com.ua/uk/park-konfliktiv-borotba-v-lisoparku/.
8. Vladislav Davidzon, "Swaggering Jewish Gangster Mayor Hennadiy Kernes, Reluctant Savior of Kharkiv, Is Felled by COVID: A Colorful Life, Summed Up in a Punchline," *Tab-*

*let Magazine*, 23 December 2020, https://www.tabletmag.com/sections/news/articles/hennadiey-kernes-obituary-covid.
9. Zhadan, "Problema Khar'kova," http://glavnoe.ua/articles/a4306.
10. http://oblrada.kharkov.ua/ua/kharkiv-region/symbolics/hymn-of-kharkiv-region.
11. Taras Kuzio, *Ukraine: Democratization, Corruption, and the New Russian Imperialism* (Santa Barbara, CA, and Denver, CO: Praeger, 2015), 240.
12. Volodymyr Kravchenko, "Kharkiv: The Past Lives On," *The Soviet and Post-Soviet Review* 64, no. 3 (2019): 324–51.
13. Ihor Kabanenko, "Kharkiv Accords. Background, Menaces, and Lessons," *Den'*, 7 April 2014.
14. http://theology.in.ua/en/index/all_news/orthodox/moscow_patriarchy/42259/.
15. Kravchenko, "Kharkiv," 340.
16. *Korrespondent*, 6 February 2011, https://korrespondent.net/ukraine/events/1182865-ross iya-namerena-otkryt-v-harkovskoj-oblasti-pyat-kabinetov-russkij-mir.
17. Tomasz Piechal, "The Kharkiv Oblast: A Fragile Stability," *OSW Commentary*, Centre for Eastern Studies, no. 172, 03.06.2015, https://www.osw.waw.pl/en/publikacje/osw-co mmentary/2015-06-09/kharkiv-oblast-a-fragile-stability.
18. http://srn.rusidea.org/?a=4025.
19. *Glavnoe*, Internet-obozrenie, 28 June 2011, https://glavnoe.ua/news/n79101ж.
20. Kuzio, *Ukraine: Democratization*, 102, 112.
21. V. Ovchinnikov and N. Oleinik, eds., *Istoriia Slobozhanshchiny i Belgorodskogo kraia. Uchebnoe posobie* (Belgorod: Belgorod Press House, 2011).
22. Ovchinnikov and Oleinik, *Istoriia Slobozhanshchiny*, 98.
23. Vasilii Bublikov, "Osobennosti identichnosti russko-ukrainskogo naseleniia prigranichnykh territorii Rossii," *Ėtnograficheskoe obozrenie*, no. 6 (2019): 138–57, here 140.
24. *Istoriia Slobozhanshchiny i Belgorodskogo kraia*, 7, 29.
25. Petr Masliuzhenko, "510 let edinstva – istoriia Slobozhanshchiny," *Russkaia pravda: informatsionno-analiticheskoe izdanie*, http://ruspravda.info/510-let-edinstva-istoriya-Slobozha nshchini-2984.html.
26. Masliuzhenko, "510 let edinstva."
27. "510 let edinstva."
28. "510 let edinstva."
29. Vladimir Bugar', "Slobozhanshchina, Novorossiia, Slavianoserbiia," https://proza.ru/20 14/06/10/1571.
30. Vladimir Putin, "Ob istoricheskom edinstve russkikh i ukraintsev," http://kremlin.ru/events/president/news/66191.
31. Zhurzhenko, "Memory Wars," 112.
32. https://www.city.kharkov.ua/en/publication/prezident-ukrayini-vidkriv-pam-yatnik-nezale zhnosti-v-harkovi-15368.html. Translation edited for clarity.
33. Zhurzhenko, "Memory Wars," 113.
34. Iuliia Skubitskaia, "Gibkost' khaosa vmesto stroinosti ansamblia: dvadsat' let postsovetskogo Khar'kova," *Neprikosnovennyi zapas*, no. 6 (2011), http://magazines.russ.ru/nz/2011/6/s5.html.
35. Vedrov, "Park konfliktiv."
36. Kravchenko, "Kharkiv."
37. Peter Dickinson, "Rejecting Russia: How Kharkiv Saved Ukraine from Putin's Partition Plan in 2014," Business Ukraine Magazine, 2 January 2017, http://bunews.com.ua/poli tics/item/rejecting-russia-how-kharkiv-saved-the-whole-of-ukraine-from-putins-partition-p lan#.WGu25NfyNgM.facebook.
38. Vladimir Socor, "Moscow Encourages Centrifugal Forces in South-Eastern Ukraine," *Eurasia Daily Monitor* 11, no. 36 (2014), http://www.jamestown.org/programs/edm/sin gle/?tx_ttnewspercent5Btt_newspercent5D=42013&cHash=d5bd15f84adc4659955af9333 ad96b4e percent23.VpdqaJOLToA#.V8tjlvkrLIU.

39. Dmitrii Volokitin, "Sevastopol'tsy zagovorili o sozdanii Malorossii," *Rabochaia gazeta* 17 (30 January 2014): 1.
40. Volodymyr Kravchenko, "Ukrainian-Russian Border after Euromaidan: Regional Perspective," in *Borders and Memories: Conflicts and Co-operation in European Border Regions*, ed. Katarzyna Stokłosa (Vienna and Zurich: LIT Verlag, 2019), 122.
41. David M. Herszenhorn, "What Is Putin's 'New Russia'?" *New York Times*, 18 April 2014, https://www.nytimes.com/2014/04/19/world/europe/what-is-putins-new-russia.html.
42. Aleksandr Shubin, *Istoriia Novorossii* (Moscow, 2015); cf. *Skhid i Pivden' Ukraïny: chas, prostir, sotsium*, ed. Valerii Smolii, 2 vols. (Kyiv, 2014).
43. Patricia Herlihy, "What Vladimir Putin Chooses Not to Know about Russian History," *Los Angeles Times*, 1 May 2014, no. http://www.latimes.com/opinion/op-ed/la-oe-herlihy-russia-ukraine-odessa-20140501-story.html.
44. Andrei Baranov, "Politicheskaia identichnost' Novorossii: sostoianie i resursy konstruirovaniia," *Kaspiiskii region: politika, ėkonomika, kul'tura* 43 (2015): 98–106.
45. Oleg Nemenskii, "Modeli iuzhnorusskogo natsionalizma na Ukraine," *Voprosy natsionalizma* 2, no. 18 (2014): 21.
46. Dickinson, "Rejecting Russia."
47. Marlene Laruelle, "The Three Colors of Novorossiya, or the Russian Nationalist Mythmaking of the Ukrainian Crisis," *Post-Soviet Affairs* 32, no. 1 (2016): 55–74.
48. David R. Marples, *Ukraine in Conflict: An Analytical Chronicle* (Bristol: E-International Relations Publishing, 2017), 57–62, https://www.e-ir.info/2017/05/01/open-access-book-ukraine-in-conflict-an-analytical-chronicle/.
49. *Korrespondent*, 1 February 2014, http://korrespondent.net/ukraine/politics/3300116-ukraynskyi-front-po-prymeru-dedov-budet-osvobozhdat-nashu-zemlui-dobkyn.
50. Kravchenko, "Kharkiv."
51. "How Yanukovych Ran from Ukraine – Investigation," UNIAN, 21 April 2014, https://www.unian.info/politics/910019-how-yanukovych-ran-from-ukraine-investigation.html.
52. Kravchenko, "Kharkiv," 2.
53. Kuzio, *Ukraine: Democratization*, 108.
54. Vijai Maheshwari, "Is Kharkiv Ukraine's Next Tipping Point?" *Daily Beast*, 13 March 2014, updated 12 July 2017, http://www.thedailybeast.com/articles/2014/03/13/is-kharkiv-ukraine-s-next-tipping-point.html.
55. Kuzio, *Ukraine: Democratization*, 112.
56. Arsen Avakov, *Mgnoveniia khar'kovskoi vesny, 2014* (Kharkiv: Folio, 2020).
57. Oleksandra Indiukhova, "Sabotazh militsioneriv u Kharkovi," *Deutsche Welle*, 10 April 2014, https://www.dw.com/uk/chomu-kharkivs'ka-militsiya-ne-zupynyla-separatystiv/a-17558327.
58. Yaroslav Hrytsak, "Ukraine in 2013–2014: A New Political Geography," in *Regionalism without Regions: Reconceptualizing Ukraine's Heterogeneity*, ed. Ulrich Schmid and Oksana Myshlovska (Budapest: Central European University Press), 367–92, here 376.
59. Iurii Butusov, "Ia skazal 'Iaguaru': 'My zashchishchaem ne pravitel'stvo, my zashchishchaem ot gibeli,' – kak 8 aprelia 2014 MVD i Natsgvardiia spasli Khar'kov ot donbasskogo stsenariia voiny," *Tsenzor.net.*, 28 April 2016, https://censor.net/ru/resonance/386630/ya_skazal_yaguaru_my_zaschischaem_ne_pravitelstvo_my_zaschischaem_ot_gibeli_vsyu_ukrainu_kak_8_aprelya.
60. Andreas Umland, "Irregular Militias and Radical Nationalism in Post-Euromaydan Ukraine: The Prehistory and Emergence of the 'Azov' Battalion in 2014," *Terrorism and Political Violence* 31, no. 1 (2019): 105–31.
61. Kuzio, *Ukraine: Democratization*, 107.
62. https://tsn.ua/ukrayina/sbu-zatrimali-teroristiv-iz-oplotu-ta-harkivskih-partizan-423206.html.
63. Natalia Shapovalova and Balázs Jarábik, "How Eastern Ukraine Is Adapting and Surviv-

ing: The Case of Kharkiv," *Carnegie Europe*, 22 December 2020, https://carnegieeurope. eu/2018/09/12/how-eastern-ukraine-is-adapting-and-surviving-case-of-kharkiv-pub-77216.
64. Hrytsak, "Ukraine in 2013–2014," 376.
65. Shapovalova and Jarábik, "How Eastern Ukraine Is Adapting."
66. UNIAN, 11 February 2014, https://www.unian.net/society/882929-bolshe-vsego-v-rod nom-gorode-nravitsya-jit-harkovchanam-opros.html.
67. Hrytsak, "Ukraine in 2013–2014"; Ihor Stebelsky, "A Tale of Two Regions: Geopolitics, Identities, Narratives, and Conflict in Kharkiv and the Donbas," *Eurasian Geography and Economics* 59, no. 1 (2018): 28–50; Nataliia Pohorila, "Political and National Identity in Ukraine's Regions: Where Does the Center Fit?" *Polish Political Science Review* 4, no. 1 (2016): 18–32; Andrii Portnov, "How 'Eastern Ukraine' Was Lost," *Open Democracy-OD Russia*, 14 January 2016, www.opende-mocracy.net/od-russia/andrii-portnov/how-eastern-ukraine-was-lost.
68. "Regiony Ukrainy: chto nas raz"ediniaet i chto ob"ediniaet? Mneniia sotsiologov. Materialy kruglogo stola. Kharkov, 18 aprelia 2014 g.," *Ab Imperio* 3 (2014): 123–60, here 136; Maksim Vikhrov, "Tri mifa ob ukrainskom iugo-vostoke," 28 April (2014): https://republic.ru/world/tri_mifa_ob_ukrain- skom_yugo_vostoke-1091432.xhtml; Oleksander Demchenko, "Pivdennoho Skhodu bil'she nemaie," *Ukraïns′ka pravda*, 22 April 2014, http://www.pravda.com.ua/articles/2014/04/22/7023182/.
69. Pohorila, "Political and National Identity." Other scholars suggest that "in the central part of Ukraine sub-ethnic identity is relatively weak." Anatoliy Melnychuck, Oleksiy Gnatiuk, and Mariia Rastvorova, "Use of Territorial Identity Markers in Geographical Researches," *Scientific Annals of "Alexandru Ioan Cuza" University of Iași* 60, no. 1 (2014), s. IIc, Geography Series (2014): 167.
70. Andrii Portnov, "Kak nachinalas' voina na vostoke Ukrainy ili pochemu Khar'kov i Dnepropetrovsk ne stali Donetskom i Luganskom?" *Gefter* 22, no. 1 (2016), http://gefter.ru/archive/17295; idem, "The New Heart of Ukraine? Dnipropetrovsk after Euromaidan," *Osteuropa* 65, no. 4 (2015): 173–87; idem, "The Ukraine and Its 'Far East': On Galician Reductionism and Its Genealogy," *Historians in UA*, 1 August 2014, www.historians.in.ua/index.php/avtorska-kolonka/1231-andrii-portnov-ukraina-ta-ii-dalekyi-skhid-pro-halytskyi-redukt-sionizm-ta-ioho-heneat.
71. John O'Loughlin, Gerard Toal, and Vladimir Kolosov, "The Rise and Fall of 'Novorossiya': Examining Support for a Separatist Geopolitical Imaginary in Southeast Ukraine," *Post-Soviet Affairs* 33, no. 2 (2016): 124–44; Kostiantyn Skorkin, "Mit Novorosiï: krai reaktsiinykh utopii," *Krytyka*, nos. 9–10 (203–204) (2015): 27–30.
72. Vladimir Dergachev and Dmitrii Kartsev, "DNR nashla sebe istoriiu: DNR provozglasila sebia preemnitsei Donetsko-Krivorozhskoi respubliki," *Gazeta. RU.*, 6 February 2015, https://www.gazeta.ru/politics/2015/02/06_a_6402557.shtml.
73. Taras Kuzio, "Rise and Fall of the Party of Regions' Political Machine," *Problems of Post-Communism* 62, no. 3 (2015): 174–86.
74. Philip Shishkin, "Head of Donetsk Separatists Says He Is Ready for 'Russian Empire,'" *Wall Street Journal – Eastern Edition*, 14 July 2014, vol. 264, issue 11 (2014): A7; Adam Taylor, "'Ukrainian Separatists Claim to Have Created a New Country: Malorossiya, or 'Little Russia,'" *Washington Post*, 19 July 2017, https://www.washingtonpost.com/news/worldviews/wp/2017/07/19/ukrainian-separatists-claim-to-have-created-a-new-country-malorossiya-or-little-russia/?utm_term=.fc9b39185448.
75. Pavel Fedosenko, "Na separatistskii forum deputatov 'Vidrodzhennia' zamanili obmanom," *Newsroom*, 24 November 2015, http://www.univer.kharkov.ua/ru/general/univer_today/news?news_id=4585.
76. [Anonymous], "Revoliutsiia na Donbasse: Osoznanie i otritsanie," *Holos natsiï* (n.d.), http://golo-sukraine.in.ua/item/20310-1477750201. The author insists that the erosion of Donbas regional identity in the territory under Kyiv's control paralleled the strengthening of Sloboda regional identity, with its center in Kharkiv.

77. Yaroslav Prytula et al., "Recent Regional Economic Development in Ukraine: Does History Help to Explain the Differences?" in *Regionalism without Regions: Reconceptualizing Ukraine's Heterogeneity* (Budapest: CEU Press, 2019), 297–366, here 299.
78. Maria Lewicka and Bartłomiej Iwańczak, "The Regional Differentiation of Identities in Ukraine: How Many Regions?" in *Regionalism without Regions*, 25–65.
79. Shapovalova and Jarábik, "How Eastern Ukraine Is Adapting."
80. "Na 'stinu Iatseniuka' vytratyly vzhe 1,3 mil'iarda – DPSU," *Ukraïns'ka pravda*, 9 April 2019, https://www.epravda.com.ua/rus/news/2019/04/9/646881/.
81. Piechal, "The Kharkiv Oblast," 7.
82. Shapovalova and Jarábik, "How Eastern Ukraine Is Adapting."
83. "How Eastern Ukraine Is Adapting."
84. "How Eastern Ukraine Is Adapting."
85. "How Eastern Ukraine Is Adapting."
86. "Dynamika nostal'hiï za SRSR," *Sotsiolohichna hrupa Reitynh*, 8 October 2015, http://ratinggroup.ua/files/ratinggroup/reg_files/rg_ussr_092016_press.pdf; Nataliya Sudakova, "Who Wants the USSR Back in Ukraine?" *Euromaidan Press*, 13 April 2018, http://euromaidanpress.com/2018/04/11/soviet-people-in-ukraine-why-do-they-miss-it-and-what-danger-does-this-pose-for-ukraine/.
87. Sudakova, "Who Wants the USSR."
88. "Dynamika nostal'hiï za SRSR."
89. *Apostrof*, 17 August 2018, https://apostrophe.ua/news/politics/political-parties/2018-08-17/partiya-za-jittya-obognala-oppoblok-v-harove-i-odesse—-sotsopros/138704.
90. Tatiana Zhurzhenko, "The Fifth Kharkiv," *The New Eastern Europe* 17, nos. 3–4 (May–August 2015): 30–37, http://www.neweasterneurope.eu/articles-and-commentary/1647-the-fifth-kharkiv.
91. "Cherhovi mistsevi vybory, 2015. Kharkivs'ka oblasna rada," Tsentral'na vyborcha komisiia Ukraïny, https://web.archive.org/web/20160304202705/http://www.cvk.gov.ua/pls/vm2015/PVM057?PID112=12&PID102=5441&PF7691=5441&PT001F01=100&rej=0&pt00_t001f01=100.
92. *Apostrof*, 17 August 2018, https://apostrophe.ua/news/politics/political-parties/2018-08-17/partiya -za-jittya-obognala-oppoblok-v-harove-i-odesse-sotsopros/138704.
93. https://upload.wikimedia.org/wikipedia/commons/5/5b/Вибори_ПУ_2019_Лідери_ОБЛ_I_II_III_I_тур.png.
94. https://www.cvk.gov.ua/pls/vp2019/wp313pt001f01=720.html.
95. https://www.cvk.gov.ua/pls/vnd2019/wp310pt001f01=919.html.
96. Harry Nedelcu, Dmytro Panchuk, and Yulia Bidenko, "Foreign Interference in Ukraine's Politics during the 2019 Elections: The Case of the Kharkiv Region," *The New Eastern Europe*, 12 February 2020, https://neweasterneurope.eu/2020/02/12/foreign-interference-in-ukraines-politics-during-the-2019-elections-the-case-of-the-kharkiv-region percentEF pe rcentBB percentBF/.
97. https://uk.wikipedia.org/wiki/Місцеві_вибори_у_Харківській_області_2020.
98. https://www.city.kharkov.ua/uk/gorodskaya-vlast/gorodskoj-sovet/frakczii.html.
99. Shapovalova and Jarábik, "How Eastern Ukraine Is Adapting."
100. "How Eastern Ukraine Is Adapting."
101. Piechal, "The Kharkiv Oblast," 4.
102. Zhurzhenko, "Memory Wars," 116.
103. Tatiana Zhurzhenko, "From Borderlands to Bloodlands," *Eurozine* 45 (2014): 1–11.
104. Vladimir Chistilin, "Kak valili Lenina," *Glavnoe*, 28 September 2015, http://glavnoe.ua/articles/a10331.
105. Zhurzhenko, "Memory Wars," 116.
106. The popular Ukrainian comedian Volodymyr Zelensky, who later became president, made fun of the Chechen leader Ramzan Kadyrov, as if the latter had wept over the toppling of the Lenin monument in Kharkiv. He subsequently apologized to Kadyrov for the incident.

107. Zhurzhenko, "Memory Wars," 119.
108. *Ukraïns'ka pravda*, 10 May 2021, https://www.pravda.com.ua/news/2021/05/10/7292999/.
109. Mariia Takhtaulova, "Vulytseiu Stusa," *Mediaport*, 16 September 2016, http://www.me-diaport.ua/vuliceyu-stusa.
110. http://www.city.kharkov.ua/uk/document/zaproponovani-nazvi-vulits-yaki-mayut-buti-zmineni-vidpovidno-do-zakonu-ukraini-pro-zasudzhennya-komunistichnogo-ta-natsional-sotsialistichnogo-natsistskogo-totalitarnikh-rezhimiv-v-ukraini-ta-zaboronu-propagandi-ikh-simvoliki-47404.html.
111. "Perelik pereimenuvan' ob'iektiv toponimiky mista Kharkova," Official site of Kharkiv City Council, http://www.city.kharkov.ua/uk/document/zaproponovani-nazvi-vulits-yaki-mayut-buti-zmineni-vidpovidno-do-zakonu-ukraini-pro-zasudzhennya-komunistich-nogo-ta-natsional-sotsialistichnogo-natsistskogo-totalitarnikh-rezhimiv-v-ukraini-ta-zaboronu-propagandi-ikh-simvoliki-47404.html.
112. "Perelik pereimenuvan' ob'iektiv toponimiky mista Kharkova."
113. "Na Bursatskom spuske ustanovili pamiatnik atamanu Ivanu Sirko," https://www.city.kharkov.ua/ru/news/na-bursatskomu-uzvozi-vstanovili-pamyatnik-otamanu-ivanovisir-ku-36337.html.
114. "Hromads'ka dumka u mistakh-mil'ionnykakh: Elektoral'ni orientatsiï ta nastroï naperedodni Dnia Nezalezhnosti Ukraïny; Rezul'taty doslidzhennia," *Ukrinform*, 17 August 2018, https://www.ukrinform.ua/rubric-presshall/2518531-elektoralni-orientacii-ta-nastroi-naperedodni-dna-nezaleznosti-ukraini-rezultati-doslidzenna.html.
115. Vera Ageeva, "Pochemu v Khar'kove ne prizhilas' stolitsa Ukrainy," *BBC Ukraine*, 27 November 2017, https://www.bbc.com/ukrainian/blog-history-russian-42135701.
116. [Anonymous], "Pochemu Khar'kov byl stolitsei. Nash otvet professoru Kievo-Mogilianki," *Status Quo*, 13 November 2017, http://www.sq.com.ua/rus/news/teksty/30.11.2017/pochemu_harkov_byl_stolitsey_nash_otvet_professoru_kievo_mogilyanki/.
117. Dickinson, "Rejecting Russia."
118. Nedelcu, Panchuk, and Bidenko, "Foreign Interference in Ukraine's Politics."
119. Peter Pomerantsev, "Kharkiv, City of Vagabonds and Poets," *Politico*, 18 December 2015, http://www.politico.eu/article/print-kharkiv-city-of-vagabonds-and-poets-ukraine-russian-border-conflict-revolution/.
120. Mykola Riabchuk, "Dvi Ukraïny: kinets' ambivalentnosty?" *Krytyka*, nos. 1–2 (207–8) (2015): 2–12.
121. Oleh Syniehubov, "Iak til'ky rosiiany vidchuiut' slabkist' oborony Kharkova, vony sprobuiut' shturmuvaty misto," *Ukraïns'ka pravda*, 21 April 2022, https://www.pravda.com.ua/articles/2022/04/21/7341146/.
122. Syniehubov, "Iak til'ky rosiiany."
123. Maksim Butchenko, "Rossiia popala snariadom v 'Rossiiu.' Khar'kovskii istorik Anton Bondarev – o realiiakh nyneshnei zhizni svoego 'russkoiazychnogo' goroda," *Novoe Vremia*, 18 March 2022, https://nv.ua/ukraine/events/harkovskiy-istorik-rasskazyvaet-o-zhizni-svoego-goroda-pod-obstrelami-50226351.html.
124. Eduard Rubin, "Ukraïns'ke misto Kharkiv," *Dzerkalo tyzhnia*, 19 March 2022, https://www.pravda.com.ua/articles/2022/04/21/7341146/.
125. Guy Chazan, "'Another Stalingrad': Assault on Kharkiv Shatters Ties That Once Bound Two Nations," *Financial Times*, 2 March 2022, https://www.ft.com/content/131068c8-5a5e-466a-a476-48de30d97760.
126. "Rosiiany vbyly u Kharkovi kolyshn'oho v'iaznia natsysts'kykh kontstaboriv," *Ukraïns'ka pravda*, 21 March 2022, https://www.pravda.com.ua/news/2022/03/21/7333336/.
127. *Segodnia*, 17 April 2022, https://ukraine.segodnya.ua/ukraine/v-harkove-snesli-i-vybrosili-na-svalku-pamyatnik-zhukovu-video-1615524.html; see also *Tsenzor*, 17 April 2022, https://censor.net/ru/video_news/3334688/v_harkove_demontirovali_pamyatnik_jukovu_videofoto.

128. Mariia Fedotova, "SKR vozbudil ugolovnoe delo iz-za snosa pamiatnika Zhukovu v Khar'kove," *Kommersant*, 17 April 2022, https://www.kommersant.ru/doc/5315745.
129. Butchenko, "Rossiia popala snariadom v 'Rossiiu.'"
130. "Net Moskovskomu prospektu: mėra Khar'kova prizvali ubrat' 'russkii mir' s ulits goroda," *Novoe vremia*, 16 March 2022, https://nv.ua/kharkiv/harkov-terehovu-predlozhili-peremenovat-moskovskiy-prospekt-i-drugie-ulicy-v-svziya-s-voynoy-50225583.html.

# Conclusions

Returning to the statement that "this city is not the first, but neither is it the second," its significance can easily be modified if one acknowledges that Kharkiv is both the first city and the second, and so on in descending order, or in no order whatsoever. Kharkiv, the capital of the borderland, is constantly in motion. In Kharkiv one can find anything at all, but nothing definite and fully formed, completed or lasting. This indefinite status is emphasized by the constant change in the region's symbolic geography, expressed in particular by the city's evolving situation on the conditional borderland between core Russian (Great Russian), Left-Bank Ukrainian (Little Russian), and South Russian (Donbas and New Russian) territories settled in the modern period.

The region's borders have changed, reflecting the zigzags of military, political, and cultural strategies deployed in the borderland by one center or another. Moreover, local elites received and "edited" signals from the center after their own fashion, striving to maintain generational continuity in their own milieu. Considering how constantly intellectuals of various generations adverted to the Sloboda region as a metaphor, using it as a basis for the construction of new historical narratives, one may conclude that regional identity was no less inherited than created by them. It is still being constructed even today, like a kaleidoscopic game of various combinations played with a limited number of symbols, to which new ones are added from time to time.

The particular conditions of the cultural and political borderland, reflecting the eclectic and multilayered composition of local identity, were probably the main reason why no political regionalism of the Siberian or Rusyn type made an appearance in the Sloboda region. There, regional identity was potent enough to correct central policy but could not and did not even attempt to oppose it with a distinct alternative. The borderland—in this case, open—character of culture and society in Kharkiv remained practically unchanged, finding stylistic expression in a certain ambivalence and eclecticism of local identity, lacking clearly delineated borders and, at the same time, capable of assimilating the innovations of every successive cultural era without rejecting the established order.

The decisive role in creating and developing the Sloboda Ukraine region was played initially by the flexible, reformist policy of the Russian imperial center, which enjoyed greater freedom of action in the periphery than in the central Great Russian regions shaped over the centuries. The government, creating conditions in the steppe borderland to attract military settlers from beyond its borders, granted them privileges unavailable to its "own," Russian population. The most important instruments of that policy were the so-called *slobody*—the complex of socioeconomic concessions and privileges that gave their name to the whole territory of the Sloboda regiments but also laid the basis for the region's identity. Hence the name of the region, Sloboda Ukraine, which distinguished it not only from "core" Russian and neighboring Cossack territories but, even more, from Tatar hordes.

As an object of the imperial elite's modernizing policy, the Sloboda region enjoyed primacy over the imperial center in many respects. More contemporary forms of administration were applied there, characterized by elements of decentralization and maintenance of local particularities. Serfdom—the price of modernization *à la russe*—was always less oppressive there than in the imperial center, and a university appeared in the Sloboda region before the one in St. Petersburg. The development of transportation facilities and financial investment turned Kharkiv into one of the most dynamically developing cities of the Russian Empire, second only, perhaps, to Odesa. All this indicates that in the case of the Sloboda region, the imperial periphery turned out to be more dynamic and open to innovation than the historical center of Russia.

The particular identity of the Sloboda region did not vanish with the incorporation of the borderlands into imperial economic, legal, and cultural space. The *slobody* and memory of them in the region long outlasted the legacy of Cossack self-government, the Crimean Khanate, and the Polish-Lithuanian Commonwealth. Moreover, the unceasing expansion of the state obstructed the consolidation of regained lands with core territories within the framework of the Russian Empire, making it more difficult to integrate them with the imperial core. Kharkiv, thanks only to its favorable geographic location, long remained the administrative, cultural, and economic center of the borderlands of the former steppe frontier, including the Sloboda region, Little Russia, the Cossack lands beyond the Dnieper Rapids, the Black Sea littoral, the Don Cossack Host, and the North Caucasus.

The example of the Sloboda region indicates the conceptual inaccuracy of the notion, advanced by some scholars, that the phenomenon of regionalism is associated with traditionalism. The development of modernizing and integrating projects in that region did not erase regional specificity but only imparted new form and content to it. On the one hand, regional identity acquired an additional ethnocultural dimension under the influence of national ideas and because of the activity of Kharkiv University, which helped deepen interest in local history, language, and ethnography. This in turn promoted the cultural rapprochement of the historical Sloboda region not only with the imperial center but also with Ukrainian ethnic territories.

On the other hand, the steppe frontier, which came to be known conventionally as South Russia, became fundamental to the local development of South Russian regional identity based not on the *slobody*, as earlier, but mainly on geographic and economic characteristics. In other words, the case of the Sloboda region does not fully support the notion of a direct link between nationalism and modernization. The latter may not necessarily lead to the formation or strengthening of national identity but to an effort to overcome it and develop transitional forms of identification.

The coexistence of various types of identity in the Sloboda region was possible, in the first place, thanks to the weakness of each of them. There, national and regional discourses did not take on an exclusive character with regard to one another—not, at least, until the fall of the Russian Empire. The transformation of the empire's political space in the years 1917–20 did not fundamentally change the picture. It only led to the gradual decline of South Russian territorial identity after the defeat of the Armed Forces of South Russia (the White movement) and the insurgent movement led by Nestor Makhno, which opposed the Whites. Thus the South Russian region never took final shape, having failed to create the institutional foundations for its development. The Ukrainian national project in turn proved unable to manifest itself on Ukrainian ethnic territory in such a way as to amalgamate old and new regional identities in a new national space.

The status of Kharkiv as a capital and the Soviet policy of Ukrainization localized the former Sloboda region in Ukrainian administrative and national cultural space. At the same time, the Soviet policy of modernization, along with the new Soviet culture and ideology, introduced the city and region into the common economic and sociocultural space of the USSR. The project of creating a "new historical community—the Soviet people," moving gradually from Marxist internationalism to the terrain of Russian imperial Slavophilism, was not completed. In the final analysis, that project returned to the point of historical bifurcation, that is to say, to the moment when the Russian imperial and Ukrainian national projects became mutually contradictory.

The historical experience of the Sloboda Ukraine/Kharkiv region shows that regional identity may in some cases promote and in other cases oppose a nation-state project of any kind. It plays a constructive role only in conjunction with successful projects and prospects of modernization, but there is no rigid interdependence between the regional, national, and modernizing components of social development: each of them remains autonomous within the framework of a given political system. Kharkiv regional discourse presented no real alternative neither to Russian imperial nor to Ukrainian national identity discourses. It merely reflected and moderated their ideological and political components. The cultural borderland remained open on all sides but not consolidated. Its identity remained weak, which, given the situation, was probably no matter for regret.

One of the reasons why local identities in Ukraine's urbanized east, including Kharkiv, were somewhat opposed to Ukrainian nation-building was not that they were based on values fundamentally different from those of the West but that the post-Soviet "Ukrainian project" itself remained, for a long time, deeply Sovietized. The Ukrainian political leadership had no well-developed regional strategy and was in no condition to assess the advantages of the country's regional diversity with regard to the effective involvement of regional potential in developing projects of innovative reform and successful modernization.

It is another question whether regional elites were capable of proposing an alternative to the nation-state projects implemented by the political regimes in Ukraine and Russia. I see no basis for a positive answer to such a question. More than Ukraine's central elites, the regional ones labor under the burden of historical tradition, based on deeply rooted stereotypes and patterns. Besides, they usually pursue not strategic but perfectly concrete tactical goals calculated for the short term. If the regional revolution was at all feasible, then it was most likely to prove conservative in character.

Russia's armed attack on Ukraine in 2014 accelerated the process of Ukrainian nation-state building, which went beyond the bounds of ethnicity to create a political nation. In the words of a contemporary scholar, "the Russian-speaking citizens of Ukraine are quite emotional when, expressing themselves in Russian, they defend Ukrainian as the sole official language, as they do all other manifestations of Ukrainian political identity."[1] The pendulum of Ukrainian political life, which swung back and forth for almost thirty years between Ukrainian nationalist and Little Russian autonomist models of the future, finally came to rest at the "independence" marker. It may be assumed that this came as a surprise to the occupiers, who had come to liberate the "good" Little Russians from the "bad" Ukrainians. The difference between them was erased, as became apparent, at the same rate as the erasure of Ukrainian towns and cities from the face of the earth.

Russian nation-state building, unlike its Ukrainian counterpart, fell into a trap set by history. The current anti-Ukrainian discourse is cultivated by those who did not learn the lessons of the nineteenth century and missed those of the twentieth entirely. By the latter century, modern Ukraine already existed alongside historical Little Russia. The Russians were aware only of Little Russia, dismissing Ukraine as an artificial product of Russia's many enemies. Even the communists headed by Lenin, whose body reposes in a mausoleum in the historical center of Moscow, were consigned to the category of enemies. That left the Ukrainians occupying the place in the structure of present-day Russian extremism that was held by the Jews in its German counterpart.

An elaborate conception of Moscow's new policy may be found in an article by Timofei Sergeitsev published by the official Russian news agency RIA Novosti in early April 2022.[2] The article argues the need to physically exterminate the Ukrainian political elite and forcibly carry out the total "denazification" of most of the Ukrainian population. According to the author, "denazification" entails total Russification and de-Europeanization by means of a system of harsh repressive measures. This means that not only the state but even the very name "Ukraine" must vanish, with the local population to be deprived of civil rights for a minimum of one generation. In general, the tone and content of the article are unprecedented in their forthright insistence on a state policy of genocide of the Ukrainian people. As such, it attests quite eloquently to the further intellectual and moral degradation of Russian society as well as the transformation of Russia into a fascist-type state.

The intellectual roots of Russian fascism can be traced back to the era of the Russian Empire's agony, with its antisemitism and Orthodox imperial chauvinism. It is apparent in the ideology of the Black Hundred, the propaganda of the White Army, and the writings of the Russian emigration. In its day, the latter had a notable influence on the intellectual evolution of German fascism.[3] Hence the considerable resemblance between Hitler's Germany, Stalin's USSR, and Putin's Russia. The current version of Russian fascism (*rashizm*) has developed as a result of the union of the historical legacy of two imperial-type systems, Russian and Soviet, now in their death agony. The ideological basis of this symbiosis was developed by the Russian Orthodox Church, and its superstructure was created through the joint efforts of Mafia capital and the Soviet secret police, the KGB. In this state, Putin's Russia is clearly destined for international isolation and further stagnation. Even in the post-Soviet wasteland, there is by no means a general impulse to raise the standards of Orthodox obscurantism and imperial chauvinism.

It is hard to tell at this point when the Russo-Ukrainian war will end and what its outcome will be, how the symbolic configuration of the former Sloboda region will change, and what postwar Kharkiv will look like. It can only be asserted that the region began as a frontier and has remained a frontier. In its three and a half centuries of existence, the Kharkiv region has not lost its immanent status as a transit territory. It is another matter that the vector of its geopolitical orientation must now change radically.

If the Sloboda frontier was oriented southward from the very beginning of its existence, serving as a bridgehead for Russian expansion and modernization, then in present-day conditions, by all accounts, it must turn into a Ukrainian-European *antemurale*, a protective bastion against Russian aggression. In order to carry out this function effectively, the Kharkiv region must again become Sloboda territory, a militarized zone of proactive modernization endowed with special socioeconomic privileges under close control of the political center.

## Notes

1. Nataliia Zverko, "Ukrainskii uchenyi: Novaia tendentsiia – russkoiazychnyi grazhdanin Ukrainy na russkom zashchishchaet ukrainskii iazyk," Lithuanian Radio and Television (LRT), 10 February 2022, https://www.lrt.lt/ru/novosti/17/1612345/ukrainskii-uchenyi-novaia-tendentsiia-russkoiazychnyi-grazhdanin-ukrainy-na-russkom-zashchishchaet-ukrainskii-iazyk.
2. Timofei Sergeitsev, "Chto Rossiia dolzhna sdelat' s Ukrainoi," RIA Novosti, 5 April 2022, https://ria.ru/20220403/ukraina-1781469605.html.
3. Michael Kellogg, *The Russian Roots of Nazism: White Émigrés and the Making of National Socialism, 1917–1945* (Cambridge: Cambridge University Press, 2005).

# Historical Timeline

1630s–40s  Belgorod defense line erected on the southern frontier of the Muscovite state

1654–55  Kharkiv founded by Ukrainian refugees as a fortified settlement

1667  Ukraine partitioned between Polish-Lithuanian Commonwealth and the Muscovite state, roughly along the Dnieper River

1679–80  Izium defense line erected

1726  Theological Collegium transferred from Belgorod to Kharkiv

1765–80  Sloboda Ukraine gubernia (reestablished 1796–1835; renamed Kharkiv gubernia in 1835)

1775  Liquidation of the Zaporozhian Cossack Host

1780–96  Kharkiv vicegerency (*namestnichestvo*) replaces former Sloboda Ukraine gubernia

1783  Russia annexes the Crimea

1785  Abolition of Ukrainian Cossack Hetmanate

1805  Kharkiv University established

1834  Kyiv University established

1869  Kursk–Kharkiv–Azov railway established

1870s  Industrial development of Donbas region begins

1885  Kharkiv Technological Institute established

1895  Kharkiv Locomotive Factory established

1900  Mykola Mikhnovsky, a Kharkiv-based lawyer and Ukrainian activist, formulates the idea of Ukrainian political independence

1906  First electrical tram begins operation in Kharkiv

1914    Outbreak of World War I

1917    Collapse of Russian monarchy and establishment of Ukrainian Central Rada

1917, 7 November    Ukrainian People's Republic proclaimed

1917, 5 December    Russian Bolshevik government declares war on Ukraine

1917, 8 December    Kharkiv captured by Russian Red Army

1917, 17 December    Kharkiv proclaimed capital of Ukrainian Soviet People's Republic

1918, 26 January    Russian Red Army occupies Kyiv

1918, 1 (14) February    Soviet Russian Donetsk-Kryvyi Rih Republic proclaimed in Kharkiv

1918, April–December    Kharkiv under control of German-supported Hetmanate of Pavlo Skoropadsky

1918, December–January    Kharkiv under control of Ukrainian units under Petro Bolbochan

1919, January–June    Kharkiv reoccupied by Russian Red Army and becomes de facto capital of Ukrainian Socialist Soviet Republic

1919, June–December    Kharkiv occupied by Russian White Army

1919, 11 December    Kharkiv recaptured by Russian Red Army and becomes capital of Soviet Ukraine

1932    Kharkiv oblast established

1932–33    Holodomor (humanmade famine) kills between 3 and 4 million people in Soviet Ukraine

1933, March    Kharkiv University reestablished

1934, June    Kharkiv loses metropolitan status to Kyiv

1941, 24 October    Kharkiv occupied by German Nazis

1943, February    Kharkiv recaptured by Russian Red Army

1943, March    Kharkiv recaptured by German Nazis

1943, 23 August    Kharkiv recaptured by Russian Red Army

1943, December    First Nazi war crimes trial in Kharkiv

1944    Deportation of Crimean Tatars from the Crimea to central Asia

1954    Administrative transfer of the Crimea from Soviet Russia to Soviet Ukraine

1986, 26 April    Chernobyl nuclear disaster

1991, 24 August    Ukrainian parliament (Supreme Council) declares independence of Ukraine from the Soviet Union

1991, December    Leonid Kravchuk elected first president of Ukraine

1994, July    Leonid Kuchma elected president of Ukraine

1994    Ukraine becomes member of NATO Partnership for Peace

1997    Treaty of Friendship signed by Russia and Ukraine (ratified in 1999), according to which Russia renounces claims to the Crimea, while Ukraine agrees that Russian military base can remain in Sevastopol for twenty years

2002, May    Ukrainian government begins process of applying for full NATO membership

2004    Ukrainian democratic Orange Revolution; Viktor Yushchenko elected president of Ukraine

2010    Viktor Yanukovych elected president of Ukraine

2014    Viktor Yanukovych's corrupt regime collapses under pressure of Ukrainian democratic revolution ("Euromaidan")

2014, February    Russia annexes the Crimea and starts undeclared ("hybrid") war on Ukraine, which leads to de facto secession of part of the Donbas

2014, May    Petro Poroshenko elected president of Ukraine

2015, May    "Decommunization" laws introduced in Ukraine

2019    Volodymyr Zelensky elected president of Ukraine

2022, 24 February    Russian invasion of Ukraine

# Selected Bibliography

Abramov, Iakov. *V. N. Karazin, ego zhizn' i obshchestvennaia deiatel'nost': Biograficheskii ocherk.* St. Petersburg: Obshchestvennaia Pol'za, 1891.

Alchevskaia, Khristina. *Peredumannoe i perezhitoe. Dnevniki, pis'ma, vospominaniia.* Moscow: I. D. Sytin, 1912.

Avakov, Arsen. *Mgnoveniia khar'kovskoi vesny, 2014.* Kharkiv: Folio, 2020.

Bagalei, Dmitrii. *Materialy dlia istorii kolonizatsii i byta stepnoi okrainy Moskovskogo gosudarstva (Khar'kovskoi i otchasti Kurskoi i Voronezhskoi gubernii) v XVI–XVIII stoletii, sobrannye v raznykh arkhivakh,* 2 vols. Kharkov: Izdanie Istoriko-Filologicheskogo Obshchestva, 1890.

———. *Ocherki iz istorii kolonizatsii i byta stepnoi okrainy Moskovskogo gosudarstva.* Moscow: Obshchestvo istorii i drevnostei, 1887.

———. *Ocherki iz russkoi istorii. Monografii i stat'i po istorii Slobodskoi Ukrainy,* 2 vols. Kharkiv: Pechatnoe delo, 1913.

———. *Opyt istorii Khar'kovskogo universiteta (po neizdannym materialam),* vol. 1 (1802-1815): 1017–18. Kharkiv: Tipografiia universiteta, 1894.

Bagalei, Dmitrii, and Aleksei Miller. *Istoriia goroda Khar'kova za 250 let ego sushchestvovaniia (s 1655 po 1905 god),* 2 vols. Kharkiv: [n.p.], 1993. Reprint edition, published originally in Kharkiv, 1912.

Bagalei, Dmitrii, Nikolai Sumtsov, and Vladislav Buzeskul, *Kratkii ocherk istorii Khar'kovskogo universiteta za pervye sto let ego sushchestvovaniia (1805–1905).* Kharkiv: Universitetskaia tipografiia, 1906.

Bahalii, Dmytro (*see also* Bagalei, Dmitrii). *Istoriia Slobids'koï Ukraïny,* ed. Volodymyr Kravchenko. Kharkiv: Osnova, 1990. Originally published in Kharkiv in 1918.

———. *Istoriia kolonizatsiï Slobids'koï Ukraïny (Vybrani pratsi. v 6 tomakh,* vol.1, ed. Volodymyr Kravchenko). Kharkiv: Golden Pages, 2007.

Bartov, Omer, and Eric D. Weitz, eds. *Shatterzone of Empires: Coexistence and Violence in the German, Habsburg, Russian, and Ottoman Borderlands.* Bloomington: Indiana University Press, 2013.

Beliaev, Konstantin, and Andrei Krasniashchikh. *Khar'kov v zerkale mirovoi literatury.* Kharkiv: Folio, 2007.

Bilaniuk, Laada. *Contested Tongues: Language Politics and Cultural Correction in Ukraine.* Ithaca, NY: Cornell University Press, 2005.

Biriova, Ol'ha. "Pomishchyts'ki sadyby Kharkivs'koï huberniï (persha polovyna XVIII–pochatok XX stolittia)." PhD diss., Karazin National University of Kharkiv, 2009.

Boiechko, Vasyl', et al. *Kordony Ukraïny: istorychna retrospektyva ta suchasnyi stan.* Kyiv: Osnovy, 1994.

Boiko, Anatolii, ed. *Opysy Stepovoï Ukraïny ostann'oï chverti XVIII–pochatku XIX stolittia.* Zaporizhia: Naukove t-vo imeni Ia. Novyts'koho, 2009.

Bolebrukh, Anatolii, et al. *Vasyl' Nazarovych Karazin (1773–1842): do 200-richchia Khar-kivs'koho universytetu.* Kharkiv: Avto-Enerhiia, 2005.

Breyfogle, Nicholas B., et al., eds. *Peopling the Russian Periphery: Borderland Colonization in Eurasian History*. London: Routledge, 2007.
Brown, Karen. *A Biography of No Place: From Ethnic Borderland to Soviet Heartland*. Cambridge, MA: Harvard University Press, 2004.
Brudny, Yitzhak M. *Reinventing Russia: Russian Nationalism and the Soviet State, 1953–1991*. Cambridge, MA: Harvard University Press, 1999.
Burbank, Jane, et al., eds. *Russian Empire: Space, People, Power, 1700–1930*. Bloomington: Indiana University Press, 2007.
Chebotarev, Khariton, ed. *Geograficheskoe metodicheskoe opisanie Rossiiskoi Imperii s nadlezhashchim vvedeniem k osnovatel'nomu poznaniiu zemnogo shara i Evropy voobshche...* Moscow: Universitetskaia tipografiiia, 1776.
Chechel'nitskii, Sergei, ed. *Arkhitektory Khar'kova*. Kharkiv: Zoloti storinky, 2008.
Chornovol, Ihor. *Komparatyvni frontyry: svitovyi i vitchyznianyi vymiry*. Kyiv: Krytyka, 2015.
Chornyi, Dmytro (*see also* Chernyi, Dmitrii). *Istoriia Slobids'koï Ukraïny: Pidruchnyk*. Kharkiv: Kharkivs'kyi universytet, 2018.
Czhizhikova, Liudmila. *Russko-ukrainskoe pogranich'e: Istoriia i sud'by traditsionno-bytovoi kul'tury (XIX–XX veka)*. Moscow: Nauka, 1988.
Danilevskii, Grigorii P. *Ukrainskaia starina: Materialy dlia istorii ukrainskoi literatury i narodnogo obrazovaniia*. Kharkiv: Izdanie Zalenskogo i Liubarskogo, 1866.
Dashkevych, Iaroslav, ed. *Istorychne kartoznavstvo Ukraïny*. Lviv, Kyiv, and New York: M. Kots', 2004.
Davies, Brian L. *Warfare, State and Society on the Black Sea Steppe, 1500–1700*. London and New York: Routledge, 2007.
Dawson, Greg. *Judgment before Nuremberg: The Holocaust in the Ukraine and the First Nazi War Crimes Trial*. New York: Pegasus Books, 2012.
D'iachenko, Nikolai T. *Ulitsy i ploshchadi Khar'kova*. Kharkiv: Prapor, 1977.
Dmytriienko, Mariia F. "Administratyvno-terytorial'nyi ustrii ukraïns'kykh zemel': istoriia, proekty, real'nist' (XIX–pochatok XX st.).ˮ *Problemy istoriï Ukraïny XIX–pochatku XX st.*, no. 6 (2003): 105–24.
Dolengo, Mykhailo. "Kyïv ta Kharkiv—literaturni vzaiemovidnoshennia.ˮ *Chervonyi shliakh*, nos. 6–7 (1923): 151–57.
Dornik, Wolfram, et al., eds. *The Emergence of Ukraine: Self-Determination, Occupation, and War in Ukraine, 1917–1922*. Edmonton: Canadian Institute of Ukrainian Studies Press, 2015.
Dreiser, Theodore. *Dreiser's Russian Diary*, ed. Thomas P. Riggio and James L. W. West III. Philadelphia: University of Pennsylvania Press, 1996.
Druzhinina, Elena I. *Iuzhnaia Ukraina v period krizisa feodalizma: 1825–1860 gg.* Moscow: Nauka, 1981.
Filaret (Gumilevskii). *Istoriko-statisticheskoe opisanie Khar'kovskoi eparkhii, v 3 tomakh*, 2nd ed. Kharkiv: Muzei Mis'koï Sadyby, 2005. Published originally in Kharkiv in five parts, 1857–1859.
Flynn, James T. *The University Reform of Tsar Alexander I, 1802–1835*. Washington, DC: Catholic University of America Press, 1988.
———. "V. N. Karazin, the Gentry, and Kharkov University.ˮ *Slavic Review* 28, no. 2 (1969): 209–20.
Fomin, Petr. *Kratkii ocherk istorii s"ezdov gornopromyshlennikov Iuga Rossii*. Kharkiv: Zilberberg & Sons, 1908.
Gel'dfanbein, Grigorii. *General i ad"iutant: rasskazy o pisateliakh*. Kharkiv: Prapor, 1966.
Georgi, Iogann Gotlib [Johann Gottlieb]. *Opisanie vsekh obitaiushchikh v Rossiiskom gosudarstve narodov: Ikh zhiteiskikh obriadov, obyknovenii, odezhd...* , 2nd ed. St. Petersburg: Russkaia Simfoniia, 2007. Published originally in St. Petersburg in 1799.

Gerasimov, Il'ia, et al., eds. *Novaia imperskaia istoriia postsovetskogo prostranstva*. Kazan: Ab Imperio, 2004.
Getmanets, Mikhail F. *Taina reki Kaialy: "Slovo o polku Igoreve,"* 2nd ed. Kharkiv: Izd. Khar'kovskogo universiteta, 1989.
Gil'denstedt, [Iohann] [Johann Anton Güldenstädt]. "Dnevnik puteshestviia po Slobodsko-Ukrainskoi gubernii v avguste i sentiabre 1774 goda." In *Khar'kovskii sbornik*, vol. 5. Kharkiv: Gubernskaia tipografiia, 1891.
Gilroy, Amanda, ed. *Romantic Geographies: Discourses of Travel, 1775–1844*. Manchester: Manchester University Press, 2000.
Glantz, David M. *Kharkov 1942: Anatomy of a Military Disaster*. Rockville Centre, NY: Sarpedon, 1998.
Gorizontov, Leonid, ed. *Regiony i granitsy Ukrainy v istoricheskoi retrospektive*. Moscow: Institut slavianovedeniia RAN, 2005.
Gorlenko, Vladimir F. *Stanovlenie ukrainskoi étnografii kontsa XVIII–pervoi poloviny XIX st.* Kyiv: Naukova Dumka, 1988.
Gusev, Aleksandr Ia. *Khar'kov: ego proshloe i nastoiashchee. Istoricheskii spravochnik-putevoditel'*. Kharkiv: Tipografiia Adol'fa Darre, 1902.
Hamm, Michael F. "Khar'kov's Progressive Duma, 1910–1914: A Study in Russian Municipal Reform." *Slavic Review* 40, no. 1 (1981): 17–36.
Hamm, Michael, ed. *The City in Late Imperial Russia: Papers from a Meeting of the American Association for the Advancement of Slavic Studies, Held in Kansas City, MO, Oct. 1983*. Bloomington: Indiana University Press, 1986.
Haxthausen, Baron von. *The Russian Empire, Its People, Institutions, and Resources*, 2 vols. London: Chapman & Hall, 1856.
Herlihy, Patricia. "Ukrainian Cities in the Nineteenth Century." In *Rethinking Ukrainian History*, ed. Ivan L. Rudnytsky with the assistance of John-Paul Himka. Edmonton: CIUS Press, 1981.
Holovko, Aleksandr, and Aleksandr Iarmysh. *Sdelal, chto mog: khar'kovskii gorodskoi golova Aleksandr Konstantinovich Pogorelko*. Kharkiv: Osnova, 1998.
Hrytsak, Iaroslav, et al., eds. *L'viv i Donets'k: sotsial'ni identychnosti v suchasnii Ukraïni. Ukraïna Moderna* 12, no. 2 (2007), special issue. Kyiv: Krytyka, 2007.
Hughes, James, and Gwendolyn Sasse, eds. *Ethnicity and Territory in the Former Soviet Union: Regions in Conflict*. London: Frank Cass, 2002.
Hulak-Artemovs'kyi, Petro. *Poetychni tvory*; Hrebinka, Ievhen. *Poetychni tvory, povisti ta opovidannia*. Kyiv: Naukova Dumka, 1984.
Hurzhii, Oleksandr. *Ukraïns'ka kozats'ka derzhava v druhii polovyni XVII–XVIII st.: kordony, naselennia, pravo*. Kyiv: Osnovy, 1996.
Iareshchenko, Artur. *Ukraïns'kyi Feniks*. Kharkiv: Prapor, 1999.
Iarmysh, Oleksandr, and Serhii Posokhov, eds. *Istoriia mista Kharkova XX stolittia*. Kharkiv: Folio, 2004.
Illiashevich, Lev. *Kratkii ocherk istorii Khar'kovskogo dvorianstva*. Kharkiv: M. Zil'berberg, 1885.
*Istoriia gorodov i sel Ukrainskoi SSR v 26 tomakh: Khar'kovskaia oblast'*. Kyiv: AN USSR, 1976.
Ivanov, Petr. *Zhizn' i pover'ia krest'ian Kupianskogo uezda Khar'kovskoi gubernii*, 2nd ed. Kharkiv: Maidan, 2007. Published originally in Kharkiv in 1907.
Janowski, Ludwik. *Uniwersytet Charkowski w początkach swego istnienia (1805–1820)*. Cracow: Akademia Umiejętności, 1911.
Jones, Martin, and Anssi Paasi, eds. *Regional Worlds: Advancing the Geography of Regions*. London: Routledge, 2017.
Kabuzan, Vladimir M. *Zaselenie Novorossii (Ekaterinoslavskoi i Khersonskoi gubernii) v XVIII–pervoi polovine XIX veka (1719–1858 gg.)*. Moscow: Nauka, 1976.
Kaganskii, Vladimir. *Kul'turnyi landshaft i sovetskoe obitaemoe prostranstvo. Sbornik statei*. Moscow: NLO, 2011.

Kalinovskii, Grigorii. *Opisanie svadebnykh ukrainskikh prostonarodnykh obriadov*. St. Petersburg: Tipografia H. F. Klena, 1777.
Kappeler, Andreas, et al., eds. *Culture, Nation, and Identity: The Ukrainian-Russian Encounter, 1600–1945*. Edmonton: CIUS Press, 2003.
Karazin, Vasilii N. *Sochineniia, pis'ma i bumagi*, ed. Dmitrii Bagalei. Kharkiv: Universitetskaia tipografiia, 1910.
Kevorkian, Konstantin E. *Pervaia stolitsa*. Kharkiv: Pervaia stolitsa, 1995; 2nd ed. Kharkiv: Folio, 1999; 3rd ed. Kharkiv: Folio, 2002.
*Khar'kov: putevoditel' dla turistov*, 3rd ed. Kharkiv: Tipografiia I. M. Anichkina, 1915.
*Kharkiv i Pol'shcha: Liudy i podiï. Mizhnarodna naukovo-praktychna konferentsiia (Kharkiv, 2005): materialy*. Kharkiv: Maidan, 2006.
Khodarkovsky, Michael. *Russia's Steppe Frontier: The Making of a Colonial Empire, 1500–1800*. Bloomington: Indiana University Press, 2002.
Khoroshkevich, Anna. *Rus' i Krym: ot soiuza k protivostoianiiu: konets XV–nachalo XVI v.* Moscow: URSS, 2001.
Kijas, Artur. *Polacy na Uniwersytecie Charkowskim, 1805–1917*, 2nd rev. ed. Poznan: PTPN Press, 2008.
Kivelson, Valerie. *Cartographies of Tsardom: The Land and Its Meanings in Seventeenth-Century Russia*. Ithaca, NY: Cornell University Press, 2006.
Klupt, Veniamin S., ed. *Ukraina (SSSR po raionam. Ėkonomicheskaia geografiia SSSR)*. Moscow-Leningrad: Gosizdat, 1928.
Kohl, Johann G. *Russia. St. Petersburg, Moscow, Kharkoff, Riga, Odessa, the German Provinces on the Baltic, the Steppes, the Crimea, and the Interior of the Empire*. London: Chapman and Hall, 1842.
Kohut, Zenon E. *History as a Battleground: Russian-Ukrainian Relations and Historical Consciousness in Contemporary Ukraine*. Saskatoon: Heritage Press, 2001.
———. *Making Ukraine: Studies on Political Culture, Historical Narrative, and Identity*. Edmonton: CIUS Press, 2011.
Kolossov, Vladimir, and Ol'ga Vendina, eds. *Rossiisko-ukrainskoe pogranich'e: dvadtsat' let razdelennogo edinstva*. Moscow: Novyi Khronograph, 2011.
Kopychko, Volodymyr P., and Iurii H. Kopychko, eds. *Kharkiv'iany: Poema pro misto v tsytatakh poetychnykh tvoriv*. Kharkiv: Slobozhanshchyna, 2007.
Koropeckyj, Iwan S., ed. *Ukrainian Economic History: Interpretive Essays*. Cambridge, MA: Harvard Ukrainian Research Institute, 1991.
Koznarsky, Taras. "Kharkiv Literary Almanacs of the 1830s: The Shaping of Ukrainian Cultural Identity." PhD diss., Harvard University, 2001.
Kravchenko, Vladimir. *D. I. Bagalei: nauchnaia i obshchestvenno-politicheskaia deiatel'nost'*. Kharkiv: Osnova, 1990.
———. "Kharkiv: The Past Lives On." *The Soviet and Post-Soviet Review* 64, no. 3 (2019): 324–51.
———. *The Ukrainian-Russian Borderland: History versus Geography*. Montreal, Kingston, London, and Chicago: McGill-Queen's University Press, 2022.
Kulinych, Ivan M. *Hubernator*. Kharkiv: Maidan, 1997.
Kurman, Mikhail, and Ivan Lebedinskii, *Naselenie bol'shogo sotsialisticheskogo goroda*. Moscow: Statistika, 1968.
Kuromiya, Hiroaki. *Freedom and Terror in the Donbas: A Ukrainian-Russian Borderland, 1870s–1990s*. Cambridge: Cambridge University Press, 1998.
Kvitka, Grigorii. *Khar'kov i uezdnye goroda: Khar'kovskaia starina*. Kharkiv: Kharkivs'ka Starovyna, 2005.
Kvitka, Hryhorii. *Zibrannia tvoriv u 7 tomakh*. Kyiv: Naukova Dumka, 1981.
Kvitka, Illia. *Zapiski o slobodskikh polkakh s nachala ikh poseleniia do 1766 g*. Kharkiv: n.p., 1812; 2nd ed. 1882.

Lavriv, Petro. *Istoriia Pivdenno-Skhidnoï Ukraïny*. Kyiv: Ukraïns'ka vydavnycha spilka, 1996.
Leckey, Colum. *Patrons of Enlightenment: The Free Economic Society in Eighteenth-Century Russia*. Newark: University of Delaware Press, 2011.
LeDonne, John P. *The Grand Strategy of the Russian Empire, 1650–1831*. New York: Oxford University Press, 2004.
Leibfreid, Aleksandr Iu., and Iuliia Poliakova. *Khar'kov: ot kreposti k stolitse. Zametki o starom gorode*. Kharkiv: Folio, 1998.
Leibfreid, Aleksandr Iu., et al. *Khar'kov: Arkhitektura, pamiatniki, novostroiki: Putevoditel'*. Kharkiv: Prapor, 1987.
Liubchenko, Arkadii. *Shchodennyk*. Lviv and New York: M. Kots', 1999.
Losievskii, Igor'. *Russkaia lira s Ukrainy: Russkie pisateli Ukrainy pervoi chetverti XIX veka*. Kharkiv: Oko Press, 1993.
Lysiak-Rudnyts'kyi, Ivan. *Istorychni ese*, 2 vols., ed. Iaroslav Hrytsak, 2nd repr. ed. Kyiv: Dukh i Litera, 2019.
Masliichuk, Volodymyr. *Altera Patria: Notatky pro diial'nist Ivana Sirka na Slobids'kii Ukraïni*. Kharkiv: Muzei Mis'koï Sadyby, 2004.
———. *Provintsiia na perekhresti kul'tur: Doslidzhennia z istoriï Slobids'koï Ukraïny XVII–XIX st*. Kharkiv: Muzei Mis'koï Sadyby, 2007.
Mel'nykiv, Rostyslav, and Iurii Tsaplin. "Severo-vostok iugo-zapada (o sovremennoi khar'kovskoi literature)." *Novoe literaturnoe obozrenie* 3, no. 85 (2007): 263–88.
Miller, Aleksei. *"Ukrainskii vopros" v politike vlastei i russkom obshchestvennom mnenii (vtoraia polovina XIX veka)*. St. Petersburg: Aleteya, 2000.
Miller, Aleksei, and Dmitrii Chernyi, eds. *Goroda imperii v gody Velikoi voiny i revoliutsii: Sbornik statei*. St. Petersburg: Nestor-istoriia, 2017.
Miller, Aleksei, et al., eds. *Ukraina–Rossiia: Istoriia vzaimootnoshenii*. Moscow: Iazyki russkoi kultury, 2003.
Mykhailyn, Ihor L. *Istoriia ukraïns'koï zhurnalistyky XIX stolittia*. Kyiv: Tsentr Navchal'noï Literatury, 2003.
Myshlovska, Oksana, and Ulrich Schmid, eds. *Regionalism without Regions: Reconceptualizing Ukraine's Heterogeneity*. Budapest: CEU Press, 2019.
Nemenskii, Oleg. "Modeli iuzhnorusskogo natsionalizma na Ukraine." *Voprosy natsionalizma* 2, no. 18 (2014): 20–31.
Novosel'skii, Aleksei A. *Bor'ba Moskovskogo gosudarstva s tatarami v pervoi polovine XVII veka*. Moscow-Leningrad: Izd. AN SSSR, 1948.
Paasi, Anssi. "The Institutionalization of Regions: A Theoretical Framework for Understanding the Emergence of Regions and the Constitutions of Regional Identity." *Fennia*, no. 164 (1986): 105–46.
———. "Place and Region: Regional Worlds and Words." *Progress in Human Geography* 26, no. 6 (2002): 802–11.
Paasi, Anssi, et al., eds. *Handbook on the Geographies of Regions and Territories*. Cheltenham: Edward Elgar, 2018.
Passek, Vadim. *Ocherk Khar'kovskoi gubernii*. Kharkiv: n.p., 1839.
Perepecha, Alla, and Artur Iareshchenko, eds. *Toponimichnyi slovnyk Kharkivshchyny*. Kharkiv: Derzhavna naukova biblioteka Korolenka, 1991.
Pirko, Vasyl'. *Kartohrafichni materialy Pivdnia Ukraïny XVIII stolittia*. Lviv: NTSh Press, 1997.
Pirko, Vasyl' O., and Oleksandr I. Hurzhii, eds. *Opysy Kharkivs'koho namisnytstva kintsia XVIII st.: Opysovo-statystychni dzherela*. Kyiv: Naukova Dumka, 1991.
Plokhy, Serhii. *The Origins of the Slavic Nations: Premodern Identities in Russia, Ukraine, and Belarus*. Cambridge: Cambridge University Press, 2006.
Portnov, Andrii. "Kak nachinalas' voina na vostoke Ukrainy ili pochemu Khar'kov i Dnepropetrovsk ne stali Donetskom i Luganskom?" *Gefter* 22, no. 1 (2016): http://gefter.ru/archive/17295.

———. "The New Heart of Ukraine? Dnipropetrovsk after Euromaidan." *Osteuropa* 65, no. 4 (2015): 173–87.
Posokhov, Sergei, and Aleksandr Iarmysh. *Gubernatory i general-gubernatory*. Kharkiv: Acta, 1996.
Posokhov, Serhii. *Obrazy universytetiv Rosiis'koï imperiï druhoï polovyny XIX–pochatku XX stolittia v publitsystytsi ta istoriohrafiï*. Kharkiv: Kharkivs'kyi universytet, 2006.
Posokhova, Liudmyla. *Kharkivs'kyi kolehium (XVIII – persha polovyna XIX st.)*. Kharkiv: Business-Inform, 1999.
Potichnyj, Peter J., et al., eds. *Ukraine and Russia in Their Historical Encounter*. Edmonton: CIUS Press, 1992.
Potrashkov, Sergei. *Khar'kovskie polki: Tri veka istorii*. Kharkiv: Oko Press, 1998.
"Regiony Ukrainy: chto nas raz"ediniaet i chto ob"ediniaet? Mneniia sotsiologov. Materialy kruglogo stola. Khar'kov,18 aprelia 2014 g." *Ab Imperio* 3 (2014): 123–60.
Reient, Oleksandr, ed. *Vid muriv do bul'variv: tvorennia modernoho mista v Ukraïni (kinets' XVIII–pochatok XX st.)*. Kyiv: Instytut istoriï Ukraïny, 2019.
Repan, O., ed. *Narysy z istoriï osvoiennia Pivdennoï Ukraïny XV–XVIII st.: kolektyvna monohrafiia*. Kyiv: K.I.S., 2020.
Riabchuk, Mykola. *Dvi Ukraïny: real'ni mezhi, virtual'ni ihry*. Kyiv: Krytyka, 2003.
———. *Vid Malorosiï do Ukraïny: paradoksy zapizniloho natsiietvorennia*. Kyiv: Krytyka, 2000.
Rodgers, Peter W. *Nation, Region, and History in Post-Communist Transitions: Identity Politics in Ukraine, 1991–2006*. Stuttgart: Ibidem Verlag, 2008.
Rommel', Kristof Ditrikh fon (Christoph Dietrich von Rommel). *Spohady pro moie zhyttia ta mii chas*, ed. Volodymyr Kravchenko, trans. Volodymyr Masliichuk and Nataliia Onishchenko. Kharkiv: Maidan, 2001.
Rudiakov, Pavel. *"V sluzhbu i vechnoe poddanstvo...": Serbskie poseleniia Novaia Serbiia i Slavianoserbiia na ukrainskikh zemliakh (1751–1764)*. Kyiv: ArtEk, 2001.
Saratov, Ivan. *Istoriia khar'kovskikh gerbov: uchebnoe posobie*. Kharkiv: Maidan, 2000.
Schmidtke, Oliver, and Serhy Yekelchyk, eds. *Europe's Last Frontier? Belarus, Moldova, and Ukraine between Russia and the European Union*. New York: Palgrave Macmillan, 2008.
Semenenko, Oleksandr. *Kharkiv, Kharkiv...* Kharkiv and New York: Berezil' and Marian Kots', 1992.
Serbina, K. I., ed. *Kniga Bol'shomu Chertezhu*. Moscow and Leningrad: AN SSSR, 1950.
Shamrai, Ahapii, ed. *Kharkivs'ka shkola romantykiv*, 3 vols. Kharkiv: DVU, 1930.
Shandra, Valentyna. *Heneral-hubernatorstva v Ukraïni, XIX–pochatok XX st.* Kyiv: Instytut istoriï Ukraïny, 2005.
Shchelkov, Konstantin P. *Istoricheskaia khronologiia Khar'kovskoi gubernii*, 2nd ed. Kharkiv: Muzei Mis'koï Sadyby, 2007. Published originally in Kharkiv in 1882.
Shchoholiv, Iakiv. *Tvory. Povnyi zbirnyk z iliustratsiiamy*. Kyiv: Rukh, 1919.
Sherekh, Iurii (*see also* Shevel'ov, Iurii). *Porohy i zaporizhzhia*, 3 vols. Kharkiv: Folio, 1998.
Shevel'ov, Iurii (*see also* Sherekh, Iurii). *Ia-mene-meni: Spohady*, 2 vols. Kharkiv and New York: Berezil'-Kots', 2001–21.
Shl'ogel, Karl (Karl Schlögel). *Ukraïns'kyi vyklyk. Vidkryttia ievropeis'koï Ukraïny*, trans. Nataliia Komarova. Kyiv: Dukh i Litera, 2016.
Shramko, Boris, and Valentin Skirda. *Rozhdenie Khar'kova*. Kharkiv: Skhidno-rehional'nyi tsentr humanitarno-osvitnikh initsiatyv, 2004.
Sklokin, Volodymyr. *Rosiis'ka imperiia i Slobids'ka Ukraïna u druhii polovyni XVIII st.: Prosvichenyi absoliutyzm, impers'ka intehratsiia, lokal'ne suspil'stvo*. Lviv: Ukrainian Catholic University Press, 2019.
Skorobohatov, Anatolii. *Kharkiv u chasy nimets'koï okupatsiï (1941–1943)*. Kharkiv: Prapor, 2004.
Sliusarskii, Anton G. (*see also* Sliusars'kyi, Anton H.). *Sotsial'no-ėkonomicheskoe razvitie Slobozhanshchiny XVII–XVIII vv*. Kharkiv: Kharkivs'ke knyzhkove vydavnytstvo, 1964.

———. *Vasilii Nazarovich Karazin: uchenyi i obshchestvennyi deiatel'*, 1773–1842. Kharkiv: Kharkivs'ke knyzhkove vydavnytstvo, 1952.

Sliusars'kyi, Anton H. (*see also* Sliusarskii, Anton G.). *Slobids'ka Ukraïna: Istorychnyi narys XVII–XVIII st.* Kharkiv: Kharkivs'ke knyzhkovo-hazetne vydavnytstvo, 1954.

Smith-Peter, Susan. *Imagining Russian Regions: Subnational Identity and Civil Society in Nineteenth-Century Russia*. Leiden: Brill, 2018.

Smolii, Valerii, ed. *Skhid i Pivden' Ukraïny: chas, prostir, sotsium*, 2 vols. Kyiv: Instytut istoriï Ukraïny, 2014.

Smolii, Valerii, et al., eds. *Ukraïna i Rosiia v istorychnii retrospektyvi*, 3 vols. Kyiv: Naukova Dumka, 2004.

Sossa, Rostyslav. *Istoriia kartohrafuvannia terytoriï Ukraïny*. Kyiv: Instytut Istoriï Ukraïny, 2007.

Søvik, Margrethe B. *Support, Resistance, and Pragmatism: An Examination of Motivation in Language Policy in Kharkiv, Ukraine*. Stockholm: Stockholm University Press, 2008.

Sreznevskii, Izmail. *Istoricheskoe obozrenie grazhdanskogo ustroeniia Slobodskoi Ukrainy so vremeni eio zaseleniia do preobrazovaniia v Khar'kovskuiu guberniiu*. Kharkiv: Gubernskaia tipografia, 1883.

Stanilov, Kiril, ed. *The Post-Socialist City: Urban Form and Space Transformations in Central and Eastern Europe after Socialism* (e-book, 2007).

Sumtsov, Mykola F. *Slobozhany: Istorychno-etnohrafichna rozvidka*. Kharkiv: Soiuz, 1918.

Sypovs'kyi, Vasyl'. *Ukraïna v rosiis'komu pys'menstvi*, pt. 1 (1801–1850). Kharkiv: DVU, 1928.

Szporluk, Roman. *Russia, Ukraine, and the Breakup of the Soviet Union*. Stanford: Hoover Institution Press, 2000.

Taliev, Valerii, ed. *Priroda i naselenie Slobodskoi Ukrainy. Khar'kovskaia guberniia. Posobie po narodovedeniiu*. Kharkiv: Soiuz, 1918.

Teslia, Mykhailo. *Oleksandr Oleksandrovych Palitsyn i "Palitsyns'ka akademiia."* Sumy: MakDen, 2010.

Turchenko, Fedir, and Halyna Turchenko. *Pivdenna Ukraïna: modernizatsiia, svitova viina, revoliutsiia (kinets' XIX st.–1921 r.)* Kyiv: Geneza, 2003.

*Ukraïns'ko-rosiis'ke porubizhzhia: formuvannia sotsial'noho ta kul'turnoho prostoru v istoriï ta suchasnii politytsi*. Kyiv: Stylos, 2003.

Uzbek, E., et al., eds. *"Ia smelo mogu stat' pred sudom potomkov. . .": Karazinskii sbornik*. Kharkiv: Maidan, 2004.

Vermenych, Iaroslava. *Teoretyko-metodolohichni problemy istorychnoï rehionalistyky v Ukraïni*. Kyiv: NANU, 2003.

———. *Terytorial'na identychnist' ukraïns'koho pohranychchia: istorychni vytoky ta heopolitychni vplyvy*. Kyiv: Instytut istoriï Ukraïny, 2019.

Wanner, Catherine. *Burden of Dreams: History and Identity in Post-Soviet Ukraine*. University Park: Pennsylvania State University Press, 1998.

Westrate, Michael T. *Living Soviet in Ukraine from Stalin to Maidan: Under the Falling Red Star in Kharkiv*. Lanham, MD: Lexington Books, 2016.

Wolchik, Sharon L., and Vladimir Zviglianich, eds. *Ukraine: The Search for a National Identity*. Lanham, MD: Rowman & Littlefield, 2000.

Zaika, Hryhorii P. *Ukraïns'ka Liniia*. Kyiv and Poltava: Arkheolohiia, 2001.

Zagorovskii, Vladimir. *Belgorodskaia cherta*. Voronezh: Izd. Voronezhskogo universiteta, 1969.

———. *Iziumskaia cherta*. Voronezh: Izd. Voronezhskogo universiteta, 1980.

Zaharchenko (Zakharchenko), Tanya. *Where Currents Meet: Frontiers in Post-Soviet Fiction of Kharkiv, Ukraine*. Budapest: CEU Press, 2016.

Zhurzhenko, Tatiana. *Borderlands into Bordered Lands: Geopolitics of Identity in Post-Soviet Ukraine*. Stuttgart: Ibidem Verlag, 2010.

# Index

Abramov, Yakov, 64, 159
Aksakov, Ivan, 85, 124, 147, 171n29, 172n61
Alchevsky, Oleksii (Aleksei), 136, 150, 170n13; Khrystyna, 145; family, 152, 278; home 157
Aleinikov, Andrei, 102
Aleksandrovskaia, Alla, 271
Aleksei Mikhailovich, tsar, 16, 22
Alexander I, emperor, 58, 61, 63–4, 67–9, 72–3, 79, 87, 99
Alexander II, emperor, 128, 157
Alexander III, emperor, 142
Antonii (Khrapovitsky), archbishop, 143
Antonovsky, Mykhailo, 96
Antonovych, Volodymyr, 154, 161; Dmytro, 155
Arseniev, Konstantin, 137
Artakov, Andrei, 66, 68–9
Aseev, Nikolai, 197
Astrakhan gubernia, 53; city, 88n10; khanate, 94
Austrian Empire, 69, 76
Avakov, Arsen, 236–7, 255, 267–8
Azov, Sea, 8, 133–4; gubernia, region, 33, 37; battalion, 279, 283

Bagration, Petr, 157
Bahalii, Dmytro, 9, 14, 16, 18, 24, 30, 37, 57, 64–5, 122, 148, 151–2, 154–5, 160–4, 178, 186, 195–6, 204, 219, 225, 227–9, 242, 278
Balakliia, town, 9, 15, 19, 139, 281
Balkans, 50, 53, 60, 62, 72
Ballu, Jacques Belin de, 80
Baltic lands, 48n124, 72, 174; gentry 68, 74, 129 n26
Bandera, Stepan, 201
Bantysh-Kamensky, Dmitrii, 103, 119, 123; Nikolai, 94
Barvinkove, town, 218

Barvinkove-Kharkiv Operation of 1942, 223
Barvinok, Cossack, 218
Barvinsky, Victor, 164
Baturyn, city, 60; university, 60
Beauplan, Guillaume Levasseur de, 12
Belarus, 225, 258
Belgorod city (town), 13–4, 21, 37–8, 52–3, 55–6, 104, 157, 201–2, 234–5, 238, 241, 258, 264, 266–7
Belgorod, gubernia, 32, 53, 96; vice-gubernia, 36; province, 24; territory, 25; *voevodstvo*, 33; *voevoda*, 26, 33, 37; region, 35, 40, 235, 259; oblast, 3, 104, 182, 199, 217, 225–6, 235, 258, 267; *Razriad* (department), 101; regiment, 234–5; eparchy, 37–8, 235; College, 53, 297; University, 259
Belgorod Line, 15–7, 21–2, 34, 37, 240, 258, 297
Belinsky, Vissarion, 98, 118, 120, 122
Bessarabia, 93–4, 134, 138
Betsky, Ivan, 118
Biletsky-Nosenko, Pavlo, 107
Biletsky, Oleksandr, 269
Black Hundred, union, movement, ideology, 144, 156, 159, 256, 258, 295
Black Sea Cossacks, 71, 135; state, 98, 137; region, 139; steppes, 119
Black Sea littoral, 1, 8, 9–10, 14, 34, 42–3, 50, 52–3, 81, 85, 93, 104–5, 107, 133–6, 177, 209, 233, 274, 292
Bobrowski, Michał, 85, 125
Bodiansky, Osyp, 96, 159
Boeck, Brian, 22
Bohodukhiv (town), 19, 62, 79, 96, 244, 257–8
Bondarev, Anton, 281
Borovykovsky, Levko, 121
Brest fortress, 241
Brest-Litovsk Peace Treaty, 184

Briukhovetsky, Ivan (hetman), 19, 100–1
Bukovyna, 260
Buonaparte, Napoleon, 72, 87

Calve, Gustav Adolf Hess de, 80–1, 110, 126
Carpathian region, 107, Rus', 219
Catherine II, also Catherine the Great, Russian empress, 36, 39, 41, 51–2, 56, 62, 68–9, 87, 92, 94, 99, 104, 110, 119; street 190
Caucasus, 50, 69, 71, 85, 125, 141, 187, 210, 292
Central Rada, 175–80, 217, 268, 298
Chaikovsky, Petr, 157
Chebotarev, Khariton, 96, 107,
Chernihiv, city, 60, 70, 73, 123, 140; gubernia, 95, 125, 175; region, 182; oblast, 198, 260
Chernihiv-Siversk Principality, 9
Chernobyl, 299
Chernyshevsky, Nikolai, 157
Chizhikova, Liudmila, 210
Chuhuiv (also Chuguev), town, 9, 13, 17, 19, 25–6, 29–30, 56, 96, 98, 128; district, 258
Chykalenko, Yevhen, 156
Crimea (territory), 9, 13, 34, 50, 69, 85, 93, 104–5, 107, 134, 137–8, 140, 185, 209, 217, 231, 233–4, 236, 240, 257, 260, 264–5, 270, 278–9, 283, 297–9
Crimean state (also Khanate, Crimean Autonomous Republic), 10, 12, 14, 19–20, 42–3, 265
Czartoryski, Adam, 72, 85

Danilevsky, Grigorii, 134, 139–40, 154, 159, 163, 184, 195, 203, 246
Daniłowicz, Ignacy, 121
Degai, Pavel, 79
Demin, Oleg, 224
Denikin, Anton, 183–4, 230, 265
Derzhavin, Gavriil, 64, 89n49, 157
*Derzhprom* (State Industry), building, vii, 191
Dickinson, Peter, 264–5, 279
Ditmar, Nikolai von, 158, 177, 181
Dnipro (Dnieper, Dnepr), river, 260
Dnipro, oblast, 38; city (formerly Dnipropetrovsk, Katerynoslav (Yekaterinoslav in Russian), 52, 220–1, 270–1
Dobkin, Mikhail (Mykhailo), 236–40, 242, 255, 258, 262, 264, 266–8, 283

Dolgoruky, Ivan, 55, 98
Don Cossack Host, 3, 10, 15–6, 19, 23–4, 26, 30, 43, 53, 71, 135; region 85, 125, 138, 180–3, 292
Don, river, 8–9, 15, 22–3, 35, 46n61, 106–7, 138
Donbas, region, 133, 135–6, 181, 183, 197, 209, 217, 219–20, 233–4, 236, 239, 243, 247, 254, 260, 264, 269, 271–4, 279, 283, 291, 297, 299
Donets: river, basin, 9, 33, 35, 103, 135, 181, 190; ridge, 8, 234; province, 36
Donets, Hryhorii, 100, 157
Donets-Kryvyi Rih, basin, 135, 181–2, 184, 186, 190; oblast, 180–1, 235, 247, 259; autonomy, 182; Soviet Republic (DKR), 180, 182, 185, 187, 219, 230, 234, 260, 270, 298
Donets-Zakharzhevsky, Cossack clan, 27–8, 58, 100; Fedir, 27, 31; Volodymyr, 62, 67
Donetsk, city, 3, 234–5, 246, 257, 267–71; oblast, 220; gubernia, 183, 188
"Donetsk People's Republic," 269–70
Dorpat (Tartu), city, 54, 70
Dorpat (Tartu), University, 67, 74, 77, 81
Dovzhenko, Oleksandr, 186
Drahomanov, Mykhailo, 138–9, 161
Dreiser, Theodore, 191
Dubrovsky, Vasyl, 201
Dugour, Antoine Jeudy (Degurov, Anton), 77–8, 80–1
Dzerzhinsky, Feliks, also street, square, 190, 200–1, 205–6, 217, 248, 277

Eastern Ukraine, 4, 174, 201, 236, 267, 271

Fedetsky, Alfred, 144
Fedor Ioannovich, tsar, 21
Fichte, Johann Gottlieb, 76
Filipović, Teodor (pseud. Božidar Grujović), 76
Flynn, James T., 72, 77
Fotiiev, Vasyl, 64
Frunze, Mikhail, 185, 277–8

Galicia (Halychyna), 106, 219, 260
Girkin, Igor (alias Strelkov), 265
Goethe, Johann Wolfgang von, 76
Gogol, Nikolai (Hohol), Mykola), 79, 96, 108, 120, 157, 247
Gonorsky, Razumnik, 81
Göttingen, 74

INDEX | 309

Gorky Park, 263, 284
Grot, Yakov, 85, 126
Güldenstädt, Johann, 103, 125
Gumilev, Lev, 230

Hamm, Michael, 145, 156
Haxthausen, August von, 87, 103–4
Herlihy, Patricia, 137, 239n101, 241n4
Hetmanate (also: Little Russia), 3–4, 14–19, 21–4, 26, 35–6, 42, 60, 81, 92, 95–7, 99, 102, 119, 151, 198, 220, 297
Hetmanate (Ukrainian state of 1918), 183, 298
Herzen, Aleksandr, 159, 217
Holodomor (human-made famine), 198–9, 219, 234, 237–8, 241, 298
Hooson, David, 208, 210
Hrebinka, Yevhen, 122
Hroch, Miroslav, 178
Hrushevsky, Mykhailo, 139, 164–5, 176, 186, 195–6; Oleksandr, 165
Hrytsak, Yaroslav, 268
Hulak-Artemovsky, Petro, 82–4, 109, 122, 163, 242, 263, 278

Ikeda, Yoshiro, 183
Illiashevich, Lev, 165
Innokentii, Metropolitan of Kharkiv, 121
Ivashko, Volodymyr, 223
Izium, town, 9, 34, 281; district, 66, 96, 128, 183, 188; province, 103; route, 8, 13; regiment, 15, 33; line, 17, 35, 297; Cossacks, 26; nobility, 69
Izmailov, Vladimir, 116

Jacob, Ludwig, 77–8
Janković-Mirijevski, Teodor, 69
Janowski, Ludwik, 55, 68, 163

Kachenovsky, Dmitrii, 124
Kaganovich, Lazar, 200
Kalinka, Walerian, 85
Karamzin, Nikolai, 109, 119
Karazin, Vasilii, vi, 62–74, 86, 98, 109–10, 115–18, 123, 125–7, 134, 139, 153, 155–9, 161–3, 165, 192–3, 195, 202–4, 211, 227, 229, 233, 245–6; Nikolai, 144
Katerynoslav (Yekaterinoslav), city, 51–2, 56, 60, 71–2, 133, 135, 141, 145, 157, 180, 270; vicegerency, 94, 97; gubernia (also region), 94, 135, 140, 146, 177, 180, 182–3; province, 103; street 150

Katsnelson, Abram, 201
Katyn, 199
Kazan, city, 70, 76; gubernia, 53; university, 77, 81
Kernes, Gennadii, 255–6, 258, 262, 264, 267–9, 273–4, 276–8
Kevorkian, Konstantin, 229–30, 242, 259, 279
Kharkiv, gubernia, vi, xi, 96, 103, 113, 122, 125, 135, 140–2, 144–6, 149, 151, 176, 182–3, 297; oblast, 3–4, 9, 17, 30, 139, 184, 186, 188, 198, 206–7, 209, 217–8, 220–5, 228, 231, 234, 236, 239, 242, 247, 254–6, 258, 260, 270–4, 281–2, 298
Kharkiv Orthodox Collegium, 60, 297
Kharkiv Romantics, 82, 120–3, 165, 195
Kharkiv University, vi, 1, 5, 50–91, 98, 109, 115, 121, 124–5, 127–8, 141, 144, 154, 159–63, 166, 179, 193, 195, 200, 202–4, 211, 229, 241, 246, 255, 257, 284, 292, 297–8
Kharko, Cossack, vi, 10, 58–9, 231–2
Kherson, city, 51, 71; gubernia 81, 94, 141, 177
Khlebnikov, Velimir, 185
Khmelnytsky (Khmelnitsky) Bohdan, 14, 17, 23, 99, 224, 257, 260
Khorvat, Osip, 79
Khotkevych, Hnat, 166, 178
Khvyliovy, Mykola, 194, 219, 227, 230
Kliuchevsky, Vasilii, 161
Kochubei, Viktor, 68, 70, 126
Kohl, Johann Georg, 40, 98
Konashevych-Sahaidachny, Petro, 278
Konev, Ivan, 223, 238, 266
Korf, Pavel, 134
Korniichuk, Oleksandr, 202
Kostiuk, Hryhorii, 194
Kostomarov, Mykola (Nikolai), 121, 138, 152, 157, 161
Kotliarevsky, Ivan, 122, 139
Kovalinsky, Mykhailo, 98, 110
Kozhedub, Ivan, 223
Kraevsky, Andrei, 112, 115
Krasicki, Ignacy, 84
Krasnov, Andrei, 141
Kravchuk, Leonid, 299
Kremenchuk, town, 52, 94, 134
Kropyvnytsky, Marko, 160
Krzemieniec Lyceum, 84
Kuban, region, 138–9, 181, 183
Kuchma, Leonid, 221, 223–4, 299
Kukol-Yasnopolsky, Fedir, 62

Kulish, Panteleimon, 96, 138, 152
Kurakin, Aleksandr, 73
Kurbas, Les, 219, 227
Kursk, city, 13, 21, 38, 52, 55, 73, 103–4, 124, 183, 225; gubernia, 81, 113–4, 123, 135, 146, 179, 182, 186; oblast, 3, 210
Kushnarev, Yevgenii, 218, 222, 229, 233, 235, 274
Kuzio, Taras, 259, 267, 269
Kuzminsky, Konstantin, 205
Kvitka (also Kvitka-Osnovianenko), Hryhorii, vi, 59, 83, 98, 105, 109–18, 120, 122–3, 125–7, 139, 153, 155, 157–8, 164–6, 193, 195, 218, 220, 227, 230, 246, 263; Illia, 100–2, 106, 110–1, 113
Kvitka, Cossack clan, 38, 100
Kyiv (also Kiev), city, 1, 38, 51–2, 59–60, 69–73, 85–6, 94–5, 98, 102, 106, 133–5, 138, 145–7, 153–5, 176–7, 179–80, 185–8, 194–5, 197–9, 202, 207–10, 217, 219, 222–4, 232, 235, 237, 242, 245–6, 255, 260, 263–8, 270, 273–4, 276–80, 283, 297–8; gubernia, 33, 36, 146, 175; principality, 13, 93; province, 36; region, 42; oblast, 198; metropolitanate, 36
Kyiv Mohyla Academy, 38, 84
Kyivan Rus', 78, 94–5, 100, 105–6, 112, 117, 235

La Harpe, Frédéric-César de, 69
Lang, Joseph, 77
Laruelle, Marlene, 265
Lavrovsky, Nikolai, 162; Petr, 159
Lazarewsky, Oleksandr, 162
Lelewel, Joachim, 85, 125
Lenin, Vladimir, vii, 180, 184, 187, 201, 206, 232–3, 235, 247, 257, 260, 274–6, 283, 294
Lermontov, Mikhail, 157–8
Lëvshin, Aleksei, 81–2
Libman, Aleksandr, 226
Limonov, Eduard, 208
Little Russia (also: Hetmanate), 14, 17–8, 23–4, 26, 31, 33, 36, 41, 43, 53–4, 70–1, 73, 81–2, 85, 92–7, 99–102, 104–6, 110, 112–5, 119, 122–8, 135, 138–40, 162, 167–8, 175, 177, 183, 188, 198, 230, 264, 270, 292, 294
Liubavsky, Matvei, 161, 196
Lopukhin, Dmitrii, 64
Lozhkin, Borys, 273
Lubny, town, 60, 70

Luhansk, oblast, 3, 182, 220, 234, 239
Lviv, 1, 38, 76, 106, 140, 146–7, 153, 200, 208–9, 219, 246, 263
Lyptsi, town, 103, 114, 281
Lysenko, Mykola, 155, 158, 160, 218
Lysiak-Rudnytsky, Ivan, 72

Maiakovsky, Vladimir, 197
Makhno, Nestor, 293
Maksymovych (Maksimovich), Mykhailo, 96, 120
Markov, Mikhail, 102
Maselsky, Oleksandr, 218, 222
Maslovych, Vasyl, 59, 83
Mazepa, Ivan, 18, 23, 101, 229
Metlynsky, Amvrosii, 96
Mickiewicz, Adam, 40, 84, 121
Mikhnovsky, Mykola, 155, 157–8, 166, 224, 227, 297
Miller, Dmitrii/Dmytro, 148, 151, 161, 164, 228, 278
Moldova (also Moldavia), 10, 42, 258
Moscow (also Muscovite), state, government, 1, 4, 11–27, 29, 31–2, 37–8, 40, 43, 59, 94, 97, 103, 114, 153, 155–6, 161, 163, 175, 179, 183, 188, 190, 199, 217–9, 234, 257, 274, 295, 297
Moscow, Grand Principality, 10; gubernia, 146–7
Moscow Patriarchate, vii, 218, 232, 244, 250, 257
Moscow, city, 33, 37–8, 52, 56, 60, 65, 70, 87, 94, 116, 119, 125–6, 146, 151, 154, 157, 185, 194, 196, 198–9, 207–8, 211, 241, 246–8, 264, 294
Moscow University, 60, 65, 76–7, 107, 161
Murava Route, 8, 11, 13–4, 18
Muraviev, Nikita, 98
Musin-Pushkin, Aleksei, 94
Mykolaiv (Nikolaev) city, 51, 236

Nekrasov, Nikolai, 157
Nemensky, Oleg, 265
Nevsky, Aleksandr, prince, 157, 232, 284
New Russia (also Novorossiia,) territory, 50, 69, 71, 86, 93–4, 96, 104, 125, 134–6, 139, 142, 184, 209, 217, 219, 234; discourse, 265, 270
Nicholas I, emperor, 87, 94, 114, 118–20, 123, 165
Noeldechen, Karl, 78
Novhorod-Siverskyi, town, 70–1

Odesa, city, 85–7; 94–5, 98, 126, 133–5, 137–8, 143, 145–7, 149, 153–4, 156, 202, 207, 219, 222, 234, 236, 245–6, 267, 270–1, 274, 292; oblast, 217
Okhtyrka (Akhtyrka), town, 9, 12, 15, 17, 23, 34–5, 38, 54, 96; regiment, 15, 18
*Oplot*, paramilitary club, 258–9, 266, 268–9, 272
Orel, town, 36, 73, 135, 137, 146, 183; gubernia, 182
Ornowski, Jan (Ivan Ornovsky), 27, 58, 100
Osipovsky, Timofei, 78, 80
Oskil (Oskol), river, 8, 21, 35, 281
Ostrogozhsk (Rybinsk), town, regiment, 15, 17–9, 34–5, 40, 101
Ostrohradsky, Mykhailo, 78
Ottoman Empire (also Sultanate), 10, 14, 34, 51, 85, 92

Passek, Vadim, 104, 124
Paul I, emperor, 58, 61–3
Pereiaslav, city, 60; Treaty (Council), 204, 257, 260; principality, 9
Pereverzev, Ivan, 104–7, 112, 114, 117, 125, 163
Perovsky, Aleksei, 71, 79
Peter I, emperor, 29, 33, 51–2, 165, 222
Petliura, Symon, 176, 229
Petrovsky, Hryhorii, 188
Piechal, Tomasz, 271
Pilger, Martin-Heinrich (Fedor), 78
Pilsky, Petr, 168
Pletnev, Petr, 85, 126
Pogodin, Mikhail, 103, 118
Poland, 15, 43, 54, 72, 85, 174, 199, 240, 272. *See also* Polish-Lithuanian Commonwealth
Polevoi, Nikolai, 119–20, 122, 126
Polish-Lithuanian Commonwealth, 3, 10, 12–6, 21, 26–8, 36–7, 40, 42, 84–5, 92, 97, 100–1, 112, 117, 121, 292, 297. *See also* Poland
Poltava, city, 15, 52, 56, 70, 73, 97, 116, 122–4, 140, 146, 157, 246; regiment, 17–8; gubernia (also region), 95, 125, 135, 141, 146, 175; oblast (also *okruh*), 3, 38, 186, 188, 198, 235, 260
Poroshenko, Petro, 273–4, 299
Potebnia, Oleksandr, 152, 193, 227
Potemkin, Grigorii, 60, 71, 97
Potocki, Seweryn, count, 69, 73–4, 76, 81
Prokopovych, Andrii, 58

Pushkin, Aleksandr, 98, 145, 157–8, 191, 203, 284
Putin, Vladimir, 225, 235, 261, 265, 282–3

Rainin, Ihor, 273–4
Reit, Bernhard, 81
Repnin, Nikolai, 126
Rittikh, Aleksandr, 142
Rizhsky, Ivan, 80, 82
Romanchenko, Borys, 283
Rommel, Christoph Dietrich, von, 41, 75, 77–81
Rozumovsky, Kyrylo, 60; Oleksii, 70
Rubin, Eduard, 281
Rumiantsev-Zadunaisky, Petr, 97
Rusov, Mykhailo, 155

Sahaidachny Konashevych, Petro, 278
Saratov, gubernia, 53
Saunders, David, 60
Savchenko, Yevgenii, 235, 258–9, 266
Schad, Johann Baptist, 77, 80
Scherer, Jean-Benoît, 81
Selivanov, Timofei, 82
Serbia, 35, 53, 76, 98
Sergeev ("Artem"), Fedor, 190, 193, 234, 278
Sevastopol, 134–5, 207, 257, 264–5, 278, 299
Severodonetsk, town, 234
Shafonsky, Afanasii (Opanas), 105
Shaginian, Marietta, 196
Shchegolev, Sergei, 168
Shcherbinin, Yevdokim, 39, 97, 157, 232–3
Shchoholiv, Yakiv, 154, 164, 259
Shelest, Petro, 223
Shevelov (Sherekh), George (Yurii), 194, 262
Shevchenko, Taras, 96, 113, 118, 138, 140, 152, 158, 160, 166, 195, 230; monument, vii, 157–8, 191–2, 224, 232; park, 245, 263
Shpyhotsky, Opanas, 126
Shumliansky, Pavlo, 82
Shveikart, Ferdinand, 70
Sirko, Ivan, ataman, 19, 227; monument, 218, 278
Siverskyi Donets, river, 8, 19, 22
Skobelev, Mikhail, 157
Skoropadsky, Ivan, 18; Pavlo, 182, 298
Skovoroda, Hryhorii, 1, 58, 97, 102, 110, 126, 139, 154, 157, 161, 163, 165, 193, 195, 211, 218, 222, 227, 241–2
Skrypnyk, Mykola, 182

Sliusarsky, Anton, 203–4
Sloboda Cossack regiments, 13, 15–20, 22–7, 29, 31–7, 39, 41–2, 99–102, 104, 108, 110–1, 113, 165, 194, 232, 234, 239, 241, 292–3
Sloboda gentry, 61–2, 64, 66–70, 74, 79, 98, 100, 115–6
Sloboda gubernia, also province, 41, 52–3, 65–7, 69, 71, 74, 81, 96–8, 108, 117, 122, 125, 176, 181, 297
Sloboda Ukraine (also Slobozhanshchina, Slobozhanshchyna, region), vi, xi, 1–5, 8–10, 12–4, 16–24–5, 27–8, 30–43, 50–3, 56, 58–62, 64–5, 67, 70–1, 73, 78, 80–1, 83–7, 92–106, 108–18, 122–8, 134–6, 138–9, 142, 148, 151–3, 160, 162–8, 175–6, 178–9, 184, 186, 193, 195–6, 198, 204–5, 219–20, 222, 224–8, 230–2, 242, 244, 256–7, 259–61, 265, 270–1, 291–2, 295
Sloboda Ukrainians (settlers, colonists, Cossacks), 17–20, 22–4, 26, 28–9, 31–2, 34–6, 40, 43, 101, 105, 109, 139, 148, 162, 218
Sokalsky, Petro, 134, 154, 184
Sreznevsky, Ivan, 82; Izmail, 82, 122–3, 126, 165
Stalin, Joseph, 190, 197, 200–1, 205–6, 230, 260; monument, vii, 205, 275
Stojković, Atanasije, 76–7, 80, 98
Sumarokov, Pavel, 55, 103, 114; Aleksandr, 58
Sumtsov, Mykola, 83, 122, 152, 155, 157, 160, 164, 178, 219, 227
Sumy, town, 3, 15, 17, 23, 26, 28, 34, 52, 54, 56, 62, 96, 134, 136, 157, 163, 176, 235, 260; regiment, 18–9, 40; oblast, 3
Suvorin, Boris, 184
Suvorov, Aleksandr, 157
Szporluk, Roman, 106, 208

Taliev, Valerii, 176, 179
Taranivka, village, 223
Tatishchev, Vasilii, 36
Terekhov, Ihor, 277, 283–4
Tolstoy, Aleksei, 183
Transcarpathia (Zakarpattia), region, 220, 260
Transnistria, 234
Tsereteli, Zurab, vi, 10, 231
Tsertelev, Nikolai, 82
Tychyna, Pavlo, 194–5
Tymkovsky, Illia, 55, 70, 77, 82
Tymoshenko, Yulia, 236, 255

Ukrainian Insurgent Army, 239, 278
Ukrainian People's Republic, 179
Ukrainian State, xii
Ukrainka, Lesia, 230
*Ukrainskii vestnik*, 83, 98, 101, 109, 166
*Ukrainskii zhurnal*, 83, 98
Uspensky, Gavriil, 81
Uvarov, Sergei (Count), 95, 119, 121

Vahylevych, Ivan, 85
Vasylkivsky, Serhii, 152, 164, 176, 193
Venelin, Yurii (Hutsa), 96
Vernadsky, Ivan, 136, 150; family, 152; Vladimir, 242
Viazigin, Andrei, 144
Vilnius, city, viii, 70, 72–3, 77, 81, 84–5, 125
Vinnytsia, town, 268
Vladimir, prince, 51
Volga, river (also region), 29, 106
Volkonsky, Mikhail, 142
Voronezh, city, 13, 21, 55, 73; oblast (territory, region), 3, 25, 38, 196, 217, 266; gubernia, 53, 81, 97, 103, 135, 146, 179, 182, 186, 196; eparchy, 37
Vovchansk, town, 281; district, 30, 66, 96
Vyhovsky, Ivan, hetman, 17, 19, 100

Wanner, Catherine, 233
Warsaw, 84, 107, 146, 174
"Wild Steppe (Field)" (*Dyke Pole*), 12, 22, 58, 97, 166, 205, 240

Yanukovych, Viktor, 216, 236, 239, 254–5, 257, 261, 264, 266–8, 273–4, 299
Yavornytsky, Dmytro, 224
Yefimenko, family, 152
Yefremov, Serhii, 194
Yekelchyk, Serhy, 119, 197–8
Yushchenko, Viktor, 236, 238–40, 254, 273, 299

Zakharashevych-Kapustiansky, Heorhii, 69
Zakharchenko, Oleksandr, 269–70
Zaporizhia, city, 140; oblast (region), 38, 105, 220, 236, 247, 271
Zaporozhian Cossacks, 13, 19, 24, 101, 165, 224, 229. *See also* Zaporozhian Host
Zaporozhian Host, 3, 10, 15–6, 19, 23, 26, 35, 54, 92, 95, 122, 139, 218, 297. *See also* Zaporizhia, Zaporozhian Sich, Zaporozhian Cossacks
Zavadovsky, Petro, 70, 72, 75

Zelensky, Volodymyr, 5, 273, 288n106, 299
Zgursky, Hennadii, 220
Zhadan, Serhii, 255–6
Zhirinovsky, Vladimir, 264–5
Zhukov, Georgii, 276–8, 283
Zhukovsky, Vasilii, 157
Zhurzhenko, Tatiana, 219, 225, 237, 255, 273
Ziablovsky, Yevdokim, 98
Zionist, movement, 144
Zmiiv, town, 15, 19, 25, 30, 56, 96, 157; district, 128, 223

www.ingramcontent.com/pod-product-compliance
Lightning Source LLC
Chambersburg PA
CBHW051527020426
42333CB00016B/1806